Mao's Little Red B

Mao Zedong's Little Red Book (*Quotations from Chairman Mao*) – a compilation of the Chinese leader's speeches and writings – is one of the most visible and ubiquitous symbols of twentieth-century radicalism. Published for the first time in 1964, it rapidly became the must-have accessory for Red Guards and revolutionaries from Berkeley to Bamako. Yet, despite its worldwide circulation and enduring presence there has, until now, been no serious scholarly effort to understand this seminal text as a global historical phenomenon. *Mao's Little Red Book* brings together a range of innovative scholars from around the world to explore the fascinating variety of uses and forms that Mao's *Quotations* has taken, from rhetoric, art, and song, to talisman, badge, and weapon. The authors of this pioneering volume use Mao's *Quotations* as a medium through which to re-examine the history of the twentieth-century world, challenging established ideas about the book to reveal its remarkable global impact.

ALEXANDER C. COOK is Assistant Professor of History at the University of California, Berkeley, where he teaches modern Chinese history. His research examines Maoism in its domestic and global contexts. His publications include the chapter on "Third World Maoism" in *Critical Introduction to Mao* (Cambridge University Press, 2010) and a forthcoming book on the Gang of Four trial in China.

Mao's Little Red Book

A Global History

Edited by

Alexander C. Cook
University of California, Berkeley

CAMBRIDGE
UNIVERSITY PRESS

CAMBRIDGE
UNIVERSITY PRESS

University Printing House, Cambridge CB2 8BS, United Kingdom

Published in the United States of America by Cambridge University Press, New York

Cambridge University Press is part of the University of Cambridge.

It furthers the University's mission by disseminating knowledge in the pursuit of education, learning and research at the highest international levels of excellence.

www.cambridge.org
Information on this title: www.cambridge.org/9781107665644

© Cambridge University Press 2014

First published 2014

Printed and bound in the United Kingdom by Clays, St Ives plc

A catalogue record for this publication is available from the British Library

Library of Congress Cataloguing in Publication data
Mao's Little Red Book : a global history / edited by Alexander C. Cook.
    pages cm
ISBN 978-1-107-05722-7 (Hardback) – ISBN 978-1-107-66564-4 (Paperback)
1. Mao, Zedong, 1893–1976. Mao zhu xi yu lu.   2. Mao, Zedong,
1893–1976–Quotations.   I. Cook, Alexander C., editor.
DS778.M3C68 2013
951.05092–dc23   2013034816

ISBN 978-1-107-05722-7 Hardback
ISBN 978-1-107-66564-4 Paperback

Contents

Illustrations

Contributors

JULIAN BOURG is Associate Professor of History at Boston College where he teaches European Intellectual History. He is the author of *From Revolution to Ethics: May 1968 and Contemporary French Thought* (2007), translator of Claude Lefort, *Complications: Communism and the Dilemmas of Democracy* (2007), and editor of *After the Deluge: New Perspectives on the Intellectual and Cultural History of Postwar France* (2004). He is currently writing a book on the history of the relationship between terror and democracy since the eighteenth century.

SREEMATI CHAKRABARTI is Professor of Chinese Studies at the Department of East Asian Studies, University of Delhi, and Honorary Fellow of the Institute of Chinese Studies, Delhi. She holds a Ph.D. in Political Science from Columbia University and Master's degrees from Delhi University (Political Science) and Harvard University (Regional Studies – East Asia). She has done post-doctoral research at Beijing Normal University. Currently, she is the Book Review Editor of the Sage journal *China Report*. Her publications include *China and the Naxalites* (1990), *Mao, China's Intellectuals and the Cultural Revolution* (1998), and *China* (2007). On academic assignments she has traveled to Russia, Japan, South Korea, Taiwan, Hong Kong, the United States, and several times to China. She is on various China-related panels in Indian universities and government-run research and educational organizations. Several television and radio news channels, including the BBC, invite her to comment on China-related issues. In the year 2010, Chinese Premier Wen Jiabao felicitated her with the China–India Friendship Award.

ALEXANDER C. COOK is Assistant Professor of Chinese History at the University of California, Berkeley. He is a graduate of Brown University (AB East Asian Studies) and Columbia University (MA Asian Languages, Ph.D. History) and formerly a Mellon Humanities Fellow at Stanford University. His research focuses on Maoism in its Chinese domestic and global contexts.

ANDREW F. JONES is Louis B. Agassiz Professor of Chinese at the University of California, Berkeley. He is the author of *Yellow Music: Media Culture and Colonial Modernity in the Chinese Jazz Age* (2001) and *Developmental Fairy Tales: Evolutionary Thinking and Modern Chinese Culture* (2011).

PRIYA LAL is Assistant Professor of History at Boston College. She is currently writing a book about Tanzania's socialist experiment, the *ujamaa* villagization initiative of the late 1960s and early 1970s. Her writing on this topic has also been published in *Africa: Journal of the International African Institute* and *The Journal of African History*.

DANIEL LEESE is Assistant Professor of Modern Chinese History and Politics at the University of Freiburg. He is the author of *Mao Cult: Rhetoric and Ritual in China's Cultural Revolution* (2011) and the editor of *Brill's Encyclopedia of China* (2009).

ELIZABETH MCGUIRE is an independent scholar teaching at San Francisco State University. She holds a Ph.D. in History from UC Berkeley and has completed a post-doctoral fellowship at the Harvard Academy of International and Area Studies. Her forthcoming first book is *The Sino-Soviet Romance: How Chinese Communists Fell in Love with the Russian Revolution*. She has also completed research for a second book, tentatively titled *Communist Neverland: History of a Russian International Children's Home, 1993–2013*.

ELIDOR MËHILLI is Assistant Professor in the History Department at Hunter College of the City University of New York. Previously, he held fellowships at Columbia University and the University of Pennsylvania (for a year-long Mellon-sponsored forum on "Peripheries"). He is completing a book on socialist globalization through the angle of Albania under Yugoslav, Soviet, Eastern bloc, and Chinese patronage, based on archival research in Tirana, Berlin, London, Moscow, Rome, and Washington.

BILL V. MULLEN is Professor of English and American Studies at Purdue University. His books include *Afro-Orientalism* (2004), a study of inter-ethnic anti-racist alliance between Asian and African Americans, and *Popular Fronts: Chicago and African American Cultural Politics, 1935–1946* (1999). He has edited five other books in collaboration with Sherry Lee Linkon, James Smethurst, and Fred Ho. He has been a Fulbright lecturer at Wuhan University in the People's Republic of China and is faculty adviser to the Purdue Students for Justice in Palestine chapter. He is currently at work on a political biography of W. E. B. Du Bois entitled *UnAmerican: W. E. B. Du Bois and the*

Century of World Revolution. His most recent publication is entitled "Building the Palestinian International" in the Social Text on-line dossier Periscope: www.socialtextjournal.org/periscope/2012/07/mullen.php.

DAVID SCOTT PALMER is Professor of International Relations and Political Science, and Founding Director of Latin American Studies at Boston University. He holds a BA from Dartmouth College, an MA from Stanford University, and a Ph.D. from Cornell University. His research and publications cover a variety of issues relating to Latin American politics, US–Latin Amerian relations, and regional conflict, but includes a major focus on Peru and Shining Path. As a Peace Corps Volunteer sent to Ayacucho in the early 1960s to teach at the recently re-founded National University of San Cristobal de Huamanga (UNSCH), he witnessed first-hand the progressive political radicalization of a unique higher education initiative designed to stimulate development of the most impoverished region of the Peruvian sierra. Fascinated by how his former colleague Abimael Guzmán Reynoso could over more than two decades apply Maoist principles to build a rural revolutionary movement that came close to victory, he has dedicated much of his research to an exploration of this phenomenon. He has several publications on the subject, including (as volume editor) *Shining Path of Peru* (1994).

DOMINIQUE KIRCHNER REILL is an Associate Professor in Modern European History at the University of Miami (Florida). She holds degrees from UC Berkeley (BA History) and Columbia University (MA, Ph.D. History). Her first monograph, *Nationalists Who Feared the Nation: Adriatic Multi-Nationalism in Habsburg Dalmatia, Trieste, and Venice,* was published in 2012 and received an Honorable Mention from the Smith Award. Currently she has been awarded the Rome Prize for Modern Italian Studies at the American Academy in Rome and the Title VIII/ACLS Fellowship in East European Studies to complete her analysis of the immediate aftermath of the dissolution of the Habsburg Empire through the lens of the independent city-state Fiume (today's Rijeka in modern-day Croatia). Previously she has received support from the Italian Academy for Advanced Studies in America at Columbia University, the Remarque Institute, the Whiting Foundation, the Delmas Foundation, the German Marshall Foundation, and the Fulbright-Hays Program among others. She specializes in nineteenth- and twentieth-century European history, with a special focus on the Mediterranean, Italy, Yugoslavia, the Habsburg Empire, nationalism, regionalism, and the idea of Europe.

QUINN SLOBODIAN is Assistant Professor of Modern European History at Wellesley College. He is the author of *Foreign Front: Third World Politics in Sixties West Germany* (2012). He has been a fellow at the Minda de Gunzburg Center for European Studies at Harvard University, the Zentrum für Zeithistorische Forschung in Potsdam, and the Dahlem Humanities Center at the Freie Universität Berlin. His ongoing work follows the movement of ideas and actors in and out of modern Germany.

BAN WANG is the William Haas Professor in Chinese Studies at Stanford University and the Yangtze River Chair Professor at East China Normal University. He is the chair of the Department of Asian Languages and Cultures. His major publications include *The Sublime Figure of History* (1997), *Illuminations from the Past* (2004), and *History and Memory* (in Chinese, 2004). He co-edited *Trauma and Cinema* (2004), *The Image of China in the American Classroom* (2005), *China and New Left Visions* (2012), and *Debating Socialist Legacy in China* (forthcoming). He edited *Words and their Stories: Essays on the Language of the Chinese Revolution* (2010). He was a research fellow with the National Endowment for the Humanities in 2000 and the Institute for Advanced Study at Princeton in 2007.

LANJUN XU is Assistant Professor of Chinese Studies at National University of Singapore, where she teaches modern Chinese literature and film. She received her Ph.D. in East Asian Studies from Princeton University in 2007 and has just completed a book manuscript tentatively titled *The Child and Chinese Modernity: Culture, Nation and Technologies of Childhood in Modern China*. She has also started to work on a new book project on the cultural interactions between China and Southeast Asian countries from the 1950s–1970s, focusing on literary translation, film, and broadcasting.

GUOBIN YANG is Associate Professor of Communication and Sociology in the Annenberg School for Communication and Department of Sociology at the University of Pennsylvania. He is the author of *The Power of the Internet in China: Citizen Activism Online* (2009) and co-editor with Ching Kwan Lee of *Re-Envisioning the Chinese Revolution: The Politics and Poetics of Collective Memories in Reform China* (2007). Previously he taught at the University of Hawaii at Manoa and Barnard College of Columbia University.

Preface

The year 2014 marks the fiftieth anniversary of the publication of *Quotations from Chairman Mao*, commonly known outside China as the Little Red Book. At the height of its influence, the decade from the mid 1960s to the mid 1970s, this compact tome was the most printed book in the world. Official editions numbered well over a billion copies in three dozen languages, plus untold numbers of unofficial local reprints and unofficial translations in more than fifty languages.[1] The book's characteristic physical form – pocket-sized, bright red, clad in sturdy vinyl – reflected its practical origins as an ideological field manual for soldiers of the Chinese military, the People's Liberation Army (PLA).[2] The canonical revised edition that first appeared in 1965 arranged its 427 quotations into 33 thematic chapters, presenting extracts from Mao Zedong's writings and speeches from 1929 to 1964, ranging in subject matter from philosophy to warfare to art.[3] This easily digestible format drew upon two distinct literary genres: an ancient Chinese genre of collected wisdom dating back to the *Analects* of Confucius, and a modern genre of ideological primers embraced especially, but by no means exclusively, by Marxist–Leninists around the world. After Mao's death, the book's unsystematic presentation of fragments torn from their historical and textual contexts was widely dismissed as a vulgarization of Maoism (not to mention Marxism). During Mao's lifetime, however, his quotations were adapted in China and elsewhere for many uses and in many forms – as a little red

---

[1] By comparison, the entire population of the world in the early 1970s did not exceed four billion people. See www.census.gov/population/international/data/idb/informationGateway.php, accessed October 1, 2012.

[2] For a history of the compilation of various editions, see Daniel Leese, *Mao Cult: Rhetoric and Ritual in Mao's China* (New York: Cambridge University Press, 2011), pp. 108–27, and his expanded discussion in the first chapter of this volume.

[3] On the distribution of quotations by source and date, see Stuart R. Schram, ed., *Quotations from Chairman Mao Tse-tung* (New York: Praeger, 1967), pp. xiv–xvii. For linguistic analysis, see John De Francis, *Annotated Quotations from Chairman Mao* (New Haven: Yale University Press, 1975).

book, of course, but also as rhetoric, art, song, performance, accessory, symbol, talisman, badge, and weapon.

This volume is the first scholarly effort to understand *Quotations from Chairman Mao* as a global historical phenomenon. A foundational premise of our work is that the Little Red Book was (and is) not just one thing. Its mass production, global circulation, and multifarious appropriation in multiple historical contexts produced meanings that cannot be exhausted from any single perspective. This demands that a global history of the Little Red Book be a collaborative effort. Each of the contributors to this volume was specially selected for his or her unique experience and expertise. The chapters that follow are the products of original research by leading scholars working around the world in a dozen different languages. As a group, we are diverse with respect to age, gender, ethnicity, and political sympathies. About half of the chapters are written by historians with various regional specializations, while the other half come from historically minded scholars of literature, area studies, political science, and sociology. While we do not pretend to provide a comprehensive history of the Little Red Book, our analytical toolkit allows us to cut sharply from a number of different angles.

From this diversity of perspectives, we have tried to identify some common themes. To this end, the contributors gathered for a conference held at the University of California, Berkeley on October 21–22, 2011, with major funding from the Townsend Center for the Humanities, the Institute for East Asian Studies, the Center for Chinese Studies, and the Department of History, and with superb logistical support by Elinor Levine. There we enjoyed intensive conversations amongst ourselves, as well as commentary and discussion from John Connelly, Brandon County, Thomas Mullaney, Daniel Sargent, Tyler Stovall, Darren Zook, and a spirited audience. (I can report that even in the twenty-first century there is no lack of public interest in the Little Red Book in Berkeley.) Later, three anonymous reviewers helped us to expand and refine our ideas. Our editors Marigold Acland and Lucy Rhymer, along with Claire Poole and the rest of the expert staff at Cambridge University Press, had the vision and skill to bring this volume to print. Throughout the process, the contributors have remained in close communication, exchanging ideas and advice. This ongoing collaboration helped us to draw together the common threads running through our work.

At the outset, we would like to draw the reader's attention to the most prominent of these threads. The Little Red Book as a global phenomenon is first and foremost a product of its era. Despite its diminutive size, perhaps no other object proved more useful for the projection and reflection of the complexities and contradictions of the global 1960s.

The story of the Little Red Book speaks to the coming of age of the postwar generation; the unresolved legacies of fascism and totalitarianism; the disenchantment with liberalism and state socialism; the descent into the Cold War and the threat of nuclear confrontation; the often unfulfilled promises of national liberation in the postcolonial world; the accelerated globalization of capitalism; and the mass production and radical appropriation of popular culture. The Little Red Book allows us to talk about these abstract issues concretely, and each is emphasized to varying degrees within and across the chapters before you. Each chapter may be read profitably on its own, but the value of each increases as it is read in conjunction with the others. The number of different threads means that shared concerns are found in chapters far apart on the global map and in the table of contents. To take just one small example, Andrew Jones' discussion of the pop song "hook" in China finds echoes in Elizabeth McGuire's dissection of bawdy socialist humor in the Soviet Union and Dominique Reill's analysis of pop culture Orientalism in Italy. This means that the chapters could have been arranged in a number of different ways.

As it stands, the chapters are organized according to a logic explained more fully in my introduction. Briefly, I argue that the Little Red Book aimed to explode the Cold War order by exploiting various fissions and fusions within and between the First World of American-style capitalism, the Second World of Soviet-style socialism, and an underdeveloped but emerging Third World. We begin with chapters that examine the Little Red Book in China. Daniel Leese details the origins, production, and dissemination of *Quotations from Chairman Mao* in China, and also explains the book's eventual demise. Andrew Jones looks at the quotations set to music, exploring the technological and ideological implications of their proliferation in cross-platform and multimedia forms. Guobin Yang turns our attention to the violence wrought by Mao's quotations, using a case study of factionalism and conflicting interpretive commitments during the height of the Cultural Revolution. Lanjun Xu's chapter, which examines the mechanisms by which the Little Red Book was translated for export, pivots from China to the rest of the world. From there, the volume considers the Third World, Second World, and First World in turn. Sreemati Chakrabarti argues that in India, where Third World Maoism had the greatest influence during the Cultural Revolution period and where Maoism continues to exert influence today, the heyday of the Little Red Book was brief. Likewise, David Scott Palmer shows that the leaders of Peru's Shining Path patterned their violent crusade on simplistic adaptations of Maoist principles, often to the detriment of those they claimed to defend. Priya Lal's study of

ujamaa socialism in Tanzania reminds us that the flow of Little Red
Books was merely a surface indicator of the ongoing exchange of people,
ideas, materials, and technologies throughout the Third World. Our
discussion of the Second World begins with Elizabeth McGuire's chapter
on Soviet reception of the Little Red Book, which was seen (like its
Chinese promoters) as primitive, dangerous, and just a little bit funny.
The scorn heaped on the Little Red Book in the Soviet Union earned it
praise in Albania, China's closest European ally in the fight against Soviet
domination of the socialist world. This poorly understood aspect of the
Cold War is detailed in Elidor Mëhilli's chapter. Dominique Reill brings
us through the Iron Curtain, revealing the Little Red Book as a symbol of
common cause for anti-imperialist partisans in socialist Yugoslavia and
capitalist Italy. On the other hand, Quinn Slobodian shows us both sides
of the Berlin Wall to argue that fashionable fascination with the Little Red
Book took fundamentally different forms in East and West Germany. In
France, as Julian Bourg explains, the Little Red Book launched a popular
intellectual movement rife with contradictions. Bill Mullen's chapter
narrates the history of Afro-Asian radicalism in the United States, where
the Little Red Book provided a textual basis for Third World solidarity in
the heart of the First World.

Ban Wang's concluding chapter, originally delivered as the keynote
address at our Berkeley conference, brings the discussion back to our
fundamental premise: the Little Red Book is what people made of it. It is
perhaps tempting to think of it as the sacred word of a totalitarian
godhead, exerting its numinous power over the mass of enslaved idol-
aters – or as an ironic accessory for the nonbelievers who know better.
Against the grain of such assumptions, Ban Wang argues that in China
the Little Red Book – as a fixed text open to interpretation – set in motion
a reformation with genuine possibilities for protest, agency, emancipation, and democracy. This volume is intended to challenge and provoke
the reader; it is an opening. In the beginning is the word – but that is only
the beginning.

1 Introduction
The spiritual atom bomb and its global fallout

Alexander C. Cook

> Once Mao Tse-tung's thought is grasped by the broad masses, it
> becomes a source of strength and a spiritual atom bomb of infinite power.
>
> Lin Biao, foreword to the second edition

This introduction is not so much about Mao's quotations themselves,
but rather the effusive foreword that introduced Chinese and foreign
readers to *Quotations from Chairman Mao* at the height of the Chinese
Cultural Revolution. Credited to Lin Biao, Mao's top military man and
tireless promoter of the Little Red Book, it described how the written
word could transform ideas into a material force for revolution.
According to the foreword, the Little Red Book was a weapon of mass
instruction – the intercontinental delivery system for a potentially
world-shattering ideological payload: "Once Mao Tse-tung's thought
is grasped by the broad masses, it becomes a source of strength and a
spiritual atom bomb of infinite power."[1] Lin Biao's metaphor was an
adulatory exaggeration, of course, but it should not be dismissed as only
that. I will show, through an extended exegesis, that the spiritual atom
bomb was in fact a coherent concept within its own Maoist intellectual
context. More broadly, I will argue that the spiritual atom bomb was
also a telling symptom of anxieties about the Cultural Revolution in
China, about the Sino-Soviet split within the socialist world, about the
larger Cold War between capitalism and socialism, and about the global
confrontation with the real prospect of nuclear Armageddon. Lin Biao's
foreword to the Little Red Book arose from historical conditions
specific to China in the 1960s, yet it was also a product of the global
Atomic Age. In that moment of global existential crisis, when faceless

---

[1] Lin Biao, Foreword to the Second Chinese Edition (December 16, 1966). Full text of the
official English translation is available at www.marxists.org/reference/archive/lin-biao/
1966/12/16.htm, accessed October 1, 2012. A rousing choral version of the foreword,
composed by Tang Ke and Sheng Mao and performed by the China Railway Art Troupe
in 1968, can be heard at www.youtube.com/watch?v=Chgz2meXKd0, accessed September
30, 2012.

technology threatened to destroy all mankind, the spiritual atom bomb was an alternate vision of the atomic that affirmed the primacy of the spiritual over the material.

The era of the spiritual atom bomb was brief but explosive, roughly corresponding to the height of the Cultural Revolution in China and including the global movements of 1968. The Little Red Book originated in the Chinese military under the leadership of Lin Biao, who helped to build the cult of Mao. Lin Biao incorporated the study of Maoist texts into daily drill and encouraged the emulation of moral exemplars such as the model soldier Lei Feng; these practices culminated in May 1964 in the internal-use publication by the General Political Department of the PLA of *Quotations from Chairman Mao*. According to the foreword added to the reprint of August 1965, and "in conformity with Comrade Lin Biao's instructions," the Little Red Book was to be issued "to every soldier in the whole army, just as we issue weapons." Amidst the nationwide campaign to "Learn from the People's Liberation Army," this handy piece of standard-issue equipment also became a prized trophy for ardent youth activists. In late August 1966, in the push that gave the Cultural Revolution its chaotic momentum, Mao approvingly reviewed throngs of young Red Guards waving Little Red Books in Tiananmen Square. The book was soon made available to the general public in order to, as Lin Biao's new foreword said, "arm the minds of the people throughout the country" with Mao Zedong Thought.[2] Mastery of Mao Zedong Thought could split the atom of the mind and unleash the power of human consciousness to destroy the old world – and create a better one in its place.

The rise and fall of the spiritual atom bomb was tied to the personal fortunes of Lin Biao, with whom the book is so closely associated. Although Lin Biao did not take an active role in creating the Little Red Book – it was not his style to take an active role in much of anything – and it is doubtful that he even wrote the foreword credited to him, nevertheless his name was the recognizable corporate mark for a particular

---

[2] The previous foreword addressed to the army had said "to arm the minds of all our commanders": General Political Department, Foreword to the Reprint of the First Edition (August 1, 1965). For a word-by-word comparison of the forewords to the first and second editions, see Stuart R. Schram, ed., *Quotations from Chairman Mao Tse-tung* (New York: Frederick A. Praeger, 1967), pp. xxxi–xxxiii. Schram, the foremost Western interpreter of Mao in the postwar era, was a polymath and polyglot who had assisted the Manhattan Project before turning to the study of politics. "Having worked on the bomb," his widow explained in his obituary, "he wanted to study more of human beings." See William Yardley, "Stuart R. Schram, Nuclear Physicist and Mao Scholar, Dies at 88," *New York Times* (July 21, 2012).

reading of Maoist ideology.[3] The appearance of the phrase "spiritual atom bomb" in PLA publications beginning in 1960 typified Lin Biao's signature brand of "politics in command" and his calls to structure all aspects of military affairs around Mao Zedong Thought.[4] Lin Biao had ascended to power in the late 1950s on the strength of his unquestioned loyalty to Mao in the Chairman's darkest moment, the collapse of the Great Leap Forward. Ever passive and deferential by disposition, Lin's reliable hold on "the barrel of the gun" proved indispensable in Mao's subsequent return to political power.[5] For while the Cultural Revolution had the appearance of a popular movement – and it is true that much of its violence unfolded in decentralized and unpredictable ways – it was Lin Biao's access to military power that secured Mao's mobilization of the masses to "bombard the headquarters" in August 1966. At key moments in Mao's attack on rivals in the power structure, which developed over the next three years, Lin Biao's loyal units protected the radical insurgents, presided over the purge of the bureaucracy, held disgruntled military commanders in check, and stepped in when internecine struggles ceased to be useful to Mao.[6] For his contributions, Lin Biao was a prime beneficiary of the Cultural Revolution, explicitly designated Mao's successor in the constitution passed by the Ninth Party Congress in April 1969. In truly dialectical fashion, however, the pinnacle of Lin Biao's rise also marked the precipice from which he fell. At the same party congress, Mao voiced annoyance with Lin Biao's insistence that the new constitution incorporate another phrase from his foreword to the Little Red Book, which stated that "Comrade Mao Zedong is the greatest Marxist–Leninist of our era. He has inherited, defended, and developed Marxism–Leninism with genius, creatively and comprehensively, and has brought it to a higher and completely new stage." The seemingly arcane debate that ensued (whether "genius" was a bourgeois concept) provided the first of several hints that the

---

[3] It was common practice among Chinese communist ideologues, including Mao, to read speeches and issue public documents edited, compiled, or written by others. Daniel Leese dispels the myth of Lin Biao as architect of the Little Red Book in *Mao Cult: Rhetoric and Ritual in China's Cultural Revolution* (Cambridge: Cambridge University Press, 2011), p. 109. On Lin Biao's plagiarism of himself or others in the foreword, see Schram, ed., *Quotations*, p. xxv–xxvi.

[4] See for example the Army Day (August 1) 1960 editorial in *PLA Daily*. On "politics in command," see Henry Yuhuai He, *Dictionary of Political Thought in the People's Republic of China* (Armonk: M. E. Sharpe, 2001), pp. 457–60.

[5] Characterization of Lin Biao based on Frederick C. Teiwes and Warren Sun, *The Tragedy of Lin Biao: Riding the Tiger during the Cultural Revolution, 1966–1971* (Honolulu: University of Hawaii Press, 1996), pp. 1–18.

[6] Roderick MacFarquhar and Michael Schoenhals, *Mao's Last Revolution* (Cambridge, Mass.: Belknap Press of Harvard University Press, 2006).

Chairman's trust in his "best student" and "closest comrade-in-arms" was less than complete.[7] Even so, no one expected the revelation in September 1971, just two-and-a-half years later, that Lin Biao had died in a plane crash – allegedly fleeing the country after an aborted assassination attempt on Mao! Naturally, Lin Biao's foreword to the Little Red Book was expunged, and the era of the spiritual atom bomb was over. Nevertheless, from the mid 1960s to the early 1970s in China, and somewhat later elsewhere, Lin Biao's doctrine of the spiritual atom bomb was the orthodox interpretation that introduced Mao's Little Red Book to the world.

The Foolish Old Man

Lin Biao's elevation of Mao Zedong Thought to the power of an atom bomb sounds like a foolish boast, emblematic of the belligerent irrationality of the Mao cult at the height of the Cultural Revolution. It would seem to vastly overestimate the power of ideology, on the one hand, and to vastly underestimate the power of the actual atom bomb, on the other. Be that as it may, Lin Biao's spiritual atom bomb metaphor is so bizarre, and yet so symptomatic of its times, that it merits serious consideration on its own terms. Mao's own defense of such "foolishness" is found in "The Foolish Old Man who Removed the Mountains" (1945), a story canonized by Lin Biao as one of the Three Constantly Read Articles. "The Foolish Old Man" is one of the longest continuous passages in the Little Red Book, and the only text to appear there in its entirety:

There is an ancient Chinese fable called "The Foolish Old Man Who Removed the Mountains." It tells of an old man who lived in northern China long, long ago and was known as the Foolish Old Man of North Mountain. His house faced south and beyond his doorway stood two great peaks obstructing the way. He called his sons, and hoe in hand they began to dig up these mountains with great determination. Another graybeard, known as the Wise Old Man, saw them and said derisively, "How silly of you to do this! It is quite impossible for you few to dig up those two huge mountains." The Foolish Old Man replied, "When I die, my sons will carry on; when they die, there will be my grandsons, and then their sons and grandsons, and so on to infinity. High as they are, the mountains cannot grow any higher and with every bit we dig, they will be that much lower. Why can't we clear them away?" Having refuted the Wise Old Man's wrongheaded view, he went on digging every day, unshaken in his conviction. God was moved by this, and he sent down two angels, who carried the mountains away on their backs. Today, two big mountains lie like a dead weight on the Chinese people. One is imperialism, the other is feudalism. The Chinese Communist Party has

---

[7] Ibid., pp. 285–336.

long made up its mind to dig them up. We must persevere and work unceasingly, and we, too, will touch God's heart. Our God is none other than the masses of the Chinese people. If they stand up and dig together with us, why can't these two mountains be cleared away?

This passage has been interpreted primarily as a story of perseverance, determination, and strength of will, as it concludes the chapter of the Little Red Book on "Self-Reliance and Arduous Struggle." But there are deeper meanings that surface when we answer possible objections to the application of this traditional fable to the socialist revolution in China: Isn't it contrary to the logic of self-reliance to invoke external forces: the literal *dei ex machina* of gods and angels? Aren't such manifestations of the spiritual alien to the materialist viewpoint of Marxism–Leninism? And isn't their sudden intervention contrary to the lesson of persistence and accumulated effort? To answer, we must reinterpret "The Foolish Old Man" as Mao's followers would, from the viewpoint of Mao's interpretation of dialectical materialism and with special attention to the *mass* character of revolutionary change.

First, the agency referred to by the fable is not external. The demystified God, as Mao explains somewhat clumsily, "is none other than the masses," and the angels are their agents, the revolutionary vanguard of the Chinese Communist Party. The party cannot succeed on its own; it needs to touch the hearts of the people and enlist their support in removing the mountains. The same idea is expressed more clearly in a metaphor from the guerrilla days: the party and its army must be like fish in the water.[8] The masses are not external, but rather are the medium in which the party operates. The revolutionary force is drawn from the masses, and the masses will become the revolutionary force; without the masses the party will flounder and die. Thus in his introductory remarks to the story of "The Foolish Old Man," Mao says, "We must first raise the political consciousness of the vanguard so that, resolute and unafraid of sacrifice, they will surmount every difficulty to win victory. But this is not enough; we must also arouse the political consciousness of the entire people so that they may willingly and gladly fight together with us for victory." The revolution is necessarily a mass movement.

Second, Mao's invocation of the spiritual is not necessarily contrary to the materialist outlook. The Chinese term "spiritual" (*jingshen*) here refers to phenomena with subjective existence in the human mind, as opposed to the material, which exists objectively outside of human consciousness. However, the material and the spiritual are not mutually

---

[8] Mao Zedong, "On Guerilla Warfare," www.marxists.org/reference/archive/mao/works/1937/guerrilla-warfare/ch06.htm.

exclusive in Maoist doctrine, but instead are dialectically intertwined by the unity of opposites. Spiritual phenomena may be ultimately reducible to manifestations of the material. As such, subjective thought can motivate human beings to know and change their objective conditions.[9] Mao proposed this relationship between the material and the spiritual, in his seminal essay on dialectical ontology, "On Contradiction" (1937), which is more fully explored in Julian Bourg's chapter on French Maoism. Mao's essay introduces two concepts: first, the notion of the "principal contradiction," the one whose resolution is decisive for unraveling the complex knot of secondary contradictions; and second, the notion of the "principal aspect of the contradiction," the side of the contradiction whose positive development will be decisive in its resolution. Mao points out that these relationships are dialectical and dynamic: the secondary acts upon the principal, and at times may even become dominant. Therefore, concludes Mao, in the contradiction between the material and the spiritual, the material is only *generally* the principal aspect:

When the superstructure (politics, culture, etc.) obstructs the development of the economic base, political and cultural changes become principal and decisive. Are we going against materialism when we say this? No. The reason is that while we recognize that in the general development of history the material determines the mental, and social being determines social consciousness, we also – and indeed must – recognize the reaction of mental on material things, of social consciousness on social being and of the superstructure on the economic base. This does not go against materialism; on the contrary, it avoids mechanical materialism and firmly upholds dialectical materialism.[10]

At the crucial moment of revolution, the spiritual can become decisive in the transformation of the material.

Third, sudden transformation is not contrary to accumulation, perseverance, and protracted struggle – it results *from* accumulation. Of the three basic laws of dialectics identified by Engels, one is transformation of quantity into quality. (Mao, following Stalin, saw this not as a separate law, but as a special case of the unity and struggle of opposites.[11])

---

[9] Mao's philosophical position of ontological monism with epistemological dualism was developed through an active but nevertheless fairly orthodox reading of the basic texts of the Soviet New Philosophy of the 1930s. See Nick Knight, *Marxist Philosophy in China: From Qu Qiubai to Mao Zedong, 1923–1945* (Dordrecht: Springer, 2005), esp. pp. 171–95.

[10] Mao Zedong, "On Contradiction" (August 1937), www.marxists.org/reference/archive/mao/selected-works/volume-1/mswv1_17.htm, accessed September 10, 2012. The latter half is excerpted in *Quotations from Chairman Mao Tse-tung*, chapter 22.

[11] See discussion at Slavoj Žižek, *On Practice and On Contradiction: Žižek Presents Mao* (London: Verso, 2007), pp. 11, 181.

The classic example is the phase change of liquid water into steam: the incremental quantitative change in temperature leads to a sudden qualitative change in form. If the masses are the water, the medium of change, then it is the agitation of myriad individual molecules that will lead to a fundamental transformation in the collective whole –in other words, a revolution.

Spiritual fission and the weaponization of ideology

Lin Biao's spiritual atom bomb refers to an exceptionally powerful kind of agitation, however, and not merely to the external application of heat or kinetic energy. Fission seeks to release vast amounts of *internal* energy, by splitting from the inside, and this process is fundamental to the Maoist worldview. For Mao, the fundamental law of dialectical materialism is the unity and struggle of opposites, sometimes manifested as "two combine into one" but more often as "one divides into two." The universe is characterized by struggle: "In any given thing, the *unity* of opposites is conditional, temporary, and transitory, and hence relative, whereas the *struggle* of opposites is universal."[12] Moreover, struggle that is sufficiently violent to break nuclear bonds can release vast amounts of energy; the key to such fission is to strike at the apparently indivisible core.

As a "universal" phenomenon in Mao's worldview, fission has spiritual manifestations. A mass change of consciousness can initiate spiritual fission, releasing tremendous material force. In this example from 1958, Mao spoke of the Chinese nation as an atom to be split:

> Now our enthusiasm has been aroused. Ours is an ardent nation, now swept by a burning tide. There is a good metaphor for this: our nation is like an atom ... When this atom's nucleus is smashed the thermal energy released will have really tremendous power. We shall be able to do things which we could not do before.[13]

Mao was talking here about a fundamental split: the struggle of self against self. For Mao, the real object of revolutionary struggle was the revolutionary's own consciousness. The Chinese communists' preferred technique for spiritual revolution was a dialectical process of "struggle–criticism–transformation," which they employed extensively for ideological indoctrination, party discipline, and social control. Ban

---

[12] Mao Zedong, "Talk on Questions of Philosophy" (August 18, 1964), www.marxists.org/reference/archive/mao/selected-works/volume-9/mswv9_27.htm, accessed September 14, 2012. Žižek (*On Practice and On Contradiction*, p. 11) likens Mao's view to Adorno's theory of negative dialectics.

[13] Mao Zedong, Speech at the Supreme State Conference (January 28, 1958), www.marxists.org/reference/archive/mao/selected-works/volume-8/mswv8_03.htm.

Wang in his chapter also considers the liberating potential of such a quasi-religious transformation. At the heart of struggle–criticism–transformation was intensive *self*-criticism, which came to be practiced constantly during the Cultural Revolution. This is why Lin Biao described the Cultural Revolution as a self-revolution, "a revolution against those of us who have been engaged in the former revolutions."[14] Here in this excerpt from *People's Daily*, Lin Biao explicitly reiterates that each person is to wage a continuing revolution against oneself:

> To look at oneself according to the law of "one divides into two" means that one must make revolution against one's own subjective world as well as the objective world. Comrade Lin Biao instructs us: "We must regard ourselves as an integral part of the revolutionary force and, at the same time, constantly regard ourselves as a target of the revolution. In making revolution, we must also revolutionize ourselves. Without revolutionizing ourselves, we cannot make this revolution."[15]

So, the most basic fissile material of the revolution is the subjective consciousness of the apparently atomistic individual, though as the story of "The Foolish Old Man" says, the process of transformation cannot be limited to the cadres. For fission to become self-sustaining, it must be concentrated on and applied to a critical mass. Thus, Lin Biao says, Mao Zedong Thought becomes a spiritual atom bomb only "once it is grasped by the masses."

It is the "grasping" of Mao Zedong Thought that allows it to be used as a weapon, says Lin Biao, and his meaning is fairly literal. Here Lin's argument invokes Engels' remarkable thesis that humans became differentiated from other animals by the dialectical co-evolution of the brain and the hand through labor.[16] According to Engels, all tools and technologies – the flint axe, the iron hoe, the spinning wheel, the steam engine, the paintbrush – are extensions of this hand–brain dyad, designed to carry out human purposes. The same principle applies to that class of tools we call weapons, from the most primitive stone to the atom bomb. Without a human being to use it, the tool (which is after all merely an extension of the person) is useless. Therefore, the power of the weapon as

---

[14] Lin Biao, "Directive on the Cultural Revolution" (September 13, 1967) in China Problems Research Center, ed., *Selected Works of Lin Piao* (Hong Kong: Chih Luen Press, 1970), p. 152.

[15] "Look at One's Self in the Light of Dividing One into Two," *People's Daily* (July 19, 1968), reproduced in David Milton, Nancy Milton, and Franz Schurmann, eds., *People's China: Social Experimentation, Politics, Entry onto the World Scene, 1966–1972* (New York: Vintage, 1974), pp. 202–05.

[16] Frederick Engels, "The Part Played by Labour in the Transformation of Ape to Man" (1876), www.marxists.org/archive/marx/works/1876/part-played-labour/index.htm, accessed October 2, 2012.

a material object is inseparable from the subjective spiritual or ideological power of the person who wields it. In Mao's own words, "Weapons are an important factor in war, but not the decisive factor; it is people, not things that are decisive. The contest of strength is not only a contest of military and economic power, but also a contest of human power and morale. People necessarily wield military and economic power."[17]

This supposition is the basis for Mao's doctrine of "people's war," which became influential among Third World revolutionaries, including the Naxalites of India (see Sreemati Chakrabarti's chapter) and the Shining Path of Peru (see David Scott Palmer's chapter). Mao's faith in the people derived in part from his belief in the historical teleology of Marxism, but it was also grounded in practical experience. In his conflicts against the vastly superior material forces of the Chinese Nationalist regime and Imperial Japan, Mao knew his rag-tag armies could not succeed, at least initially, by using standard positional warfare. Victory required the mobile tactics of guerrilla warfare, but also a long-term strategy of protracted conflict in which the enemy could be weakened through attrition and his own forces strengthened through accumulation. But the rebels could survive long enough for this to happen only at the sufferance of the local populace. Therefore, the military doctrine of people's war rests on a social proposition: the "people's army" must provide benefits that outweigh the costs of provisioning them. More than that, even, the army must be embraced by the people as a necessary part *of* the people. In the present-day parlance of insurgency and counter-insurgency, you win the war by winning hearts and minds. In the language of Mao, if the soldiers are at home like fish in the water, then the people are the sustaining medium that will eventually overwhelm and drown the enemy. People's war proved successful in the war of resistance against Japan and in the subsequent civil war against the Nationalists, so it is no surprise that Mao should return to it in his confrontation with the nuclear superpowers.

By the outset of the Cold War, Mao had established his view that people's war could overcome the atomic threat. Consider, for example, his comments to the American journalist Anna Louise Strong in August 1946, just a year after the atomic bombing of Hiroshima and Nagasaki: "The atom bomb is a paper tiger which the US reactionaries use to scare people. It looks terrible, but in fact it isn't. Of course, the atom bomb is a weapon of mass slaughter, but the outcome of a war is decided by the

---

[17] Mao Zedong, "On Protracted War" (May 1938), www.marxists.org/reference/archive/mao/selected-works/volume-2/mswv2_09.htm, accessed September 14, 2012. This passage appears in chapter 12 of the Little Red Book.

people, not by one or two new types of weapon."[18] Here we have one half of the "foolish" boast, the apparent underestimation of the atomic bomb. The second half, the apparent overestimation of ideology, was introduced by Lin Biao in his famous paean to Mao, "Long Live the Victory of People's War" (1965):

Even if US imperialism brazenly uses nuclear weapons, it cannot conquer the people, who are indomitable. However highly developed modern weapons and technical equipment may be and however complicated the methods of modern warfare, in the final analysis the outcome of a war will be decided by the sustained fighting of the ground forces, by the fighting at close quarters on battlefields, by the political consciousness of the men, by their courage and spirit of sacrifice. Here the weak points of US imperialism will be completely laid bare, while the superiority of the revolutionary people will be brought into full play. The reactionary troops of US imperialism cannot possibly be endowed with the courage and the spirit of sacrifice possessed by the revolutionary people. The spiritual atom bomb which the revolutionary people possess is a far more powerful and useful weapon than the physical atom bomb.[19]

Mao had already stated that people matter more than weapons, and implied that ideological weapons could overcome physical weapons, but he left it to Lin Biao to state explicitly that the people were best armed with Mao Zedong Thought.

"Military affairs are a constituent part of politics, while politics includes more things, encompasses a wider scope. What is the best weapon? It's not the airplane, not artillery, not the tank, not the atom bomb. The best weapon is Mao Zedong Thought. What is the greatest military force? The greatest military force is people, armed with Mao Zedong Thought; it's courage and fearlessness of death."[20]

The Little Red Book was a weapon to be grasped by the hands of the people, so that Mao Zedong Thought could be grasped by their minds. But how could a sheaf of paper bound in vinyl be elevated to the status of an atom bomb, while the actual atom bomb was dismissed as a flimsy "paper tiger"?

---

[18] Mao Zedong, "Talk with American Anna Louise Strong" (1946), www.marxists.org/reference/archive/mao/selected-works/volume-4/mswv4_13.htm, accessed September 24, 2012.

[19] Lin Biao, "Long Live the Victory of People's War! In Commemoration of the 20th Anniversary of Victory in the Chinese People's War of Resistance Against Japan" (September 3, 1965), www.marxists.org/reference/archive/lin-biao/1965/09/peoples_war/ch08.htm, accessed September 24, 2012. The authorial attribution to Lin Biao is again questionable: see Teiwes and Sun, *The Tragedy of Lin Biao*, p. 27.

[20] Lin Biao, "Dui yijiuliuliu nian quanjun gongzuo tichu de wu xiang yuanze" [Five Principles Addressed to the All-Army Work Conference of 1966] (November 18, 1965), in *Lin Biao wenxuan* [Selected works of Lin Biao] (Hong Kong: Zhong-Gang chuanmei chubanshe, 2011), p. 413.

Paper tigers of the atomic age

Mao's supposedly cavalier attitude toward atomic weapons was a major point of contention with the Soviet Union, which withdrew its nuclear experts from China in 1960. However, Mao's negative assessment of the atom bomb was by no means based on a naïve underestimation of its capacity for physical destruction. In 1955, to the consternation of his Soviet allies, Mao asserted:

> The Chinese people are not to be cowed by US atomic blackmail. Our country has a population of 600 million and an area of 9,600,000 square kilometers. The United States cannot annihilate the Chinese nation with its small stack of atom bombs. Even if the US atom bombs were so powerful that, when dropped on China, they would make a hole right through the earth, or even blow it up, that would hardly mean anything to the universe as a whole, though it might be a major event for the solar system.[21]

We may be appalled at Mao's cosmic indifference toward human life, but we cannot say he thought the atom bomb powerless.[22] Nor did Mao's bravado arise from a confident belief that atomic bombs would never be used against China. In hindsight we know that not a single nuclear weapon was detonated in combat during the Cold War; but in Mao's time nuclear war seemed like a very real possibility, and China appeared to be one of the more likely targets. In the 1950s, China fought the US to a bloody stalemate on the Korean peninsula, and the Eisenhower administration pursued a New Look policy calling for heavy reliance on nuclear weaponry as a "virtually conventional" force.[23] Yet in 1958, as the confrontation over the Taiwan Strait teetered on the brink of open war, Mao spoke of the coming atomic holocaust as an eventuality, noting insolently that it was "not a bad thing":

> We have no experience in atomic war. So, how many will be killed cannot be known. The best outcome may be that only half of the population [of the world] is left and the second best may be only one-third. When 900 million are left out of 2.9 billion, several five-year plans can be developed for the total elimination of capitalism and for permanent peace. It is not a bad thing.[24]

---

[21] Mao Zedong, "The Chinese People Cannot be Cowed by the Atom Bomb" (January 28, 1955), www.marxists.org/reference/archive/mao/selected-works/volume-5/mswv5_40.htm, accessed September 14, 2012.

[22] See also Slavoj Žižek, "Mao Zedong: The Marxist Lord of Misrule," in *On Practice and On Contradiction*, pp. 9–10, 27–28.

[23] John Wilson Lewis and Xue Litai, *China Builds the Bomb*, Illustrated edn. (Stanford: Stanford University Press, 1988), pp. 16–19.

[24] Mao Zedong, "Speeches at the Second Plenum of the Eighth Party Congress: Second Speech" (May 17, 1958), www.marxists.org/reference/archive/mao/selected-works/volume-8/mswv8_10.htm, accessed October 1, 2012. See also Chen Jian, *Mao's China and the Cold War* (Chapel Hill: University of North Carolina Press, 2001), pp. 189–90.

Socialists do not want war, said Mao, but the destruction will only strengthen the socialist cause. Just as World War I gave birth to the Bolshevik revolution, and World War II to the Chinese revolution and anti-colonial movements worldwide, World War III might very well bring the global revolution to completion. Moreover, by the early 1960s the Sino-Soviet rift had become irreparable, with Mao accusing the Kremlin of practicing revisionism or "phoney" socialism. Sino-Soviet relations declined precipitously, and in 1969 border skirmishes even erupted into a brief shooting war. In the era of the Little Red Book, nuclear attack by either the United States or the Soviet Union seemed a very real possibility.

So, in Mao's entirely realistic assessment, atomic weapons could (and very possibly *would*) be used against China in the foreseeable future, and if so, the result would be massive death and destruction.[25] We need no further proof of Mao's appreciation of the atom bomb's military value than the fact that the People's Republic of China invested at great cost in a nuclear weapons program of its own. The PLA successfully tested its first atom bomb in 1964, without Soviet assistance, becoming just the fifth nation to do so, and in 1967 China became the fourth nation to successfully detonate a thermonuclear fission–fusion device. Neverthe-less, the Chinese military still gave preference to the spiritual: "China's material atom bomb has had a tremendous effect, but we always maintain that the significant human factor and the policy of turning the whole people into fighting men constitute a powerful spiritual atom bomb which we have long had in our possession. Our enemies have never had such a spiritual atom bomb."[26] Chinese rhetoric caused the Soviets and Americans to fear a nuclear-armed loose cannon in the East – an inscrut-able "Mr. China A-Bomb."[27] However, a more sober RAND report from 1963 proved prescient, insisting that "*the Chinese do understand the significance of nuclear warfare and are not inclined to be reckless.*"[28] China

[25] For a discussion of how Mao's view evolved over time, see Shu Guang Zhang, "Between 'Paper' and 'Real Tigers': Mao's View of Nuclear Weapons," in John Lewis Gaddis, Philip Gordon, Ernest May, and Jonathan Rosenberg, eds., *Cold War Statesmen Confront the Bomb* (Oxford: Oxford University Press, 1999), pp. 194–215.

[26] Xinhua report on a conference of the General Political Department of the PLA, quoted in "People's Militia: A Spiritual Atom Bomb" in *Radio Free Europe Research: Communist Area* (CHINA) (October 20, 1964).

[27] "Mr. China A-Bomb" epithet from "South of the Mountains to North of the Seas: Excerpts from American Journalist Edgar Snow's Interview with Mao Tse-tung" (January 9, 1965) in *Selected Works of Mao Zedong*, vol. IX, www.marxists.org/reference/archive/mao/selected-works/volume-9/appendix.htm, accessed October 2, 2012.

[28] Alice Langley Hsieh, *Chinese Nuclear Force* (Santa Monica: RAND Corporation, 1963), p. 15 (italics in original). On American nuclear Orientalism, see Hugh Gusterson, "Nuclear Weapons and the Other in the American Imagination," in *People of the Bomb:*

entered the age of the spiritual atom bomb with a first-hand knowledge of the physical atom bomb – there can be no question of foolishness on that count – yet Mao continued to denigrate the atom bomb as a paper tiger. Nuclear weapons could destroy the world, he argued, but still they could not *win* it.

This did not mean that China could ignore the atomic threat, of course, but Mao treated the atom bomb the same as any paper tiger: tactically it is dangerous, but strategically it is vulnerable. "Despise the enemy strategically," was his mantra, "but take full account of it tactically." Beginning with the Korean War in the 1950s and continuing through the realignment of the 1970s, China made definite preparations to weather a nuclear storm. To the tactical and logistical provisions, "Dig tunnels deep, store grain everywhere," Mao added a strategic imperative: "Never seek hegemony."[29] It was this word "hegemony" that best summarized the Cold War for Mao, and it was the world order of superpower hegemony that stood to be annihilated by the spiritual atom bomb. "Mao Tse-tung's thought is Marxism–Leninism of the era in which imperialism is heading for total collapse and socialism is advancing to world-wide victory," explained Lin Biao's foreword.[30] Less than three years later, speaking on the anniversary of Russia's October Revolution and at the height of China's Cultural Revolution, Lin Biao boasted that the blast radius of the spiritual atom bomb was global: "Once Marxism–Leninism–Mao Zedong Thought is integrated with the revolutionary practice of the people of all countries, *the entire old world* will be shattered to smithereens."[31]

Three worlds apart

The dropping of the atom bomb at the conclusion of World War II left the globe divided into the First World of capitalism, the Second World of socialism, and a "developing" Third World, which served as the battleground of a Cold War between them. The leaders of the First and Second Worlds – the United States and the Soviet Union – were

Portraits of America's Nuclear Complex (Minneapolis: University of Minnesota Press, 2004), pp. 21–47.

[29] See, for example, www.marxists.org/reference/archive/mao/selected-works/volume-5/mswv5_22.htm, accessed September 28, 2012. The USA and other Cold War belligerents made similar plans to weather an attack.

[30] The ordering of the phrases suggests a two-stage revolution, first anti-imperialist (anti-hegemonic), then socialist (anti-revisionist).

[31] Lin Biao, "Speech at Peking Rally Commemorating the Fiftieth Anniversary of the October Revolution" (November 7, 1967) in China Problems Research Center, ed., *Selected Works of Lin Piao*, p. 172.

Fig. 1. Arming the people with Mao Zedong Thought; the warhead reads:
"Down with American imperialism! Down with Soviet revisionism!"
Source: Revolutionary Committee of the Cultural Office of the
Shenyang Revolutionary Committee, "Organize contingents of the
people's militia on a large scale," ca. 1969. (Stefan R. Landsberger
Collection, International Institute of Social History, Amsterdam.)

supposed paradigms of capitalism and socialism, and they were "superpowers" by virtue of their nuclear arsenals. All other nations had joined one armed camp or the other, or soon would do so. This was the conventional wisdom, at least; Mao offered a different assessment. China had entered World War II with a united front between the Chinese Communist Party and Chiang Kai-shek's Nationalist Party, reasoning that the clash between socialism and capitalism must take a back seat to the fight against Japanese imperialism. After World War II, Mao once again turned to civil war and socialist revolution in China. On a global scale, however, Mao remained convinced that for the time being the principal contradiction in the world was not between capitalism and socialism, but between imperialism and anti-imperialism.

The Sino-Soviet split added a new dimension to Mao's understanding of global imperialism. With the Soviet Union abandoning revolution at home and seeking peaceful accommodation with the capitalist world abroad, Mao spoke of three ideological worlds: capitalism, socialism, and revisionism. Even more troubling to Mao was the increasingly forceful imposition of cultural chauvinism and military domination by the revisionist Soviets over the genuinely socialist states. Now Mao began to distinguish between two types of imperialism. The "old" imperialism, which Lenin had identified as the globalization of capitalism, was clearly in decline as waves of national liberation movements attended the postwar dissolution of the great maritime empires. However, the "new" imperialism of superpower hegemony had risen to take its place. This superpower hegemony consisted of both American capitalist imperialism and Soviet social-imperialism. Superpower hegemony was postwar imperialism par excellence, and the atom bomb its most terrible weapon. "The US and Soviet Union both have nuclear weapons," Mao stated plainly, "and they want to dominate the world."[32] Unless a third way could be found between the Americans and the Soviets, the Cold War – and possibly the world – would end with the atom bomb.

Confronted with the existential threat of nuclear war, Albert Einstein and several key Manhattan Project scientists had pleaded in 1946, "The unleashed power of the atom has changed everything save our modes of thinking, and we thus drift toward unparalleled catastrophe ... A new type of thinking is essential if mankind is to survive and move toward

---

[32] "There are Two Intermediate Zones," part II, excerpt from talk with Kikunami Katsumi, Politburo member of the Japanese CP (January 5, 1964) in Ministry of Foreign Affairs of the People's Republic of China and Party Literature Research Center of the Central Committee of the Communist Party of China, *Mao Zedong on Diplomacy* (Beijing: Foreign Languages Press, 1998), pp. 388.

higher levels."[33] The search for a third way took many forms, including the Third World movement for national liberation on its own terms, and the Non-Aligned Movement touted by Tito, Nehru, and others. But it was the spiritual atom bomb, Mao Zedong Thought, that presented itself as more than an opt-out or a political compromise – as above all a new way of *thinking*. Mao's thinking on the atomic age constellated in 1964. This was the year that he spoke openly of defying superpower hegemony, the year that China acquired the physical atom bomb, and the year that Lin Biao's military first issued its soldiers the Little Red Book.

Mao's unorthodox interpretation of the Cold War order revealed worlds in contradiction and susceptible to fission. The division *between* the two superpowers was obvious, delineating the two sides of the Cold War. Mao's innovation was to argue that this Cold War division was actually the manifestation of the unity of opposites. The Soviet Union and United States were dialectical poles of an underlying unity, he said, and the struggle between them was a contradiction *internal* to the world of superpower hegemony. Moreover, while the United States and Soviet Union appeared to lead two insoluble global alliances, in fact the superpowers were isolated in their hegemony, with the entire rest of the world caught between them. Mao sketched out his theory of the "intermediate zone" in January 1964 in a talk with a visiting Japanese communist:

When we talk about intermediate zones, we refer to two separate parts. The vast economically backward countries in Asia, Africa, and Latin America constitute the first. Imperialist and advanced capitalist countries represented by Europe [and Japan] constitute the second. Both are opposed to American control. Countries in Eastern Europe, on the other hand, are against control by the Soviet Union. This trend is quite obvious.[34]

The idea of intermediate zones would be formalized some ten years later as Mao's Theory of Three Worlds, but already we see the precursors of a radical reconfiguration.[35] At the very least, common cause against superpower hegemony opened up the possibility of alliances between

---

[33] Albert Einstein, writing as chairman of the Emergency Committee of Atomic Scientists, quoted in "Atomic Education Urged by Einstein: Scientists in Plea for $200,000 to Promote New Type of Essential Thinking," *New York Times* (May 25, 1946), p. 11.

[34] "There are Two Intermediate Zones," part II, excerpt from talk with Kikunami Katsumi, Politburo member of the Japanese CP (January 5, 1964) in Ministry of Foreign Affairs, *Mao Zedong on Diplomacy*, pp. 388.

[35] See Yang Kuisong, "Zhong-Mei hejie guocheng zhong de Zhongfang bianzou: Mao Zedong sange shijie lilun tichu de Beijing tanxi" [A variation on the Chinese side during Sino-American reconciliation: An analysis of the background of Mao's Three Worlds theory] in *Cuiruo de lianmeng: Lengzhan yu Zhong-Su guanxi* [Fragile alliance: the Cold War and Sino-Soviet relations] (Beijing: Social Sciences Academic Press, 2010), pp. 457–81.

the old imperialist states of the capitalist world, the non-revisionist states of the socialist world, and the oppressed nations of the Third World.

However, hegemony could not be challenged without first breaking the superpowers' exclusive hold on atomic weapons. The United Kingdom had tested its own atom bomb in 1952, drawing heavily on their wartime cooperation in the Manhattan Project, but the British remained close allies with the Americans. More significant was French acquisition of the atom bomb in 1960, by which France sought to reassert its traditional Great Power status and to announce its independence within the capitalist world.[36] Similarly, China's acquisition of the atom bomb in October 1964 safeguarded its breakaway from the world of Soviet revisionist socialism. Earlier in the year, when Chinese and French diplomats met to discuss the normalization of relations, Mao compared the two nations' efforts to break the thrall of the superpowers:[37]

The US is frightening some countries, forbidding them to do business with us. The US is a paper tiger; don't take it seriously; it will break at the slightest touch. The Soviet Union is a paper tiger, too; we don't trust it at all. I'm not superstitious. Perhaps you are religious. I'm an atheist and afraid of nothing. It's not acceptable if big powers try to control us. France is a small country. China, too. Only the US and Soviet Union are big powers. Do we have to seek their approval on everything and go on pilgrimage to their land?[38]

Only an inveterate underdog such as Mao could describe France and China as "small" countries, but his point was that nuclear arsenals had made the United States and Soviet Union seem "big" in a way that was qualitatively different. Expressing defiance against the superpowers in the language of religious disillusionment ("I'm not superstitious ... I'm an atheist ... Do we have to ... go on pilgrimage?"), Mao suggests the demystification of false gods, the awakening of consciousness to alienation and exploitation, and the emboldened grasp of one's own destiny. The acquisition of the physical atom bomb in the intermediate zone secured the possibility of spiritual conversion by the Little Red Book.

The global proliferation of the Little Red Book in the late 1960s and early 1970s, expertly detailed by Lanjun Xu in her chapter, reflected widespread disenchantment with the postwar status quo: the persistent inequalities that belied the promises of liberal capitalism, the less-than-utopian repression and drudgery of "actually existing" socialism, and the

---

[36] Philip H. Gordon, "Charles De Gaulle and the Nuclear Revolution," in Gaddis et al., eds., *Cold War Statesmen Confront the Bomb*, pp. 216–35.

[37] Jeremi Suri, *Power and Protest: Global Revolution and the Rise of Détente* (Cambridge, Mass.: Harvard University Press, 2003), pp. 73–79.

[38] Talk with French National Assembly Delegation (January 30, 1964) in Ministry of Foreign Affairs, *Mao Zedong on Diplomacy*, p. 398.

realization that Third World liberation had not allayed the poverty and violence engendered by an imbalanced world system. Mao's China increasingly self-identified with the Third World, throwing in its lot with the oppressed nations of the intermediate zone, and Lin Biao drew up grand visions of people's war on a global scale, with the world's hinterland surrounding and destroying its cities.[39] Third World rulers and revolutionaries for their part made mixed use of the spiritual atom bomb – donning its symbolic accoutrements, playing the Mao card to extract aid from China or others, engaging in dogmatic imitation, or attempting creative application of Mao's doctrines to local circumstances.[40] Our chapters show that for serious Maoists in the Third World, the Little Red Book was merely an entrée into more systematic study of revolutionary texts, especially the multi-volume *Selected Works of Mao Zedong*. In places where the Chinese state maintained a lasting relationship with the postcolonial regime, as in the case of Tanzania (see Priya Lal's chapter), Maoism provided the idioms and concepts of an alternative "shared imaginary" of the nation.

Within the socialist world, the Little Red Book exacerbated the potentially explosive fissure between revolution and revisionism. Mao argued that the Soviet Union had abandoned revolution at home and abroad, and in so doing had abandoned its comrades still fighting the good fight. By early 1964 Mao could speak of generalized discontent within the socialist world against the Soviet Union:

In fact, Khrushchev has not secured a big majority among the countries in the socialist camp. Romania has differing views; Poland can be counted as only half a supporter. Like the Americans, he wants to control others and tries to make them develop single-product economies, which is not feasible. Romania does not accept it. Cuba is quarreling with him.[41]

Only Albania would side decisively with China in the Sino-Soviet split, as discussed in Elidor Mëhilli's chapter, but heavy-handed Soviet imposition of its ideologies and institutions (and especially the invasion of socialist ally Czechoslovakia in August 1968) drew condemnation from a range of fraternal communist parties on both sides of the Iron Curtain. This feeling of common cause is explored in Quinn Slobodian's chapter on East and West Germany and in Dominique Reill's comparison of Italy and Yugoslavia. Moreover, as Elizabeth McGuire argues, while the Little

---

[39] Lin Biao, "Long Live the Victory of People's War!"

[40] See Alexander C. Cook, "Third World Maoism," in Timothy Cheek, ed., *Critical Introduction to Mao* (Cambridge: Cambridge University Press, 2010).

[41] Mao Zedong, Statement (January 17, 1964) in Ministry of Foreign Affairs, *Mao Zedong on Diplomacy*, p. 393.

Red Book was universally dismissed in the Soviet Union itself, the thoroughgoing denunciation of Maoism there provided a dress rehearsal for later dissident critiques of Soviet socialism.

The Little Red Book played well to divisions within capitalist society as well. Rocked by postwar decolonization, the waning of former imperial powers such as France and Japan that constituted the more developed part of the intermediate zone exemplified the shift from old imperialism to new: "On the one hand these countries oppress others; on the other hand they are oppressed by the United States and have contradictions with it."[42] In addition to external pressures of superpower hegemony and internal struggles between the proletariat and the bourgeoisie, the nations of the capitalist world also faced the internal effects of imperialism's external decline: economic shocks, military loss, social unrest, and political uncertainty. Moreover, groups representing oppressed minorities in the First World, such as the *Quotations*-toting Black Panthers, readily appropriated the language of Third World national liberation. Bill V. Mullen's study of Afro-Asian radicalism in the USA shows how the book could be a catalyst for both the fusion and split of identities. This, encompassing also generational disenchantment with the postwar order, helps to explain why the Little Red Book was picked as an appropriate symbol for the student movements of the late 1960s. However, the *ubiquity* of the Little Red Book is due not only to the prodigious printing power of the Foreign Languages Press in Beijing, but also to its remarkable form. Andrew Jones' provocative thesis about the Mao quotation as a prototype of the modern pop song is echoed in our chapters on Italy, the Soviet Union, and especially in Quinn Slobodian's discussion of "brand" books and "badge" books in Germany. This thread raises the intriguing question of whether the popularity of the Little Red Book represents the appropriation of radicalism by the commodity form or the appropriation of the commodity form by radicalism. What is certain is that the Little Red Book, as a flexible and dynamic script for revolution, travelled easily from its contingent and specific origins in China to a great many different kinds of places.

Conclusion

Maoist culture has afterlives in China and elsewhere, as shown here in the chapters by Guobin Yang and Julian Bourg. But the "spiritual atom bomb" belongs to a bygone era, the peculiar shadow of a *Zeitgeist* long

---

[42] Ibid.

past. Nevertheless, its internal logic is still discernible to us today through the schematic plans laid out in the Little Red Book. The essential elements were a theoretical understanding of spiritual fission (Mao's take on dialectics), the application of dialectical analysis to a particular set of historical conditions (Mao Zedong Thought), the accumulation of a critical mass (Cultural Revolution), and the engineering of a global delivery system (the Little Red Book). Wherever deployed, the spiritual atom bomb proved a powerful fission device, initiating chain reactions of escalating violence that threatened to destroy, for better or worse, the established structures of the world order. At times it even functioned like a spiritual hydrogen bomb, a spiritual fission–fusion device that joined unlikely allies to even greater effect. However, true to Mao's doctrine of "one divides into two," such fusion events were transitory, and never sufficiently sustained to hold together the imagined socialist collective. Instead, worldwide detonation of the spiritual atom bomb produced the characteristic mushroom cloud of water vapor, fissile material, and detritus – which soon fell back to the barren, irradiated landscape, its most lasting legacy being the half-lives of human trauma. Earlier we saw the dialecticians' metaphor of revolution as the mass agitation of myriad individual particles, like the phase change of water from liquid to gas. Perhaps this metaphor explains how the builders of the bomb could have mistaken the deadly mushroom cloud for the outward manifestation of a revolution.

BIBLIOGRAPHY

Chen Jian, *Mao's China and the Cold War* (Chapel Hill: University of North Carolina Press, 2001)
China Problems Research Center, ed., *Selected Works of Lin Piao* (Hong Kong: Chih Luen Press, 1970)
Cook, Alexander C., "Third World Maoism," in Timothy Cheek, ed., *Critical Introduction to Mao* (Cambridge: Cambridge University Press, 2010), pp. 288–312
Engels, Frederick, "The Part Played by Labour in the Transformation of Ape to Man," www.marxists.org/archive/marx/works/1876/part-played-labour/index.htm
Gaddis, John Lewis, Philip Gordon, Ernest May, and Jonathan Rosenberg, eds., *Cold War Statesmen Confront the Bomb* (Oxford: Oxford University Press, 1999)
Gordon, Philip H., "Charles De Gaulle and the Nuclear Revolution," in Gaddis et al., eds., *Cold War Statesmen Confront the Bomb*, pp. 216–35
Gusterson, Hugh, "Nuclear Weapons and the Other in the American Imagination," in *People of the Bomb: Portraits of America's Nuclear Complex* (Minneapolis: University of Minnesota Press, 2004), pp. 21–47

He, Henry Yuhuai, *Dictionary of Political Thought in the People's Republic of China* (Armonk: M. E. Sharpe, 2001)

Hsieh, Alice Langley, *Chinese Nuclear Force* (Santa Monica: RAND Corporation, 1963)

Knight, Nick, *Marxist Philosophy in China: From Qu Qiubai to Mao Zedong, 1923–1945* (Dordrecht: Springer, 2005)

Leese, Daniel, *Mao Cult: Rhetoric and Ritual in China's Cultural Revolution* (Cambridge: Cambridge University Press, 2011)

Lewis, John Wilson, and Xue Litai, *China Builds the Bomb*, illustrated edn. (Stanford: Stanford University Press, 1988)

Lin Biao, "Directive on the Cultural Revolution," in China Problems Research Center, ed., *Selected Works of Lin Piao*, pp. 147–58

"Dui yijiuliuliu nian quanjun gongzuo tichu de wu xiang yuanze" [Five principles addressed to the All-Army Work Conference of 1966] (November 18, 1965), in *Lin Biao wenxuan* [Selected works of Lin Biao] (Hong Kong: Zhong-Gang chuanmei chubanshe, 2011), pp. 412–13

"Long Live the Victory of People's War! In Commemoration of the 20th Anniversary of Victory in the Chinese People's War of Resistance Against Japan," www.marxists.org/reference/archive/lin-biao/1965/09/peoples_war/ch08.htm

"Look at One's Self in the Light of Dividing One into Two," *People's Daily*, July 19, 1968; reproduced in David Milton, Nancy Milton, and Franz Schurmann, eds., *People's China: Social Experimentation, Politics, Entry onto the World Scene, 1966–1972* (New York: Vintage, 1974), pp. 202–05

"Speech at Peking Rally Commemorating the Fiftieth Anniversary of the October Revolution," in China Problems Research Center, ed., *Selected Works of Lin Piao*, pp. 167–76

MacFarquhar, Roderick, and Michael Schoenhals, *Mao's Last Revolution* (Cambridge, Mass.: Belknap Press of Harvard University Press, 2006)

Mao Zedong, "The Chinese People Cannot be Cowed by the Atom Bomb," www.marxists.org/reference/archive/mao/selected-works/volume-5/mswv5_40.htm

"On Contradiction," www.marxists.org/reference/archive/mao/selected-works/volume-1/mswv1_17.htm

"On Guerilla Warfare," www.marxists.org/reference/archive/mao/works/1937/guerrilla-warfare/ch06.htm

"Khrushchev is Having a Hard Time," in Ministry of Foreign Affairs, *Mao Zedong on Diplomacy*, pp. 392–95

"On Protracted War," www.marxists.org/reference/archive/mao/selected-works/volume-2/mswv2_09.htm

"South of the Mountains to North of the Seas: Excerpts from American Journalist Edgar Snow's Interview with Mao Tse-tung," in *Selected Works of Mao Zedong*, vol. IX, www.marxists.org/reference/archive/mao/selected-works/volume-9/appendix.htm

"Speeches at the Second Plenum of the Eighth Party Congress: Second Speech," www.marxists.org/reference/archive/mao/selected-works/volume-8/mswv8_10.htm

"Talk with American Anna Louise Strong," www.marxists.org/reference/archive/mao/selected-works/volume-4/mswv4_13.htm

"Talk on Questions of Philosophy," www.marxists.org/reference/archive/mao/selected-works/volume-9/mswv9_27.htm

"There are Two Intermediate Zones," excerpts from talks with Kikunami Katsumi, Politburo member of the Japanese CP," in Ministry of Foreign Affairs, *Mao Zedong on Diplomacy*, pp. 387–89

Ministry of Foreign Affairs of the People's Republic of China and Party Literature Research Center of the Central Committee of the Communist Party of China, *Mao Zedong on Diplomacy* (Beijing: Foreign Languages Press, 1998)

Schram, Stuart R., ed., *Quotations from Chairman Mao Tse-tung* (New York: Frederick A. Praeger, 1967)

Suri, Jeremi, *Power and Protest: Global Revolution and the Rise of Détente* (Cambridge, Mass.: Harvard University Press, 2003)

Teiwes, Frederick C., and Warren Sun, *The Tragedy of Lin Biao: Riding the Tiger during the Cultural Revolution, 1966–1971* (Honolulu: University of Hawaii Press, 1996)

Yang Kuisong, "Zhong-Mei hejie guocheng zhong de Zhongfang bianzou: Mao Zedong sange shijie lilun tichu de Beijing tanxi" [A variation on the Chinese side during Sino-American reconciliation: an analysis of the background of Mao's Three Worlds theory], in *Cuiruo de lianmeng: Lengzhan yu Zhong-Su guanxi* [Fragile alliance: the Cold War and Sino-Soviet relations] (Beijing: Social Sciences Academic Press, 2010), pp. 457–81

Zhang, Shu Guang, "Between 'Paper' and 'Real Tigers': Mao's View of Nuclear Weapons," in Gaddis et al., eds., *Cold War Statesmen Confront the Bomb*, pp. 194–215

Žižek, Slavoj, "Mao Zedong: The Marxist Lord of Misrule," in *On Practice and On Contradiction: Žižek Presents Mao* (London: Verso, 2007), pp. 1–28

2   A single spark
Origins and spread of the Little Red Book in China

Daniel Leese

> Comrade Mao Tse-tung is the greatest Marxist-Leninist of our era. He has inherited, defended and developed Marxism-Leninism with genius, creatively and comprehensively and has brought it to a higher and completely new stage.
>
> Preface to the first English edition

Quotations from Chairman Mao (*Mao Zhuxi Yulu*), known colloquially as the "red treasure book" (*hong baoshu*) in Chinese, was the most prominent icon of the Cultural Revolution. It was printed just over one billion times[1] between 1966 and 1971, and in terms of print circulation ranks second only to the Bible. In China in the late 1960s it achieved supreme importance as the ultimate guide to political action and moral behavior. Several factors explain the Little Red Book's enormous distribution numbers and its resonance with the Chinese populace. First, the compilation was not a novel phenomenon in Chinese culture; collected sayings dating back to the Confucian *Analects* frequently were employed to spread the wisdom of religious or secular sages. Second, communist claims to represent the absolute truth of a scientific world-view encouraged utmost reverence for works in the Marxist–Leninist canon. The ingenious physical format of the *Quotations* presents a third distinctive feature. Fourth, and without doubt the most important reason, was the political environment. As the former propaganda establishment came under heavy attack for having hampered the spread of Mao Zedong Thought, the new leadership raised production numbers as proof of revolutionary loyalty. Finally, in the absence of a functioning party bureaucracy, the decontextualized quotations could be employed for highly diverse aims, and supplied skillful orators with a means of empowerment in local power struggles. This chapter traces the

---

[1] Numbers vary between 1.02 and 1.09 billion official copies; see for example Fang Houqu, "Mao Zedong zhuzuo chuban jishi (1949–1982 nian)" [Recollections of publishing Chairman Mao's works (1949–1982)], www.pubhistory.com/img/text/2/1062.htm, last accessed 27 September 2011.

fascinating and contingent history of the Little Red Book in China, from its traditional predecessors and its humble origins in the General Political Department of the People's Liberation Army (PLA) in May 1964, through the high tide of its cult status during the Cultural Revolution, and finally on to its withdrawal from circulation in February 1979.

Quotations traditions

Quotations from Chairman Mao belongs to the traditional Chinese genre of *yulu* (literally "records of utterances"): the speeches, sermons, or anecdotes of a particular philosophical school or master, recorded and later edited for didactic purposes. The classic example is the *Analects* of Confucius, compiled by disciples of the legendary sage, probably during the Warring States Period (475–221 BCE). The *yulu* genre gained unprecedented importance more than a thousand years later, during the Song dynasty, with the canonization of the *Analects* and the discourses of a second-generation Confucian disciple named Mencius. These *yulu* soon became the main basis for the imperial civil service examination, and consequently were associated with rote learning and the stifling of original thought in the late imperial period. Originally, however, the genre was highly popular and challenged established practices of intellectual discourse.

The first works consciously classified as *yulu* emerged in the late Tang and early Song dynasties. During this period of crisis, Chan Buddhist factions relied on the oral transmission of teachings in the form of public sermons or dialogues between teacher and students rather than on sutra recitation or written commentaries. The novelty of the genre was strongly related to its focus on immediate application and the possibility of embedding Buddhist scriptural truths in specific contexts. The records of conversations turned out to be highly successful in winning over new adherents, and therefore came to influence other traditions as well. The most renowned *yulu* were compiled by Neo-Confucian philosophers, such as the *Reflections on Things at Hand*, edited by Zhu Xi and Lü Zuqian.[2] While the Buddhist challenge presented an important stimulus for appropriating the new literary genre, the reasons behind the compilation of the Neo-Confucian *yulu* were manifold. Similar to the Buddhist tradition, the freewheeling conversation records were a welcome alternative to the highly restricted genre of in-line textual commentaries. The compilation of *yulu* allowed Song literati to "reflect on the canon

---

[2] Wing-Tsit Chan (trans.), *Reflections on Things at Hand: The Neo-Confucian Anthology compiled by Chu Hsi and Lü Tsu-ch'ien* (New York: Columbia University Press, 1967).

and to engage in dialogue with it, but at a greater distance and with more independence from its authority."[3]

The flourishing of *yulu* in the Song dynasty signified the confidence of the literati to take command of transmitted orthodoxy and develop it in new directions. As the voice of the canon receded, the importance of contemporary thinkers was elevated. The new genre still invoked the authority of the classics, but truth was no longer "simply a function of the moral platitudes that Confucius delivered";[4] instead, truth was derived from the active selection and arrangement of parts of the canon within new contexts. The *yulu* exemplified the intellectual ambitions of the day, to attain unity of knowledge through systematic thinking and move beyond the limitations of the classics. However, the *yulu* were not meant to stand alone. In his preface to the *Reflections on Things at Hand*, Zhu Xi emphasizes that the compilation provides a point of entry to the classics: having mastered the basics, the reader is to proceed to the complete works. Thus he warned against mistaking the study of selected quotations with grasping the whole: "Someone may shrink from effort and be contented with the simple and convenient, thinking that all he needs is to be found here, but this is not the purpose of the present anthology."[5] His co-editor Lü Zuqian added that one must not cull quotes without sufficient clarity as to vocabulary and context. Those who failed to follow these prescriptions would most certainly be "drifting in emptiness and vacuity, without anything to rely on."[6] The *yulu* genre therefore did not replace the classics, but offered a less orthodox way of assessing them.

The emergence of *yulu* thus signified, first, the effectiveness of transmitting moral truths orally; to a certain extent the records retained this flavor even after they had been written down and edited. Second, they offered space for exegesis and strengthened the voice of the present vis-à-vis the canonic writings, based on the premise that truth or a unity of knowledge could be achieved through present-day thinkers. Therefore, the genre took a novel approach that emphasized independent thinking, though the new texts lost their emancipating impact as they were elevated to orthodoxy. A similar pattern of development can be seen in the emergence of the Little Red Book within the Chinese Communist Party (CCP) some eight hundred years later.

[3] Daniel K. Gardner, "Modes of Thinking and Modes of Discourse in the Sung: Some Thoughts on the 'Yü-lu' ('Recorded Conversations') Texts," *Journal of Asian Studies* 50.3 (August 1991), p. 574.
[4] Albert Welter, *The* Linji lu *and the Creation of Chan Orthodoxy: The Development of Chan's Records of Sayings Literature* (Oxford: Oxford University Press, 2008), p. 73.
[5] Chan, *Reflections*, p. 2.   [6] Ibid., p. 3.

Marxist orthodoxy and creative exegesis

With the abolition of the traditional examination system in 1905 and the fall of the monarchy in 1912, Confucianism lost its position as the predominant ideology. During this period of political tumult and intellectual crisis, various parties emerged and presented themselves as agents of providence. The two main political contenders were the Nationalist Party (Guomindang) and the CCP. Both parties, as well as several others, strengthened their claims to ideological primacy by compiling collections of their leaders' speeches (though none of these bore the name *yulu*). Both the Nationalist Party and the CCP organized as Leninist parties, and here the Chinese tradition of *yulu* intersected with the newer genre of Marxist primers. Works such as the Russian *ABC of Communism*, written by Nikolai Bukharin and Yevgeni Preobrazhensky in October 1919 and shortly after translated into Chinese, offered a coherent introduction to the main topics and terminology of Marxism. While it contains only a few quotations from the Marxist canon, the frequent use of rhetorical questions gives the feeling of a lively dialogue between student and teacher. Deng Xiaoping later claimed that the Chinese translation of the *ABC of Communism* was highly instrumental in convincing him of the Marxist approach.[7]

Within the communist movement more broadly, quotes from the Marxist–Leninist canon played an important part in establishing the veracity of an argument, and naturally favored the experiences of the Soviet Union as the first state to have established a dictatorship of the proletariat. After a series of political and military failures ensued from attempts to follow the Soviet example too rigorously, differences emerged within the CCP over how to apply the new Marxist orthodoxy to national circumstances. During the late 1930s, it was Mao Zedong who achieved preeminence among his colleagues through the proven success of his guerrilla tactics and his strong reliance on nationalist sentiments, and not least through carefully crafting his public media image as the party's foremost theoretician. In October 1938, he first employed the classical quotation "seek truth from facts" to shake off the restraining impact of Soviet communist doctrines, and argued for the adaptation of Marxism–Leninism according to local conditions. Forty years later, Deng Xiaoping would quote the same sentence to free himself from the shackles of orthodox Maoism.

---

[7] Deng Xiaoping, *Deng Xiaoping wenxuan* [Selected writings of Deng Xiaoping], vol. III (Beijing: Renmin chubanshe, 1993), p. 382.

During the late 1930s and early 1940s, articles and speeches by Mao Zedong and several of his aides came to constitute the core of what was to emerge as the CCP's new guiding ideology, hailed as the "Sinicization" of Marxism. Mao acceded that his writings did not yet represent a complete system of thought. He therefore decided against the term "Maoism" and favored "Mao Zedong Thought" (*Mao Zedong sixiang*) to indicate its evolving nature. Mao quoted from both the communist canon and Chinese tradition to substantiate his arguments. The effect of emancipating himself from Soviet orthodoxy considerably advanced Mao Zedong's power, as exemplified by the Yan'an Rectification campaign in 1942–43, when guided study of Mao texts and self-criticism of erroneous thought and practice were used to integrate a massive influx of party recruits.

The reprint of Mao's writings and speeches in comprehensive fashion started in the wake of the Seventh Party Congress in 1945. The *Selected Works of Mao Zedong* are too long to be exemplary *yulu*, but within daily party work fragments of his speeches came to be employed to bolster the authority of arguments. The successful founding of the People's Republic of China (PRC) in 1949 further added to Mao's sage-like status in public perception. His works were officially published in three volumes between 1951 and 1953, selling ten million copies by 1965. In the early 1950s, Mao still accepted the superior standing of the Soviet Union, especially with regard to foreign affairs and economic policy. Official discourse was littered with quotes from *Pravda* and other Soviet news media. Yet with the turning away from the Soviet Union during the Great Leap Forward, the balance shifted to quotations from Chinese leaders. The years 1959 and 1960 witnessed renewed efforts to establish Mao's writings as orthodoxy, as revealed by the hype surrounding the publication of volume four of Mao's *Selected Works* in 1960. However, the deaths of tens of millions in the famine that resulted from the Great Leap Forward proved that Mao was far from infallible. Still most party cadres retained their belief in the basic correctness of Marxist theory and its Maoist adaptation to Chinese circumstances. Mao conducted a half-hearted self-criticism, which was never made public, and his profile within the party media was reduced. His authority as the living source of correct Chinese communist thought, however, remained intact.

Manufacturing the *Quotations from Chairman Mao*

The impetus for compiling the Little Red Book came from the fallout of the Great Leap Forward. Mao replaced Minister of Defense Peng Dehuai, who had voiced sharp criticism of the Leap strategy, with Lin

Biao. Lin had taken a low profile in the early days of the PRC, astutely aware of the dangers of conducting politics within a system centered on Mao's authority. Lin had worked closely with Mao since the late 1920s, although they occasionally had differed on questions of strategy. The most famous occasion of dissent was recorded in a letter written by Mao on January 5, 1930, in which he accused Lin of insufficient faith in the socialist revolution by virtue of his "underestimating subjective forces and overestimating objective forces to a certain extent."[8] The letter, later scrubbed of references to Lin Biao and published in Mao's *Selected Works* under the title "A single spark can start a prairie fire," marks an important turning point in Lin's career. From this time on he publicly acceded to Mao's criticism and championed the importance of man and willpower.

Lin had long since displayed a penchant for employing short quotations within military education. He emphasized the importance of creating a lively, emotional response among the audience, for example through employing enemy materials for didactic purposes.[9] The communist interpretation of events could be rendered much more effective and trustworthy by eliciting and continuously molding soldiers' raw emotions than by studying textbooks. Like Mao, Lin relied on more than the Marxist–Leninist canon. Though far from an erudite scholar, he kept a card box of his favorite classical sayings that could be employed as universally valid moral precepts. Thus the lack of comprehensive study of Marxist–Leninist works in the PLA could be justified by a quotation from the Daoist classic *Daodejing*: "Scarcity results in achievement; abundance results in confusion."[10]

Lin Biao is often credited with being the mastermind behind the compilation of *Quotations from Chairman Mao*, since he appears as author of the preface to the revised second edition. However, Lin's main influence was the style of study that he introduced in order to contain the impact of the Great Leap among the largely rural-based rank and file of the PLA. He strengthened political education through a wide variety of persuasive means, including emotional comparisons of past and present and oral presentations on carefully selected model heroes. These stories were instruments to secure the political loyalty of the PLA,

---

[8] Stuart Schram and Nancy Hodges, eds., *Mao's Road to Power: Revolutionary Writings 1912–1949*, vol III: *From the Jinggangshan to the Establishment of the Jiangxi Soviets, July 1927–December 1930* (Armonk: M. E. Sharpe, 1995), p. 237.

[9] Anonymous, *Yi Lin futongshuai wei guanghui bangyang wuxian zhongyu weida lingxiu Mao zhuxi* [With Vice-Commander Lin as glorious example boundlessly loyal to the Great Leader Chairman Mao], vol. I (Beijing: n.p. [1970]), p. 42.

[10] Ibid., p. 316.

and the bottom line was always the same: failures in recent policies were due to a failure to keep in step with Mao's ideas, rather than the opposite. The hallmark of Lin's approach was frequent study of short Mao quotations that could immediately be acted upon in daily work; this became known as "lively study, lively application" of Mao Zedong Thought.

In 1961, Lin Biao ordered the army organ *PLA Daily* to come up with a daily Mao quote to underscore the main gist of the day's editorial. These catchphrases turned out to be highly popular. In a political environment that in the wake of the famine was characterized by uncertainty about the future path of Chinese communism, these vague yet authoritative sayings were elevated to the rank of unshakable truths. Lin Biao's instruction placed great stress upon the working staff of the *PLA Daily*, and turned out to be a clarion call for the compilation of the *Quotations from Chairman Mao*. The need for a daily Mao quote on a certain topic required the systematic accumulation of quotes from Mao's officially published works and speeches. Although no index of Mao's works had been compiled to that date, the editors were lucky to hear about a *Tianjin Daily* catalogue of Mao quotes arranged according to certain topics, such as the "mass line," "people's war," or "class struggle." The catalogue was copied and came to constitute the core of the Little Red Book.[11]

The compilation process was similarly contingent. As Mao became increasingly dissatisfied with political developments in China, he elevated the army as a model for the civilian apparatus, calling for a nationwide campaign in 1964 to "Learn from the PLA." In the meantime, the PLA leadership had earned its model position by way of attaching supreme importance to political work. In December 1963, at a work conference of the General Political Department of the PLA, deputy editor-in-chief of the *PLA Daily* Tang Pingzhu presented the idea of compiling a selection of Mao quotes in book form for use within the army. The delegates greeted the proposal with great enthusiasm and, as a result, a first draft was produced entitled *200 Quotations from Chairman Mao*. In the following months the booklet was revised several times, based on the feedback of conference participants and military study activists, who applied it in political work in trial units. The first official edition of the *Quotations from Chairman Mao* finally appeared in May 1964.[12] The original foreword,

---

[11] See Wei Meiya, "Fengmi quanguo quanqiu, faxing 50 yu yi ce: 'Mao zhuxi yulu' bianfa quancheng xunzong" [Enticing all China and [the] whole world; delivering over 5 billion copies: traces of the compilation of the "Quotations from Chairman Mao"], *Yanhuang chunqiu* 17 (August 1993), pp. 10–24.

[12] On the earliest variants and different color-bindings see Oliver Lei Han, "Sources and Early Printing History of Chairman Mao's 'Quotations'," January 10, 2004, www.bibsocamer.org/bibsite/han/index.html, last accessed September 27, 2011.

published in the name of the PLA General Political Department, referred to several recent instructions of Lin Biao, namely that "in order to truly master Mao Zedong Thought, one has to repeatedly study several of Chairman Mao's most basic viewpoints. One should even learn by heart a few key sentences, repeatedly study and make use of them."[13] The book contained a collection of 355 quotations, most of them previously published in the *PLA Daily*, assembled under 30 topics.

The *Quotations* were not sold officially, and were only distributed within the PLA. The print run of 4.2 million was to ensure that every squad would receive one copy. However, the enormous excess demand of requests from military and civilian units quickly overexerted the capabilities of the PLA Publishing House. From September 1964 onward, printing molds were on occasion handed out to civilian publishing houses to relieve the pressure. By August 1965, over twelve million copies of the *Quotations* had been printed – three times the amount envisioned one year earlier.

Lin Biao was commissioned to write a calligraphic dedication drawn from the diary of model soldier Lei Feng: "Study Chairman Mao's writings, follow Chairman Mao's teachings, act according to Chairman Mao's instructions, and be a good fighter for Chairman Mao." For reasons unknown, Lin stopped short after the third phrase. Only after the book had been distributed did readers' letters alert the editors that Lin had skipped a sentence and also misspelled a character by adding a superfluous dot. As the book had been distributed to every squad already, the mistake was only removed in the second edition, published from August 1965 onward. By this time, the white paperbound volumes were being replaced by red plastic cover versions to render the book more durable in fieldwork, and the size had been reduced to neatly fit into a uniform pocket. The updated foreword now included an authoritative evaluation of Mao Zedong Thought in present world affairs, which hailed Mao as "a great contemporary Marxist–Leninist."[14] Three chapters had been added and the number of entries had been expanded to 427 quotations. Thus by August 1965 the Little Red Book had gained its distinctive appearance and content.

The quotations were drawn from volumes I to IV of Mao's *Selected Works*, covering the years 1926–49, as well as offprints of more recent articles and speeches. Stuart Schram, in his insightful introduction to

---

[13] Mao Zedong, *Mao zhuxi yulu* (Beijing: Zhongguo renmin jiefangjun zongzhengzhibu, 1964), p. 1.

[14] Mao Zedong, *Mao zhuxi yulu* (Zhengzhou: Zhongguo renmin jiefangjun zongzhengzhibu, February 1966), p. 1.

Fig. 2. Lin Biao's calligraphic dedication to first edition (1964).

a non-official English edition of the *Quotations* published in 1967, has shown that the texts are fairly evenly distributed in terms of chronology, with 62 items drawn from volume I of the *Selected Works*, 72 from volume II, 86 from volume III, 81 from volume IV, and 123 quotations dating from the period between 1949 and 1964.[15] However, the selection by no means paid equal attention to Mao's most important speeches and essays. Given the aim of employing the *Quotations* within PLA political work, the selected passages had to be of a highly general nature and therefore disadvantaged texts dealing with specific historical or political circumstances. For use in group study and recitation, most quotations were devoid of concrete political analysis, and instead stated moral truths to be learned by heart and "applied" in everyday life. The fragments were not aimed at provoking critical inquiry or analysis and did not add up to a general introduction to Mao Zedong Thought.

There was considerable opposition both within the CCP and PLA leadership to the reduction of Mao Zedong Thought to a set of moral platitudes. Already in March 1960, Deng Xiaoping characterized Lin

[15] Stuart Schram, ed., *Quotations from Chairman Mao Tse-tung*, with an introductory essay and notes by Stuart Schram (New York: Praeger, 1967), p. xv.

Biao's ritualistic approach as "vulgarization"[16] of Mao Zedong Thought, while propaganda head Lu Dingyi compared the unprincipled cherishing of Mao quotes during the Great Leap Forward with the superstitious belief by the turn-of-the-century Boxer rebels in magic words.[17] Both Deng and Lu perceived the danger to the larger project of socialist construction in debasing the truth-value of its ideology. Within the army, it was especially Marshal Luo Ronghuan, Lin Biao's former political commissar, who opposed a formalistic appraisal of Mao Zedong Thought and challenged Lin more than once on the subject. It is probably no coincidence that the *PLA Daily* editors advanced the *Quotations* project only days after Luo's death in December 1963.

After the first edition of the *Quotations* gained enormous attention, attempts were made from within the civilian administration to advance the knowledge of Mao Zedong Thought in more comprehensive fashion – and occasionally even to limit the influence of the army volume. In June 1964, two editions of *Selected Readings from Mao Zedong's Works* (*Mao Zedong zhuzuo xuandu*) appeared. The editions contained longer sections of Mao's essays and continued to be printed alongside the *Quotations* throughout the Cultural Revolution, finally adding up to another 211 million copies. The same year, the People's Press published a two-volume edition entitled *Thematic Excerpts from Mao Zedong's Writings* (*Mao Zedong zhuzuo zhuanti zhailu*), a compilation supervised by Mao's secretary Tian Jiaying that was supplied only to party cadres ranked at provincial secretary and above.[18] This rare 1,347-page edition bears the closest resemblance to the Neo-Confucian gateway of learning envisioned by Zhu Xi. Later, Tian Jiaying was accused of having tried to usurp the interpretation of Mao Zedong Thought; he hanged himself on May 23, 1966.

In 1965, central institutions compiled two alternative quotations editions in hopes of supplanting the army version. The first was compiled by staff of the Central Propaganda Department and the Ministry of Culture in cooperation with the People's Press. This edition received

---

[16] Zhonggong zhongyang xuanchuanbu bangongting (ed.), *Zhongguo gongchandang xuanchuan gongzuo, 1957–1992* [Chinese Communist Party propaganda work, 1957–1992], vol. IV (Beijing: Xuexi chubanshe, 1996), pp. 184f.

[17] *Da pipan ziliao xuanbian: Lu Dingyi fangeming xiuzhengzhuyi jiaoyu yanlun zhaibian* [Selection of great criticism materials: extracts from Lu Dingyi's counterrevolutionary revisionist speeches on education] (Shanghai: "Neikan" fanxiu bing, May 1967), p. 2.

[18] Leng Quanqing, "Wo suo zhidao de zhongyang zhengzhi yanjiushi" [The Central Political Research Office I knew], www.cssn.cn/news/385660.htm, last accessed September 27, 2011.

the political backing of the cultural establishment and high-ranking party leaders such as Deng Xiaoping and Peng Zhen. By February 28, 1966, the edition included 646 entries divided under 47 headings and was ready for print. However, Mao's former secretary Chen Boda at the party journal *Red Flag* was greatly dissatisfied with an earlier draft of this edition, claiming it had failed to embody the theoretical system of Mao Zedong Thought. He ordered the *Red Flag* staff to compile yet another alternative edition comprising 300,000 characters, more than three times longer than the army volume.

All three editions were supplied to the Central Secretariat and various provincial party committees for critical scrutiny in early 1966. The Central Secretariat under Deng Xiaoping approved a revised version of the Propaganda Department's edition, along with an abbreviation called *100 Quotations of Chairman Mao*. Although printing plans were drawn up, the Propaganda Department's version never appeared; during the following months party leaders and institutions associated with this *yulu* edition came under severe criticism for having hampered the advancement of Mao Zedong Thought. By May 1966, most of them had been either purged or severely criticized. The fate of the rival editions was finally sealed in a meeting of the Cultural Revolution Small Group around Mao's wife Jiang Qing, who decided on December 15, 1966 to have the army edition reprinted with a "new" foreword by Lin Biao. This featured slight modifications of the foreword originally credited to the General Political Department. Mao Zedong was no longer merely a "great contemporary Marxist–Leninist" but the "greatest Marxist–Leninist of our era." On December 17, 1966, the *People's Daily* fronted the "Foreword to the Second Edition" and the Little Red Book came to be printed in ever-greater quantities.

A single spark can start a prairie fire

The main reason why internal party criticism of the army edition proved futile was that Mao Zedong himself was rather fond of the book. Although he had not been involved in its compilation, he had received a copy through one of his secretaries. He was aware of its intellectual pedigree within the classical Chinese tradition, and obviously enjoyed his sage-like status. In a discussion with local cadres in November 1965 he compared the *Quotations* to the *Analects* and the *Daodejing*: "This book has thirty-three chapters altogether. That is sufficient. It is even longer than Kongzi's works. Laozi's writings consist of only 5,000 characters, even less than this edition. The writings of Marx, Engels, Lenin, and Stalin are too long. I advise to write short articles. This book is not bad."[19] In September 1965, Mao personally approved distribution of the army edition's printing molds to factories in Anhui province to alleviate pressure from the PLA Publishing House, and other provinces followed shortly afterwards. It was this low-key distribution of printing molds that effectively gained the army edition its supremacy.

The enormous demand for the *Quotations* had come as a surprise to the party leadership. Although the campaign to learn from the PLA and the renewed emphasis on studying Mao Zedong's writings had created an atmosphere conducive to the sale of Mao's works, no other edition of his writings achieved similar prominence. By March 1966, 28 million copies of the second edition had been printed and resources had been allocated for another 51 million copies. The demand for the *Quotations* skyrocketed, but still it remained an internal army publication until April 1966, when the People's Publishing House, after having failed to secure the success of its own set of Mao quotations in collaboration with the Propaganda Department, was effectively ordered by the CCP Center to take over printing and to supply the book to the general public through the Xinhua bookstores.

As the content of the book consisted of previously published items only, it did not present riveting new insights. The attraction of the *Quotations from Chairman Mao* owed more to form than content. The simple layout popularized Maoist phrases within the PLA, where drill naturally took precedence over philosophical acumen and where, as a recent Chinese article sarcastically puts it, "primary school graduates counted as intellectuals."[20] The decontextualized utterances eased memorization and group recitation, but also allowed for near-infinite recombination and thus provided the fundaments for creative exegesis. The lack of a coherent philosophical framework permitted free association of the quotations, even within contradictory arguments. Ideological "vacuity" was thus one unforeseen consequence of the instrumental approach to spread Mao Zedong Thought. As for its design, the book's red vinyl cover presented a fashionable novelty that along with other army accessories resonated with contemporary youth culture. Prior to the outbreak of the Cultural Revolution, its

[19] Mao Zedong, "Mao Zedong zai yi ci jiancha ge di gongzuo shi de zhishi" [Instructions made by Mao Zedong while observing work in various localities] (November 1965), in Song Yongyi, ed., *Chinese Cultural Revolution Database* (Hong Kong: Chinese University Press, 2006), available at ccrd.usc.cuhk.edu.hk/Fulltext.aspx.

[20] Wan Yanzhu, "'Mao zhuxi yulu' hongbian quanguo de beihou" [Behind the "Quotations from Chairman Mao" that colored the whole nation in red], *Dangshi bolan* 3 (2009), p. 56.

secret and hard-to-obtain nature only increased the appeal; later it became an indispensable badge of loyalty.

As late as March 1966, the Little Red Book was not actively promoted outside the army. The Ministry of Culture specifically ordered that there was to be "no notice within the papers, no advertising, no public displays, and no sale to foreigners. A small amount may be used for outlet sales."[21] The attempts to prevent the book from being distributed to foreigners are of particular interest. In March 1966, the State Council's Foreign Affairs Department issued a circular requesting all foreigners who had managed to obtain a book to return it, since it did not represent a comprehensive rendering of Mao Zedong Thought and was for internal study and education only. Moreover, the Little Red Book was not to be read in the presence of foreigners, or even mentioned in conversation. On April 20, the Central Propaganda Department loosened the regulations considerably. It had been impossible to regain all copies, and the efforts occasionally had tarnished the image of Mao. Therefore, in the future, all "foreign experts and exchange students may request to borrow or possibly buy a copy of the *Quotations from Chairman Mao* at their respective units."[22] Copies already handed out should not be recalled, but the book should be distributed only following an explicit request. Furthermore, while handing out copies, local staff were to explain the special nature of the book as internal study material.

With the outbreak of the Cultural Revolution in May 1966, the former CCP propaganda and cultural institutions were accused of deliberately hindering the enhancement of Mao Zedong Thought. In the assault on "the palace of Yama" (the seat of the king of the Buddhist hell, as the Central Propaganda Department came to be called), a deadly sin was its less than enthusiastic attitude in propagating the Little Red Book. The tiny percentage of Mao's works within the whole publishing industry was taken as a prime example of their heinous crimes. Accordingly, Mao's works had only accounted for 0.5 percent of all published books in 1962. A mere 70 tons of paper had been allocated to the reprint of the CCP Chairman's works that year, while the classical novels *Dream of the Red Chamber* and *Romance of the Three Kingdoms* had been given one hundred times the amount with a total of 7,500 tons.[23] In order to avoid

[21] Daniel Leese, *Mao Cult: Rhetoric and Ritual in China's Cultural Revolution* (Cambridge: Cambridge University Press, 2011), p. 119.

[22] "Zhongyang xuanchuanbu guanyu waiguo zhuanjia, liuxuesheng su yao 'Mao zhuxi yulu' de wenti de tongzhi" [Central Propaganda Department notice on the problem of foreign experts and students plainly wanting the *Quotations from Chairman Mao*], April 20, 1966, Hebei Provincial Archives 864–2–340.

[23] Fang, "Mao Zedong zhuzuo chuban jishi."

humiliation and torture for committing similar "crimes," cadres in charge of propaganda stepped up the printing of Mao's works and the Little Red Book as proof of their revolutionary attitude. Between 1966 and 1970, the amount of paper used for the official print of Mao's works amounted to 650,000 tons, slightly more than had been used between 1949 and 1965 for all published items in China.[24]

By late June 1966, basically the whole Chinese publishing industry was geared toward the production of Chairman Mao's works, even at the expense of school textbooks. The target number of the *Quotations* had been raised to 200 million copies for the two-year period 1966 and 1967. Every ministry and department tried to outshine the others by proving their utmost dedication to facilitate the spreading of Mao Zedong Thought. Materials used for the production of Mao's works were exempted from all taxes. Transport of raw materials and finished products via railway or air, including packaging and distribution costs, was conducted free of charge.[25] State banks offered interest-free loans to institutions manufacturing or distributing Mao's works. Prices were set only slightly above manufacturing costs, thus turning the biggest book hype in history into a financial losing deal.[26]

During the early Cultural Revolution, the *Quotations* were frequently donated to representatives of the "revolutionary masses" to demonstrate the correct class standpoint. On National Day 1966, for example, one million copies were handed out to Red Guards traveling to the capital.[27] Although the orders specified that no one in possession of a plastic-covered edition was to be supplied with an additional copy, distribution clearly defied a strictly planned allocation process. By the end of the year, the publishing goals had long since been overfulfilled; in 1966, the civilian party apparatus published no less than 234.6 million *Quotations* copies. The year 1967 witnessed the climax, with 370 million officially published copies, and by 1968 statistically every Chinese had been supplied with a copy.[28]

---

[24] Fang Houqu, "'Mao zhuxi yulu' chuban shihua" [True account of publishing the "Quotations from Chairman Mao"], *Zhonghua dushu bao*, July 7, 2004.

[25] Liu Gao and Shi Feng, eds., *Xin Zhongguo chuban wushi nian jishi* [Recollections about fifty years of publishing in new China] (Beijing: Xinhua chubanshe, 1999), p. 101.

[26] Ibid.

[27] "Guanyu zengsong waidi lai jing geming shisheng 'Mao zhuxi yulu' he 'xuexi shiliu tiao shouce' de tongzhi" [Notice on presenting revolutionary students and teachers arriving at the capital from afar with "Quotations from Chairman Mao" and the "Study Handbook for the 16 Articles"], Beijing Municipal Archives 182–20–240.

[28] The official publication number from 1966 to 1968 was given with over 740 million: see "Mao Zedong xuanji jin san nian chuban yi yi wu qian wan bu" [Mao Zedong's selected works have been published 150 million times in the past three years], *Renmin Ribao* (January 3, 1969), p. 1.

In fact, however, many urbanites owned multiple copies, while in the countryside, despite frequent donation campaigns designed to reach even to the most remote peasant huts, the volume remained in short supply.

Quotation wars and rituals of loyalty

Besides the official print run, there were hundreds of unofficial editions printed by local organizations that did not appear in the above statistics. A survey conducted in 1970 revealed no less than 440 local editions, 53 percent of which had been compiled by Red Guard organizations, while the remaining 47 percent had been printed in the name of temporary state institutions such as revolutionary committees.[29] While at the outset of the Cultural Revolution Red Guard organizations had compiled handy references to the official *Quotations* for quick answers to frequently encountered problems, they later adopted more comprehensive approaches. Through raids against "reactionary scholarly authorities" and CCP "capitalist-roaders" in the early phase of the Cultural Revolution, some had acquired previously unpublished or not yet redacted Mao speeches that now were reprinted in so-called *wansui* (Long Live) editions. These speeches considerably widened the scope for employing the Chairman's quotations in local conflicts. Red Guard and rebel organizations naturally favored quotes that empowered them to overthrow party structures, such as: "Erroneous leadership, which brings harm to the revolution, should not be accepted unconditionally but should be resisted resolutely."[30] Defenders of the party's leadership monopoly, on the other hand, emphasized quotations that drew on the necessity of continued party leadership, most importantly: "The force at the core leading our cause forward is the Chinese Communist Party."[31]

The *Quotations* had originally been designed for the army, to be recited in groups, with political commissars or activists providing guidance on correct understanding. Now the book came to be used without guidance from above. The phenomenon of local editions reveals that at least in late 1966 and 1967 the *Quotations* not only served as a means of indoctrination and rote learning, but also as a means of empowerment. Mao's sayings offered ample opportunities to substantiate opposing viewpoints once they were no longer applied within a hierarchical setting. Since with the outbreak of the Cultural Revolution Mao Zedong Thought had become the only criterion of truth, "quotation wars" turned Mao's sayings into ideological weapons in ways never intended. Victory

---

[29] Fang, "'Mao zhuxi yulu' chuban shihua."   [30] Mao Zedong, August 5, 1966.
[31] *Quotations from Chairman Mao Tse-tung* (Beijing: Foreign Languages Press, 1966), p. 1.

in such battles was based on the skillful manipulation of quotations that were no longer aimed at a faithful application of Mao Zedong Thought but at gaining rhetorical advantages in struggles for political power.

The only way to regain control over the cult anarchy surrounding the Little Red Book was to rely on the coercive force of the PLA. Military rule was imposed starting in late 1967 by local military authorities who relied on mandatory group study of official Mao quotations to establish their authority. The focus was no longer study but guided application. China was to be turned into a "great school" of the PLA, a term that concealed the brutality with which many former contestants for power were either banished or persecuted during the campaign to "cleanse the class ranks" in 1968–69. This period witnessed the apogee of elevating the Little Red Book to the rank of a sacred icon. The unprincipled employment of Mao's quotations had resulted in anarchic quotation wars, and now order was restored with ritual demonstrations of loyalty and faith in the Chairman.

Maoism shared in the universal yet contradictory aspirations of ideology, "the determination to make everyone think the same correct thoughts, and the desire that they should do so spontaneously."[32] The attempt at resolution failed on a massive scale. Instead of critical debates about the meaning of certain passages, ritual praise of Mao and his thought came to dominate public discourse as a safe haven to avoid political persecution. Under PLA guidance, standardized Mao quotes came to penetrate even the most mundane linguistic exchanges to secure the conformity of speech and conduct.[33] In a climate where people were sentenced to long years in prison for having accidentally destroyed a *Quotations* volume or a Mao idol, the book had to be carried and quoted at all times. Similarly, the disposal of damaged books or images had to take place in utmost secrecy in order not to be seen as counter-revolutionary behavior.[34] Thus at the time that the international acclaim of the Little Red Book as a symbol of youth rebellion and world

[32] Schram, ed., *Quotations*, p. xix. Compare *Analects* 2.4.

[33] See for example: "**Serve the people**. Comrade, could I have two pounds of pork, please?" "**A revolution is not a dinner party**. That makes 1.85 yuan altogether. **To rebel is justified**. Here you are." "**Practice frugality while making revolution**. There's your change, and there's your meat." Quoted in Michael Schoenhals, *Doing Things with Words in Chinese Politics: Five Studies* (Berkeley: Institute of East Asian Studies, 1992), p. 19.

[34] In Beijing, special personnel were sent at night to collect such items after being alerted by local leadership: see Beijing shi wuzi huishou gongsi geming weiyuanhui, "Guanyu qingshi huishou gongzuo zhong yudao de zhengcexing de wenti baogao" [Instruction on a report regarding problems of political character encountered during recollection work], February 25, 1969, BMA 182–15–112.

revolution reached its apex in the summer of 1968, in China it had completely lost its emancipating impact and had become a symbol of imposed worship to discipline the masses, conducted under the auspices of the PLA.

The importance attached to the *Quotations* volume only started to decrease around the Ninth Party Congress in April 1969, after a new party leadership had been decided upon and revolutionary committees had come to secure their power in the provinces. The excessive cult had become a major embarrassment for the CCP's claim to represent a scientific ideology rather than idol worship. Once the new power structures had been set in place, Mao no longer needed to rely on this extra-bureaucratic means of mobilization, and the most extreme expressions of the cult were diminished. Zhou Enlai was the first to criticize the rampant waste of printing resources in March 1969; he called upon citizens to donate their quotation copies to remote villages.[35] On May 1, 1969 postal fees were no longer waived for the distribution of Mao's writings, and the railroad administration followed suit one year later. The print run decreased markedly, and by 1971 the *Quotations* basically went out of print.

After the attempted flight of Lin Biao and his family in September 1971, the compilation and distribution of the *Quotations* became part of the accusations against the "hypocrite" and "careerist" Lin, who was said to have manipulated the cult to amass personal political capital. While traces of Lin Biao's influence were destroyed, for example by crossing out his name in the foreword or ripping out his calligraphic dedication, the huge number of volumes did not simply fade from view. An inventory conducted in March 1970 revealed that there were still 123.44 million copies held in storages all over China.[36] Since the official reverence paid to Mao Zedong and his sayings had by no means diminished, the volumes retained a "shelf life" until after Mao's death and Deng Xiaoping's ascent to power in the late 1970s.[37] As Mao had frequently criticized Deng in the past, Deng stood little chance of consolidating his power in an environment that considered Mao infallible. The revived Maoist slogan "seek truth in the facts" once again played an important

---

[35] Leese, *Mao Cult*, p. 227.

[36] Fang Houqu, "'Wenge' shi nian Mao Zedong zhuzuo, Mao Zedong xiang chuban jishi" [Recollections about the publication of Mao Zedong's works and Mao Zedong images during the ten years of the 'Cultural Revolution'], in Song Yuanfang et al. (eds.), *Zhongguo chuban shiliao (xiandai bufen)*, vol. III.1 (Jinan: Shandong jiaoyuchubanshe, 2001), p. 235.

[37] Geremie Barmé, ed., *Shades of Mao: The Posthumous Cult of the Great Leader* (Armonk: M. E. Sharpe, 1996), pp. 6f.

role in the "truth criterion controversy" of 1978, this time freeing the post-Mao leadership from the strains of orthodox Maoism and its conservative gatekeepers.

Between 1978 and 1981, a series of official directives ordered a thorough de-Maoification of the publishing industry. In response to an inquiry from the State Publishing Bureau about how to deal with the huge volume of Little Red Books clogging up storage space needed for other publications, a Central Propaganda Department circular dated February 12, 1979 officially announced the withdrawal from circulation of the *Quotations from Chairman Mao*. The Propaganda Department further described the *Quotations* as distortion of Mao Zedong Thought that had exerted a "widespread and pernicious influence."[38] Foreigners were not to be provided with additional copies either, but were to be offered instead the more comprehensive *Selected Works*; foreign bookstores were allowed to continue sales of current stock so as to avoid a negative reaction. Domestically, however, most remaining copies were to be pulped. Thus by early 1979 over a hundred million copies of the *Quotations* were destroyed. Many citizens, who had suffered during the Cultural Revolutionary turmoil, followed suit and got rid of their volumes. This explains how, fifty years after its initial publication, the Little Red Book has once again become a scarce commodity.

Conclusion

The *Quotations of Chairman Mao* were originally compiled to supply PLA soldiers with a set of moral guidelines to act upon in military drill. The compilation and distribution of the Little Red Book within the army evaded scrutiny of CCP propaganda institutions, officially in charge of guarding the heritage of Mao Zedong Thought. Yet Mao's implicit backing of the volume secured its success, especially after publishing authorities were purged in May 1966. Publishing ever-greater quantities of the *Quotations* now became imperative to survive in an increasingly unpredictable environment. Moreover, the book's ingenious design gained widespread attention among the Chinese populace and turned the *Quotations* into a revolutionary icon, aided by a political climate that championed Maoist ideology as ultimate wisdom. The short and decontextualized quotations provided neither a hidden gateway to enlightenment nor a systematic approach to Maoist ideology. Within the hierarchical setting of the army, they served as moral mnemonics to secure loyalty to

---

[38] Ibid., p. 130.

Mao Zedong outside the ambit of party institutions. Yet once the volume spread beyond the army, the fragments lent themselves to political manipulation. Steering mass movements with an incoherent set of quotations proved futile, however, and the Cultural Revolutionary experiment ended in military suppression enforced by the ritual acceptance of Mao's sayings. Orthodoxy was reestablished through coercive means, and the *Quotations'* potentially empowering impact was curbed. After Mao's death the CCP leadership tried to distance itself from the *Quotations* and blamed Lin Biao for the excessive worship of Mao. In so doing, the party denied the causal linkage between its self-appointed avant-garde role, based on its investment of absolute truth claims in Marxist–Leninist–Maoist doctrines, and the eventual apogee of this development in the Little Red Book. The post-Mao leadership might have been advised to ponder a memorable quotation attributed to the Tang dynasty Chan Buddhist master Linji:

Students today don't get it. How futilely they seize upon words and letters for their understanding! They transcribe some dead old guy's words in a big notebook, wrap it up in three or five layers of cloth and don't let anyone else see it. They refer to it as the "profound meaning," and guard it with their life. What blunderous blind idiots they are! What sort of juice do they expect from dried up old bones?[39]

BIBLIOGRAPHY

Barmé, Geremie, ed., *Shades of Mao: The Posthumous Cult of the Great Leader* (Armonk: M. E. Sharpe, 1996)

Chan, Wing-Tsit (trans.), *Reflections on Things at Hand: The Neo-Confucian Anthology compiled by Chu Hsi and Lü Tsu-ch'ien* (New York: Columbia University Press, 1967)

Da pipan ziliao xuanbian: Lu Dingyi fangeming xiuzhengzhuyi jiaoyu yanlun zhaibian [Selection of great criticism materials: extracts from Lu Dingyi's counterrevolutionary revisionist speeches on education] (Shanghai: "Neikan" fanxiu bing, May 1967)

Deng Xiaoping, *Deng Xiaoping wenxuan* [Selected writings of Deng Xiaoping], vol. III (Beijing: Renmin chubanshe, 1993)

Fang Houqu, "'Wenge' shi nian Mao Zedong zhuzuo, Mao Zedong xiang chuban jishi" [Recollections about the publication of Mao Zedong's works and Mao Zedong images during the ten years of the "Cultural Revolution"], in Song Yuanfang et al. (eds.), *Zhongguo chuban shiliao (xiandai bufen)*, vol. III.1 (Jinan: Shandong jiaoyuchubanshe, 2001), pp. 215–36

Gardner, Daniel K., "Modes of Thinking and Modes of Discourse in the Sung: Some Thoughts on the 'Yü-lu' ('Recorded Conversations') Texts," *Journal of Asian Studies*, 50.3 (August 1991), pp. 574–603

[39] Welter, *The* Linji lu, p. 158.

Leese, Daniel, *Mao Cult: Rhetoric and Ritual in China's Cultural Revolution* (Cambridge: Cambridge University Press, 2011)

Liu Gao and Shi Feng, eds., *Xin Zhongguo chuban wushi nian jishi* [Recollections about fifty years of publishing in new China] (Beijing: Xinhua chubanshe, 1999)

Mao Zedong, "Mao Zedong zai yi ci jiancha ge di gongzuo shi de zhishi" [Instructions made by Mao Zedong while observing work in various localities], in Song Yongyi, ed., *Chinese Cultural Revolution Database* (Hong Kong: Chinese University Press, 2006), available at ccrd.usc.cuhk.edu.hk/Fulltext.aspx

Mao zhuxi yulu, with foreword by Lin Biao (Beijing and Zhengzhou: Zhongguo renmin jiefangjun zong zhengzhibu, 1964 and 1966)

Quotations from Chairman Mao Tse-tung (Peking: Foreign Languages Press, 1966)

Schoenhals, Michael, *Doing Things with Words in Chinese Politics: Five Studies* (Berkeley: Institute of East Asian Studies, 1992)

Schram, Stuart, ed., *Quotations from Chairman Mao Tse-tung* (New York: Praeger, 1967)

Schram, Stuart, and Nancy Hodges, eds., *Mao's Road to Power: Revolutionary Writings 1912–1949*, vol III: *From the Jinggangshan to the Establishment of the Jiangxi Soviets, July 1927–December 1930* (Armonk: M. E. Sharpe, 1995)

Wan Yanzhu, "'Mao zhuxi yulu' hongbian quanguo de beihou" [Behind the 'Quotations from Chairman Mao' that colored the whole nation in red], *Dangshi bolan* 3 (2009), pp. 54–58

Wei Meiya, "Fengmi quanguo quanqiu, faxing 50 yu yi ce: 'Mao zhuxi yulu' bianfa quancheng xunzong" [Enticing all China and [the] whole world; delivering over 5 billion copies: traces of the compilation of the "Quotations from Chairman Mao"], *Yanhuang chunqiu* 17 (August 1993), pp. 10–24

Welter, Albert, *The Linji lu and the Creation of Chan Orthodoxy: The Development of Chan's Records of Sayings Literature* (Oxford: Oxford University Press, 2008)

Yi Lin futongshuai wei guanghui bangyang wuxian zhongyu weida lingxiu Mao zhuxi [With Vice-Commander Lin as glorious example boundlessly loyal to the Great Leader Chairman Mao], vol. I (Beijing: n.p. [1970])

Zhonggong zhongyang xuanchuanbu bangongting, ed., *Zhongguo gongchandang xuanchuan gongzuo, 1957–1992* [Chinese Communist Party propaganda work, 1957–1992], vol. IV (Beijing: Xuexi chubanshe, 1996)

3 Quotation songs
Portable media and the Maoist pop song

Andrew F. Jones

> Singing Chairman Mao's quotation songs, we think of Chairman Mao; singing Chairman Mao's quotation songs, we remember Chairman Mao's instructions; singing Chairman Mao's quotation songs, it's as if Chairman Mao himself is by our side.
>
> *People's Daily*, September 30, 1967

At the Ninth National Congress of the Communist Party of China in April 1969, Chairman Mao's wife Jiang Qing issued a surprising broadside against a form of music that had once seemed to embody the political passions of the Great Proletarian Cultural Revolution: the quotation song. These songs, which had been promoted nationwide since September 1966, set the Chairman's maxims to music, and were deliberately conceived as a musical analogue and mnemonic device for *Quotations from Chairman Mao*, more popularly known as the Little Red Book. Upon watching a televised song-and-dance program extolling the Chairman, Jiang Qing is reported to have said:

> Don't you believe that they are singing about Mao Zedong thought – that's not really what it is at all. It's yellow music. We've already dealt a blow to the emperors and feudal lords, and now they're doing this sort of thing? In future, we need to get rid of folk tunes, we need to be rid of this swing music. They say they're eliminating the old and ringing in the new. What's new here? Some of their movements are based entirely on swing dancing.[1]

She continued, "They're wearing red stars and waving red flags, but they're swing dancing. They may as well be naked."[2]

We may surmise that Jiang Qing's ire had something to do with the fact that these enormously popular songs were one of the few forms of mass-produced culture not yet under her direct control. Yet it would be a mistake to dismiss these comments wholesale. Indeed, I argue that Jiang

---

[1] Liang Maochun, "Lun 'yulu ge' xianxiang" [On the quotation songs phenomenon], *Huangzhong: Wuhan yinyue xueyuan xuebao* 1 (2003), pp. 46–47. Jiang Qing's comments were made on April 15, 1969.

[2] Ibid., p. 46.

Qing's tirade – which drew on a long tradition of leftist critique of popular music in China and not incidentally led to the immediate proscription of quotation songs throughout the country – may help us understand not only quotation songs as a form of popular music, but also pose new questions about the relation between musical modernity and media culture in the Chinese 1960s.[3]

At first blush, of course, Jiang Qing's identification of "quotation songs" as "yellow," or off-color, jazz seems unlikely in the extreme. What could possibly be promiscuous or even pleasurable about a choral march in duple meter entitled – to cite just one of the more than one hundred such compositions that were published and recorded between 1966 and 1969 – "Ensure that Literature and Art Operate as Powerful Weapons for Exterminating the Enemy"?[4] Part of the underlying affinity may lie not just in the ecstatic movement that sometimes accompanied the performance of such music, but also in the deliberate promiscuity of their *form*. By form, I indicate not only their musical, lyrical, and ideological characteristics, but also the way in which these qualities made use of the new technological possibilities and ever-expanding reach of the socialist mass media in the 1960s. Quotation songs, in a manner not radically different from popular music in the same years in the West, were designed for promiscuous movement, for effortless portability. And as with the mass-mediated pop songs of the 1960s in the USA and Europe, the revolutionary songs of the 1960s owed their popularity in part to the self-conscious crafting of a hook that rendered a song not only recognizable but also replicable in disparate media and contexts. In fact, the use of melodic hooks drawn from the urban folk-song (*xiaodiao*) tradition is precisely what incensed Jiang Qing about the performances to which she and other party activists were privy at the Ninth Party Congress.[5] Her sense of the affinity of such music with Western pop may well have extended to the linguistic qualities and rhetorical mode of

---

[3] On the politics of popular music in the pre-1949 era, see Andrew F. Jones, *Yellow Music: Media Culture and Colonial Modernity in the Chinese Jazz Age* (Durham: Duke University Press, 2001).

[4] This particular composition is included on a 7-inch 45 rpm record released under the title "Wei Mao zhuxi yulu puqu" (Quotations from Chairman Mao set to music). See China Records S-103, 1966.

[5] Her comments of April 15 were followed by an equally vehement summary the following day: "Last night I saw a TV program, watched for the first time in my life, as they adopted unbearably bourgeois techniques to distort the solemnity of the great Ninth Party Congress ... in reality what they were singing were just popular folk tunes, vulgar 'yellow' folk songs, tunes that are all about 'my darling man' and 'my little girl.' I have nothing against talking love, but to use these tunes to sing of the Ninth Party Congress, to sing quotations, is not to praise Chairman Mao, it's an insult to the thought of Chairman Mao. And to dance so crazily is actually swing dancing." See Liang, "Lun 'yulu ge' xianxiang," p. 47.

these songs, in that the quotation song did in fact lend itself uniquely well to the performative and citational logic on which pop songs are premised, and by which they are able to circulate.

This portability, as envisioned by those who originally promoted these songs at the very height of the Red Guard movement of September 1966 in the pages of the *People's Daily*, would not only annihilate spatial and temporal limitations, but also penetrate psychological barriers as well: "We believe that with the hard work of musical workers, the sound of songs of Chairman Mao's quotations will resonate across the entire country. This will make the thought of Chairman Mao penetrate ever deeper into people's hearts, so as to forever radiate its brilliance."[6] Interestingly enough, this description, in its emphasis on the ability of these songs to record, broadcast, and enable Mao Zedong thought to saturate social, somatic, and psychological space, reads almost uncannily like an account of the ethereal yet ubiquitous powers of mass media itself. This is not merely a rhetorical accident. Quotation songs were in fact the product and the logical conclusion of a system of what we might now call "media interactivity" (or even more anachronistically, "cross-platform marketing") that took shape in the 1960s, and their power was premised on the ease with which they traveled across different media, from print to performance, from radio to records, from the revolutionary postures of the "loyalty dance" to poster art.[7]

The Little Red Book

In the beginning, there was the Little Red Book. Compiled at the behest of the then minister of defense Lin Biao, as part of a larger effort to promote Mao Zedong Thought, the volume in its final form brought together 427 excerpts from Chairman Mao's published writings and speeches, organized under 33 thematic rubrics, and was first published in April 1964 by the General Political Department of the People's Liberation Army. As such, the work was originally conceived as a kind of standard-issue ideological field manual for PLA soldiers, and this accounts for its handy, durable design, and water- and wear-resistant red vinyl cover. With the explosion of the popularity of the *Quotations*

---

[6] "Yiwan renmin qi huan chang, Mao Zedong sixiang fang guangmang" [The multitudes of the people sing joyfully in unison, Chairman Mao's thought radiates brilliance], *People's daily* (September 30, 1966).

[7] Paul Clark makes much the same point in exploring the centrality of the model operas (*yangbanxi*) as a locus of cultural production in forms as diverse as fiction, film, painting, sculpture, and so on. See *The Chinese Cultural Revolution: A History* (Cambridge: Cambridge University Press, 2008), p. 74.

after 1966, this emphasis on pocket-size portability was taken to almost fetishistic extremes: one edition squeezed not only the *Quotations*, but also the Chairman's regulated verse and lyrical poetry, as well as the Five Works (a set of short essays) into a single, and no doubt nearly illegible, matchbox size edition of 256 *kai*, measuring one by one-and-a-half inches. The quantities in which the book was produced during the high tide of the Cultural Revolution are equally staggering: by 1967, 628 million copies were in circulation, and by the end of the following decade, the official figure (not counting offprints and unauthorized copies) had swollen to 1.5 billion.

The portability (and perhaps even the talismanic character) of the material object itself, however, represented in some sense an extension of the underlying logic of the quotation as a literary genre. For what is the function of the quotation, if not to remove a textual extract from its original context, and allow it to *circulate* beyond the original and particular historical circumstances in which it was produced, rendering it available for reuse, recitation, and re-contextualization? The *Quotations* achieve precisely this function, bringing together words spoken or written from the mid 1920s to the mid 1960s, torn from the often quite specific and complex tactical situations for which they were crafted, and offered instead as trans-historical scripts for revolutionary praxis, organized under abstract rubrics such as "Classes and Class Struggle," "War and Peace," "Women," or simply "Study." The "catchiest" of these catchphrases, injunctions, and maxims, moreover, often detach themselves even from the longer quotation of which they were originally a part, traveling seemingly without effort across linguistic and temporal boundaries, and attaining (like the Little Red Book itself) iconic status: "Revolution is not a dinner party"; "It's right to rebel"; "All reactionaries are paper tigers"; "Political power grows out of the barrel of a gun."

Quotations, in short, are made by their medium, and once mediated, they take on an itinerant life of their own.[8] In the case of the *Quotations*, that life is indelibly politicized. It is perhaps symptomatic of the quotation's function as what we might now call a viral linguistic media that Lin Biao, in his oft-quoted introduction to the 1966 edition of the *Quotations* (which was itself later set to music as quotation song), emphasizes the

---

[8] I am deliberately misquoting the work of the Bakhtin scholar Gary Paul Morson, who asserts that "Cited expressions become quotations, they are not automatically so. Becoming a quotation is a change in status, which may involve a change in form. When a set of words achieves that status, we typically remember it in its quoted form, which takes on a life of its own": "The Quotation and its Genres," *Sun Yat-sen Journal of Humanities* 21 (Winter 2005), p. 129.

bringing to life of Chairman Mao's word through repetition, memorization, and "live application":

In studying Chairman Mao's work, we need to learn through problem-solving, through live study and live application, uniting the two together, learning what is of urgent use, so that the results are immediately visible, always putting fierce emphasis on the character for "use." In order to really put Mao Zedong thought to hand, we need to repeatedly study Chairman Mao's many fundamental standpoints, and preferably memorize some of his maxims, repeatedly studying them, and repeatedly using them.[9]

With repetition comes mastery, and with mastery, Lin famously concludes, Mao Zedong Thought will be mobilized as "a spiritual atom bomb" against the enemies of the revolution.[10] The metaphor, of course, speaks directly to the Cold War context in which this mobilization took place, as well as to the centrality of such metaphors in effecting what Lin calls the "weaponization of the minds of the people of the entire nation."[11]

In practice, this weaponization was brought about by way of the unprecedented integration, centralization, and degree of saturation of everyday life of the socialist mass media by the mid 1960s. The roll-out of the quotation song as a new genre is itself a primary case in point. A set of ten "quotation songs," set to music by the prominent composer Li Jiefu (1913–76), was introduced on the pages of the *People's Daily* a little more than a month after the first of the massive Red Guard rallies on Tiananmen Square which marked the beginning of the high tide of the Cultural Revolution. Released on September 30, 1966, the songs were set to simplified notation and accompanied by an introduction.[12] This presentation deliberately mirrored the sequencing of the Little Red Book itself, by citing the aforementioned quotation from the Lin Biao preface to the *Quotations*, before presenting the very first entry in the *Quotations*, "The Force at the Core Leading our Cause Forward is the Chinese Communist Party," in musical form.

To some extent, quotation songs partook of a long and ongoing tradition of quotation literature (*yulu*) in China, one whose genealogy might be said to include the Confucian *Analects*, Buddhist hagiographies dating back to the Tang, and Republican-era compilations of the sayings of prominent leaders such as Sun Yat-sen. Perhaps more relevant to the

---

[9] Lin Biao, "Zaiban qianyan" [Preface to the second edition], in *Mao Zhuxi Yulu* [*Quotations from Chairman Mao*] (Guangzhou: Zhongguo renmin jiefang jun zong zhengzhi bu, 1967), p. 2.

[10] Ibid., p. 3.   [11] Ibid., p. 1.

[12] Liang Maochun, "Lun 'yulu ge' xianxiang" [On the quotation songs phenomenon], part 2, *Huangzhong: Wuhan yinyue xueyuan xuebao* 2 (2003), pp. 91–93.

emergence of the form was the practice of exhortatory choral singing that, having been introduced by Christian missionaries in the nineteenth century, had gone on to become a staple of Chinese school life and political ritual in the early decades of the twentieth.[13] Yet, as Liang Maochun points out, the appearance of the songs was accompanied by a "theoretical" apparatus – outlined in a series of articles in prominent publications – that insisted (as the *People's Daily* put it) on the unprecedented "novelty of the form."[14]

To the extent that quotation songs were designed from the start as modular participants in a larger, and unprecedently integrated national media landscape, this was undoubtedly true. This initial fusillade of songs, released on the day before National Day, was followed by a barrage of follow-up reports in the print media, which were disseminated through a variety of visual and aural media, including but not limited to neighborhood and work unit bulletin and chalk boards, paintings, posters, study sessions, and public readings of newspapers and official reports.[15]

These forms of dissemination were reinforced by the printing not only of a series of songbooks which allowed for public singing, but also by monaural vinyl records (in both 7- and 10-inch formats) of orchestrated choral performances produced by China Records. The packaging of these products, moreover, were to a large degree standardized across different media: songbooks also sported red vinyl covers, while the covers of the records featured much the same layout and typography as the Little Red Book itself. Vinyl long-playing records of the quotation songs, moreover, were exported with bilingual sleeves by China International Books.

While home ownership of phonographs remained relatively rare in the 1960s, especially in rural areas, these recordings reached listeners across the country by way of China's extensive radio rediffusion network.[16]

---

[13] For an illuminating history of revolutionary song and its roots in Christian hymnal, see Isabel K. F. Wong, "*Geming gequ:* Songs for the Education of the Masses," in Bonnie Macdougal, ed., *Popular Chinese Culture and Performing Arts in the People's Republic of China, 1949–1979* (Berkeley: University of California Press, 1984).

[14] Liang Maochun, "Lun 'yulu ge' xianxiang," pp. 45–46. "Lingdao women shiye de hexin liliang shi Zhongguo gongchandang" [The force at the core leading our cause forward is the Communist Party of China], *People's Daily* (September 30, 1966).

[15] On an exhibition of "quotations paintings" held in Shanghai in the summer of 1967, see "'Mao zhuxi yulu huazhan' zai Shanghai zhanchu shoudao relie huanying" [Opening of the 'Chairman Mao quotations paintings' exhibit is warmly welcomed in Shanghai], *People's Daily* (June 5, 1967).

[16] Recordings of quotation songs became more accessible to domestic listeners in 1968, when China Records began to produce inexpensive flexi-discs for the domestic market. Referred to as *baomo changpian,* these records, mostly in the 7-inch format, were pressed on a thin sheet of vinyl. China Records developed their process for manufacturing flexi-discs in house, and by 1968 had manufactured 1.8 million such records. For a

By the early 1970s, this wired or in-line (as opposed to wireless) system, radiating from Radio Peking at the center, and penetrating deep into the interior, broadcast to (by one estimate) over one hundred and forty million loudspeakers, mounted on utility poles and street-light standards in urban streets, schools, train and bus stations, army barracks and factory floors, and even rural fields and village lanes.[17] By the late 1960s and early 1970s, many rural homes were also wired for sound, for which no off-switch was provided.[18] When the *People's Daily* breathlessly reported on October 25, 1966 that "the sound of the singing of quotation songs is ringing out across the nation, from the interior to the borderlands, from country to city, in factories and fields, from barracks to schools," reality had in fact already overtaken rhetoric.[19]

The establishment of a wired rediffusion network was the culmination of a 1955 decision by the Chinese Communist Party (CCP) to radically expand the reach of the mass media into the countryside.[20] In the first

handy comparative chart of technical developments in the Chinese and Taiwanese record industries, see Huang Guolong (Kh'o), "Ershi shiji er zhan hou liang an leibi changpian fazhan gaiyao" [A summary of the development of analogue records in China and Taiwan after World War II], blog.sina.com.tw/wiwienen/article.php?pbgid=323 &entryid=580588, accessed July 30, 2012.

[17] Estimates as to the number of loudspeakers vary, and are based of necessity on (not always entirely reliable) official statistics. According to Alan P. Liu, China had installed 6 million loudspeakers by 1964. Andrew Nathan estimates that that figure had mushroomed to 141,000,000 by the mid-1970s, reaching 95 percent of production units and 65 percent of rural homes. See Andrew Nathan, *Chinese Democracy* (London: I. B. Tauris, 1986), p. 163.

[18] For a history and description of this radio network, see Alan Liu, *Communications and National Integration in Communist China* (Berkeley: University of California Press, 1971), pp. 119–29. The penetration of everyday life by this speaker system even reached into the most intimate spaces of the home. As the anthropologist Yan Yunxiang notes in regard to the collectivization of individual space in an agricultural commune, "Wired broadcasting is a typical example. In the early 1970s, Dadui village installed a loudspeaker in every home, typically right above the *kang* bed. The loudspeakers had no on/off switches, and both the content and times of the programming was determined by the county broadcast station. The Dadui station was just a relay for the county broadcast system. And so the villagers had no control over what they could hear or when they would hear it. They were forced to listen everyday to official news, political propaganda, speeches by cadres, entertainment programs, and the like. But as time went on, everyone not only got accustomed to the wired broadcasts, but came to depend upon them." See Yan Yunxiang, *Siren shenghuo de biange: yige zhongguo cunzhuang li de aiqing, jiating yu qinmi guanxi, 1949–1999* [The transformation of everyday life: love, family, and intimacy in a Chinese village, 1949–199] (Shanghai: Shanghai shudian, 2006), p. 41.

[19] See "Mao zhuxi de shu shi ti women pinxia zhong nong shuo hua de" [Chairman Mao's book speaks for us poor and middle peasants], *People's Daily*, October 1, 1966. This article appeared, it is worth noting, just the day after the roll-out of the first ten quotation songs on September 30.

[20] The policy is laid out in an editorial in *Wuxiandian* (Wireless) entitled " Dali fazhan nongcun guangbo wang" [Vigorously develop the rural broadcasting network], *Wuxiandian* 2 (1956), pp. 4–5.

five years of CCP rule, an extensive system of monitored "radio listening stations" had been set up for collective listening, often using commandeered pre-liberation radio sets, and reliant on wireless broadcasts. Wired broadcasting networks, through which local relay stations could pick up broadcasts from the center wirelessly, and then rediffuse the signal across a wired network of loudspeakers, however, offered several advantages. First, they were less costly to establish and maintain – simple tongue-and-groove loudspeakers were much easier to manufacture than wireless receivers, and these systems could sometimes piggyback atop existing electrical and telephone lines. Second, they controlled the flow of information by preventing individuals from using radio-receiving sets to access shortwave broadcasts from abroad, or from simply turning off the radio. Third, they allowed authorities a limited ability to customize broadcasts, inserting announcements and information pertaining to local conditions and interests.

For this reason, the wired radio network grew hand in hand with the establishment of rural communes in the late 1950s. By the time of the Great Leap Forward in 1959, 9,435 communes and 1,689 county wired relay stations had been established, linked to 4,570,000 in-line loudspeakers. But a second, and largely unheralded, "leap forward" was to take place throughout the 1960s – the transistorization of the radio broadcasting network. Transistors – first invented at Bell Labs in 1947 – were not only smaller and more durable than the vacuum tube technology they replaced, but also far more energy efficient. This fact was of crucial importance to the expansion of rural mass media in China, because electrical mains power supplies remained in many areas insufficient, unreliable, or simply nonexistent. Transistor devices could be run far more effectively from batteries than their tubed counterparts, and provided far more volume than crystal sets. By 1957, China had already begun to produce transistorized sound equipment, most notably in the East German-designed North China Wireless Electronics Materials Factory, which for the tenth anniversary celebration of the revolution in 1959 designed, produced, and installed the loudspeaker systems for Beijing's Chang'an Avenue and the wired sound columns that still define Tiananmen Square as a politically and socially resonant space.[21]

By the time of the Cultural Revolution, battery-powered portable transistor radios, microphones, portable public address systems, and, above all, loudspeakers were not only widely available, but had also reached remote rural areas. This was a matter of deliberate policy, in

---

[21] This factory complex is now globally famous in its repurposed form as the 798 arts district.

that transistors allowed the revolution to reach areas remote from or insufficiently supplied by electric mains services.[22] In the classic anthropological account of an isolated and impoverished village in Guangdong province, *Chen Village*, the installation of a broadcast network takes place precisely in 1966, in the immediate wake of rural electrification, and the beginning of an intensive campaign to promote Mao Zedong Thought among the villagers: "The system consisted of thirty loudspeakers positioned throughout the village, with four large ones installed in the village's main meeting places. The volume was tuned loud enough that even while indoors people could hear the announcements."[23]

In the context of a village in which clocks were not yet common, the loudspeaker system quickly imposed on the villagers a newly regimented sense of "industrial" time. Operated by a single sent-down youth named Ao, the system served as a "mouthpiece" for the movement, providing not only music and reports from the provincial broadcast station, but also customized political admonitions directed at local conditions and targeted toward specific villagers.[24]

The case of Chen Village suggests some of the ways that transistorized electronics helped to transform rural life. By the late 1960s, the ubiquity of portable amplification and public address equipment had also opened the possibility of a newly mobile and even interactive media landscape. Designed to mobilize the masses, these devices were quickly commandeered by Red Guard activists and pressed to the service of a new kind of politics in the streets of Beijing and other cities. In a poster produced in the fall of 1966 in the wake of Chairman Mao's exhortation to the Red Guard insurgents to "Bombard the Headquarters!" and thus escalate the scope and scale of the Cultural Revolution, for instance, we see Mao's broadside, visualized as a kind of free-standing column or billboard, presiding over a kind of frenzy of revolutionary representation. Insurgents write and paste "big-character posters" (*dazibao*) on a wall, as if in response to Mao's words, and perhaps reinforcing Mao's sense that his own sloganeering was itself a *dazibao*: an unofficial, insurrectionary, temporary, portable text-event, directed against his own party apparatus. A worker speaks animatedly to his cohorts through a PA system. Wind-blown red banners blazoned with slogans form phalanxes above the crowd. A truck, wired for sound with a set of battery-powered

[22] A spate of articles on the problem of rural electrification and the expansion of the broadcasting network appear in the pages of *Wuxiandian* (Wireless) throughout 1966.

[23] Anita Chan, Richard Madsen, and Jonathan Unger, *Chen Village: The Recent History of a Peasant Community in Mao's China* (Berkeley: University of California Press, 1984), pp. 84–85.

[24] Ibid., pp. 85–86.

loudspeakers, presumably blares out more messages or perhaps music, its sonic barrage aimed at the ubiquitous wired loudspeakers mounted on the wall directly opposite.

Such an image suggests how transistorized and portable media might have begun by the late 1960s to challenge the fixed networks of the party-state, threatening to surround and thus displace the "headquarters." This is an aspect of the media culture of the Cultural Revolution that merits further research. Yet the ubiquity of transistors and portable media could not displace Mao himself as the "master" or "transcendent signifier" of the media system. Indeed, as the cover image of the October 1966 edition of *Wireless Magazine* (*Wuxiandian*) illustrates, that relation was seen – and practiced – as a kind of "closed circuit." We see workers reading and reciting from Chairman Mao's *Quotations* as part of the production process of manufacturing solid-state transistor circuits – circuits which would no doubt power the radios and loudspeakers broadcasting vocal as well as musical renditions of the *Quotations from Chairman Mao*. What this sort of circuituous loop suggests is that "Mao" himself becomes a kind of "media effect," a product of his constant citation as text and as image.

Another way to approach this idea is through what the French philosopher Jacques Derrida called "iterability." Language, Derrida tells us in his essay "Signature Event Context," works because each of our speech acts is a kind of "citation" of the speech acts of everyone else.[25] When I say "Mao," I am citing previous usages of the term, not merely creating the term out of nowhere. I am "reiterating" the word "Mao." But its iterability in the first place is a function of having been constantly repeated. So, how is it possible to speak of a real Mao? Is his presence (and his power) merely an effect of linguistic or other types of mediation? What Derrida wants to get at here is an interesting contradiction, and he uses the example of a signature to further underline the problem. A signature is supposed to be the unique possession of its owner – the legal mark of his or her individuality. But in order to function, the signature must be consistently replicable, it has to proliferate, to be used and re-used in multiple contexts, and thus, by definition, what had initially looked like the guarantor of individual identity is not and cannot be entirely unique. In other words, a signature must be replicable to be authentic. And if a signature is replicable, it can also be forged. For Derrida, citation is like a signature: when we quote someone, we both invoke and displace the original source, so that the words can take on a promiscuous life of their own.

[25] See Jacques Derrida, "Signature Event Context," in *Limited Inc* (Evanston, Ill.: Northwestern University Press, 1988), pp. 1–24.

Fig. 3. A closed circuit: reciting Mao quotations.
Source: Front cover, *Wuxiandian* 10, 1966. (Hoover Library, Stanford University.)

This may be why the phenomenon of quotation songs was often accompanied by a persistent and perhaps compensatory trope of presence. Over and over in the news media from this period, citizens are quoted as celebrating the way in which the *Quotations* have rendered Chairman Mao himself portable: "Chairman Mao's book speaks for us poor and middle peasants. Reading Chairman Mao's book everyday is like seeing Chairman Mao himself everyday," begins one such ventriloquized report.[26] Editorializing on the activities of the "little generals" leading the revolutionary charge, another article captures the extent to which the very act of citation in song was seen as transformative:

[The Red Guards] sing the *Quotations of Chairman Mao*, and they are imprinted upon their hearts ... they say "we love most of all to sing and to listen to Chairman Mao's quotations. Singing Chairman Mao's quotation songs, we think of Chairman Mao; singing Chairman Mao's quotation songs, we remember Chairman Mao's instructions, singing Chairman Mao's quotation songs, it's as if Chairman Mao himself is by our side."[27]

Here, not only does the song effect the Chairman's teleportation, but the body of the singer itself becomes a resonant medium upon which the quotation is printed.

How, then, is this rhetoric of mass-mediated intimacy – one which repeatedly evokes the spiritual *and* somatic effects of song – registered in the compositions themselves and their recorded renditions? How do we account for the undeniable popularity of this music? Part of the answer lies, as Jiang Qing herself suggested, in the effects generated by listening and singing in unison with loud (and especially amplified) music. As Liang Maochun has noted, the distinct musical aesthetics of the Cultural Revolution have been characterized as "high, fast, hard, and loud."[28] This phrase, of course, could easily be applied to rock and roll, and for reasons that are not entirely coincidental. For when one turns to the recorded versions of the quotation songs released by China Records in 1966, it is immediately apparent that the music has been engineered so as to wring the maximum aural impact from limited technical means.

---

[26] "Mao Zhuxi de shu, shi ti women pinxia zhong nong shuo hua de, tiantian du Mao Zhuxi de shu, jiu haoxiang tiantian jiandao Mao Zhuxi" [Chairman Mao's book speaks for us poor and middle peasants. Reading Chairman Mao's book everyday is like seeing Chairman Mao himself everyday], *People's Daily* (October 1, 1966).

[27] "Dangdai zui weida de Malie zhuyizhe Mao zhuxi de yulu pucheng de gequ shi woguo renmin zui xin'ai de geming zhange" [The quotations set to music of the greatest Marxist–Leninist thinker of our time, Chairman Mao, are the most beloved battle hymns of our people], *People's Daily* (September 30, 1967). This article was published exactly one year after the initial introduction of the genre to China's reading public in 1966.

[28] Liang Maochun, "Lun 'yulu ge' xianxiang," p. 48.

The production is perfectly suited to unison singing, melding choral voices and orchestral accompaniment together into a monophonic wall of sound, one pitched high enough and with enough amplitude to penetrate the public spaces in which these songs were usually broadcast on monaural in-line loudspeaker systems. The shrillness of the music, with its tendency to emphasize the frequencies well above the midrange, almost certainly reflects the inability of compact loudspeakers and megaphones to reproduce low-frequency band with any degree of fidelity. The lack of stereo separation and internal space between instruments or individual voices is also an artifact of this technology. The resultant block-like solidity of the sound, coupled with duple, marching rhythms, serves as an aural analogue of their ideological insistence on the collectivity. The consistently "overdriven" timbres of climactic vocal phrases (perhaps an artifact of the soft-clipping of tubed recording equipment) seem to emulate the high pitch to which revolutionary energy has been driven in this moment of self-conscious historical emergency.[29] In many of these songs, finally, the choral harmonies are punctuated by a fanfare in brass, serving perhaps as heralds of the arrival of the revolutionary army, or of Chairman Mao himself.

Before these technical constraints, of course, came the compositional and political challenge of setting Chairman Mao's words to music. Certain keywords (the "Communist Party of China," for instance) had to be sung at a higher pitch in order to underscore their sacred position in the political lexicon. Melodies, in turn, needed not only to be limited in terms of range (to facilitate mass singing), but also to be structured around preexisting, and not always terribly melodious or even metrical, prose. The most obvious consequence of this particular constraint is that a composer like Li Jiefu has deftly selected for adaptation just those quotations that are the most portable, quotations which on account of their brevity and rhetorical nicety travel most readily across media. A singular and self-reflexive example is his setting of "We Should Support Whatever the Enemy Opposes and Oppose Whatever the Enemy Supports" (*Fan shi diren fandui de, women jiu yao yonghu, fanshi diren yonghu de, women jiu yao fandui*) as a choral round, in which the chiasmus of the original phrase is mirrored by a catchily chiastic melodic line.

Quotation songs – not unlike their contemporary pop musical counterparts in the West – exploited both formal limitations and new technological possibilities in order to forge a new musical language, one

---

[29] On the types and uses of distortion in the recording process, see Jay Hodgson, *Understanding Records: A Field Guide to Recording Practice* (New York: Continuum Books, 2010), pp. 97–116.

predicated on the power of the "hook." A hook is a musical or lyrical phrase, particular rhythmic figure, harmonic modulation, or timbral effect that catches the listener's attention and lodges a song in his or her memory.[30] One example might be the rhythmic "stutter-step" of eighth-notes we hear in the fanfare-like introduction to "The Force at the Core Leading our Cause Forward is the Chinese Communist Party." The "earworm" metaphor captures the invasive way pop music can make its way into our heads and reshape our subjectivities. The hook, finally, having been internalized as memory, often comes to stand in for the song itself, functioning as a kind of sonic synecdoche or self-reflexive citation. In this sense, we might see the quotation song as pop music in its purest most politically effective form. Citational from the very start, the typical quotation song is short, seldom extending much beyond a single minute, brutally repetitive, and compressed to the point that nothing is left *except* the hook itself.

And yet, as Derrida seems to augur, citation is not as stable as it may seem. The very portability of the Chairman's words, of his ideological signature – across time, space, and different sorts of media – may allow for the possibility of a new sort of semantic promiscuity. In his provocative study of Soviet culture, *Everything was Forever, Until it was No More*, the anthropologist Alexei Yurchak makes just such a claim, arguing that the increasingly rigid formalization of socialist language and visual iconography effected what he calls a "performative shift" after Stalin's death.[31] The more Soviet citizens internalized propaganda as repetitive ritual formulae that needed to be performed, the less their "original" constative meaning (the signature, if you will) mattered. Indeed, the meaning of icons or slogans or ritual behaviors gradually became "open-ended, indeterminate, or simply irrelevant." More interestingly, they also became subject to re-signification and reinterpretation, to a kind of performative drift.

The Chinese literary critic Huang Ziping, in a memoir about everyday language in the early 1970s, gives us an interesting example of this sort of drift. Remembering his years as a sent-down youth on Hainan island, he cites a love letter written by a friend who was trying to seduce a young

---

[30] Gary Burns, "A Typology of 'Hooks' in Popular Records," *Popular Music* 6.1 (January 1987), pp. 1–20.

[31] Alexei Yurchak, *Everything was Forever, Until it was No More: The Last Soviet Generation* (Princeton: Princeton University Press, 2006), pp. 24–26. Jason McGrath observes a similar phenomenon underlying the increasing formalization of revolutionary realism, as evinced by the model opera films. See his "Cultural Revolution Model Opera Films and the Realist Tradition in Chinese Cinema," *The Opera Quarterly* 26.2–3 (Spring–Summer 2010).

woman. The letter consisted of three lines of text, each of which is quoted verbatim from Chairman Mao's *Quotations* and Highest Directives:

1. Hailing from the five lakes and the four seas, for a common revolutionary aim, we come together.
2. We must share information.
3. We must first have a firm grasp, and secondly be attentive to politics.[32]

As Huang Ziping points out, this is a fine example of Lin Biao's notion of the "live study and live application" of Maoist dicta through their recontexualization and reuse in daily life.[33] Is there a "common revolutionary aim"? In order to find out, the lovers will need to share "information" (*qingbao*) – which, in a clever play on words, can also be understood as a "declaration of love." Having understood one another, they can hold to one another with a firm grasp, an embrace which trumps the business of politics and (in a phrase that has been expediently clipped from the original directive) "cleansing the class ranks." In this light, Jiang Qing's worries as to the promiscuity of the quotation song form were not entirely unjustified.

But what of her sense that quotation songs resembled Western pop music? This chapter has suggested some underlying formal similarities. Moreover, despite the enormous gulf separating China from the capitalist West, quotation songs and the youth culture with which they were associated were very much participants in the global 1960s. This contemporaneity is most easily illuminated by looking at some of the pathways along which Chairman Mao – as citation, signature, and song – journeyed to the West in those same years. The global diffusion of the Little Red Book is well known, as is its iconic status as a handbook for activists in locales as far-flung as Paris, Prague, Mexico City, and Berkeley. In the USA and Western Europe in particular, the China of the Cultural Revolution was read as a radically "other," and potentially utopian, alternative to capitalism, yet it reached the West largely by way of mass mediated products for overseas markets: the Little Red Book; 10-inch LPs of revolutionary music, including quotation songs; pictorial magazines such as *China Reconstructs*; and iconic posters of Chairman Mao.

---

[32] Huang Ziping, "Qishi niandai richang yuyan xue" [Everyday linguistics in the 1970s], in Bei Dao and Li Tuo, eds., *Qishi niandai* [The seventies] (Beijing: Sanlian, 2009), p. 324. Huang's essay has been translated by Nick Admussen as "Practical Linguistics of the 1970s" in *Renditions* 75 (Spring 2011).
[33] Ibid.

John Lennon of the Beatles was famously dismissive of the hollowness of such radical chic in his 1968 anthem "Revolution," singing "If you want to go around carrying pictures of Chairman Mao, you're not going to make it with anyone anyhow." It was Jean-Luc Godard, however, who sensed an underlying formal promiscuity linking Maoist iconography and late 1960s pop culture, between quotation songs and the Beatlesque music known as "yé-yé-yé" in French. In his prophetic 1967 film about a failed assassination plot perpetrated by an underground cell of self-styled Maoist revolutionaries in Paris, *La Chinoise*, Godard meticulously works to situate these aspiring insurgents within the globalized media cultures they avidly consume. Whether posed in front of Chinese revolutionary posters, assiduously taking notes as they listen to the broadcasts of Radio Peking, foregrounded against shelves of European novels from Goethe's *Wilhelm Meister* to Dostoevsky's *The Possessed*, intercut with imagery from American comic books, replicating laundry detergent commercials, modeling the latest fashions, or unwittingly replaying the plot structures of Hollywood thrillers, these characters do not so much inhabit a world as consume a global media landscape, in which revolution (and, indeed, social reality) are always already misrecognized as a form of citation, a performance.

The point is driven home in an early scene, in which Godard gives us a quotation song of his own, performed by the yé-yé-yé singer Claude Channes in a distinctly "high, fast, hard, and loud" style. As the song suffuses the soundtrack, the face of a stylish would-be revolutionary is tightly framed in close-up, distractedly worrying a red pen. She is foregrounded against a bookshelf in which copies of the Little Red Book are interspersed with assorted paperbacks, hard-bound tomes, and a blurred photograph of Chairman Mao. Each successive cut, keyed to the frenetic tempo of the song, shifts backwards to reveal more of the room. Each cut also reveals marked discontinuities. In the second shot the woman (with a new hairstyle and different-colored sweater) is seated at a table taking notes of Maoist dicta. Across the table a man draws a poster, and to the side a portable phonograph turns. The picture of Mao has been moved to the middle of the bookshelf and a tape transcription machine looms above it. The other books have been removed, leaving only runs of bright red, vinyl-clad *Quotations*. The third tableau pulls back to a medium shot in which the Mao photo is top-center, and the shelves are filled by monolithic and utterly superfluous stacks of Little Red Books. Meanwhile, our heroine (with new hair and sweater again) drinks tea with a female companion, seemingly unconscious of the proliferation of books behind her.

Channes' rapid-fire lyrics echo the reduplicative logic and parodic intent of Godard's carefully constructed series of images:

> Vietnam burns and I spurn Mao Mao
> Johnson wiggles and me I wriggle Mao Mao
> The napalm runs and me I gun Mao Mao
> Cities die and me I cry Mao Mao
> Whores cry and me I sigh Mao Mao
> The rice is mad and me a cad
> It's the Little Red Book
> That makes it all move
> Imperialism lays down the law
> Revolution is not a dinner party
> The A-bomb is a paper tiger
> The masses are the real heroes
> The Yanks kill and me I read Mao Mao
> The jester is king and me I sing Mao Mao
> The bombs go off and me I scoff Mao Mao
> Girls run and me I follow Mao Mao
> The Russians eat and me I dance Mao Mao
> I denounce and renounce Mao Mao
> It's the Little Red Book
> That makes it all move[34]

Mao's name and Mao's book have quite literally become the hook in this uneasy fusion of revolutionary ethos and pop art, ideological purity and the *au courant*, the austerity of dogma and the pleasure of primary colors. Mao is the means by which Godard reflects on the complex interactions between print, mediated sound, and the photographic image, not only in his own cinematic art, but in the unfolding of a particular historical moment. And Mao is finally the hook with which Godard skewers his own formal contradictions, along with the utopian longings of his generation of intellectuals. Yet this is also the same hook on which hangs the possibility of a politics beyond the merely performative.

BIBLIOGRAPHY

Burns, Gary, "A Typology of 'Hooks' in Popular Records," *Popular Music* 6.1 (January 1987), pp. 1–20

Chan, Anita, Richard Madsen, and Jonathan Unger, *Chen Village: The Recent History of a Peasant Community in Mao's China* (Berkeley: University of California Press, 1984)

Clark, Paul, *The Chinese Cultural Revolution: A History* (Cambridge: Cambridge University Press, 2008)

---

[34] Translation from the original French, adapted from the Australian DVD edition of the film, released by Madman Cinema.

Derrida, Jacques, "Signature Event Context" (1971), in *Limited Inc.* (Evanston, Ill.: Northwestern University Press, 1988), pp. 1–24

Hodgson, Jay, *Understanding Records: A Field Guide to Recording Practice* (New York: Continuum Books, 2010)

Huang Ziping, "Qishi niandai richang yuyan xue" [Everyday linguistics in the 1970s], in Bei Dao and Li Tuo, eds., *Qishi niandai* [The seventies] (Beijing: Sanlian, 2009), pp. 319–30; trans. Nick Admussen as "Practical Linguistics of the 1970s," *Renditions* 75 (Spring 2011), pp. 72–88

Jones, Andrew F., *Yellow Music: Media Culture and Colonial Modernity in the Chinese Jazz Age* (Durham: Duke University Press, 2001)

Liang Maochun, "Lun 'yulu ge' xianxiang" [On the quotation songs phenomenon] *Huangzhong: Wuhan yinyue xueyuan xuebao* 1 (2003), pp. 43–52

"Lun 'yulu ge' xianxiang" [On the quotation songs phenomenon], part 2, *Huangzhong: Wuhan yinyue xueyuan xuebao* 2 (2003), pp. 91–94

Lin Biao, "Zaiban qianyan" [Preface to the second edition], in *Mao Zhuxi Yulu* [*Quotations of Chairman Mao*] (Guangzhou: Zhongguo renmin jiefang jun zong zhengzhi bu, 1967), pp. 1–3

Liu, Alan, *Communications and National Integration in Communist China* (Berkeley: University of California Press, 1971)

McGrath, Jason, "Cultural Revolution Model Opera Films and the Realist Tradition in Chinese Cinema," *The Opera Quarterly* 26.2–3 (Spring–Summer 2010), pp. 343–76

Morson, Gary Paul, "The Quotation and its Genres," *Sun Yat-sen Journal of Humanities* 21 (Winter 2005), pp. 125–39

Nathan, Andrew, *Chinese Democracy* (London: I. B. Tauris, 1986)

Wong, Isabel K. F., "*Geming gequ*: Songs for the Education of the Masses," in Bonnie Macdougal, ed., *Popular Chinese Culture and Performing Arts in the People's Republic of China, 1949–1979* (Berkeley: University of California Press, 1984), pp. 112–43

Yan Yunxiang, *Siren shenghuo de bianqe: yige zhongguo cunzhuang li de aiqing, jiating yu qinmi guanxi, 1949–1999* [The transformation of everyday life: love, family, and intimacy in a Chinese village, 1949–1999] (Shanghai: Shanghai shudian, 2006)

Yurchak, Alexei, *Everything was Forever, Until it was No More: The Last Soviet Generation* (Princeton: Princeton University Press, 2006)

4 Mao quotations in factional battles and their afterlives

Episodes from Chongqing

Guobin Yang

> Comrades throughout the Party must never forget this experience for which we have paid in blood.
>
> War and Peace

The rhetoric of revolution was a ubiquitous presence in the Chinese Cultural Revolution. Red Guard papers exploded with such rhetoric. Revolutionary slogans, posters, and plaques were the indispensable props of rallies, demonstrations, and mass meetings. They dotted public spaces. The Cultural Revolution would not have been what it was without its rhetoric. Yet few scholars have examined how this rhetoric may be integral to the revolutionary process. By examining the uses of the *Quotations from Chairman Mao*, or the Little Red Book, in the Red Guard press, this chapter shows that Mao quotations, and revolutionary rhetoric more generally, were not meaningless propaganda, but a constitutive part of the factional dynamics of the revolution. My analysis will focus on two episodes of factionalism in 1967 in the city of Chongqing, which witnessed some of the most violent battles in the Red Guard movement in the entire country. Armed with Mao quotations, Red Guards and rebels engaged in intense verbal and physical conflicts. The combatants would recite Mao quotations to give themselves strength and inspiration. The escalation of Red Guard factionalism to violence had much to do with the intensification of this rhetoric of revolutionary violence. It seemed as if Mao quotations had taken on an incantatory power. I will argue that they were the core of an entire script of the Chinese revolution. This script took on its power because by the eve of the Cultural Revolution, it had been sanctified. Like the word "revolution," Mao quotations became holy symbols of the Chinese nation.[1] In the end, Red Guards made a revolution by performing the sacred script of revolution.

---

[1] Liu Xiaobo, "That Holy Word, 'Revolution'," in Jeffrey N. Wasserstrom and Elizabeth J. Perry, eds., *Popular Protest and Political Culture in Modern China*, 2nd edn. (Boulder: Westview Press, 1996).

For Mao quotations and the revolutionary script to realize their power, however, there must be appropriate social conditions and contexts. The uncertainty and vicissitudes of the Cultural Revolution provided the contexts. They compelled public displays of revolutionary faith and called for the enactment of the script. The significance of political context to revolutionary performances becomes obvious once the context changes. In the post-Mao period, the Little Red Book quickly lost its sacred aura. Indeed, at the height of the de-Maoification in the early 1980s, a party circular ordered that with the exception of some limited numbers to be held by provincial-level Xinhua bookstores, all copies and editions of the *Quotations from Chairman Mao*, which by then had taken up too much valuable warehouse space, were to be pulped.[2] Once without their sacred aura, the *Quotations* became worthless and had to be dispensed with. In time, however, in the process of commercialization and marketization, it has taken on new, commercial value. It has become a cultural relic and a collector's item with a price tag. While the dimming of its sacred aura reflects the fading of an ideological era, its revaluation in the commercial era reflects the emerging logic of the market.

The Red Guard movement in Chongqing

The Red Guard movement in Chongqing fell roughly into four stages. The first stage, from early June to December 4, 1966, marked the rise and fall of conservative Red Guard organizations and the rise of rebel groups. The most important rebel organization to emerge at this stage was called August Fifteenth at Chongqing University, so named because rebels there had staged a major protest event on that day. In the second stage, from December 4, 1966 to May 16, 1967, the rebel groups that came to dominate the Cultural Revolution in Chongqing split into two opposing factions. August Fifteenth was the core of the more moderate and more powerful faction, known as the United Committee (*ge lian hui*). Opposing it was the Smashers (*za pai*), later known as Fight-to-the-End, which was the minority and more radical faction. The leading organization of the Smashers was called August Thirty-First of the Southwest Teachers' College.

The third stage, from May 16, 1967 to October 15, 1968, was a prolonged factional warfare between these two rebel factions. The warfare sucked into its orbit not only college students, but middle school students, workers, peasants, government employees, and the military. The last stage, from mid-October 1968 to April 1969, was a period of settling accounts.

---

[2] Geremie Barmé, "The Irresistible Rise and Fall of Mao," in Geremie Barmé, ed., *Shades of Mao: The Posthumous Cult of the Great Leader* (Armonk: M. E. Sharpe, 1996), p. 7.

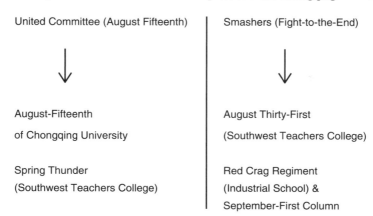

Fig. 4. Factional alignment in Chongqing in 1967–1968, showing only factions mentioned in this chapter.

Red Guard organizations were disbanded throughout the country. New power structures were established at different bureaucratic levels. Youth were sent down to rural areas. Unlike Beijing, where the first contingent of Red Guard organizations was the result of bottom-up student organizing, in Chongqing, the earliest Red Guard organizations were sponsored by local party authorities and thus were viewed as conservative groups by their opponents. Like Beijing, however, and unlike places such as Guangzhou, the main stage of factional warfare happened between two rebel factions, not between conservative and rebel factions. My analysis will focus on two episodes in the third stage, which was characterized by intense warfare between the two factions.

Red Guard factionalism had multiple causes. Mao and top party leaders evidently played a central role through their support of local rebel factions.[3] From the perspective of class conflicts, some scholars find that Red Guards and rebels were divided along the lines of class interests formed prior to the Cultural Revolution.[4] Perry and Li use social network, social interest, and psycho-cultural perspectives to explain different aspects of labor activism in Shanghai.[5] Walder's works on Beijing Red Guard factionalism show that the decisive factor was not people's

[3] Roderick MacFaquhar and Michael Schoenhals, *Mao's Last Revolution* (Cambridge, Mass.: Belknap Press of Harvard University Press, 2008).

[4] Anita Chan, Stanley Rosen, and Jonathan Unger, "Students and Class Warfare: The Social Roots of the Red Guard Conflict in Guangzhou (Canton)," *The China Quarterly* 83 (1980).

[5] Elizabeth Perry and Li Xun, *Proletarian Power: Shanghai in the Cultural Revolution* (Boulder: Westview Press, 1997).

social-class positions, but rather the choices they made under the uncertain political conditions of the initial period.[6] My study of the role of the revolutionary script in factional violence draws on studies of political culture in modern China and the formation of Maoist discourse and revolutionary tradition.[7] I argue that the revolutionary culture formed before the Cultural Revolution, dating back to the Yan'an period[8] and dominating the media discourse of the early 1960s, had direct influences on Red Guard radicalism, because it was that culture that created the holy symbols of Mao and the "revolution."

Two factional battles in Chongqing

The first battle to be examined here was called the June 5–8 Incident. On those days in 1967, the August Fifteenth and the Smashers fought each other at the Southwest Teachers' College. The main faction of August Fifteenth at the Southwest Teachers' College was called Spring Thunder, which had occupied the college's newly built library. Spring Thunder's opponent at the college was August Thirty-First. In the afternoon of June 5, August Thirty-First attacked Spring Thunder and took control of the two lower levels of the library, but could not take over the two upper floors occupied by Spring Thunder. As the battle continued on June 6–7, reinforcements from other August Fifteenth groups in the city arrived, but were initially blocked outside the campus by August Thirty-First. Finally, on the night of June 7, major reinforcements from the August Fifteenth at Chongqing University arrived on the scene. Under attack above from Spring Thunder and below from the reinforcements, August Thirty-First could no longer hold on. Some of its members were captured while others made their escape by jumping off the building. Although no military weapons were used, the battles from June 5–8 marked the beginning of large-scale factional violence in Chongqing.

The second case was the July 25 Incident. On July 25, 1967, members of the August Fifteenth faction, armed with knives, pistols, rifles, machine guns and submachine guns, attacked four hundred unarmed members of two Smashers groups, called Red Crag Regiment and

---

[6] Andrew Walder, *Fractured Rebellion: The Beijing Red Guard Movement* (Cambridge, Mass.: Harvard University Press, 2009).

[7] Jeffrey N. Wasserstrom and Elizabeth J. Perry, eds., *Popular Protest and Political Culture in Modern China*, 2nd edn. (Boulder: Westview Press, 1994); David E. Apter and Tony Saich, *Revolutionary Discourse in Mao's Republic* (Cambridge, Mass.: Harvard University Press, 1998). Hung Chang-tai, *Mao's New World: Political Culture in the Early People's Republic* (Ithaca: Cornell University Press, 2011).

[8] Apter and Saich, *Revolutionary Discourse*.

September First Column, at the Industrial School in Chongqing.[9] After half a day's battle, August Fifteenth defeated the Smashers and took over control of the Industrial School. August Fifteenth killed ten members of the Smashers and lost two lives on its own side.[10]

In each case, after the battle each side was engaged in publicity work, attacking the opponent and commemorating its own dead. Those who died in action were conferred with "martyr" status. The commemoration included both public memorial services and newspaper pages devoted to the incident and the martyrs. The newspaper pages contained narratives about the incident in the form of editorials, reportage, and eyewitness accounts. The narratives published by each side viewed the other side as the enemy, yet except for that they were very similar. They would condemn the cruelty and fierceness of the enemy, extol the bravery and fearlessness of their own fighters, and end with expressions of determination to defend Mao and the cause of the revolution and avenge the martyrs.

The narratives were invariably interspersed with quotations from Mao's verse or prose works, which seemed to have a fitting quote for praising all heroic and revolutionary behavior and condemning every reactionary act. Some samples were: "Be resolute, fear no sacrifice and surmount every difficulty to win victory"; "Bitter sacrifice strengthens bold resolve, Which dares to make sun and moon shine in new skies"; and "Wherever there is struggle there is sacrifice, and death is a common occurrence." A not-so-poetic but no less forceful remark by Lin Biao was also a favorite quote to express one's fearlessness in the face of death: "When called upon to die, then be brave enough to die, including losing your own life. To hell with death! On the battlefield, once fighting starts, old-man me just gets ready to die on the battlefield!"

The narratives usually contain descriptions of battle scenes. These battle scenes bear such close resemblance to those in Chinese war films and fiction of the revolutionary romanticism style that they seemed to be mimetic of art, suggesting that Red Guard factional warfare was the enactment of scripts familiar to these youth.

Below is a description of the battle scene at the Southwest Teachers' College on June 6, 1967. It was from a story in the June 16, 1967 issue of *August 15 Battle News*, the leading newspaper of the August Fifteenth faction, to which the Spring Thunder group at the Southwest Teachers'

---

[9] The above is based on a story published in the inaugural issue of *Shancheng Nuhuo* on August 14, 1967.

[10] The number of casualties is based on He Shu, *Fighting for Chairmao Mao* [Wei Mao Zhuxi er zhan] (Hong Kong: Sanlian Shudian, 2010), p. 197. He surmises that the two deaths on the side of August Fifteenth might have been caused by friendly fire due to the confusion of the situation.

College belonged. The first part of the story describes how ruthlessly Spring Thunder's opponents "August 31" had attacked Spring Thunder. Now, a day's battle had come to an end:

Night fell on the campus of Southwest Teachers' College. The situation is getting more and more serious. "Looking up, we see the north star, in our heart we think of Mao Zedong ..." Spring Thunder fighters could all be wiped out. But to die, what is so scary about that! Spring Thunder fighters have all made up their mind. "When called upon to die, then be brave enough to die, including losing your own life. To hell with death! On the battlefield, once fighting starts, old-man me just gets ready to die on the battlefield!"[11]

Besides narratives about battle scenes, Red Guard papers devoted to these incidents contained photos, obituaries, diaries, and occasionally letters of the dead, as well as memorial speeches. These mnemonic genres similarly glorify the dead and exalt heroism and sacrifice for the cause of revolution. The standard scripts used in these remembrances were Mao's remarks about the need to memorialize the dead in the Little Red Book. Coming from "Mao the storyteller," in the words of Apter and Saich, these remarks seemed to cast a spell on their readers like incantations inviting them to act.[12] The following passage from "Serve the People," for example, was printed in the middle of the page devoted to the "martyrs" of the July 25 battle in the August 8, 1967 issue of *August 15 Battle News*:

From now on, when anyone in our ranks who has done some useful work dies, be he soldier or cook, we should have a funeral ceremony and a memorial meeting in his honour. This should become the rule. And it should be introduced among the people as well. When someone dies in a village, let a memorial meeting be held. In this way we express our mourning for the dead and unite all the people.

Another quotation from Mao, which appeared at the end of the story reporting the August Fifteenth memorial service for its martyrs, is a famous eulogy of martyrdom: "Thousands upon thousands of martyrs have heroically laid down their lives for the people; let us hold their banner high and march ahead along the path crimson with their blood!" As factional warfare intensified and casualties increased, these Mao quotations became the staples in the Red Guard press.

The reality of the role

Mao quotations were not mere rhetoric with which Red Guards randomly and freely used to embellish their narratives. It would be difficult

[11] *August 15 Battle News* (June 16, 1967), p. 2.
[12] Apter and Saich, *Revolutionary Discourse*, p. 69.

to imagine the violent warfare between opposing factions without this rhetoric. One need not have to argue that Mao quotations *caused* the factional violence to see their essential role in Red Guard factionalism.

These young rebels were performing a role in a revolutionary drama, often doing things in imitation of the role in the script. When they were in battle, they often consciously imitated the actions of soldiers in the battle scenes in the many Chinese war films and fiction that they had grown up with. To argue that they were performing the revolution by no means implies that their action lacked authenticity. For them, performance and reality had become one and the same thing. Their role in the drama of the Cultural Revolution was their reality. This unity of performance and reality is evident in the story of Li Shengpin, who died several days after the battle of July 25, 1967.

On July 29, 1967, Li Shengpin, a member of the August Fifteenth at Chongqing University, was killed in an accident while he was training high school students to use homemade hand-grenades. Li was one of the three people given "martyr" status in a decision published in the *August 15 Battle News*. The same issue also published excerpts of Li's diaries, as well as a letter to a friend he wrote shortly before his death. Zhou Ziren, the editor of the newspaper, revealed in his memoir that the friend was in fact Li's girlfriend. The letter provided a valuable glimpse into the inner world of the factional warriors at that time. Li Shengpin was fully aware of the dangers. His letter expressed intimations about possible death. He also recalled the sufferings of his parents and grandparents in the "old society" and mentioned specifically that his mother had to beg for food in the streets when she was ten years old. After this, Li wrote:

I often thought, if our country doesn't have a future, all talk about personal future is deceitful nonsense ... The question now is whether to carry the Cultural Revolution to the end or to let it die prematurely ... We must exert ourselves, struggle hard, and not fear death.[13]

Li told his girlfriend not to tell his family if he died. He ended the letter by saying that she should not feel too sad about his death and should look to the future.

Li's letter had a calm, intimate, and conversational tone, untypical of the Red Guard writing style at that time. It conveyed a sense of touching authenticity about the meaning of revolution and sacrifice to the young generation. This letter shows the difficulty, and perhaps the meaningless-ness, of any attempt to draw a sharp line between performance and

[13] *August 15 Battle News* (August 8, 1967), p. 3.

reality. One might argue that Li Shengpin, in writing the letter, and in his use of language, was following a script that he had learned through socialization and education. Yet if he was acting a role, he had certainly taken that role to heart. His role was his reality.

Political culture

In the imagination of the Cultural Revolution generation, violence was an integral part and ultimate manifestation of revolution. The sacred tradition of the Chinese revolution, carefully crafted by the party in the period in which this generation was coming of age, celebrated martyrdom and revolutionary heroes. It exalted violence as a necessary means of revolution and glorified death for the cause of revolution. The entire education of this generation in the seventeen years prior to the Cultural Revolution, whether it was formal education at school or informal education through films, arts, and children's picture books, was suffused with these messages of heroic martyrdom.[14]

In his study of Chinese political culture, Chang-tai Hung examines the "cult of the red martyr" in the first decade of the PRC. A top-down political project, this cult was created through a whole set of practices from the establishment of a Martyrs' Memorial Day to the building of war memorials, the publication of martyrs' biographies, and public trials of "counterrevolutionaries."[15] By the eve of the Cultural Revolution, a whole edifice of "revolutionary tradition" had been erected. Indeed, by 1964, with Mao's warnings about the dangers of a Soviet-style revisionism and the American strategy of peaceful evolution of communist nations, the inculcation of the revolutionary tradition took on a new urgency as a way to train "revolutionary successors."[16] Hence the launching of the campaign to revolutionize Chinese youth in 1964.[17]

---

[14] It should be noted that other cultural traditions also fed into the socialization of China's young generation in the 1950s. These included the May Fourth tradition and world literature, especially Russian revolutionary literature. But as Qian Liqun points out, what his generation learned from these cultural resources was that "the world consisted of 'oppressors and the oppressed,' the former being our enemies and the latter our brothers, sisters, and friends. Our ideal and our historical mission was to eliminate all of that, both in China and abroad: all the phenomena of oppression, exploitation, and slavery." Qian also stresses the utter sincerity of his generation in their aspirations to eliminate oppression. See Qian Liqun, "The Way our Generation Imagined the World," *Inter-Asia Cultural Studies* 6.4 (2005), p. 528.

[15] Hung, *Mao's New World*.

[16] Roderick MacFarquhar, *The Origins of the Cultural Revolution* (New York: Columbia University Press, 1997), p. 611.

[17] James R. Townsend, *The Revolutionization of Chinese Youth: A Study of Chung-kuo Ch'ing-nien* (Berkeley: University of California Center for Chinese Studies, 1967).

Hung points out that the "cult of the red martyr" seldom presents a story of bereavement, but instead "extols war's glory and warriors' sacrifice to the lofty political goal of socialism."[18]

Various art forms in that period, such as the revolutionary model opera, not only enacted revolutions through artistic representation but, as Xiaomei Chen writes, "was intended to spur the Chinese people to a continued revolution, the Great Proletarian Cultural Revolution."[19] A careful study of the emulation of heroes published in early 1968 shows that Chinese political culture prior to the Cultural Revolution had built an image of revolutionary heroism that directly fed and fired Red Guard factional struggles. Analyzing the diaries of officially promoted heroes, Mary Sheridan wrote that "a hero openly courts death, and when it comes it elevates him to a higher plane. There is a thrill of achievement which overrides the sense of loss … for a revolutionary hero, death holds neither pain, nor fear, nor disfigurement. Transfixed by inner visions, the hero watches himself pass into immortality. He dies in spiritual certainty."[20] This revolutionary romanticism had always been in the Maoist vision of revolution, but was carried to new extremes in the Red Guard period.[21]

The institutions and practices of the "cult of the red martyr" built in the 1950s not only remained in place during the Cultural Revolution; the Cultural Revolution was in fact the ultimate manifestation and proof of the profound effects of the revolutionary tradition. Of all aspects of the Cultural Revolution, the factional battles were the manifestations in their most radical and concrete form. They reenacted familiar scenes in the representations of war and revolution that had become an integral part of the social and mental landscape of the Cultural Revolution generation prior to the Cultural Revolution itself.

Political context

Political culture, specifically the building of a sacred revolutionary tradition, was a necessary but insufficient condition for enacting a revolution. The political context itself mattered in critical ways by giving the tradition a sense of reality and immediacy.

[18] Hung, *Mao's New World*. p. 233.
[19] Xiaomei Chen, "Operatic Revolutions: Tradition, Memory, and Women in Model Theater," in *Acting the Right Part: Political Theater and Popular Drama in Contemporary China, 1966–1996* (Honolulu: University of Hawaii Press, 2002), p. 75.
[20] Mary Sheridan, "The Emulation of Heroes," *The China Quarterly* 33 (1968), pp. 60, 61.
[21] Ibid., p. 71.

One crucial feature of the Cultural Revolution was its intense revolutionary atmosphere. Addressing an audience in London in 1856, Marx said, "The atmosphere in which we live weighs upon every one with a 20,000-pound force, but do you feel it? No more than European society before 1848 felt the revolutionary atmosphere enveloping and pressing it from all sides."[22] If everything else was uncertain and unclear, the revolutionary atmosphere of the Cultural Revolution was not. The *feeling* of the onset of a revolution permeated the air through newspapers, radio, the Red Guard press, the mass rallies and assemblies, and the factional violence. The visceral feeling of a surging revolution, combined with the uncertainty about how to make the revolution, left the participants with one clear option only: be true revolutionaries. Never having experienced a revolution and self-conscious of their historical mission as revolutionary successors, Red Guards and rebels needed to imagine themselves to be making a revolution and to be true revolutionaries in it. They also needed to demonstrate through their own action that this was a real revolution, and they were its true practitioners.

Another important feature of the political context was the political uncertainty in the course of the Cultural Revolution. Despite official documents about the methods of conducting the Cultural Revolution, such as the May 16th Notice and the "16 Articles," its goals, process, and anticipated outcomes were both vague and open to multiple interpretations. They were left to the participants themselves to decide and find out.

In the early period, participants, whether they were rebels or conservatives, party authorities or students, fought among themselves about their own and their opponents' revolutionary credentials and loyalty. When suppressed by local authorities, many rebel groups traveled to Beijing to *gaozhuang*, or petition, central leaders. This happened in Chongqing too. Central leaders from Zhou Enlai to members of the Cultural Revolution Small Group (CRSG), which was charged with leading the Cultural Revolution, met numerous times with these Red Guards to hear their complaints, give instructions and advice, and explain central policies.

At these meetings, petitioners sought confirmation from central leaders that their actions were revolutionary, not counterrevolutionary. They also asked for advice about how to carry out the revolution. Central leaders rarely just used their power to give orders and directives to Red Guard petitioners, however. More often than not, they resorted to persuasion, and sometimes goading. Like dramatic directors, their approach was not simply to tell the actors how to put on a particular act, but to

---

[22] Karl Marx, "Speech at the Anniversary of the People's Paper," in Robert C. Tucker, ed., *The Marx–Engels Reader*, 2nd edn. (London: Norton, 1978 [1856]), p. 577.

help the actors "enter their role" in order to get the feel of the game and then perform successfully. They did so by invoking the familiar myth of the revolutionary struggles of the Chinese Communist Party, by adding their reinterpretations, and by offering tips about concrete methods.

In their speeches, central leaders often talked about the meaning and nature of revolution during the Cultural Revolution. They emphasized that the Cultural Revolution was an unprecedented, world-shaking event, that it had to be made by people themselves rather than being directed from above, and that the best test of the true revolutionaries was through their own revolutionary practice. When asked whether the central party leadership should intervene in the struggles in Chongqing by directly removing local party leaders, CRSG member Wang Li responded:

It is better not to remove them yet. Why? Because that should come as a result of your own struggle. In my view, you haven't struggled enough ... Usually we do not use the method of removing people from top down. This would not solve the problem. Problems in the revolution should be resolved by Chongqing people themselves.[23]

At the same meeting, Qi Benyu talked about the necessity of revolution and dangers of capitalist revision by citing the history of class exploitation in Sichuan. Referring to a work of sculpture about the exploitation of peasants by landlords, which inspired a documentary film called *Rent Collection Courtyard*, Qi said:

One thing I want to say is that we support your rebellion. Your rebellion was well done, but not yet done enough. You should have bigger rebellions. I have seen Sichuan's *Rent Collection Courtyard*. Have you seen it? It is a living textbook for class education. If we do not carry the Cultural Revolution thoroughly, then it is possible that capitalism and feudalism will have a comeback. Our country will change color.[24]

In their responses to questions about who was or was not revolutionary, central leaders called on the young people to prove themselves by going through the trials of the revolutionary process. A speech given by Tao Zhu, one-time head of the CRSG, contained the following remarks:

What is counterrevolutionary? ... You can't say you are the true revolutionaries and they are fake. This is mass organizing. Their organizations may also be revolutionary. You may have a revolutionary competition. Good ones will grow, bad ones will collapse ... True or fake revolutionaries will be distinguished in revolutionary practice.[25]

---

[23] *Hong wei bing zi liao: xu bian* (Red Guard publications: supplement II), vol. IV (Okaton, Va.: Center for Chinese Research Materials, 1992), p. 2374.
[24] Ibid., p. 2376.   [25] Ibid., p. 2294.

In a way, these remarks by Tao Zhu captured the hidden logic of the Cultural Revolution. During it, nothing could be taken for granted; individuals had to prove whether they were "fake" or true revolutionaries. The proof had to come from people's observable behavior – their performances.

Thus it was true that central leaders did a great deal to mobilize the young rebels, but that was not the whole story. In the later stage of the movement in Chongqing, when factional warfare broke out among the rebel ranks, both sides in the rebel camp fought each other just as ferociously and as earnestly as they had done when they were battling the conservatives. Nor was the struggle for power the only or even the main reason for the split among the rebels. There was certainly grappling for power. But power was an essential component in the script of revolution. If a true revolution was about the change of power, then for these believers, that should happen in Chongqing as well for the Chongqing revolution to merit its name. Thus even the struggles for power, a factor often cited as a major cause of the escalation of factional violence, had a performative rationale. It was part of the sacred code of revolution.

Afterlives: red culture in Chongqing

The story of Mao quotations in Red Guard factionalism happened several decades ago. Soon after Mao died in 1976, China embarked on an alternative developmental path, rejecting revolution and class struggle in favor of market economic development. The fate of the Little Red Book in this process epitomizes the broader patterns of transformation. In the Red Guard movement, the Little Red Book was a symbol of political capital, of which ownership, familiarity with its contents, and readiness to follow its directions, were signs. Yet because others also possessed this capital, people had to be engaged in competitive performances in order to retain and grow it. Violence was a radical form of revolutionary competition. Thus factional violence escalated in the process of these competitive performances.

In the power struggles between Mao's successor Hua Guofeng and the rehabilitated Deng Xiaoping, part of Deng's strategy to oust Hua and launch the reform program was de-Maoification and the settling of accounts with the Cultural Revolution. In this process, the Little Red Book not only lost its sacred aura, but was cast aside and pulped as historical garbage. In February 1979, an official party document was issued to suspend the distribution of the Mao quotation books.[26]

---

[26] See Duo Chunsheng, *Zhongguo gaige kaifang shi* [A history of China's reform and opening up] (Beijing: Hongqi chubanshe, 1998), p. 320. See CCP Central

Another party directive issued in July 1980 to cut back on "propagating individuals"[27] ordered the reduction of the number of Mao portraits and statues in public spaces.

The Little Red Book and all that it symbolized, however, did not die out, despite the official policy of renouncing the Cultural Revolution. On the contrary, in the process of the market transformation, it gains new mnemonic value as a memento of a complicated past as well as commercial value as a collectable relic of China's "red culture." Original or reprint copies of the Little Red Book, along with other relics of the Cultural Revolution, have become common consumer items in popular tourist sites. A token of revolution endowed with sacred political power is thus desacralized and turned into an item with mere monetary and sentimental value, an appropriate footnote to the ideological and cultural transformations of China's economic reform.

It was quite another thing, however, when Bo Xilai, the now-disgraced former party secretary of Chongqing, decided to make "red culture" a core element of his campaign to build a Chongqing model. Bo assumed his position in Chongqing in November 2007. Shortly afterwards, he launched a campaign to "sing red songs" and "crack down on criminals." The campaign to "sing red songs" was supposed to revive China's revolutionary culture to counter the corrosive influences of contemporary commercialism and consumerism. Red culture was billed as the core of new socialist values, and inculcating these values was seen as necessary for building a harmonious and prosperous society, the new vision of China propounded under Hu Jintao.

Bo's campaign used Cultural Revolution-style methods to mobilize Chongqing residents to join group singing of "red songs." According to one estimate, by the end of 2010, Chongqing had organized 155,000 activities for the singing of red songs. By head count, these involved almost all of Chongqing's adult population. In addition, 170 million text messages of "red classics" were reportedly sent to and by Chongqing residents on their mobile phones and the online texting service QQ.[28] In May 2009, 13 million mobile phone subscribers in Chongqing received Bo Xilai's personal texting, in which he shared a few of his favorite Mao quotations and commented, "These words are very concise,

Committee, "Decision Concerning the Great Proletarian Cultural Revolution," *Peking Review* 33 (1966), pp. 6–11.

27 See CCP Central Committee, "Decision Concerning the Great Proletarian Cultural Revolution."

28 Zhou Yong, "Chongqing de 'chang, du, jiang, chuan' yu guojia wenhua ruan shili" [Singing, reading, story-telling, and disseminating [red culture] in Chongqing and national soft power], *Chong Social Sciences* 5 (2011), p. 93.

very true, and very elevating."[29] In its scale if not in its violence, then, the "red culture" campaign in Chongqing approached the proportions of the Cultural Revolution. Whether intentionally or unintentionally, Bo Xilai seems to have tried to play the role of Mao in mobilizing participation through personal charisma and mass campaigns.

It is a historical irony that a red culture that once was the bible of militancy and revolutionary violence is now mobilized to promote social harmony and stability. Yet although the "red culture" campaign in Chongqing fell flat and then collapsed when Bo Xilai met his downfall in his much-publicized scandal in 2012,[30] it still managed to gain supporters. At the height of the building of the Chongqing model, left-leaning intellectuals in China and abroad saw new hopes of countering Chinese capitalism. At the personal level, at least among the generation who experienced the Mao era, the rhythms and tunes of the red songs were an emotional tie both to a national history and to personal lives long gone but hard to forget.[31] This may well be a testimony to the lingering incantatory power of the once anointed Little Red Book. If nothing else, singing and hearing the same songs today among members of a generation who grew up with those rhythms gives at least a modicum of continuity to a life course disrupted by campaign after campaign.

BIBLIOGRAPHY

Apter, David E., and Tony Saich, *Revolutionary Discourse in Mao's Republic* (Cambridge, Mass.: Harvard University Press, 1998)

Barmé, Geremie, "The Irresistible Rise and Fall of Mao," in Geremie Barmé, ed., *Shades of Mao: The Posthumous Cult of the Great Leader* (Armonk: M. E. Sharpe, 1996), pp. 3–74

CCP Central Committee, "Decision Concerning the Great Proletarian Cultural Revolution," *Peking Review* 33 (1966), pp. 6–11

Chan, Anita, Stanley Rosen, and Jonathan Unger, "Students and Class Warfare: The Social Roots of the Red Guard Conflict in Guangzhou (Canton)," *The China Quarterly* 83 (1980), pp. 397–446

Chen, Xiaomei, "Operatic Revolutions: Tradition, Memory, and Women in Model Theater," in *Acting the Right Part: Political Theater and Popular Drama*

---

[29] "Why is Chongqing so Red?" *Vista (Kan tianxia)* 2 (2011), available at www.vistastory.com/index.php/Ebook/details/news_id/1719, accessed October 10, 2013.

[30] On media coverage of the scandal, see "Bo Xilai" in "Times Topics," *The New York Times*, updated November 6, 2012: topics.nytimes.com/top/reference/timestopics/people/b/bo_xilai/index.html.

[31] For an analysis of the contemporary meaning of "red songs," see Andreas Steen, "'Voices of the Mainstream': Red Songs and Revolutionary Identities in the People's Republic of China," in Christian Utz and Frederick Lau, eds., *Vocal Music and Cultural Identity in Contemporary Music: Unlimited Voices in East Asia and the West* (London: Routledge, 2013).

in Contemporary China, 1966–1996 (Honolulu: University of Hawaii Press, 2002), pp. 73–122

Duo Chunsheng, *Zhongguo gaige kaifang shi* [A history of China's reform and opening up] (Beijing: Hongqi chubanshe, 1998)

He Shu, *Fighting for Chairmao Mao* [Wei Mao Zhuxi er zhan] (Hong Kong: Sanlian Shudian, 2010)

Hong wei bing zi liao: xu bian [Red Guard publications: supplement II], vol. IV (Okaton, Va.: Center for Chinese Research Materials, 1992)

Hung Chang-tai, *Mao's New World: Political Culture in the Early People's Republic* (Ithaca: Cornell University Press, 2011)

Liu Xiaobo, "That Holy Word, 'Revolution'," in Wasserstrom and Perry, eds., *Popular Protest and Political Culture in Modern China*, pp. 309–24

MacFarquhar, Roderick, *The Origins of the Cultural Revolution* (New York: Columbia University Press, 1997)

MacFarquhar, Roderick, and Michael Schoenhals, *Mao's Last Revolution* (Cambridge, Mass.: Belknap Press of Harvard University Press, 2008)

Marx, Karl, "Speech at the Anniversary of the People's Paper," in Robert C. Tucker, ed., *The Marx–Engels Reader*, 2nd edn. (London: Norton, 1978 [1856]), pp. 577–78

Perry, Elizabeth, and Li Xun, *Proletarian Power: Shanghai in the Cultural Revolution* (Boulder: Westview Press, 1997)

Qian Liqun, "The Way our Generation Imagined the World," *Inter-Asia Cultural Studies* 6.4 (2005), pp. 524–34

Sheridan, Mary, "The Emulation of Heroes," *The China Quarterly* 33 (1968), pp. 47–72

Steen, Andreas, "'Voices of the Mainstream': Red Songs and Revolutionary Identities in the People's Republic of China," in Christian Utz and Frederick Lau, eds., *Vocal Music and Cultural Identity in Contemporary Music: Unlimited Voices in East Asia and the West* (London: Routledge, 2013), pp. 225–47

Townsend, James R., *The Revolutionization of Chinese Youth: A Study of Chung-kuo Ch'ing-nien* (Berkeley: University of California Center for Chinese Studies, 1967)

Walder, Andrew, *Fractured Rebellion: The Beijing Red Guard Movement* (Cambridge, Mass.: Harvard University Press, 2009)

Wasserstrom, Jeffrey N., and Elizabeth J. Perry, eds., *Popular Protest and Political Culture in Modern China*, 2nd edn. (Boulder: Westview Press, 1994)

"Why is Chongqing so Red?" *Vista (Kan tianxia)* 2 (2011), available at www.vistastory.com/index.php/Ebook/details/news_id/1719

Zhou Yong, "Chongqing de 'chang, du, jiang, chuan' yu guojia wenhua ran shili" [Singing, reading, story-telling, and disseminating [red culture] in Chongqing and national soft power], *Chongqing Social Sciences* 5 (2011), pp. 93–94

5   Translation and internationalism

Lanjun Xu

> The people who have triumphed in their own revolution should help
> those still struggling for liberation. This is our internationalist duty.
>
> Patriotism and Internationalism

From its founding in 1949, the young People's Republic of China (PRC)
fully recognized the importance of translation and treated it as a significant part of its cultural diplomacy and exchange. In hopes of creating a
global language of Maoist revolution, the Chinese government subsidized
the publication and distribution of numerous foreign-language publications, such as *China Pictorial*, *China Reconstructs*, and *Peking Review*. But
none of these could rival Mao Zedong's Little Red Book in visibility and
influence. China's Foreign Languages Press translated *Quotations from
Chairman Mao*, otherwise known as the Little Red Book, into dozens of
languages and arranged for global distribution of the book, and in the
eight months from October 1966 to May 1967, the International Bookstore successfully sent copies to more than a hundred countries.[1] This
major translation undertaking was seen as an invaluable contribution to
socialist internationalism and to the development of global revolution.
This chapter details how, when, and by whom the text of the Little Red
Book was translated, and how the book itself, as a material object, came to
stock bookshelves around the world. Drawing on oral history interviews,
memoirs, and archival research, this chapter argues that the global success
of the Little Red Book should be seen as part of New China's extended
efforts to translate Chinese literature, revolutionary theory, and Mao's
works into different languages, potentially serving as a common and
universal currency of revolution. In other words, the popularity of the
Little Red Book in the 1960s was based on the cumulative efforts of the
PRC since its establishment to build a global book distribution network

---

[1] Xinhuashe, "Guojigongchanzhuyi yundongshi shang de dashijian, wuchanjieji
wenhuadageming de xinsheng" [The big event in the history of the internationalist
movement and the new victory in the proletarian cultural revolution], *People's Daily*
(July 2, 1967).

through the International Bookstore, as well as its consistent emphasis on the role of translation in promoting Mao's work under the auspices of the Foreign Languages Press. In my discussion, I am particularly interested in these two important institutions, which played crucial roles in promoting *Quotations from Chairman Mao*. The development of these two institutions and the evolution of some major policies related to the translation will be mapped out. Moreover, complementary to these two institutions, I will also discuss other ways of spreading the content of the Little Red Book to the world, such as radio broadcasts and by sailors.

I further argue that the Chinese Communist Party (CCP) treated systematic translation as an important way to transcend and transgress the boundaries of First World capitalism, Second World socialism, and Third World development, and as a result, one essential element of the monumental project to "export Chinese revolution to the world" was to transmit to a global audience a wide range of Chinese literature, and in particular Mao's writings. Since its beginning, the Foreign Languages Press made it very clear that their target readers were not those in the socialist bloc, but rather those people who were politically between the radical leftists and the rightists, and geographically in the "in-between" regions including those in the capitalist and imperialist countries, as well as in the developing countries, mainly in Asia, Africa, and Latin America, that were fighting for independence from imperialism.

Translation in the young PRC and the Foreign Languages Press

The Foreign Languages Press was originally one part of the International News Bureau (Guoji xinwen ju), which was established in October 1949. The main purpose of the International News Bureau was to publicize New China globally, including editing news in foreign languages for international use, establishing journals for foreign readers, and regulating foreign journalists in China. The reason for setting up this press was to increase the convenience of international distribution, especially to and in non-socialist countries.[2] In December of the same year, the International Bookstore was built, through which all the books published by the International News Bureau were released to the world. In 1952, the International News Bureau was officially reorganized into China's Foreign Languages Press under the Publicity Department, focusing on translating

---

[2] Dai Yannian and Chen Rinong, eds., *Zhongguo waiwenju wushinian: dashiji* [Fifty years of the Chinese Foreign Languages Bureau: memorabilia] (Beijing: Xinxing chubanshe, 1999), p. 1.

and publishing journals and books. The stated purpose of the press's publications was "to broadly introduce the achievements of the New China, the policies of the Communist Party and also the central government, as well as the experiences of Chinese revolution to the world." The main contents of its publications included: the bulletin of policy documents of the central government; the works of important Chinese politicians, scientists, and theorists; articles, reports, and literary works introducing New China's achievements; and works of propaganda.[3]

The main target audience of Chinese propaganda, according to a report on internal discussions at the Foreign Languages Press in 1962, were those in three so-called "in-between regions": the socialist countries; the "developing countries that are fighting for independence"; and "also the capitalist countries."[4] But there were disputes about how to define the term "in-between" and how to differentiate it from the other two categories of "left" and "right." The report mentions internal discussions related to this issue and lists the following three attributes of this "in-between" audience: they are (1) friendly to China and willing to know more about China; (2) anti-imperialist and anti-colonialist; and (3) anti-war.[5] In socialist countries, the translations of Chinese books were often conducted locally, enabling each country to more easily select topics based on their needs.[6]

In relation to this discussion, Mao's evolving analysis of imperialism as the principal contradiction in global politics deserves some special attention. The concept of "in-between regions" may be traced back to his conversation with the American journalist Anna Louise Strong in 1946. In that conversation, Mao proposed this concept based mainly on his anticipation of the coming complex rivalry between two superpowers, the United States and the Soviet Union. In his view, there existed broad regions between the two superpowers, which included "many capitalist countries, colonial, and semi-colonial countries. If it does not first

---

[3] General Publication Administration, "Guanyu zhongyang yiji gechubanshe de zhuanye fengong jiqi lingdaoguanxi de guiding (cao'an)" [Stipulation on the division of work and administrative relationship of all central-level presses [draft]], in Zhou Dongyuan, ed., *Zhongguo waiwenju wushi nian: shiliao xuanbian* [Fifty years of the Chinese Foreign Languages Bureau: selected archives documents; hereafter *Shiliao xuanbian*] (Beijing: Xinxing chubanshe, 1995), pp. 51–52.

[4] "Guanyu waiwen chubanshe yewu sixiang wenti taolun qingkuang de huibao" [Report on the internal discussions on the business and ideological issues of the Foreign Languages Press], in *Shiliao xuanbian*, pp. 238–39.

[5] Ibid., p. 245.

[6] "Waiwen chubanshe yijiuwujiunian zai tushuqikan fangmian de chuban gongzuo guihua (cao'an)" [Working plan on the publication of books and journals of the Foreign Languages Press in 1959 [draft]], in *Shiliao xuanbian*, p. 140.

control these regions, it is impossible for America to conquer the Soviets."[7] This idea became more visible and was enlarged after 1958, especially after the Sino-Soviet split. For instance, in 1963, Mao pointed out that "we have two in-between regions: one is Asia, Africa, and Latin America, and the other is Europe. Japan and Canada are not satisfied with America."[8] We may see this concept as an early form of his later "Three Worlds" theory in the 1970s. Still, during the whole of the 1960s, Mao did not use the categories of "class struggle" and "revolution" to define and explain this concept.[9]

Translation during this period included two tasks: translating foreign works into Chinese[10] and introducing Chinese works globally. This chapter will focus mainly on the latter. What, then, did the Foreign Languages Press translate and publish? First, it initiated new journals with different target audiences, including *People's China* (*Renmin zhongguo*), *China Pictorial* (*Renmin huabao*), *China Reconstructs* (*Zhongguo jianshe*), and *Peking Review* (*Beijing zhoubao*). The Foreign Languages

---

[7] Mao Zedong, "Conversation with the American Journalist Anna Louise Strong," in *Mao Zedong xuanji* [Selected works of Mao Zedong] (Beijing: Renminchubanshe, 1991), vol. IV, p. 1191.

[8] Mao Zedong, *Mao Zedong waijiao wenxuan* [Selected writings of Mao Zedong on foreign affairs] (Beijing: Zhongyang wenxian chubanshe, 1994), pp. 506–07.

[9] For a more detailed analysis of the evolution of Mao's analysis of the world order, especially his Three Worlds theory, see Yang Kuisong's excellent piece, "A Variation on the Chinese Side during Sino-American Reconciliation: An Analysis of the Background of Mao Zedong's 'Three Worlds Theory'," in Shen Zhihua and Douglas A. Stiffler, eds., *Fragile Alliance: The Cold War and Sino-Soviet Relations* (Beijing: Social Sciences Academic Press, 2010), pp. 457–81.

[10] During this period, a large number of science and technology textbooks and literary works of Soviet origin were translated into Chinese. According to one report, in 1961, in all the books imported from the Soviet Union and other Eastern European countries, science and technology themes occupied 80.9 percent and literature only 4.7 percent; in terms of nationality, the Soviet Union dominated, reaching 97.3 percent of the total number of books imported. For more details, please see Cao Jianfei, ed., *Zhongguo guoji tushu maoyi zonggongsi sishizhounian: shilunji* [The fortieth anniversary of the China International Publishing Company: selected papers on its history] (Beijing: China International Publishing Group, 1989), pp. 68–69. In terms of the literary works, the themes of representing the achievements of socialist industry as well as socialist rural reforms were particularly well received by the Chinese audience. Classics of Russian literature were also quite popular; for instance, Gorky's 'Mother', Mayakovsky's poems, and Chekhov's short stories were all bestsellers. In addition, Soviet children's literature and adventure stories also occupied an important place in the market. Between October 1949 and September 1955, more than 2,300 Russian and Soviet literary works, classics, and contemporary pieces were translated, and works such as *How the Steel was Tempered*, *The Story of Zoya and Shura*, and *The Seagull* were extremely successful. For more details on the translation of Soviet literature into Chinese, please see Nicolai Volland, "Translating the Socialist State: Cultural Exchange, National Identity, and the Socialist World in the Early PRC," *Twentieth-Century China* 33.2 (April 2008), pp. 51–72. Between 1949 and 1966, large numbers of works by important English authors were also translated into Chinese.

Press also translated and published Chinese literature into foreign languages, and it initiated an English-language journal, *Chinese Literature* (*Zhongguo wenxue*), in order to help do so. The four main categories of translations can be identified as classics, May Fourth authors, socialist realists, and Stalin Prize winners.[11] Among these journals, *China Pictorial* had the largest circulation.

The choice of languages of these journals was determined by the target readers. For instance, in order to reach most Eastern European countries, and other places where Russian, English, and French were not so widespread, the monthly *El Popola Ĉinio* (*People's China Report* or *Renmin Zhongguo baodao*)[12] was published in Esperanto. As a press official explained, "The reason we chose Esperanto as an important tool of our international propaganda is that the languages we are able to translate are not enough. For instance, in the regions such as northwestern Europe, Japan, and middle South America, we haven't produced any publications in their languages, so quite a few readers of these regions use Esperanto to know the new China as well as to publicize China."[13] In 1962, the issue of Esperanto was brought up again and was treated as an important language to attract politically in-between intellectuals.[14] If *People's China* mainly attracted leftists and those who were very much policy oriented, some journals tried to dilute their political tone in the name of non-government organizations. *El Popola Ĉinio* was published through the All China Esperanto League. After the Sino-Soviet split, Esperanto played a more important role: "The revisionist countries blockade us and don't permit us to distribute anti-revisionist articles. Therefore, editions in Russian, English, and French cannot enter those countries, and the same applies to broadcasting. Using Esperanto can allow us to get in through the side door, so they can have some fresh air."[15] In addition, Song Qingling initiated another journal, *China Reconstructs* (*Zhongguo jianshe*), in Shanghai in order to engage readers or even liberal intellectuals in "capitalist countries and colonial countries" who might not be politically progressive but "pursued world peace." Song Qingling emphasized that the new

---

[11] Volland, "Translating the Socialist State," p. 67.

[12] The journal was suspended in June 1951 because the Soviet Union and Eastern European countries prohibited it. The journal resumed in 1957.

[13] "Liu Zunqi tongzhi zai quanshe dahuishang zongjie waiwen chubanshe yijiuwuernian gongzuo" [Liu Zunqi's summary of the Foreign Languages Press's achievements in 1952 at a general meeting of the press], in *Shiliao xuanbian*, p. 43.

[14] "Duiwai wenwei tongzhi tan guanyu shijieyu duiwaixuanchuan de yijian" [The Foreign Affairs Committee of the China Cultural Council's opinions on international propaganda in Esperanto], in *Shiliao xuanbian*, pp. 212–13.

[15] Chen Yi, "Chen Yi tongzhi zai shijieyu gongzuo zuotanhuishang de jianghua" [Chen Yi's talk in the colloquium on Esperanto], in *Shiliao xuanbian*, p. 302.

journal would not publish any political and military reports or essays, to differentiate it from the journal *People's China*.[16]

Besides the above journals, the Chinese Foreign Languages Press also translated and published policy documents from China's central government, the works of important Chinese politicians, and Chinese literature of different periods. In terms of literature, beginning in 1953, the press made plans to translate and publish classical literary works and also works by May Fourth writers such as Lu Xun, Guo Moruo, Mao Dun, and Ding Ling, among others.[17] Its main target audience was readers in the non-socialist countries: "Our translations of Chinese literary works are also received widely, mostly in English. They are especially of interest to readers in capitalist countries."[18] In 1957, when the journal *Chinese Literature* was moved from a quarterly schedule to publication once every two months, the plan was that "contemporary literary work should make up 50%, the classics and May Fourth literary works 20–25%, and other literary reviews as well as reports of new publications 20–25%."[19] From this composition, we can very clearly see that contemporary literary work was particularly emphasized. According to a report in the *People's Daily*, the three best-known Chinese writers in the Soviet Union were Lu Xun, Ding Ling, and Zhao Shuli. Their works reached a combined print run of 500,000 and were translated, in addition to Russian, into twelve minority languages in the Soviet Union.[20] Those works which represented socialist achievements were translated in a much more systematic fashion than works with other themes.

One main problem in the translation projects of the 1950s was the shortage of experienced translators in many foreign languages, especially some Asian languages. Aside from Indonesian, translations into other Asian languages such as Vietnamese, Korean, and Burmese had not even started by 1954. In terms of Western languages, until 1954, only English, German, Russian, and French were available. As a result, choices about what should be translated were often based on what the current translators could translate, rather than on what the target audience might be interested in. The work plan of the Foreign Languages Press for the year 1959 states that the

---

[16] "Song Qingling tongzhi zhuchi zhongguojianshe choubei gongzuo huiyijiyao" [Minutes of the preparation meeting for the journal *Chinese Reconstructs* hosted by Song Qingling], in *Shiliao xuanbian*, p. 43.

[17] "Waiwen chubanshe yijiuwusannian gongzuo zongjie yu yijiuwusinian de fangzhenrenwu" [The Foreign Languages Press's summary of its work in 1953 and its working plan and principles in 1954], in *Shiliao xuanbian*, p. 97.

[18] "Waiwen chubanshe yijiuwusannian zhi yijiuwusinian tushu bianyichuban gongzuo zongjie" [The Foreign Languages Press's summary of its achievements in publishing and editing books between 1953 and 1954], in *Shiliao xuanbian*, pp. 109–110.

[19] Dai and Chen, eds., *Zhongguo waiwenju wushinian*, p. 75.

[20] Xinhuashe, "Woguo zuojia daibiaotuan yu Sulian zuojia huiwu" [Our country's writers' delegation meets with Soviet writers], *People's Daily* (December 15, 1951).

press planned to set up some footholds of translation in India, Indonesia, Latin America, and the Arabic-speaking areas in order to hire local talent to help do the translations. It is not known whether this strategy was eventually put into practice or not.[21] Another way to solve this problem of the lack of translators was to hire foreign experts, but the requirements for such experts were often quite strict. As Zhou Enlai stated: "We should employ two kinds of foreign translators: those who are politically correct can help us polish our translation, and those who are politically in-between can help us train our own translation talents."[22] On October 25, 1954, he required that the employment of foreign experts for the translation project be approved by the Publicity Department. The number of these foreign experts was not so small. For instance, according to one planning document, "between 1956 and 1967, the Foreign Languages Press is planning to create forty-two positions for foreign experts (including eleven nationalities)."[23] The foreign experts came from the following categories: (1) overseas Chinese who came back to New China;[24] (2) foreign experts from both capitalist and socialist countries;[25] and (3) short-term foreign translators.[26]

[21] "Waiwen chubanshe yijiuwujiunian zai tushuqikan fangmian de chubangongzuo guihua (cao'an)," p. 141.

[22] Foreign Affairs Committee of the State Council, "Guanyu jiaqiang waiwenshukan chubanfaxing gongzuo de baogao" [Report on strengthening the publication and distribution of foreign language journals and books], in *Shiliao xuanbian*, p. 290.

[23] Dai and Chen, eds., *Zhongguo waiwenju wushinian*, p. 62.

[24] In the 1950s, quite a few overseas Chinese returned from regions such as Southeast Asia, Japan, France, and Germany, and some of them became important translators in the Foreign Languages Press. For instance, Ye Junjian, who returned from England, joined the English-language group and was an important translator of Mao's poems in the 1960s. (See Sun Xuchun, "Tamen de gongji buke momie" [Their contributions should not be forgotten], in *Gongtong zouguo de lu: 'wo yu waiwenju' zhengwenxuan* [The road we walk together: selected works on the theme "The Foreign Languages Bureau and I"] (Beijing: Zhongguo waiwenju, 2009), p. 437. The extreme case is the Indonesian group, whose members were all overseas Chinese.

[25] Some of them came to China before 1949 and remained because of family reasons. Gladys B. Tayler from England and Sidney Shapiro from the USA could be seen as typical examples. They represent a few translators who came from capitalist countries such as the United States and Japan but stayed in communist China for a long time. Sidney Shapiro came to China in 1947 and became a Chinese citizen in 1963. He was one editor of the journal *Chinese Literature* mentioned above. His first translation was *Daughters and Sons*, and later on, he translated both famous May Fourth works such as Bajin's *Family* and Mao Dun's *Silkworm*, and popular socialist works like those of Zhao Shuli. He stayed in China for more than sixty years and was a translator at the Foreign Languages Press until his retirement (for more details, see Sun, 'Tamen de gongji buke momie', p. 438). Gladys B. Tayler was another prestigious translator of Chinese literary classics. She translated Lu Xun's *The True Story of Ah Q* and also Ding Ling's famous piece *The Sun Over the Sanggan River* into English. Some of these translators were originally Communist Party members but quite a few of them were not.

[26] Some of them were hired directly from overseas and helped the Foreign Languages Press to translate one specific project. A typical example was the group of translators from the

The International Bookstore and its global distribution network

The International Bookstore, founded in December 1949, was mainly responsible for "cultural exchanges between the new China and other countries."[27] It defined itself as a trade organization rather than a propaganda institution. In the 1950s and 1960s, however, the International Bookstore faced a continual conflict between its business activities and its political function. To a certain degree, its self-definition as a trading company facilitated its relationship with capitalist countries. For instance, in August 1953, the Translation and Editing Bureau of the General Publication Administration gave a very clear statement about the role of the International Bookstore: "The International Bookstore is a trade organization for the importation and exportation of books and journals, there to satisfy the needs of nation-building and the people's cultural life, and also to strengthen international propaganda. The International Bookstore conducts only commercial activities and achieves the abovementioned political mission by means of trade. In principle, it cannot conduct non-commercial work."[28] Throughout the 1950s, the International Bookstore consciously developed its distribution network in non-socialist countries "by building international trade connections with more countries and exchanges with conservative foreign book traders in order to break through geographical and political boundaries."[29] Generally speaking, in the 1950s, the International Bookstore followed the principle of "focusing only on business activity" and avoided "political distribution."[30] For instance, in October 1953, the leaders of the International Bookstore went so far as to investigate those activities that did not follow this principle.[31]

A turning-point was the year 1959, in which the International Bookstore broke away from the Ministry of Culture and was included in the newly established Foreign Affairs Committee of the China Cultural Council. As a result, the mission of the International Bookstore was changed to be "cooperation with foreign affairs."[32] In 1962, its mission became the principle that "distribution should coordinate international revolutionary movements," and then during the Cultural Revolution period, it transformed into the principle that "distribution should accelerate world revolution."[33] This principle was very different from the

Soviet Union. They played important roles in training the younger generation of Chinese translators, but were required to leave China after the Sino-Soviet split.

[27] Cao, ed., *Zhongguo guoji tushu maoyi zonggongsi sishizhounian*, p. 37.
[28] Ibid.   [29] Ibid., p. 39.   [30] Ibid., pp. 16–17.   [31] Ibid., p. 17.
[32] Ibid., p. 47.   [33] Ibid., p. 59.

former one of strengthening the international publicity of the new China through trade. The translation of Chinese literature followed a similar trajectory. For instance, in 1964, when Zhang Yan, the director of the Foreign Affairs Department of the State Council, talked about the publication of Chinese literature and arts, he particularly emphasized that the translation of Chinese literature should prioritize works representing two revolutionary periods: the nationalist revolution and the socialist revolution. Among Chinese classical literature and the literary works produced in the May Fourth period, he said, only the most representative ones should be published; according to Zhang, fewer readers would be interested in that non-revolutionary literature.[34] Between 1964 and 1965, the International Bookstore set six main objectives; the first two were as follows: make great efforts to publish works by Mao and by anti-revisionists; and set up a global network in two years and strengthen its distribution agents overseas. In the report, the International Bookstore claimed that it had established a business relationship with 738 agencies in 91 countries and offered 75 exhibitions in 37 countries in order to broaden the influence of Chinese books and journals.[35]

Translation of the Little Red Book

Following its costly involvement in Korea and Vietnam, the PRC was unable, and perhaps unwilling, to provide substantial military and economic support for global revolution abroad. During the Cultural Revolution, Mao's China continued to offer vocal support, expertise, and very limited material aid to communist parties overseas, but its main intervention in global politics was a small vinyl-covered book. In the 1960s, the proportion of Mao's works in the Foreign Languages Press's intended translations annually increased, and in 1961, Mao's works made up 70 percent of exported books.[36] Correspondingly, the 1962 report by the Foreign Affairs Committee of the China Cultural Council stated that "the export of foreign language books should be done in cooperation with the development of international revolutionary movements. The priority of the categories exported overseas should be those in foreign languages, especially Mao's works."[37] In September 1962, at the meeting of the Eighth Plenum of the CCP Central Committee,

[34] Dai and Chen, eds., *Zhongguo waiwenju wushinian*, p. 180.   [35] Ibid., p. 78.
[36] Foreign Affairs Committee, "Guanyu jiaqiang," p. 266.
[37] Cao, ed., *Zhongguo guoji tushu maoyi zonggongsi sishizhounian*, p. 44.

Zhou Enlai claimed that the center of world revolution had moved from Moscow to Beijing.[38]

In 1963, the Foreign Languages Press made an important step in expanding its distribution network. In its "Report on Increasing the Publication and Distribution of Foreign Language Books and Journals," the Office of Foreign Affairs in the State Council advanced the slogan "Surge Out" (*chong chuqu*),[39] and required all the institutions related to foreign affairs to work together with the International Bookstore to reorganize and expand their global distribution network. The report suggested a few important strategies to strengthen the dissemination of foreign-language books. One was to establish branches of the International Bookstore overseas, for example in Hong Kong, Switzerland, and Berlin. Hong Kong, for a long period, was an important intermediary base for importing Mao's works into Southeast Asia: Singapore, the Philippines, Malaysia, etc. Another strategy, intended to counter revisionism, was that the International Bookstore should build up connections with revolutionary bookstores and subsidize local progressive agents to enable them to open different kinds of bookstores to sell foreign-language books from China. The International Bookstore also tried to take advantage of connections with capitalist book dealers, provided that the latter adhered to their contracts.[40] In addition, the International Bookstore developed a direct-mailing service for readers abroad, and donated foreign-language books from China as gifts through organizations of women, youth, or workers in other countries. This push was quite effective, and by the end of 1963, the International Bookstore had established trade relations with 545 bookstores in 87 countries.[41] In the late 1960s, the International Bookstore added a large number of African countries to its list. Relying on this expanding distribution network, according to the *People's Daily*,[42] during the period from October 1966 to May 1967, the International Bookstore distributed more than 800,000 copies of the Little Red Book in 14 languages to 117 countries. In addition, the newspaper

---

[38] For more background, see part 2 of Cheng Yinghong's "Xiang shijie shuchu geming: wege zai Yafeilayingxiang de chutan" [Exporting the revolution to the world: a preliminary study on the influence of the Cultural Revolution on the regions of Asia, Africa and Latin America], in *Mao zhuyi yu shijiegeming* [Maoist revolution: China and the world in the twentieth century] (Hong Kong: Tianyuanshuwu, 2009).

[39] Cao, ed., *Zhongguo guoji tushu maoyi zonggongsi sishizhounian*, p. 16.

[40] Foreign Affairs Committee, "Guanyu jiaqiang," pp. 290–91.

[41] Cao, ed., *Zhongguo guoji tushu maoyi zonggongsi sishizhounian*, p. 69.

[42] Xinhuashe, "Guojigongchanzhuyi yundongshi shang de dashijian, wuchanjieji wenhuadageming de xinsheng" [The big event in the history of the internationalist movement and the new victory in the proletarian cultural revolution], *People's Daily* (July 2, 1967).

reported that in 16 countries, such as England and France, some progressive organizations had started to translate *Quotations from Chairman Mao* on their own. In Japan, for instance, from November 1966 to March 1967 there appeared four different editions of the Little Red Book. Chinese reportage celebrated its wide distribution as "the most joyful thing in the whole world."[43]

The translation of *Selected Works of Mao Zedong* played a significant role in setting up the means of translation and distribution of Mao's writings in the 1950s and 1960s. To a certain degree, the organization of the translation of *Quotations from Chairman Mao* followed the same format. In May 1953, at the invitation of the Foreign Languages Press, a Mr. Russell, the manager of a British communist bookstore, came to China and, representing the publisher Lawrence & Wishart, signed a contract to translate into English and publish the *Selected Works of Mao Zedong*. This was the first time that China had entrusted a foreign press with translating Mao's work. Chinese translators such as Qian Zhongshu and Wang Zuoliang worked together with experts in Britain, and translated the first three volumes of the *Selected Works*. Communist China built up good connections with a number of similar communist bookstores in Europe, such as the Fenghuang (Phoenix) Bookstore in France, which greatly aided the spread of Mao's works in Europe and other regions.[44] In 1960, the fourth volume in the Chinese edition was published. In 1961, the Foreign Affairs Department of the State Council and the International Department both wrote to Zhou Enlai to persuade him that translating Mao's work into different languages was an important political mission. Accordingly, the Foreign Languages Press finished the translations of the four volumes in five languages: English, Spanish, Japanese, French, and Russian. Very soon, the translation of Mao's work expanded dramatically. In October 1966, the Foreign Languages Press was required to arrange for the translations of the four volumes into twelve foreign languages and also of *Quotations from Chairman Mao* into thirteen foreign languages within two years.[45]

In 1967, the Publicity Department and the International Department of the Central Committee of the Communist Party set up a special institution called the Office for the Translation of Chairman Mao's Works to organise the translation of Mao's work. For this, the central

---

[43] Xinhuashe, "The Most Joyful Thing in the Whole World," *The Liberation Army Daily* (July 2, 1967).

[44] He Mingxing, *Xinzhongguo shukan haiwai faxing chuanbo liushinian* [The sixty-year history of Chinese books' distribution and circulation overseas] (Beijing: zhongguo shuji chubanshe, 2010), pp. 153–56.

[45] Dai and Chen, eds., *Zhongguo waiwenju wushinian*, p. 223.

government even set up a five-person leading group for the translation of the *Selected Works*, although this group did not play any significant role because it was quickly disbanded by the rebels of the Cultural Revolution. All the translators were called up to stay together in a hotel, and were organized into groups based on language. By 1967, seventeen such groups had been set up.[46] According to a memoir by one participant, there were many steps designed to guarantee the quality of the translation: an initial draft, revision, verification, group discussion, polishing by foreign experts, universalizing the format, finalizing through discussion among group members, proofreading, and so on. For some marginal languages for which translators were not easily found, the group worked with progressive agents in the individual countries, asking them to translate first; the Publicity Department and the International Department retained the rights to review and approve the final versions before they were published. For instance, in 1967, the International Department telegraphed Chinese embassies in Eastern European countries such as Czechoslovakia, Poland, and Bulgaria, and told them to organize the translation of *Quotations from Chairman Mao* into local languages. Though the translation was done locally, the books were still published through the Foreign Languages Press.[47]

The translations of the Little Red Book were done mostly by the same translation groups as the *Selected Works*. According to my interviews,[48] most translators were between thirty and forty years old. The criteria for selection included proficiency of translation skills, as well as political correctness. All the members worked together as a group and each of their projects went through all the processes, including translation, proofreading, and finalizing. Each language group consisted of approximately twenty members. Taking the Spanish group as an example, there were about twenty core members and four foreign experts. In order to do the translation, they gathered all the translators into a hotel, such as the Friendship Hotel. The Central Compilation and Translation Bureau and the Foreign Languages Press were responsible for organizing the different translation groups. They could ask the Publicity Department, the Ministry of Foreign Affairs, and the International Department for permission to borrow these translators from their original workplaces.[49] In addition to the translation group, there was also an "inquiry group."

---

[46] Ibid., p. 228.   [47] Ibid., p. 233.

[48] Yin Chengdong participated in the Spanish translation of the *Selected Works of Mao Zedong* (volumes 1–3). Interviewed August 2011.

[49] For more details, see part 2 of "On the arrangements for translators" in the document "On the planning of the translating and publishing of Chairman Mao's works" made in October 1966 by the five-person leading group, in *Shiliao xuanbian*, pp. 406–10.

This group often collected questions from the translation group, mostly related to how to understand content. Any questions the inquiry group could not answer, they passed to their superiors. In order to answer specific questions related to military issues, two specialists from the Chinese Academy of Military Science were invited to join the inquiry group.

The work was divided as follows. The Central Compilation and Translation Bureau took charge of translations into English, French, Spanish, and Russian; the International Department was responsible for Japanese, Vietnamese, Burmese, Thai, and Indonesian; all the other languages went to the Foreign Languages Press. According to Zhang Xingshi,[50] who participated in the inquiry group for English translation, the group usually met once every two weeks and discussed the questions they had collected. Those they could not answer would be submitted to the International Department and the Ministry of Foreign Affairs.

On February 28, 1967, the State Council sent out a notice[51] rescinding three earlier notices which had restricted sending copies of the Little Red Book as gifts to foreigners. The new reasoning was that these former notices did not accord with the spirit of actively promoting Mao Zedong Thought globally and were therefore completely wrong. At the same time, the Council required that all the organizations related to foreign affairs should take the international promotion of Mao Zedong Thought as the most important political task. On September 18, 1968, an editorial in the *People's Daily* stated that the most important mission of China's ambassadors and experts was to "propagandize Chairman Mao's thought."

In order to promote Mao's work more broadly, the International Bookstore posted advertisements in local newspapers abroad. For instance, in March 1966, in order to further promote the English version of the four-volume *Selected Works of Mao Zedong*, the Foreign Affairs Office of the State Council approved the International Bookstore's application to advertise in more than forty newspapers in nineteen countries.[52] Figure 5 shows an example of an advertisement in a Tanzanian newspaper. They also built around sixty agencies in Anglophone and European countries, Latin America,

---

[50] Interview conducted September 19, 2011.

[51] In March, April, and June 1966 the State Council's Foreign Affairs Department sent out three notices related to issues about foreigners' requests for *Quotations from Chairman Mao*. In the beginning, access to the Little Red Book by foreigners was prohibited, but later the restrictions were gradually loosened.

[52] Cao, ed., *Zhongguo guoji tushu maoyi zonggongsi sishizhounian*, p. 86.

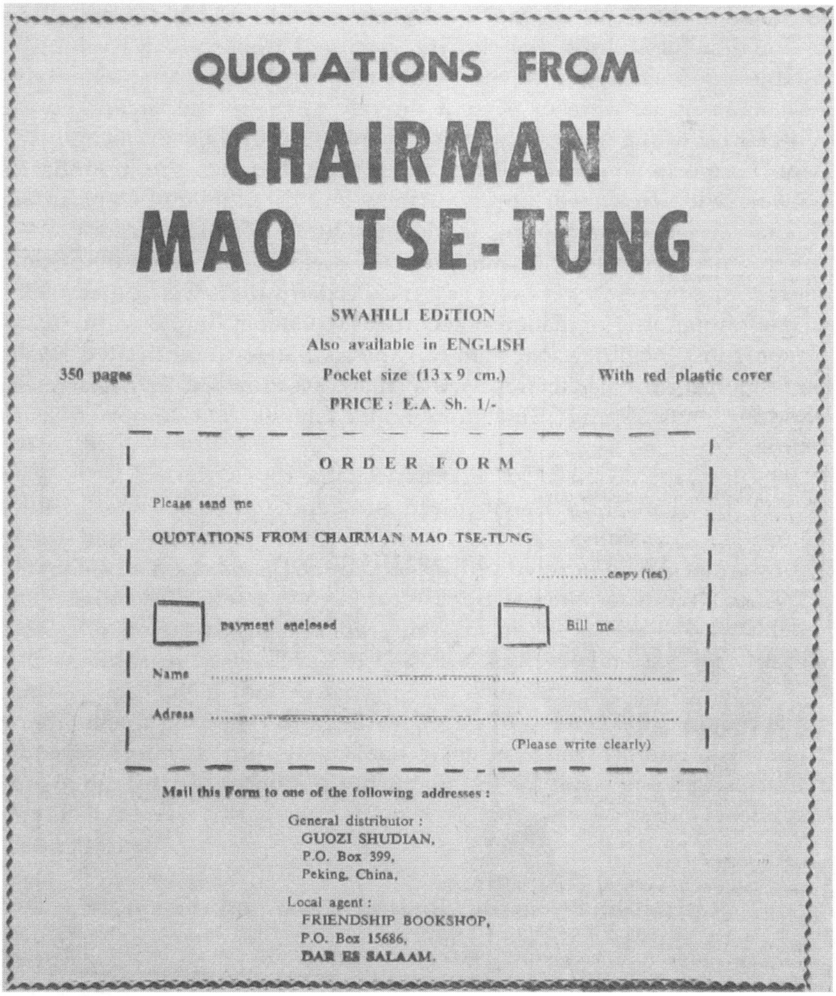

Fig. 5. Order form for Swahili edition of the Little Red Book.
Source: The Nationalist (Tanzania), February 20, 1968. (Priya Lal.)

and North Africa. The global distribution network included the
following levels: distribution headquarters, agencies, and individual
dealers.[53] Furthermore, sailors also played an important role in disseminating the Little Red Book. In January 1967, the State Council

[53] Ibid., p. 74.

announced when they met with representatives of various international sailors' clubs that the International Bookstore was going to establish connections with such clubs all over the world, and books as well as journals were to be sent directly to them; this facilitated the radical rise of the non-commercial distribution of their publications.[54] More importantly, the Communists even blurred the boundaries between the Ministry of Foreign Affairs and the Publicity Department in the service of promoting world revolution. Chinese embassies in different countries took on a big role in spreading the Little Red Book, most copies of which were sent as gifts. Certainly there were other means of dissemination. For instance, according to Cheng Yinghong, there was a report in a local newspaper in Singapore that some Little Red Books and stamps with Chairman Mao's image were found in packages of children's snacks that Singapore and Malaysia had imported from China.[55]

In 1969, the Ministry of Foreign Affairs reported that there were serious problems of waste involved in sending Mao's work to other countries. According to the example they provided, one small bookstore in Africa ordered only 50 copies of *Quotations from Chairman Mao* from the International Bookstore, but were sent 500 copies. The result was 450 copies left in customs, which charged the small store a storage fee – an outcome that was said to have caused resentment.[56] It was certainly not the only such case in that period. In July 1971, Zhou Enlai required the Bureau of Foreign Affairs to reflect on the emerging chauvinism and arrogance of using books and journals for propaganda purposes, and as a result the International Bookstore took steps to reduce such behaviour.[57]

Revolutionary sound: Radio Beijing and the spread of Mao's Little Red Book

In addition to the International Bookstore discussed above, broadcasting was a very important – or even more powerful – way to spread Mao Zedong Thought. In December 1949, China's Central Broadcasting Station (*Zhongyang renmin guangbo diantai*) was built, including domestic and international departments. The Central Committee required that the

[54] Ibid., p. 91.
[55] Cheng Yinghong, *Mao Zhuyi geming: Ershi shiji de zhongguo yu shijie (Maoist Revolution: China and the World in the Twentieth Century)* (Hong Kong: Tianyuan Bookstore, 2008), p. 114.
[56] Dai and Chen, eds., *Zhongguo waiwenju wushinian*, p. 250.   [57] Ibid., p. 266.

station first satisfy the needs of surrounding countries and overseas Chinese. In April 1950, the international broadcasting department started programs in four languages for listeners in Vietnam, Thailand, Burma, and Indonesia, under the name Radio Beijing (*Beijing guangbo diantai*). Many of the initiators of these programs were returned overseas Chinese from Southeast Asian countries. On the same day in April 1950, programs in four dialects (Cantonese, Teochew, Hakka, and Hokkien) were launched for the overseas Chinese in East Asia. All of this programming was restructured into the Southeast Asia Group (*Dongnan yazu*) in 1952. Early in February 1950, the editorial board of Radio Beijing reported to the central government that its three main working principles were as follows: first, it would promote revolutionary victories and the achievements of socialist constructions; second, it would propagandize the fact that the Chinese government supports all anti-colonial fights and the struggles of oppressed peoples; third, it would propagandize China's peaceful foreign policies, which were there to encourage world peace. These efforts were all made to introduce the new China to the world, just as Mao proclaimed in the mid-1950s, "Control the globe and let the whole world listen to our voices."[58] Following this principle, in 1956, Radio Beijing already included four main departments (Asian, European, Soviet, and Overseas Chinese), which altogether covered fourteen languages.

In 1958, there were some changes in the guidelines, and one of the new emphases was on lending more support to in-between regions.[59] With the financial support of the central government, the decade between 1957 and 1967 witnessed the increasingly expanding influence of Radio Beijing.[60] In addition to building a new building, Radio Beijing increased its languages to twenty-seven in 1958, and the interactions with overseas audiences were also active. According to statistics provided by Radio Beijing, in 1965 they received 2,860,000 letters from audiences in 135 countries.[61] In terms of the content, with the start of the Cultural Revolution Radio Beijing canceled most of its regular programs and turned its main attention to the promotion of Mao's works.[62] The International News department initiated some new programs such as "All the People of the World Love Chairman Mao," "China in the Eyes of Foreign Friends," and "Quotations from Chairman Mao: On Imperialism and All Reactionaries are Paper Tigers." Beginning in February

---

[58] Zhongyang guoji guangbo diantai shizhi congshu bianweihui, ed., *Zhongguo guoji guangbo diantai zhi (The History of China Radio International)* (Beijing: Zhongyang guoji guangbo chubanshe, 2001), vol. I, p. 5.
[59] Ibid., p. 33.   [60] Ibid., p. 7.   [61] Ibid., pp. 8–9.   [62] Ibid., vol. II, p. 16.

1967, the various language sections of Radio Beijing initiated the program "Quotations from Chairman Mao Zedong" and more importantly, the content of this program was broadcast at a very slow speed in order to let the audience write down what they heard.[63] According to one report titled "*Quotations from Chairman Mao* is the Revolutionary People's Steering Wheel" in the internal journal *Reflections from Foreign Audiences* (*Guowai tingzhong fanying*),[64] a few Japanese listeners wrote letters to Radio Beijing to show their appreciation for the broadcasts from *Quotations* before the news: "The broadcasting of *Quotations from Chairman Mao* is a must-listen for me. It is very valuable. In particular, it is extremely helpful that it tells listeners the specific volume and page for each quotation they broadcast. That way, we can immediately find it in the *Collection of Chairman Mao's Works*, whenever necessary." Another listener expressed his hope that *Quotations* could be broadcast more often and wrote that it would be even better if the announcer read the quotations a little slower so that he could take notes in order to repeatedly read and understand them more deeply.[65] According to a report in the *People's Daily*, the local communist publishing house of the guerrilla force in Malaysia collected quotations from Mao one by one by listening to Radio Beijing, and eventually edited them together for publication.[66] Another letter from a Japanese audience member even described the Chairman's thoughts as powerful missiles that Radio Beijing sent out to the whole world: "This is the most powerful and irresistible weapon."[67]

---

[63] Ibid., vol. I, p. 123.

[64] Radio Beijing, *Guowai guangzhong fanying* (*Reflections from foreign audiences*), 78 (1966), p. 7.

[65] There were a few reports of how foreign listeners wrote to Radio Beijing showing their passion to learn *Quotations from Chairman Mao*. For instance, there was an essay titled "Revolutionary Truth is Transmitted Overseas and the People of Different Countries Listen Avidly" (*People's Daily* [January 10, 1967], p. 5). The essay includes citations from letters by listeners from countries such as Japan, France, England, and Afghanistan. Another report titled "Zuo Mao Zedong sixiang de xuanchuanyuan" [Volunteer to spread Chairman Mao's thoughts] (*People's Daily* [January 10, 1967], p. 5) tells how a Japanese worker insisted on listening to *Quotations* on Radio Beijing every night, and if he needed to work at night, he brought the radio with him.

[66] Xinhuashe, "Malaiya geming genjudi daliang di chuban Mao zhuxi zhuzuo" [The Malay revolutionary forces published a large number of Chairman Mao's works], *People's Daily* (December 29, 1969), p. 6.

[67] Xinhuashe, "Wudazhou geming renmin ba Beijing guangbo dangzuo buke queshao de jingsheng shiliang" [Revolutionary people treat Radio Beijing as essential spiritual food], *People's Daily* (December 10, 1966), p. 4.

Conclusion

In the 1960s, China was under threat from both of the world's superpowers, the United States and the Soviet Union. The young PRC conceived of translation as an important strategy in pursuing the larger agenda of achieving a kind of "solidarity" in the in-between regions, especially in the nations of Asia, Africa, and Latin America. Behind this large translation drive, an internationalist spirit could be seen through the participation of foreign experts and distributors, quite a few of which were communist bookstores in foreign countries. In other words, the new China's translation activities and the distribution of its publications were mostly a transnational collaboration, even though these translation activities were very systematic and often organized as an internal, national project. Internationalism has often referred to mutual help and cultural cooperation among nations struggling for national independence from imperial forces and for social reforms. Historically, internationalism has meant the global attempts led by the Soviet Union to counter imperialism and fascism. New China identified itself as one part of that internationalist movement, especially after the Sino-Soviet split, claiming that Beijing was the new center of the world revolution, and putting on its own shoulders the great mission of leading and helping the developing countries in Asia, Africa, and Latin America. Mao's thoughts and revolutionary ideas, moreover, were to serve as the ideological basis for their struggle for national liberation. As one part of the transnational print culture of the socialist movement, the International Bookstore made great efforts to set up a network of distribution in order to foster exchanges in the cultural field designed to promote the new China. The mechanisms used by the Foreign Languages Press to distribute publications across the capitalist world, socialist world, and developing world were quite effective, such as emphasizing the International Bookstore as a trade organization, using Esperanto, the common language of the "in-between" intellectuals, to initiate a special journal, as well as maintaining diversity in its translation content, especially in literature. Beijing Radio was another powerful transmitter of Chairman Mao's Little Red Book through the medium of sound, which to a certain degree can more easily transcend geographical boundaries and ideological differences. It connected the different continents through revolutionary sound in the air.

To a certain degree, in my discussion above, I have put the myth of the Little Red Book of the 1960s back into the longer history of New China's ongoing efforts to translate Chinese literature and Mao's works globally. As such, I argue that the success of the Little Red Book did not occur all at once. Rather, it relied on the global distribution network and translation mode that the new China had been developing since its establishment. Certainly, despite my emphasis on continuity, there are some significant differences between the translation activities of the 1950s and 1960s. Most important, in terms of what should be translated and exported, whereas in the 1950s China tried to keep a balance between political and non-political materials, in the 1960s the dissemination of Mao's works played a dominant role, which is seen most clearly in the case of the Little Red Book.

BIBLIOGRAPHY

Cao Jianfei, ed., *Zhongguo guoji tushu maoyi zonggongsi sishizhounian: shilunji* [The fortieth anniversary of the China International Publishing Company: selected papers on its history] (Beijing: China International Publishing Group, 1989)

Cheng Yinghong, *Mao Zhuyi geming: Ershi shiji de zhongguo yu shijie (Maoist Revolution: China and the World in the Twentieth Century)* (Hong Kong: Tianyuan Bookstore, 2008)

"Xiang shijie shuchu geming: wege zai Yafeilayingxiang de chutan" [Exporting the revolution to the world: a preliminary study on the influence of the Cultural Revolution on the regions of Asia, Africa and Latin America], in *Mao zhuyi yu shijiegeming* [Maoist revolution: China and the world in the twentieth century] (Hong Kong: Tianyuanshuwu, 2009), pp. 59–100

Chen Yi, "Chen Yi tongzhi zai shijieyu gongzuo zuotanhuishang de jianghua" [Chen Yi's talk in the colloquium on Esperanto], in Zhou, ed., *Shiliao xuanbian*, pp. 302–09

Dai Yannian and Chen Rinong, eds., *Zhongguo waiwenju wushinian: dashiji* [Fifty years of the Chinese Foreign Languages Bureau: memorabilia] (Beijing: Xinxing chubanshe, 1999)

Foreign Affairs Committee of the China Cultural Council, "Duiwai wenwei tongzhi tan guanyu shijieyu duiwaixuanchuan de yijian" [The Foreign Affairs Committee of the China Cultural Council's opinions on international propaganda in Esperanto], in Zhou, ed., *Shiliao xuanbian*, pp. 212–13

Foreign Affairs Committee of the State Council,"Guanyu jiaqiang waiwenshukan chubanfaxing gongzuo de baogao" [Report on strengthening the publication and distribution of foreign language journals and books], in Zhou, ed., *Shiliao xuanbian*, pp. 285–92

General Publication Administration, "Guanyu zhongyang yiji gechubanshe de zhuanye fengong jiqi lingdaoguanxi de guiding (cao'an)" [Stipulation on the division of work and administrative relationship of all central-level presses [draft]], in Zhou, ed., *Shiliao xuanbian*, pp. 48–50

"Guanyu waiwen chubanshe yewu sixiang wenti taolun qingkuang de huibao" [Report on the internal discussions on the business and ideological issues of the Foreign Languages Press], in Zhou, ed., *Shiliao xuanbian*, pp. 236–56

He Mingxing, *Xinzhongguo shukan haiwai faxing chuanbo liushinian* [The sixty-year history of Chinese books' distribution and circulation overseas] (Beijing: Zhongguo shuji chubanshe, 2010)

Liu Zunqi, "Liu Zunqi tongzhi zai quanshe dahuishang zongjie waiwen
   chubanshe yijiuwuernian gongzuo" [Liu Zunqi's summary of the Foreign
   Languages Press's achievements in 1952 at a general meeting of the press],
   in Zhou, ed., *Shiliao xuanbian*, pp. 57–69
Mao Zedong, "Conversation with the American Journalist Anna Louise Strong,"
   in *Mao Zedong xuanji* [Selected works of Mao Zedong] (Beijing:
   Renminchubanshe, 1991), vol. IV, pp. 1191–96
Mao Zedong waijiao wenxuan [Selected writings of Mao Zedong on foreign
   affairs] (Beijing: Zhongyang wenxian chubanshe, 1994)
"Song Qingling tongzhi zhuchi zhongguojianshe choubei gongzuo huiyijiyao"
   [Minutes of the preparation meeting for the journal *Chinese Reconstructs*
   hosted by Song Qingling], in Zhou, ed., *Shiliao xuanbian*, pp. 43–44
Sun Xuchun, "Tamen de gongji buke momie" [Their contributions should not
   be forgotten], in *Gongtong zouguo de lu: "wo yu waiwenju" zhengwenxuan*
   [The road we walk together: selected works on the theme "The Foreign
   Languages Bureau and I"] (Beijing: Zhongguo waiwenju, 2009), pp. 437–39
Volland, Nicolai, "Translating the Socialist State: Cultural Exchange, National
   Identity, and the Socialist World in the Early PRC," *Twentieth-Century China*
   33.2 (April 2008), pp. 51–72
"Waiwen chubanshe yijiuwusannian gongzuo zongjie yu yijiuwusinian de
   fangzhenrenwu" [The Foreign Languages Press's summary of its work in
   1953 and its working plan and principles in 1954], in Zhou, ed., *Shiliao
   xuanbian*, pp. 94–104
"Waiwen chubanshe yijiuwujiunian zai tushuqikan fangmian de chuban gongzuo
   guihua (cao'an)" [Working plan on the publication of books and journals of
   the Foreign Languages Press in 1959 [draft]], in Zhou, ed., *Shiliao xuanbian*,
   pp. 152–54
"Waiwen chubanshe yijiuwusannian zhi yijiuwusinian tushu bianyichuban
   gongzuo zongjie" [The Foreign Languages Press's summary of its
   achievements in publishing and editing books between 1953 and 1954], in
   Zhou, ed., *Shiliao xuanbian*, pp. 108–17
Yang Kuisong, "A Variation on the Chinese Side during Sino-American
   Reconciliation: An Analysis of the Background of Mao Zedong's 'Three
   Worlds Theory'," in Shen Zhihua and Douglas A. Stiffler, eds., *Fragile
   Alliance: The Cold War and Sino-Soviet Relations* (Beijing: Social Sciences
   Academic Press, 2010), pp. 457–81
Zhongyang guoji guangbo diantai shizhi congshu bianweihui, ed., *Zhongguo guoji
   guangbo diantai zhi (The History of China Radio International)*, vol. I (Beijing:
   Zhongyang guoji guangbo chubanshe, 2001)
Zhou Dongyuan, ed., *Zhongguo waiwenju wushi nian: shiliao xuanbian* [Fifty years
   of the Chinese Foreign Languages Bureau: selected archives documents]
   (Beijing: Xinxing chubanshe, 1995)

6 Maoism in Tanzania
Material connections and shared imaginaries

Priya Lal

> We stand for self-reliance. We hope for foreign aid but cannot be
> dependent on it; we depend on our own efforts, on the creative power of
> the whole army and the entire people.
>
> Self-Reliance and Arduous Struggle

In December 1966, President Julius Nyerere embarked on a six-week tour
of half of the regions in the newly independent East African country of
Tanzania, which the national press enthusiastically dubbed his "Long
March."[1] During this journey to both major regional centers and remote
rural outposts, Nyerere called upon Tanzanians across the countryside to
unite in pursuit of the country's new developmental imperatives: self-
reliance and socialism. In a pamphlet published several years earlier,
Nyerere had already begun to outline these political principles, introducing
the concept of *ujamaa*, or "familyhood," into national discourse as the
foundation for a proposed program of African socialism.[2] It was not until
the conclusion of his "Long March," however, that Nyerere officially
inaugurated the policy of *ujamaa* that would structure life in Tanzania over
the next decade. On February 5, 1967, in a widely publicized manifesto
issued in the northern town of Arusha, President Nyerere – popularly
known as Mwalimu (Teacher) – announced the ideological contours of a
radical approach to national development based upon collective hard work,
popular agrarian transformation, and a resolutely anti-colonial stance.

Though in theory the *ujamaa* project elaborated in the Arusha Declaration sought to recuperate a lost ideal of traditional African socialism, it was
very much the product of the global circumstances of the 1960s. As the
Tanzanian initiative evolved, it borrowed from the Chinese developmental
model symbolically and ideologically – invoking Chinese historical mile-
stones such as the Long March and the Cultural Revolution, and drawing

---

[1] Nsa Kaisi, "Mwalimu's Long March," *The Nationalist* (February 4, 1967).
[2] Julius Nyerere, "*Ujamaa*: The Basis of African Socialism," in *Freedom and Unity: A Selection from Writings and Speeches, 1952–65* (Dar es Salaam: Oxford University Press, 1966).

upon key themes of Maoism such as self-reliance, mass politics, and peasant primacy. The discursive circulation of Maoist idioms and concepts among state officials and broader publics in Tanzania during the early postcolonial era was accompanied and enabled by the simultaneous material circulation of Chinese cultural, political, and economic resources throughout the country. Mao's Little Red Book was one such resource; in the late 1960s, English and Swahili translations of the text were advertised for sale (for the highly affordable price of one shilling) in major Tanzanian newspapers such as *The Nationalist*,[3] and copies of the *Quotations* were stocked at the National Central Library, opened in December 1967.[4] The contents of Mao's Little Red Book embodied China's innovative, unorthodox approach to socialism – an approach that resonated with officials of Tanzania's ruling political party, TANU, but also captured the attention of young people and intellectuals in cities such as Dar es Salaam.

Given low literacy rates and the poor condition of transportation infrastructure in the countryside, the book itself, as a physical object, was not always – or even often – the vehicle for the spread of Maoist ideas and symbols throughout Tanzania. Instead, the *Quotations* traveled across radio airwaves to reach rural communities and illiterate urban publics across the country in oral form. Most importantly, the influence of the Chinese socialist model on *ujamaa*-era Tanzania was entrenched through, and manifested itself in, the circulation of a wide range of people and resources between China and Tanzania from 1964 to 1975. The Chinese–Tanzanian relationship was, importantly, an asymmetrical one; though Tanzanian diplomatic missions and student groups paid multiple visits to the PRC during this period, China flooded Tanzania with teachers, doctors, technological support, monetary aid, cultural productions, and a range of other collaborative and unilateral assistance. Rather than passively absorbing this aid, cultivating a position of economic and ideological dependency on China, Tanzanian actors imported, incorporated, and transformed these Chinese elements to forge their own project of African socialism.

Background

The United Republic of Tanzania was born in 1964, three years after the former British colony of Tanganyika became a sovereign country, and

---

[3] *The Nationalist*, the primary newspaper referenced here, was one of four daily newspapers in Tanzania until the press was fully nationalized in 1972. *The Nationalist*, along with *Uhuru*, its Swahili-language counterpart, was owned and operated by TANU, the ruling party at the time.

[4] "No Censorship of Books in Tanzania," *The Nationalist* (December 12, 1967).

several months after the island territory of Zanzibar also gained independence from British rule. Though mainland Tanganyika's transition to independence in 1961 was a fairly smooth and peaceful affair, in Zanzibar decolonization was accompanied by a tumultuous, violent leftist revolution – with racial overtones – against the ruling elite and landed classes on the island. In the context of political turbulence, ongoing civil war, and foreign involvement in the neighboring country of the Congo, as well as the escalation of liberation struggles against Portuguese imperialism and apartheid-style governance immediately to the south of Tanzania, the Zanzibar revolution drew new international attention to East Africa. Nyerere and other TANU officials, like their counterparts across the African continent, felt the pressures of the Cold War quite acutely, and pursued a platform of global engagement that would preserve the geopolitical and ideological autonomy of their young country. At the same time, the Tanzanian leadership sought to formulate an agenda for domestic development that accorded to the ideals informing their foreign policy (an emphasis on self-reliance combined with an idealization of community) but remained compatible with the on-the-ground realities of a poor, largely rural, society.

By 1967, *ujamaa* had emerged as the philosophy and strategy that TANU leaders felt would best respond to the opportunities and constraints of the early postcolonial period. *Ujamaa* simultaneously drew upon standard socialist themes – by rejecting exploitation and inequality in favor of collective effort and welfare – and departed from the conventional global repertoire of development policy – by proposing a decentralized, pastoral version of socialist democracy. Tanzanian political elites styled *ujamaa* as a flexible, improvisational utopian project driven by a shifting dialectic between state-directed policy and popular subjective transformation, rather than proclaiming it a fixed blueprint for revolutionary change. Immediately following the Arusha Declaration, the implementation of *ujamaa* began with the one-party state's nationalization of banks, major industries, and natural resources. The centerpiece of the *ujamaa* initiative, however, was the longer-term undertaking of reorganizing the Tanzanian countryside into socialist villages. The *ujamaa* village was to be defined by collective ownership of property and communal organization of agriculture; the hard work and unified dedication of *ujamaa* villagers would fuel national development.

Whereas villagization began as an experimental and voluntary effort, it morphed into a compulsory drive (known as Operation Vijiji [Villages]) between 1973 and 1975 in which millions of peasants were forcefully resettled. By the end of Operation Vijiji, the Tanzanian rural landscape had been superficially transformed, but substantive *ujamaa* had not been achieved, since TANU had exchanged the original goal of establishing functional socialist villages for the objective of achieving a mere spatial reconfiguration of the countryside. The fate of the individual *ujamaa* village paralleled that of the Tanzanian nation-state at large. By the mid 1970s Tanzania, like many other newly independent states in sub-Saharan Africa, had lost its developmental momentum largely due to a number of structural, institutional, and ideological constraints – all of which reflected local factors but were deeply connected to the increasing unevenness of the world economy and the restrictiveness of global geopolitics.

Shared imaginaries

Before the disappointments and closures of the 1970s, however, Tanzanian politics were marked by a spirit of experimentation and possibility. Without reproducing Mao's vision wholesale, Nyerere transposed a number of key themes of Chinese socialism onto Tanzanian soil, combining them with popular local idioms, colonial practices, and other borrowed developmental ideologies into the distinctive *ujamaa* imaginary. Moreover, as the *ujamaa* project was translated into practice, the state officials and youth militants who interpreted and implemented official development policy further injected a Maoist flavor into their endeavors, demonstrating the broad reach of the Chinese socialist model among Tanzanian populations. In many ways, the Tanzanian *ujamaa* experiment mirrored and overlapped with other African Socialist projects in countries such as Ghana, Guinea, Mali, and Zambia – which all drew upon a common continental repertoire in which Maoist ideology and symbolic citations figured prominently. Yet *ujamaa* was easily the most ambitious and sustained version of African Socialism, and featured an especially striking affinity with the Chinese configuration at multiple levels.

Equally committed to the task of forging an "alternative" path to socialist development, Tanzania and China shared a political language of anti-colonialism and self-reliance, and their domestic agendas both valorized the countryside as the primary site of economic and ideological transformation. Like Mao, Nyerere realized the unsuitability of Soviet strategies in a predominantly agrarian society, and refused to countenance the intensification of urban–rural discrepancies, class tensions, and general hardship for the average citizen that a straightforward policy of industrialization and proletarianization would produce. Rather than deferring the establishment of socialist forms of social organization until the reconfiguration of productive forces had been achieved, both

Mao and Nyerere insisted that the cultivation of socialist subjectivities could itself be a lever of economic development. "In a socialist society it is the socialist attitude of mind, and not the rigid adherence to a standard political pattern, which is needed,"[5] Nyerere insisted, echoing Mao's position that "the people, and the people alone" – rather than abstract historical logic, or technological capacity – "are the motive force in the making of world history."[6] *Ujamaa* and Maoism alike held that the historical "backwardness" of their countries – their largely unindustrialized character – actually represented circumstances particularly favorable to socialist revolution. Though Mao urged the abolition of any traces of outdated Confucian beliefs and traditional practices among the mostly "poor and blank" Chinese peasantry, Nyerere maintained that an African heritage of "tribal socialism" dating to the precolonial era could underpin a modern developmental program that was simultaneously restorative and transformative.

Despite this difference, however, TANU officials during the *ujamaa* era and their Chinese counterparts during and after the Great Leap Forward both promoted popular dedication and discipline as an inherently rural ethos to be generalized as a national imperative. By relying upon themselves and working hard, Tanzanian and Chinese citizens would, in theory, be able to secure the self-reliance of their countries in a 1960s world marked by the rise of new threats to national sovereignty, the deepening of capitalist-fueled global inequalities, and geopolitical turbulence (apparent in dynamics such as the Sino-Soviet split). Of course, Mao and Nyerere carried this logic to different extremes; while Mao urged modified rural and urban industrialization to allow the Chinese to "catch up" to the West, Nyerere felt that hard work and a dedicated socialist ethos alone were sufficient ingredients for longer-term economic progress. At times, the urgency of these developmental missions, and the tense regional and global circumstances in which they unfolded, lent a militaristic character to official campaigns for increased agricultural production or cultural reform in both China and Tanzania.

However, this militarism was hardly managed and applied by a centralized state apparatus. The aggression and energy of young Chinese student activists during the Cultural Revolution, and of members of TANU's Youth League during villagization, exposed the limits of state control over revolutionary activity in both countries. Indeed, both the Maoist and Tanzanian political imaginaries privileged revolutionary spontaneity; the philosophy of the mass line elaborated in Mao's

---

[5] Nyerere, "*Ujamaa*: The Basis of African Socialism."
[6] Mao Zedong, *Quotations from Chairman Mao*, www.marxists.org/reference/archive/mao/works/red-book/ch11.htm.

Quotations was mirrored in Nyerere's faith in peasant initiative and suspicion of bureaucratic elitism. Both Maoism and *ujamaa* were, at heart, utopian formulations; as such, they ended up exhibiting a number of similar contradictions – between a tendency toward decentralized openness and an impulse toward the centralization and top-down application of power, for instance. Ultimately, both the Chinese and Tanzanian socialist projects assumed a thoroughly hybrid form, blending unwieldy state planning and a strong party apparatus with an idealization of popular creativity and improvisation.

Material connections

The particularly close Tanzania–China relationship of the 1960s manifested and produced these overlapping approaches to socialism and national development. The Chinese link with Tanzania was the deepest of its numerous relationships with African countries at this time;[7] in 1964 alone, China provided $45.5 million in aid to Tanzania, comprising nearly half of its total annual aid on the African continent.[8] In 1965, Nyerere and Zhou Enlai signed a ten-year friendship treaty that would solidify Tanzania's status as the largest African recipient of Chinese economic assistance, and China's as the most significant donor to Tanzania, over the course of the *ujamaa* era. In subsequent years this support arrived in a variety of forms: as donations ranging from books and broadcasting equipment to services such as visiting rural medical teams; interest-free loans and investment in a labor-intensive textile mill; a joint shipping line and state farms; and the Chinese design and construction of a major regional railway. Diplomatic and cultural exchanges between the two countries demonstrated that this relationship was more than one of mere financial dependence, however. Between 1964 and 1967, a number of visits between Tanzania and China established and deepened these material and ideological connections. During these meetings, TANU leaders often referred to the parallel, intertwined histories and common challenges faced by the two countries – a narrative also cultivated by Chinese officials to substantiate Mao's Three Worlds theory in the wake of the Soviet-Sino split. In 1964, Second Vice-President Rashidi Kawawa greeted Premier Zhou Enlai in Dar es Salaam, proclaiming that "your great and famous country throughout

---

[7] Jamie Monson, *Africa's Freedom Railway: How a Chinese Development Project Changed Lives and Livelihoods in Tanzania* (Bloomington: Indiana University Press, 2009).

[8] Tareq Y. Ismael, "The People's Republic of China and Africa," *Journal of Modern African Studies* 9.4 (1971), pp. 507–29 at p. 515.

Fig. 6. Chinese dancers welcome Tanzanian president Julius Nyerere to Beijing. Banner reads, "Welcome, Tanzanian brothers!"
Source: Daily News (Tanzania), February 17, 1965.

world history has had cordial relations with both Tanganyika and Zanzibar for over a thousand years." He concluded that since "this relation was disrupted by imperialists and colonialists," it was a "sacred duty" for "we peoples of Asia and Africa in this century to restore our former friendly relationship."[9] In 1965, on a visit by Nyerere and other TANU officials to Beijing, Zhou remarked of China and Tanzania that "we have similar past experience, face common fighting tasks, and so can most easily understand and trust each other."[10] Nyerere agreed, noting that "China is the biggest and the most powerful of the developing countries – indeed, it is the only developing country which can challenge imperialism on equal terms" and that "China is undergoing the greatest ideological revolution the world has ever seen, with anti-imperialism as its core."[11]

By 1967, TANU leaders sought to reinforce their new calls for rural sacrifice and self-reliance in the name of *ujamaa* by repeatedly pointing to

[9] Rashidi M. Kawawa and Chou En-Lai, *Hotuba Zilizotolewa Wakati wa Matembezi ya Bwana Kawawa Katika China* [Speeches made during the visit of Mr. Kawawa to China] (Dar es Salaam: TANU pamphlet, 1964).
[10] "US Imperialism Sure to Fail: Chou Tells Isle Rally," *The Nationalist* (June 7, 1965).
[11] Pressman's Commentary: "The Cold War Politics," *The Nationalist* (August 25, 1967).

China as both a model of the correct path of self-reliance and an illustration of the concrete benefits of pursuing such a developmental path. After visiting Beijing and touring southern China as part of a TANU friendship delegation in 1967, Executive Party Secretary P. Msekwa proclaimed that "China has set an excellent example for us in taking the road of self-reliance . . . Tanzania must take this road too. It's the only road to make our country strong and prosperous."[12] After his 1965 visit, Nyerere contrasted a Chinese ethos of discipline and austerity with the "list of needs and requests for assistance" he encountered in Tanzanian rural settlement schemes, commenting that the Chinese

are a frugal people; they husband their resources very carefully indeed, and only spend money on things which are absolutely essential. Workers who do not need to spend all their money on food, clothing and housing do not buy a lot of unnecessary things just because they would be nice to have or because someone else has one; they lend their money to the Government instead so that more investment, more education, and more health facilities can be provided.[13]

"This attitude we have to adopt too," he continued, explaining that "the only way to defeat our present poverty is to accept the fact that it exists, to live as poor people."[14]

Nyerere's admiration of "the conscious and deliberate frugality"[15] he witnessed in China extended to the attitude of the political leaders he encountered; his observations that Chinese government elites "were never richly dressed and were not luxuriously spending on cars"[16] prefigured the Arusha Declaration's stipulation that every TANU and government leader hold limited property, earn a single salary, and "be either a peasant or a worker." During the early years of *ujamaa*, public and official critiques of the conspicuous consumption of wealthy TANU members – known derisively as *wabenzi* for the flashy Mercedes-Benz vehicles they drove – escalated, culminating in the release of a 1971 set of Party Guidelines known as the *Mwongozo*, which provided further sanction against the "arrogant, extravagant, contemptuous, and oppressive" behavior of these officials, and urged the latter to practice self-reliance rather than "exploitation" in their personal lives. The decadent lifestyle of the *wabenzi* appeared particularly egregious when held up against the public displays of rugged self-sufficiency by Nyerere, members of

---

[12] "TANU Team Flies to S. China," *The Nationalist* (December 22, 1967).
[13] "Union Being Cemented, Says Mwalimu: Union Making Great Progress," *The Nationalist* (April 27, 1965).
[14] Ibid.
[15] "We Admire People of Tanzania – Chou," *The Nationalist* (June 5, 1965).
[16] "Invest your Cash Here: President Call to Tanzanians," *The Nationalist* (March 9, 1965).

TANU's Youth League (TYL), students, and rural people across the country in the wake of the President's "Long March" leading up to the Arusha Declaration in 1967. Later that year, these Tanzanians embarked upon a series of long-distance walks in support of the new *ujamaa* program, culminating in Nyerere's seven-day trek from his birthplace in Butiama to the northern city of Mwanza over 130 miles away. The editors and staff of *The Nationalist* – TANU members including Nyerere's successor, Benjamin Mkapa, and his future advisor, Nsa Kaisi – celebrated these "heroic" marches in their typically militant language, noting that the people's "leader believes in hard work and struggle and is himself in the forefront of this hard work and struggle."[17] The symbolism was clear: in *ujamaa*'s "war on poverty," the Chinese revolutionary spirit of self-reliance, exemplified by the physical endurance evident in "the Long March which the beleaguered Red Army undertook in 1934/5,"[18] would comprise the most effective weapon in the Tanzanian arsenal.

Despite China and Tanzania's mutual commitment to self-reliance as a developmental strategy for their rural populations, their very relationship was premised upon a recognition that national self-reliance could only realistically comprise a developmental goal for a poor country such as Tanzania. During the 1960s, Chinese aid to Tanzania arrived in many forms. In Dar es Salaam and Zanzibar, Chinese money built factories such as the Urafiki (Friendship) Textile Mill, whose operations were organized and guided by Chinese managers and technical experts. A large state farm (Ruvu) just outside Dar es Salaam – one of several exceptions to Nyerere's policy of small-scale, village-level agriculture – relied upon Chinese tractors and other equipment, as well as the labor of Chinese agricultural advisors and workers. Chinese medical missions extended aid into remote areas of the countryside, resulting in the circulation of over thirty doctors, six nurses, and five interpreters throughout the regions of Mara, Dodoma, and Mtwara.[19] These highly visible forms of aid were accompanied by regular donations of more mundane, but hardly less significant, materials such as books and radio equipment.

A number of cooperative ventures between China and Tanzania emphasized the commitment to symbolic and substantive solidarity between the two countries. A joint shipping line, whose vessels were given names such as the *Asia/Africa*, was one such undertaking; more

---

[17] Editorial: "On the March," *The Nationalist* (October 4, 1967).
[18] "We Admire People of Tanzania – Chou," *The Nationalist* (June 5, 1965).
[19] "Chinese Doctors Call on Shaba," *The Nationalist* (April 18, 1968).

notable was the construction of what came to be known as the Uhuru (Freedom) Railway. Although the public marches of 1967 foregrounded an almost anti-modern strand of *ujamaa* ideology, which echoed Gandhi's ascetic traditionalism by rejecting "dependency" on transportation infrastructure and machinery, they were staged at precisely the moment at which Tanzania signed a pact with China and Zambia to develop the longest rail link in the country – the Tan–Zam (or TAZARA) railway from Dar es Salaam to Lusaka. Preliminary discussions of Chinese financing of the proposed TAZARA railway began in 1965. After the World Bank and other potential donors rejected Tanzanian and Zambian requests for investment, the Chinese deal was formalized, and the railway was built between 1969 and 1974.

The TAZARA railway embodied the complexity and depth of the Sino-Tanzanian relationship during this period. The project – like the relationship more broadly – participated in and helped constitute the ideas and initiatives of the Third World in its "second chapter,"[20] marked by its members' shared preoccupation with attaining and preserving national sovereignty, yet materialized through their commitment to transnational engagement and internationalism. In this spirit, TANU promoted regionalism – a building-block of pan-Africanism – as an economic tool in both the larger pursuit of geopolitical and ideological autonomy from Cold War bipolarities and the ongoing struggle against imperialist formations on the African continent. In particular, the work of combating formal colonialism and apartheid in southern Africa was inextricable from the project of strengthening regional economic ties with neighboring states, such as Zambia, that would otherwise be dependent on trade with Rhodesia and South Africa. TAZARA was a key element of the effort to bring down the Rhodesian and South African regimes, offering a route of access for imports and exports to and from Zambia that bypassed southern Africa, and thus promised to whittle down the latter's economic base. The Chinese support for this initiative – via money, technology, technicians, and laborers – thus benefited the Tanzanian and Zambian economies, aided southern African liberation struggles, and bolstered China's anti-colonial credentials.

These credentials had been secured earlier, in more covert and direct ways. Since its independence, Tanganyika had been a leader in regional and later continental efforts to aid liberation struggles in southern Africa,

---

[20] For this periodization see Mark Berger, "After the Third World? History, Destiny and the Fate of Third Worldism," *Third World Quarterly* 25.1 (2004), pp. 9–39; Vijay Prashad, *The Darker Nations: A People's History of the Third World* (New York: The New Press, 2007).

spearheading the Pan African Freedom Movement of East, Central, and Southern Africa (PAFMECSA) and hosting the Liberation Committee of the Organization of African Unity in Dar es Salaam from 1963 onward. Tanzania served as a base for anti-colonial and anti-apartheid movements from South Africa, Namibia, Angola, Zimbabwe, and Mozambique, housing their operational headquarters and facilitating their militarization by running training-camps as well as acting as a conduit for arms and supplies provided by a range of radical foreign sources.[21] Chinese aid was particularly substantial among the latter. In 1964, China began training soldiers of the Zanzibar Island's People's Liberation Army and the Tanzania People's Defence Forces (many of whom would later go on to secure Tanzania's southern border with Mozambique and train freedom fighters in refugee camps) as well as providing instruction to southern African guerrillas at the mainland Moshi Police College and in training-camps in sites such as Kongwa.[22] By 1970, the Chinese had become the largest contributor of weapons and training to Tanzania-based freedom fighters.[23] They had also entirely replaced Canadian aid, previously the primary source of military assistance in mainland Tanzania, to hold "a monopoly in field training and the supply of sophisticated military equipment for the armed forces,"[24] and also worked to provide coastal patrol boats and jet fighters to the Tanzanian forces.

This military aid raised eyebrows among American and British officials, particularly when it was covertly channeled through Tanzania toward groups such as the Simba rebels from the Eastern Congo. Nyerere and other Tanzanian officials remained alert to the lessons of the recent Congo crisis, which starkly illustrated the potential perils of inviting anti-communist intervention from the West.[25] Within Tanzanian borders, TANU leaders maintained that the TAZARA deal,

---

[21] See Shubi L. Ishemo, "'A Symbol that Cannot be Substituted': The Role of Mwalimu J. K. Nyerere in the Liberation of Southern Africa, 1955–1990," *Review of African Political Economy* 27.83 (2000), pp. 81–94; Piero Gleijeses, *Conflicting Missions: Havana, Washington, and Africa: 1959–1976* (Chapel Hill: University of North Carolina Press, 2002); Paul Bjerk, "Postcolonial Realism: Tanganyika's Foreign Policy under Nyerere, 1960–1963," *International Journal of African Historical Studies* 44.2 (2011), pp. 215–47.

[22] "Russians and Chinese use Tanzania as Arms Centre," *Sunday Telegraph* (March 21, 1965).

[23] UK National Archives. Foreign and Commonwealth Office (FCO) 31/690. "Anglo-US Talks on China. The Chinese in Tanzania." East African department, November 1970. Background Notes.

[24] Ibid., Speaking Notes.

[25] Ludo deWitte, *The Assassination of Lumumba* (New York: Verso, 2003).

along with the proliferation of other material ties to China, did not compromise the country's position of self-reliance, commitment to ideological sovereignty, and policy of non-alignment. Responding to perceived alarm and anticipated pressure by the USA in the wake of the TAZARA agreement, Nyerere maintained, repeatedly and insistently, that "a railway was a railway whether it was built by Chinese or Italians and it was not necessarily 'Red'."[26] In the context of such debates about China's influence on Tanzania, the cultural and political symbolism associated with *ujamaa* took on a particular importance. In 1965, Nyerere remarked that "large sections of the Western Press and some Western politicians have been examining us through microscopes"; he laughed off scrutiny of his penchant for Mao-style suits, scoffing that "I gather that even the suits I wear have been adduced as evidence of pernicious Chinese influence."[27] Yet, given the politicization of dress across sub-Saharan Africa and within Tanzanian borders throughout the 1960s,[28] Nyerere's sartorial choices spoke through a fairly clear visual language to express an ideological affinity for the evolving Maoist developmental model.[29]

Culture and revolution

The popularity of Mao suits was hardly the only evidence of Chinese cultural and political influence in 1960s Tanzania. China's revolution reached Tanzanians more concretely through the distribution of books and other media, especially radio and film. The Chinese operated the radical Tanganyika Bookshop in Dar es Salaam and the Mapinduzi (Revolution) Bookshop in Zanzibar, which sold "Chinese publications of a wide and useful variety in both Swahili and English," ranging from technical manuals to *China Pictorial* magazine.[30] Chief among these publications was Mao's *Quotations*, which was also sold in smaller towns throughout Tanzania, and remained widely available by mail order in Swahili and English. Though such a text would have been irrelevant to many illiterate Tanzanians, a number of young intellectuals and activists

[26] "Tan-Zam Railway is Not 'Red' Says Nyerere," *The Nationalist* (October 20, 1968).

[27] "President Nyerere Speaks out on Remaining Colonies: Bloodshed? It's up to West," *The Nationalist* (June 24, 1965).

[28] Jean Allman, ed., *Fashioning Africa: Power and the Politics of Dress* (Bloomington: Indiana University Press, 2004).

[29] The "Kaunda suit," popularized by Zambian president Kenneth Kaunda, was another popular sartorial choice for male officials at the time.

[30] UK National Archives. Dominion Office (DO) 213/100. "Tanzania: Chinese Influence in Tanzania." British High Commissioner in Tanzania to the Secretary of State for Commonwealth Relations, March 19, 1965.

in urban centers avidly read the Little Red Book, with students at the University of Dar es Salaam gathering outside of the classroom to discuss related texts such as Mao's "On Contradiction" in weekend study groups.[31] The Little Red Book also inspired African imitations. In the autumn of 1967, the State Publishing Corporation released a Swahili pamphlet prepared by the Political Department of the Zanzibar Contingent of the Tanzanian People's Defence Forces, entitled *Mateuo ya Rais Karume* (Quotations from President Karume). Consisting of fifty pages of quotations from speeches given by Tanzania's First Vice-President and Zanzibar's leader Abeid Karume in 1965, the pamphlet measured six inches by four and one-half inches, and was known informally as the "little blue book."[32] Across the continent in Ghana, a pamphlet entitled the *Axioms of Kwame Nkrumah*, containing eighty-five quotations from Nkrumah's writings grouped under headings such as "African Revolution" and "African Unity," was published at roughly the same time. The layout and content of these texts unquestionably invoked Mao's *Quotations*.[33]

On the whole, radio was a more effective medium than text for reaching large segments of the Tanzanian population, and the Chinese were active in this sector as well. Broadcasts in Swahili from Beijing began in September 1961. By 1967, Radio Peking was transmitting twenty-one hours weekly in English to East Africa, with transmissions occurring every day between the hours of six and nine in the evening, and programming consisting of news and commentary interspersed with intervals of recorded music. The impact of Radio Peking was circumscribed by the fact that in rural areas radio ownership remained a relative luxury, and qualified by the popularity of other foreign radio stations, including the BBC and Radio Cairo.[34] Yet the Chinese also played a role in Tanzania's domestic radio operations, assisting with the reconfiguration of the colonial-era Tanganyika Broadcasting Corporation as Radio Tanzania, donating radio equipment, and even supplying technical training to radio

---

[31] Karim Hirji, ed., *Cheche: Reminiscences of a Radical Magazine* (Dar es Salaam: Mkuki na Nyota, 2010).

[32] US National Archives and Records Administration, College Park. State Department records. Box 2513, Central Foreign Policy Files 1967–69, Political and Defense. "'Blue Book' of Karume Sayings Issued." October 12, 1967: American Embassy Dar es Salaam.

[33] FCO 31/155. "Socialist Concepts in Zambia, East Africa, and Ghana." African Section, Joint Research Department, June 21, 1967.

[34] George Yu, "Dragon in the Bush: Peking's Presence in Africa," *Asian Survey* 8.12 (1968), pp. 1018–26; James Brennan, "Radio Cairo and the Decolonization of East Africa, 1953–1964," in Christopher Lee, ed., *Making a World after Empire: The Bandung Moment and its Political Afterlives* (Athens: Ohio University Press, 2010).

staff. Additionally, though television access was minimal in Tanzania, the Chinese used film to advertise the depths of the Sino-African relationship and extol the benefits of Maoism. The Chinese embassy in Dar es Salaam applied for permission to build a cinema adjoining their ambassador's house, but this request was refused. Nonetheless, Chinese and Chinese-themed films were screened in Dar es Salaam cinemas alongside Bollywood movies and select Western features; these included a 1965 color documentary of Nyerere's visit to China (dubbed in Swahili), a Chinese feature film entitled *Youth in the Flames of War*, and propaganda shorts praising China's doctors, such as *The Reattachment of a Completely Severed Hand*.[35] Outside of the cinema, theater, dance, and musical events captured the attention of urban elites. In 1967, for instance, Chinese cultural troupes performed *The East is Red* to audiences composed of members of the public and TANU leaders.

The image of Mao himself also became a charged symbol of Tanzania's radical inclinations. In a bit of political theater in late 1967, officials in neighboring Kenya "called for the immediate closure of the Chinese Embassy in Nairobi," charging that Chinese officials "had been trying to persuade Kenyans to 'study the thoughts of Mao Tse-tung'" and "engag[ing] in 'gross interference in Kenya's internal affairs'."[36] At the same moment, TANU leaders staged their own counter-theater by speaking out in favor of the distribution of badges emblazoned with Mao's portrait in Tanzanian secondary schools; Nyerere announced that "the Government will not tolerate attempts by any foreign country to try and influence the policies of the United Republic but it will not draw iron curtains around Tanzania to stop foreign propaganda."[37] *The Nationalist* issued a response to the Ministry of Education's reported attempt to prohibit the wearing of foreign badges by Tanzanian schoolchildren, asking, "how does a whole Ministry of the Government of the United Republic of Tanzania panic over badges of Mao Tse Tung when there is not a single Chinese teacher in Tanzania as compared to ... hundreds of American Peace Corps teachers and others from foreign countries?"[38] Letters to the editor, similarly, questioned the assumption that "to refrain from wearing a foreign badge proves loyalty to Tanzania and vice versa," asking, "what about those thousands of Christians who wear

[35] DO 213/100. Extract from "Communist Activities in Africa." December 1965.
[36] "Close Down Chinese Embassy – Mboya," *The Nationalist* (September 1, 1967).
[37] "Mwalimu Warns Against Foreign Influence ... but Assures: No Iron Curtains Around Tanzania," *The Nationalist* (August 22, 1967).
[38] Editorial: "Foreign Badges," *The Nationalist* (September 21, 1967).

badges – medals if you like – bearing the heads of Jesus Christ (a foreigner), Virgin Mary (a foreigner) – are they disloyal to Tanzania?"[39]

That Tanzanian schoolchildren were wearing badges featuring Mao's image is hardly surprising given the range of Chinese cultural and political resources in circulation in Dar es Salaam in the late 1960s. Moreover, debates over Maoist adornment reflected the emergent politicization of dress in Tanzania more generally, as TYL militants embarked upon a number of cultural policing campaigns that became known in some circles as Tanzania's own "cultural revolution." TANU launched Operation Vijana (Youth) in late 1968 to eradicate symbols of "cultural enslavement" among Dar es Salaam residents; the operation particularly targeted items of female adornment including miniskirts, wigs, tight pants, and cosmetics, but ostensibly condemned all signs of "imperialist" behavior, comportment, and dress. While the focus of these campaigns in Tanzania, unlike in China, was the revival and restoration of traditional African cultural practices, the Tanzanian "cultural revolution" was also accompanied by initiatives to purge national culture of indigenous elements deemed insufficiently compatible with socialist modernity – such as Operation Dress-Up, which forced Maasai citizens to wear "proper" clothing.[40] Officials and press reports referred to the TYL policers as "Green Guards"; just as the Chinese Communist Party struggled to regain control over the students, workers, and activists emboldened and authorized by Mao's call for Cultural Revolution, the senior TANU leadership began to express anxiety about the increasing numbers of unsanctioned beatings and arrests staged by Youth Leaguers in the name of Operation Vijana.[41]

Tensions and translations

While *ujamaa* and Maoism overlapped ideologically, they also generated similar patterns and contradictions as they unfolded in practice. The tension between inciting and managing popular activism in the name of cultural reform and agrarian reorganization was a recurring theme in

---

[39] Mwana-wa-Mkulima, Dar es Salaam, letter to the editor, "Ban on Foreign Badges," *The Nationalist* (September 29, 1967).

[40] Leander Schneider, "The Maasai's New Clothes: A Developmentalist Modernity and its Exclusions," *Africa Today* 53.1 (2006), pp. 100–31.

[41] Andrew Ivaska, *Cultured States: Youth, Gender, and Modern Style in 1960s Dar es Salaam* (Durham: Duke University Press, 2011); James Brennan, "Youth, the TANU Youth League, and Managed Vigilantism in Dar es Salaam, Tanzania 1925–1973," *Africa: Journal of the International Africa Institute* 76.2 (2006), pp. 221–46.

both national contexts, and manifested itself especially clearly in Operation Vijana and Operation Vijiji (the latter also entrusted TYL militants with its implementation). In both China and Tanzania, concern over cultural policing campaigns in cities bled into broader official anxieties about urban unemployment. TANU officials, drawing in part upon older colonial "repatriation" policies, urged young urban-dwellers without formal employment to "return" to the countryside throughout the 1960s; this strategy was designed not only to emphasize the rural orientation of Tanzanian socialism – to "counteract" the likelihood "that the towns might attract more people from rural areas and thus discourage effort in nation-building"[42] – but also offered party leaders an effective means of defusing unrest in cities. In this respect periodic urban removal campaigns in *ujamaa*-era Tanzania mirrored the "sent-down" (*xia fang*) rustication movements in Mao's China. TANU also adopted a national service program designed to introduce young people to military training and require them to spend time farming in *ujamaa* villages. After growing accusations of elitism among students at the University of Dar es Salaam (paralleling Mao's concerns about the cultivation of "bourgeois" mentalities among Chinese intellectuals) the party made national service compulsory for all secondary school graduates. These policies targeted young women as well as men; however, as in China, national policy toward matters of gender and family remained ambiguous and often paradoxical during the 1960s. The concept of *ujamaa* itself – like the Maoist vision of socialist egalitarianism – theoretically called for the socialization of household functions; however, both Tanzanian and Chinese policies continued to preserve the centrality of the nuclear family structure and assign women the double burden of fulfilling reproductive (or domestic) and productive duties.[43]

Some Tanzanians pointed out these contradictions of official policy to criticize Nyerere's regime, leading to presidential mandates to ban or detain opposition groups or activists such as the University Students' African Revolutionary Front and Oscar Kambona. Similarly, the Sino-Tanzanian relationship, like the project of Afro-Asian solidarity more broadly, was punctuated by points of friction and acts of dissent. Reports

---

[42] Tanzania National Archives, Prime Minister's Office, Dodoma. RARD/UV/U24. "TANU National Conference 1969. May 30, 1969."

[43] Priya Lal, "Militants, Mothers, and the National Family: *Ujamaa*, Gender, and Rural Development in Postcolonial Tanzania," *Journal of African History* 51.1 (2010), pp. 1–20.; Gail Hershatter, *The Gender of Memory: Rural Women and China's Collective Past* (Berkeley: University of California Press, 2011).

of labor trouble at the Friendship Mill began as early as 1965, consisting of a range of "complaints about unfairness and discrimination in Mill personnel policies."[44] Other rumors pointed to popular disillusionment concerning the terms and conditions of Chinese aid, ranging from disappointment at the quality of donated machinery to frustration with the importation and conduct of Chinese laborers. Some Tanzanians bristled at what they saw as unwelcome Chinese propaganda. "Only recently I listened to the Kiswahili Service of Radio Peking about the work which was being done by the Chinese doctors here in Tanzania," one Dar es Salaam resident wrote in a letter to the editor of *Ngurumo*, a popular Swahili newspaper. "Perhaps Radio Peking forgot that in our country we have our own President and our own Party." The author claimed that Chinese doctors "inject the sick people and present them with the gift of small red books," although Tanzanians "do not want any propaganda," noting that "it will be better if they sincerely treat the sick people and not mix their medical profession with Chinese politics."[45] A number of residents of the mainland, like this angry letter-writer, also expressed dismay over Zanzibar's seemingly immoderate embrace of brash revolutionary rhetoric and policy, often manifested in what appeared to many to be an excessive tilt toward China.

This wariness could be compounded by logistical challenges hindering Sino-Tanzanian communication and expressions of solidarity. Despite the work of interpreters and language-exchange programs among Chinese and Tanzanian students, linguistic differences created a social barrier between citizens of the two countries, and could easily lead to instances of confusion or misunderstanding. In May 1967, the American embassy in Dar es Salaam reported a benign case of mistranslation that nonetheless hinted at the potential for larger problems in communication. Describing "a big-character banner draped on the front of the Chinese Communist Embassy," the memo wryly noted that "since there are no tigers in East Africa, and thus no word for 'tiger' in Swahili, the translation appearing below the Chinese ideographs solemnly declares that 'Imperialism and all enemies of progress are paper leopards'."[46] In this case, the essential meaning of Mao's maxim had been preserved though its referents had been modified; in other instances, however,

---

[44] DO 213/100. Telegram 1242, August 9, 1965, from Dar es Salaam to Commonwealth Relations Office.

[45] Idi Yusufu, Dar es Salaam, letter to the editor, "Wageni Wangu" [Our Guests], *Ngurumo* (June 10, 1969).

[46] NARA: Box 2513, Central Foreign Policy Files 1967–69, Political and Defense. "This Week in Tanzania, May 29–June 4, 1967," American Embassy Dar es Salaam. A-310.

the act of linguistic translation paralleled the conversion – both intentional and inadvertent – of Chinese ideology as it entered the cultural and political framework of *ujamaa*-era Tanzania.

Afterlives

Though Maoism comprised but one of a whole range of ideological models available to Tanzanian leaders and publics during the early postcolonial period, the influence of Chinese socialism on the political imaginary of *ujamaa* proved singularly unmistakable. A particularly close material relationship between the two countries throughout the 1960s and early 1970s enabled and deepened the conceptual, discursive, and symbolic impact of Maoism on politics and everyday life in Tanzania. Yet Tanzanian socialism was hardly a wholesale reproduction or crude derivative of Maoism. Just as officials, intellectuals, and activists in Dar es Salaam translated Mao's *Quotations* into Swahili, and converted the book into an oral text, TANU leaders and Tanzanian citizens modified and adapted elements of the rich and varied ideological field of Maoism as they incorporated them into the evolving *ujamaa* project. Blending Chinese concepts such as self-reliance, mass politics, and cultural revolution with local discourses of parasitism, colonial strategies of resettlement, Gandhian village republicanism, Soviet-style planning, and multiple elements of other African Socialist projects, Tanzanians remade Maoist ideas and symbols in the process of adopting them.

The heyday of the Sino-Tanzanian relationship – the mid 1960s until the early 1970s – coincided with the apex and subsequent rapid decline of Maoism and *ujamaa* socialism as dominant political discourses and actual policies in each country. Nyerere's 1967 Arusha Declaration inaugurated the *ujamaa* project at the height of the Cultural Revolution in China; while Chinese officials and publics turned away from the ambitious ideals and succinct imperatives contained in Little Red Book during the early 1970s, the *ujamaa* villagization initiative simultaneously mutated from a utopian vision of agrarian socialism into a compulsory resettlement drive focused solely on the superficial spatial reordering of the countryside. After 1975, which marked the conclusion of Operation Vijiji, Tanzanian politics preserved much of the earlier language of *ujamaa* but evacuated it of meaningful content. Though liberation struggles in southern Africa persisted and even escalated through the 1970s, rendering the TAZARA project more critical than ever, during the second half of the decade *ujamaa* appeared increasingly irrelevant as Tanzania followed the course of many of its independent African counterparts, falling into a condition of economic decline and deepening indebtedness to foreign donors.

In the 1980s, Tanzania (under the leadership of Nyerere's successor, Benjamin Mkapa) succumbed to these pressures by submitting to the austerity measures and liberalization regimen prescribed by IMF and World Bank-imposed structural adjustment policies. Meanwhile, the Chinese rejection of substantive socialism during the 1980s and 1990s so thoroughly transformed the country's political and economic position that by the late 1990s the Chinese "return to Africa"[47] had completely reversed the ideological and material terms of the Sino-Tanzanian relationship during the 1960s era of Third World anti-imperialist solidarity. Whereas earlier Chinese aid built factories such as the Friendship Textile Mill to strengthen Tanzanian manufacturing capacities for Tanzanian gain, and railroads such as the TAZARA for the purpose of pan-African integration, Chinese capital now employs casualized Tanzanian labor in enclaves of industrial production, resource extraction, and infrastructure construction on unfavorable terms that conform precisely to *ujamaa* conceptions of capitalist exploitation.

The breadth and depth of the earlier connection between the two countries, however, is evidenced in the durability of popular memories of Mao's example and *ujamaa*-era Chinese aid – which hold continued appeal among Tanzanians as varied as former national officials in Dar es Salaam and elderly villagers in the peripheral region of Mtwara. Popular experiences of neoliberalism over the past few decades have produced a growing nostalgia among many Tanzanians about the utopian promise of the *ujamaa* period; even while sentiments of fear and resentment toward contemporary Chinese managers and workers spread among rural and urban publics, a widespread appreciation of previous Chinese aid and the Maoist developmental model persists. In contemporary Tanzania, thus, resurgent socialist idioms of self-reliance, hard work, and exploitation can have paradoxical connotations and uses – ranging from invoking a sense of continuity and solidarity in Chinese–African relations to critiquing policies of privatization and labor casualization at the hands of foreign capitalists.[48]

---

[47] Ching Kwan Lee, "Raw Encounters: Chinese Managers, African Workers and the Politics of Casualization in Africa's Chinese Enclaves," *The China Quarterly* 199 (2009), pp. 647–66 at p. 647.

[48] Priya Lal, "Self-Reliance and the State: The Multiple Meanings of Development in Early Post-Colonial Tanzania," *Africa: Journal of the International African Institute* 82.2 (2012), pp. 212–34.

BIBLIOGRAPHY

ARCHIVAL SOURCES

Tanzania National Archives, Prime Minister's Office, Dodoma. RARD/UV/U24
UK National Archives, Kew. Dominion Office (DO) 213/100
UK National Archives, Kew. Foreign and Commonwealth Office (FCO) 31/690
UK National Archives, Kew. Foreign and Commonwealth Office (FCO) 31/155
US National Archives and Records Administration, College Park. RG 59, State
  Department records. Box 2513, Central Foreign Policy Files 1967–69,
  Political and Defense

GENERAL SOURCES

Allman, Jean, ed., *Fashioning Africa: Power and the Politics of Dress* (Bloomington:
  Indiana University Press, 2004)
Berger, Mark, "After the Third World? History, Destiny and the Fate of Third
  Worldism," *Third World Quarterly* 25.1 (2004), pp. 9–39
Bjerk, Paul, "Postcolonial Realism: Tanganyika's Foreign Policy under Nyerere,
  1960–1963," *International Journal of African Historical Studies* 44.2 (2011),
  pp. 215–47
Brennan, James, "Radio Cairo and the Decolonization of East Africa, 1953–
  1964," in Christopher Lee, ed., *Making a World after Empire: The Bandung
  Moment and its Political Afterlives* (Athens: Ohio University Press, 2010), pp.
  173–95
  "Youth, the TANU Youth League, and Managed Vigilantism in Dar es
  Salaam, Tanzania 1925–1973," *Africa: Journal of the International Africa
  Institute* 76.2 (2006), pp. 221–46
deWitte, Ludo, *The Assassination of Lumumba* (New York: Verso, 2003)
Gleijeses, Piero, *Conflicting Missions: Havana, Washington, and Africa: 1959–1976*
  (Chapel Hill: University of North Carolina Press, 2002)
Hershatter, Gail, *The Gender of Memory: Rural Women and China's Collective Past*
  (Berkeley: University of California Press, 2011)
Hirji, Karim, ed., *Cheche: Reminiscences of a Radical Magazine* (Dar es Salaam:
  Mkuki na Nyota, 2010)
Ishemo, Shubi L., "'A Symbol that Cannot be Substituted': The Role of
  Mwalimu J. K. Nyerere in the Liberation of Southern Africa, 1955–1990,"
  Review of African Political Economy 27.83 (2000), pp. 81–94
Ismael, Tareq Y., "The People's Republic of China and Africa," *Journal of
  Modern African Studies* 9.4 (1971), pp. 507–29
Ivaska, Andrew, *Cultured States: Youth, Gender, and Modern Style in 1960s Dar es
  Salaam* (Durham: Duke University Press, 2011)
Kawawa, Rashidi M., and Chou En-Lai, *Hotuba Zilizotolewa Wakati wa
  Matembezi ya Bwana Kawawa Katika China* [Speeches made during the visit
  of Mr Kawawa to China] (Dar es Salaam: TANU pamphlet, 1964)
Lal, Priya, "Militants, Mothers, and the National Family: *Ujamaa*, Gender, and
  Rural Development in Postcolonial Tanzania," *Journal of African History*
  51.1 (2010), pp. 1–20

"Self-Reliance and the State: The Multiple Meanings of Development in Early Post-Colonial Tanzania," *Africa: Journal of the International African Institute* 82.2 (2012), pp. 212–34

Lee, Ching Kwan, "Raw Encounters: Chinese Managers, African Workers and the Politics of Casualization in Africa's Chinese Enclaves," *The China Quarterly* 199 (2009), pp. 647–66

Monson, Jamie, *Africa's Freedom Railway: How a Chinese Development Project Changed Lives and Livelihoods in Tanzania* (Bloomington: Indiana University Press, 2009)

Nyerere, Julius, *"Ujamaa*: The Basis of African Socialism," in *Freedom and Unity: A Selection from Writings and Speeches, 1952–65* (Dar es Salaam: Oxford University Press, 1966), pp. 162–171

Prashad, Vijay, *The Darker Nations: A People's History of the Third World* (New York: The New Press, 2007)

Schneider, Leander, "The Maasai's New Clothes: A Developmentalist Modernity and its Exclusions," *Africa Today* 53.1 (2006), pp. 100–31

Yu, George, "Dragon in the Bush: Peking's Presence in Africa," *Asian Survey* 8.12 (1968), pp. 1018–26

7 Empty symbol
The Little Red Book in India

Sreemati Chakrabarti

The Little Red Book gained popularity in India with the outbreak of the Naxalite Movement, named for the hamlet of Naxalbari (in the Darjeeling district of the eastern Indian state of West Bengal), where in the early summer of 1967 a local communist unit led poor peasants to overthrow the local gentry in a land dispute.[1] This so-called victory of the peasant insurgents was short-lived, but it had significant consequences. It split the communist movement in India for a second time, following the Sino-Soviet split of the mid-1950s, and introduced violent revolutionary Maoism (or Naxalism) into Indian politics. The Indian state considers Naxalism a security threat even today, with twelve of its twenty-eight states under some degree of pressure. However, the first phase of the Naxalite Movement ended with the death of its leader, Charu Majumdar, in 1972, after which the Little Red Book rapidly declined in popularity. As chief leader of the Naxalite Movement, Majumdar treated the *Quotations* like gospel, insisting in his writings and speeches that his comrades keep a copy of the Little Red Book on their persons at all times, to be studied in indoctrination classes and also read aloud to aid the illiterate peasants in the midst of their "armed struggle." A good many students and intellectuals recruited to the organization took this directive seriously and did follow it. However, as will be shown later, no other senior functionary of the Naxalites put so much stress on reading the *Quotations*; in fact, as revealed later, many of them were opposed to reducing the entire Maoist ideology to the short passages in the Little Red Book. Majumdar's closest comrades believed the Little Red Book to

The author wishes to thank Professor Manoranjan Mohanty, Chairperson, Institute of Chinese Studies, Delhi for his suggestions.
[1] On the early phase of the Naxalite Movement, see Biplab Dasgupta, *The Naxalite Movement* (Bombay: Allied Publishers, 1974); Sumanta Bannerjee, *In the Wake of Naxalbari* (Calcutta: Subarnarekha, 1980); Sohail Jawaid, *The Naxalite Movement in India* (New Delhi: Associated Publishing House, 1974); Manoranjan Mohanty, *Revolutionary Violence* (New Delhi: Sterling, 1977); and Sreemati Chakrabarti, *China and the Naxalites* (New Delhi and London: Radiant Publishers and Sangam Books, 1990).

be of little consequence to the movement, and after his demise the importance of the *Quotations* among the Naxalites faded.

Nonetheless, during this early phase *Quotations from Chairman Mao* was popular among students and intellectuals who supported and sympathized with the movement, whether they joined or not. Thousands of copies of the book entered India and reached bookstores in the College Street area of Calcutta (now Kolkata), probably arriving from Nepal, Burma, and East Pakistan (now Bangladesh); the book has been banned in India since the mid 1970s and bookstore owners in Calcutta are extremely hesitant to reveal much about its distribution.[2] What is certain is that, next to the *Communist Manifesto*, in the entire history of the communist movement in India from the mid 1920s to the present, the Little Red Book is the one text that most captured the imagination of young revolutionaries. This chapter compares Naxalite propaganda from the Majumdar era with the recollections and interpretations of some former Naxalites to consider the rise and demise of the Little Red Book in India.

Indian Maoism and the rise of the Naxalites

Maoist ideology took roots within the Indian communist movement some years before the outbreak of the Naxalite Movement in West Bengal, with the Telengana Movement (1946–51) in the southeastern state of Andhra Pradesh and the Tebhaga Movement in the state of Bengal (1946–50). The Telengana Movement was a localized peasant insurrection in which communist leaders liberated two districts of Andhra Pradesh from the rule of Nizam, a local despot patronized by the British colonial government. According to historian Mohan Ram, the communists of Andhra Pradesh modeled their movement on Mao's essay "On New Democracy" (1940):

The Telengana struggle incorporated all the basic elements of what later came to be formalized as the Maoist strategy – a two-stage revolution based on a clear understanding of the differences between the stages and their interrelation; liberated bases from where peasant struggles could be conducted to achieve proletarian hegemony and the triumph of the democratic revolution; and a close alliance between the working class and the peasant masses towards a revolutionary front with the national bourgeoisie against imperialism.[3]

However, says Ram, the Telengana Movement was at heart an indigenous struggle retrofitted to the language of Maoism: "The Andhra

---

[2] Efforts by the author and others to gather further information from booksellers were futile. A few said categorically that since the movement has become a serious matter of internal security, they preferred not to talk about it.

[3] Mohan Ram, *Indian Communism: Split Within a Split* (Delhi: Vikas Publications, 1969), p. 2.

communists had discovered a uniquely Indian idiom of revolution [and] were in search of a theoretical basis to legitimize it in the eyes of the international communist movement."[4]

The Tebhaga Movement began around the same time in Bengal. This was a peasant campaign for a greater share of the produce from the land they tilled. Landlords there conventionally claimed half of the crops, but tenant farmers and sharecroppers now demanded that only a third be taken. ("Tebhaga" means one-third in the local language.) Here again the peasantry acted with support from the local communist leadership, and some landlords who protested this demand had their land expropriated. The rapid spread of the movement across various districts threatened the power base of the local gentry, who turned to the police. In the end, many peasant activists and their party supporters were arrested and jailed. Although the direct connection to Maoist doctrine was less clear in this case, the attempt by peasants to seize power from the local gentry resembled the insurrectionary peasant activism depicted in Mao's famous "Report on an Investigation of the Peasant Movement in Hunan" (1927).[5] However, both the Telengana and the Tebhaga Movements were soon overshadowed by political developments at the national level: independence from British colonial rule and the partition of the former Indian empire into India and Pakistan.

Barely two decades into its independence, India in the mid-1960s was confronted by a perfect storm of economic crisis and political instability. Huge defense expenditures resulting from two disastrous wars (against China in 1962 and Pakistan in 1965) had adversely affected development programs. Lack of growth in the industrial and service sectors led to unemployment among the educated. Massive droughts in some parts of India caused food shortages. The economy stalled under the weight of budget deficits, trade deficits, and aggravated inflation. In the political arena, electoral reverses in more than half of the states cost the ruling Congress Party its monopoly on power. Independent India's government had failed to address issues of development and equity. Discontent spread widely, particularly among the youth and students, and anti-government protests erupted all over the country.[6]

---

[4] Ibid.

[5] Asok Mazumdar, *The Tebhaga Movement: Politics of Peasant Protest in Bengal, 1946–50* (Delhi: Aakar Books, 1993); D. N. Dhanagre, "Peasant Protest and Politics: The Tebhaga Movement in Bengal, 1946–47," *Journal of Peasant Studies* 3.3 (1976).

[6] Sreemati Chakrabarti, "From Radical Politics to Liberal Economics: China as a Model," in S. Narsimhan and G. Balatchandirane, eds., *India and East Asia: Learning from Each Other* (Delhi: Manak, 2004).

It was in this environment of economic, political, and social turmoil that the Naxalite Movement broke out. In 1964, the Communist Party of India (CPI) split as a result of the Sino-Soviet dispute. The breakaway group that did not unquestionably support the Soviet Union took the name CPI (Marxist), and contested the general elections of 1967 on its own. It was during the preparations for the elections that serious differences in ideology, strategy, and tactics arose between the top leadership of the CPI (Marxist) and its local units in Darjeeling and Siliguri. Some of the local leaders, led by district general secretary Charu Majumdar, not only questioned Moscow but were outright Maoists. Majumdar and others split from the CPI (Marxist) and later in April 1969 formed the Maoist-oriented CPI (Marxist–Leninist).[7]

Majumdar announced that the uprising in Naxalbari marked the beginning of the armed revolution in India – a Maoist revolution. He subsequently became the ideologue of his party, and coined the slogan "China's path is our path, China's Chairman is our Chairman." Majumdar denounced the parliamentary system and completely rejected the Indian constitution. In his view Mao Zedong's strategy of revolution, which was successful in China's case, was fully applicable to India. Since only the Chinese model could save India, it was important for Indian revolutionaries to completely immerse themselves in Maoist philosophy and ideology. Mao's works were essential readings, and *Quotations from Chairman Mao* was the indispensable document to be owned by all of them and carried on their persons at all times.

Appeal and popularity of the Little Red Book

Political indoctrination through reading and discussion (and sometimes debate) has been a notable aspect of Leninist party practice. Before being initiated into the party organization, it is almost mandatory for all activists and cadres to become well versed in the writings of Marx, Engels, and Lenin. Depending on the orientation of the movement, this might also include the writings of other Marxist ideologues such as Stalin, Trotsky, Luxemburg, Gramsci, Mao, etc. In the Indian communist movement, despite the proximity to China, until the 1940s works of western (including Russian) Marxist thinkers formed the bulk of the reading list. Even when the Chinese revolutionary experiences were discussed in political classes, the leadership put little weight on reading Mao's writings. Nevertheless, some emerging leaders from educated

---

[7] Bhabani Sengupta, *Communism in Indian Politics* (New Delhi and Stockholm: Young Asia Publications, 1978), pp. 319–28.

backgrounds came on their own to read works of Chinese communism. Liu Shaoqi's *How to be a Good Communist* (1939) was well known, as were Mao's articles on guerrilla warfare and military strategy. Other essays by Mao that attracted interest were "Analyses of Classes in Chinese Society" (1926), which purportedly showed the striking similarity between the Chinese and Indian rural situations in early twentieth century; Mao's treatise on dialectical ontology, "On Contradiction" (1937); a textbook called "The Chinese Revolution and the Chinese Communist Party" (1939); and "On New Democracy" (1940), a wartime analysis of the Chinese revolution's past, present, and future. The audience for these works was, again, young and educated. Peasant communists, even those with some education, showed little if any enthusiasm for Mao's writings. A major reason for this was that Mao's works were available mostly in English, and not in Bengali or Telugu.

Under Majumdar, the Naxalites adopted the Maoist canon promoted by Lin Biao, the military leader named Mao's successor during the Cultural Revolution. The Little Red Book formed the foundation, of course, but other important works were Lin Biao's paean, "Long Live the Victory of the People's War" (1965) and the so-called Three Constantly Read Articles – a brief compilation of "In Memory of Norman Bethune" (1939), "Serve the People" (1944), and "The Foolish Old Man who Removed the Mountains" (1945). Initially the Little Red Book was available only in English, but soon a Bengali version appeared, followed by Nepali, Sinhalese, Tamil, Malayalam, and Urdu. Most often, the Little Red Book was presented free of cost to younger recruits when they joined the movement or in their first indoctrination session. Sometimes this was accompanied by Lin Biao's essay on people's war. Even among peasants with a sincere interest in Maoism, the Little Red Book and other texts were received tepidly, while young, urban, educated, middle-class, would-be "revolutionaries" were willing to pay to purchase a copy.

In fact, it is likely that urban, educated youth were familiar with the Little Red Book before joining the Naxalite Movement. A former Naxalite recalls this introduction to the Little Red Book as Bible:

We came to revolutionary ideas via a re-assessment of Marxism and China played a major role in this. I remember the hubbub caused on Delhi University campus when [British economist] Joan Robinson visited the Delhi School of Economics wearing a Mao cap. She was on her way back from a trip to China, and full of enthusiastic admiration for the Great Proletarian Cultural Revolution. I didn't get to see her but my close friend (the late Arvind Das) did, and told us all about it. She was actually brandishing a copy of the highly prized Little Red Book of *Quotations from Chairman Mao Tse-tung*, he said. And whenever someone threw her a critical question about China, she would read out an appropriate quotation. For example when someone asked her: "Don't you think Marxism is dogmatic?" her answer was "Chairman Mao says dogma is worse than cow dung!" And so on.[8]

Likewise, Indian Maoists were expected to see Mao's Little Red Book as their Bible – both the source of all answers and the symbol of a greater cause. An essay in an early issue of the Naxalite Bengali periodical *Deshabrati* (also published in English as *Liberation*) describes the valiant death of a peasant guerrilla after a four-hour standoff with the police: "A true revolutionary and a true disciple of Chairman Mao, Comrade Babulal died with a gun in one hand and the little Red Book of quotations from Chairman Mao in the other. The Red Book was his constant companion. He was hardly thirty at the time of his death."[9] A later issue describes the killing by police of a young recruit named Niranjan Rao. He was a bright thirteen-year-old boy who worked as a tailor, says the article, and "whenever free he read *Quotations from Chairman Mao Tsetung*, recited and explained them to his mother even while taking his food. He fought with his parents who were reluctant in consideration of his age to allow him to join a guerrilla squad. He was killed the same day he got the permission."[10] According to an informant who quit the movement early, these sorts of reports were meant to show that non-intellectuals were also enamored by the Little Red Book. Majumdar called young, fresh recruits of whatever class "revolutionary intellectuals," and stated again and again that reading the *Quotations* was of utmost importance for learning Mao Zedong Thought and spurring revolutionary activism.

In an article titled "To the Youth and Students" published in *Liberation*, Majumdar projects the Little Red Book as the essential guide for the young and educated Naxalites who in substantial numbers were leaving colleges and universities to join the movement.[11] In this article, Majumdar repeats the Maoist argument that since Stalin's death the Soviet Union has abandoned Marxism–Leninism, established a "bourgeois dictatorship," and emerged as the number one accomplice of American imperialism. Due to these developments Mao's thought is now the "only Marxism–Leninism," which Mao has greatly developed and enriched through the Cultural Revolution. Echoing Lin Biao, Majumdar says the world has entered into the era of Mao Zedong Thought – the Marxism of the era of the complete collapse of

---

[8] Dilip Simeon, "Glory Days," in Ira Pande, ed., *India China Neighbours Strangers* (New Delhi: Harper Collins Publishers India with India Today Group and India International Centre, 2010), p. 441.

[9] *Liberation* 1.12 (October 1968).   [10] *Liberation* 2.9 (July 1969).

[11] *Liberation* 2.6 (April 1969).

imperialism.[12] "The political task of the student and youth workers," at this stage of history, "is to study this new and developed Marxism, the thought of Chairman Mao and put it into practice. He who shuns this task can never acquire the knowledge about the principles of Marxism. They must, therefore, study the *Quotations of Chairman Mao Tse-tung*."[13] Majumdar put particular emphasis on the quotations "On People's War," which apparently were published separately in an even littler, pocket-sized booklet with a red plastic cover. This booklet, available in English or Bengali, "is meant for revolutionary workers and peasants," said Majumdar. "We should make this our propaganda and agitation material. *Whether a worker is revolutionary or not will be judged on the basis of the number of workers and peasants to whom he has read out and explained this book.*"[14] Majumdar advised young recruits to form small squads of four or five students from each school or college in every locality, and each member of the squad must possess a copy of the *Quotations*. They were instructed to go to the villages whenever they found free time, to live and work among the poor and landless peasants, to learn from them, and to "read out quotations of Chairman Mao to them to acquaint them with Mao Tsetung Thought as much as you can."[15] For Majumdar, the Little Red Book was the glue to hold together the revolutionary intellectuals and youth with the workers and peasants. If Naxalite propaganda is to be believed, Majumdar's emphasis on reading the Little Red Book created enthusiasm among a large number of his young followers. According to an article called "Story of a Red Guard Squad of Youths and Students" written by a "Revolutionary Student Organizer," reading out relevant sections of *Quotations from Chairman Mao* to poor and landless peasants was an important task carried out zealously.[16]

Majumdar may have felt encouraged in his promotion of the Little Red Book by a report filed by a *Xinhua* news correspondent based in Beijing. Titled "Revolutionary Indian People are Advancing," the report was republished in *Liberation* in January 1969:

This year has witnessed the extensive spread of Marxism–Leninism, Mao Tsetung's thought in various places in India ... The Indian revolutionaries have translated and published Chairman Mao's brilliant works in large quantities and reproduced Chairman Mao's writings and quotations in their revolutionary journals. They have spread the revolutionary truth among the broad masses of the Indian people, especially among the poor laboring people most brutally

---

[12] Ibid., pp. 94–95. Compare Lin Biao, "Speech at the Peking Rally Commemorating the 50th Anniversary of the October Revolution" (November 6, 1967), www.marxists.org/reference/archive/lin-biao/1967/11/06.htm.

[13] *Liberation*, 2.6 (April 1969), pp. 94–95.   [14] Ibid. (emphasis added).

[15] Ibid., pp. 87–88.   [16] *Liberation* 3.6 (April 1970).

oppressed and exploited. It has been leaked out in the Indian press that among the 'adivasi' (indigenous) peasants living in Chota Nagpur area, Bihar state, many can recite quotations from Chairman Mao.[17]

Majumdar may have interpreted the report as a signal that the Chinese leadership supported and endorsed his stress on the Little Red Book. *Liberation* also republished a similar report on the Malaysian Maoist movement from *Peking Review*. The article said that many fighters in the Malaysian National Liberation Army were new recruits, and also that many were women. They lacked military training, combat experience, weapons, and equipment. In order to overcome these shortcomings, the fighters followed Lin Biao's advice: take firm hold of the study of Mao's works in order to arm yourself with Mao Zedong Thought. The fighters read the Three Constantly Read Articles and *"Quotations from Chairman Mao* on people's war, people's army, revolutionary heroism and other subjects *over and over."*[18] Only then was the fighters' confidence strengthened, and they found more and more ways of overcoming difficulties.[19]

Emphasis on the Little Red Book is most evident through the summer of 1970. After the Naxalites suffered setbacks in a series of violent clashes with the police and other security forces, Majumdar published a write-up in the party mouthpiece titled "Rely Fully on Landless and Poor Peasants and Combat Revisionism." He stressed the need to make sacrifices and accept bloodshed as part of the revolution.

Educate the landless and poor peasant in Mao Tsetung Thought. Let him learn to fight with guidance from the *Quotations*. Teach him to plan on his own. Help him so that he can develop into a leader. In order to do this it is necessary to help him read the quotations and the three constantly read articles; it is also equally necessary to politically educate the masses. Today the oppressed masses who have suffered from exploitation and tyranny for thousands of years yearn for their liberation and want revolution. Never hesitate to give them politics.[20]

In waging people's war, the people themselves are the main asset of the partisans. Majumdar envisioned the Little Red Book as the way to make and train new soldiers for revolution.

Decline of the Little Red Book

The rise and fall of the Little Red Book in the Naxalite Movement was linked with the personal fortunes of Charu Majumdar. Not all of

---

[17] *Liberation* 2.3 (January 1969).
[18] "Fighters Armed With Mao Tsetung Thought are Invincible," *Peking Review* 3 (January 16, 1970), reproduced in *Liberation* 5.3 (March 1970) (emphasis added).
[19] Ibid.
[20] *Liberation* 10.3 (August 1970), p. 2, speech dated July 14.

Majumdar's comrades in the Naxalite leadership agreed with his approach, which emphasized the Little Red Book almost to the exclusion of other Marxist literature. Majumdar seemed to be more Maoist than Mao himself – and he abandoned other Marxists for the cult of Mao. Majumdar's attachment to the Little Red Book is perhaps inexplicable on the face of it; some of his erstwhile supporters and admirers consider it to have been an obsession. One former comrade speculates that the attraction lay in the overall form of the Little Red Book – nothing else was published in that distinctive color, size, shape, and weight. Moreover, it was inexpensive (often distributed free), easily carried in one's pocket, and no dictionary was required to understand its contents. Majumdar himself may have found it far more readable than the denser writings of Marx, Engels, or Lenin. A pocket edition of Mao's thoughts was most convenient for the formulation of political instructions: one had only to pull out the Little Red Book and read a few passages.

Dissatisfaction with Majumdar's "short-cut" revolutionary methods certainly contributed to the disunity and factionalism that became visible by mid 1971. Majumdar answered his critics in a piece titled "Strengthen the Party Organization" written in October 1971. He expressed dismay at his colleagues for conceit and arrogance, and unhappiness with the fact that his comrades underplayed the importance of the Little Red Book.

We have united for making a revolution. That is why our relation should be of mutual respect and cooperation. Each of us must study deeply the chapter titled "Communists" in the *Quotations from Chairman Mao Tsetung*. It is then that the unity of our Party will be as strong as steel ... The struggle between the two lines exists within the party and it will always be so.[21]

Majumdar attacks those who think that enough political work has been done and there should be more stress on military work. This to him was clearly a deviation which could not take the struggle forward. Following Lin Biao's doctrine of people over weapons, and politics as the most important aspect of military work, Majumdar argues: "Our people's Liberation Army will be able to achieve success only when the number of guerrilla units in the villages increases through political work. There is no way of building guerrilla units except through political propaganda. Political work must be given priority at every stage of the class struggle. This is the Chairman's teaching."[22]

By that time, however, Majumdar's position on the Little Red Book already had been undercut by the Chinese. Sometime in 1970, a Naxalite leader named Souren Bose made a secret visit to China. In one of his

[21] *Liberation* 5.1 (July 1971–January 1972).   [22] Ibid.

long meetings with Zhou Enlai, Bose was told in no uncertain terms that the Indian revolutionaries must refrain from calling China's Chairman their Chairman, and must find an Indian path to revolution rather than mechanically copying the "Chinese model."[23] Naxalite propaganda did not publicize anything pertaining to this – most likely due to Majumdar's objections – but the fact that the Chinese leadership no longer approved of his position became well known, and in many formal as well as informal party meetings it led to heated discussions and acrimonious debates. As Majumdar's influence waned, there was less and less mention of the Little Red Book in Naxalite discourse.

Majumdar was now vulnerable over another contentious issue: his policy of "annihilation of the class enemy." Under the pretext of this so-called Maoist principle, all opponents of the Naxalites, regardless of class, could be killed. Police constables, primary school teachers, petty shopkeepers – people who by no definition belonged to India's exploiting classes – were frequent targets of the revolutionaries. Actually, Mao had never advocated such indiscriminate annihilation, and the main target in Mao's writings on guerrilla warfare was the Japanese occupation army. Majumdar seems to have missed this point rather deliberately, as the annihilation policy initially helped him retain his dominant position within the party. Even within his own flock, however, Majumdar's annihilation line eventually came under attack as patently un-Maoist, and his leadership was challenged by other sections of the party.[24]

The final blow against the Little Red Book was the unexpected death of Lin Biao in September 1971 and the incredible revelation that he had been a traitor conspiring with the Soviet Union to kill Chairman Mao. That Mao's "comrade-in-arms and successor" could be a traitor left many Indian Maoists confused, disappointed, and disillusioned. According to some former Naxalites, the Lin Biao incident raised questions about the infallibility of the "great, glorious and correct Communist Party of China" and troubling doubts about Mao Zedong himself.[25] Majumdar's own opinion of the Lin Biao incident is not clear from his writings, but when his erstwhile comrade Ashim Chatterjee split from Majumdar in 1972, Chatterjee made a scathing and insinuating remark about those who were "supporting the black conspiracy of Lin Biao and, in actuality, registering their approval of the vile attempt on the life of Chairman Mao."[26] Majumdar had hitched his star to Lin Biao and the

---

[23] Chakrabarti, *China and the Naxalites*, pp. 110–18.
[24] Mohan Ram, *Maoism in India* (New Delhi: Vikas Publications, 1971), pp. 132–33.
[25] Chakrabarti, *China and the Naxalites*, pp. 118–22.
[26] Ashim Chatterjee, "A Statement," *Frontier* 7.4 (May 18, 1974).

Lin Biao version of Maoism. After Lin Biao's star fell, and the aura of China, the Chinese Revolution, and Mao Zedong began to fade, the Little Red Book lost its revered status in the hearts and minds of Indian Maoist intellectuals. Charu Majumdar was arrested on July 16, 1972, and he died ten days later in police custody, under mysterious circumstances. The Majumdar era was over.

The Little Red Book was formally banned in India in 1975, but even prior to that those who merely owned the book were harassed by the police, especially in the city of Calcutta. Many activists or suspected activists had their houses raided by the police looking for copies of Mao's *Quotations* and other "incriminating" documents. By the late 1970s, due to various domestic and international factors, the Naxalite Movement had become more or less dormant. The ban on the Little Red Book continues today, but those who possess copies of it are no longer secretive about it. This latter fact is somewhat surprising, since the Naxalite Movement has reemerged after more than two decades of quiescence and is today considered by some to be a greater threat to India's internal security than cross-border terrorism. Reportedly twelve of India's twenty-eight states have come under Naxalite influence in varying degrees, and periodic incidents of violence between insurgents and security personnel have brought death and destruction on both sides.

However, the Naxalite Movement is no longer a peasant revolution led by the so-called petty-bourgeois intellectuals, but an insurrection of tribal locals whose livelihood has been compromised by the Indian state due to liberalization and globalization. There is an ongoing debate whether Maoism in India today should be viewed as a social problem or as a law-and-order issue. Many, including this author, believe that the so-called Maoist movement is now devoid of specifically Maoist characteristics.[27] What is clear is that Maoist ideology itself, as represented by its vector the Little Red Book, is no longer considered a fearsome weapon on its own.

Conclusion

The popularity of the Little Red Book peaked in the period 1969–72. Its readers included members of the Naxalite Movement, as well as its sympathizers and not a few curious observers. Of the latter two groups,

---

[27] Recent works on the reemerged Maoist/Naxalite movement include: Bidyut Chakraborty and Rajat Kumar Kujur, *Maoism in India: Re-incarnation of Ultra-left wing Extremism in the 21st Century* (Oxford and New York: Routledge Contemporary Asia Series, 2010); Santosh Paul, *The Maoist Movement in India: Perspectives and Counter-Perspectives* (New Delhi: Routledge India, 2012); and Nirmalangshu Mukherjee, *The Maoists in India: Tribals Under Siege* (London: Pluto Press, 2012).

nearly all were educated – mostly college and university students – and from middle-class or affluent backgrounds. The Little Red Book played an important role in the radicalization of reasonably large numbers of urban students and intellectuals in the late 1960s. Classes for ideological indoctrination at that time included the writings of Marx, Engels, Lenin, and Stalin, but Mao's *Quotations* had a special kind of appeal due to the proximity and supposed similarity of China, and because Mao was projected as the charismatic chairman of India's most ardent, anti-revisionist Marxist–Leninists. According to some former Naxalites, Charu Majumdar was solely responsible for the propagation of the cult of Mao, the elevation of the Little Red Book to the status of relic, and the overly mechanical application of the Chinese model to India. As a result, some blame him for the precipitous decline of the movement in Bengal in the early 1970s.

Integrating the views of former Naxalites, the problem with the Little Red Book is clear: it encapsulates thought without context. First, the historical context of revolution in India was quite different. In China, the Little Red Book was used to mobilize social forces against the entrench-ment of a ruling communist party; in India, the Maoists were a minor faction within a minor faction of a minority party. Second, the textual context was absent. In China, the Little Red Book was a pocket reference to a much larger and well-known corpus of works; in India, it became an inadequate substitute for systematic ideological indoctrination. Mao's ideological vigor comes out in his long essays and speeches (which form part of his selected works) and not from a few loose quotations. Third, the philosophical content without context could not be translated into meaningful action. The Little Red Book reduced Maoism to a derivative and inert system of thought, rather than a creative and vibrant system of thinking, ready to be put to use in new situations. As one former Naxalite activist put it, the "revolutionary" exercise of reading and recitation was at best symbolic.

BIBLIOGRAPHY

Bannerjee, Sumanta, *In the Wake of Naxalbari* (Calcutta: Subarnarekha, 1980)
Chakrabarti, Sreemati, *China and the Naxalites* (New Delhi and London: Radiant Publishers and Sangam Books, 1990)
    "From Radical Politics to Liberal Economics: China as a Model," in S. Narsimhan and G. Balatchandirane, eds., *India and East Asia: Learning from Each Other* (Delhi: Manak, 2004), pp. 505–19
Chakraborty, Bidyut, and Rajat Kumar Kujur, *Maoism in India: Re-incarnation of Ultra-left wing Extremism in the 21st Century*, Routledge Contemporary Asia Series (Oxford and New York: Routledge, 2010)

Dasgupta, Biplab, *The Naxalite Movement* (Bombay: Allied Publishers, 1974)

Dhanagre, D. N., "Peasant Protest and Politics: The Tebhaga Movement in Bengal, 1946–47," *Journal of Peasant Studies* 3.3 (1976), pp. 360–78

Jawaid, Sohail, *The Naxalite Movement in India* (New Delhi: Associated Publishing House, 1974)

Mazumdar, Asok, *The Tebhaga Movement: Politics of Peasant Protest in Bengal, 1946–50* (Delhi: Aakar Books, 1993)

Mohanty, Manoranjan, *Revolutionary Violence* (New Delhi: Sterling, 1977)

Mukherjee, Nirmalangshu, *The Maoists in India: Tribals Under Siege* (London: Pluto Press, 2012)

Paul, Santosh, *The Maoist Movement in India: Perspectives and Counter-Perspectives* (New Delhi: Routledge India, 2012)

Ram, Mohan, *Indian Communism: Split Within a Split* (Delhi: Vikas Publications, 1969)

Ram, Mohan, *Maoism in India* (New Delhi: Vikas Publications, 1971)

Sengupta, Bhabani, *Communism in Indian Politics* (New Delhi and Stockholm: Young Asia Publications, 1978)

Simeon, Dilip, "Glory Days," in Ira Pande, ed., *India China Neighbours Strangers* (New Delhi: Harper Collins Publishers India with India Today Group and India International Centre, 2010), pp. 438–45

8   The influence of Maoism in Peru

David Scott Palmer

The revolutionary war is a war of the masses; only mobilizing the masses and relying on them can wage it.

People's War

Peru's Maoist guerrilla movement, known as Shining Path, was far and away the most radical and violent in Latin America. The group's founder and leader, Abimael Guzmán Reynoso, claimed to be a devoted Maoist and a faithful interpreter of Mao Zedong's ideology, strategy, and tactics as he directed a people's war based largely in rural, impoverished, and predominantly indigenous areas of Peru between 1980 and his capture in 1992.

However, Guzmán was trained in China as a potential Third World guerrilla during several extended visits beginning just before the Cultural Revolution (1966–76) and continuing during it, as were several other members of his organization.[1] As a result, he and other Shining Path central committee members were much more influenced by the post-revolutionary ideological dogmatism of the Gang of Four than by *Quotations from Chairman Mao*, also known as the Little Red Book, or Mao's reflections on the course of the Chinese revolution itself. However, by 1976 the Gang of Four had lost its struggle for political control in China, which meant that Shining Path was cast adrift and left to fend for itself.

This experience led Guzmán to conclude that revisionist forces had betrayed the communist revolution in China, as had occurred earlier in the Soviet Union. Therefore, he concluded, the only route to a true

The original paper from which this chapter emerged was presented at the Little Red Book: A Global History conference sponsored by the Center for Chinese Studies and the Institute of East Asian Studies at the University of California, Berkeley, October 21–22, 2011. The conference presentations and discussions assisted greatly in the preparation of the final manuscript for this chapter, as did the extensive comments by Professor Cook on the penultimate draft. The author is grateful for the invitation to participate in this project, as well as to Boston University graduate assistant Kaitlin Dinota for her tireless efforts to track down important references.

[1] Gustavo Gorriti, "Shining Path's Stalin and Trotsky," in David Scott Palmer, ed., *Shining Path of Peru*, 2nd edn. (New York: St. Martin's Press, 1994), pp. 156–58.

communist revolution was for him to direct a people's war that maintained the purity of its ideology at all times.[2] His vision was that by
waging such a properly conceived war in Peru, he would provide a model
for a new generation of guerrilla struggles that remained faithful to core
Marxist–Leninist–Maoist principles, unlike what had occurred in the
Soviet Union, Cuba, or China.

Guzmán's attraction to ideology was furthered by his background as a
provincial university academic steeped in a detailed reading of Marxist–
Leninist theory originally passed on by his mentors during his undergraduate days at the public university in Arequipa, a major city in the
south of Peru. He was also a product of his country's Spanish culture,
dominant since colonial times over the historically much larger Indian
population. Until he arrived in the indigenous highlands provincial capital of Ayacucho for his first teaching position in 1962, he had had little
contact with that component of Peruvian society.[3]

Such experiences – growing up in a Spanish-speaking milieu and becoming a committed Marxist–Leninist during his university days – contributed
to his insistence on defining Peruvian rural reality exclusively in the more
abstract class terms of landlord and peasant rather than on ethnic grounds
of mestizo and Indian, even though the latter reflected highland Peru much
more accurately. A class-based ideological perspective resonated among
many university faculty and students in Peru during the 1960s and 1970s, as
elsewhere during the ascendency of Marxism among scholars, which contributed to the formation of a significant band of committed supporters.
However, it proved to be much less convincing to Peru's indigenous peasantry, supposedly the principal beneficiaries of a Maoist revolution.[4]

All of these experiences influenced Guzmán as he moved from an
extended period of organization building, going back to the early 1960s
from his base as a professor of education at Ayacucho's recently
reopened University of San Cristóbal de Huamanga, to beginning preparations in 1977 for a full-scale, protracted guerrilla war. Although
multiple factors influenced the course of the war after its formal launching in May 1980, as we shall see, Guzmán's insistence on ideological
purity was a constant from beginning to end and, in the final analysis, a
major reason for Shining Path's ultimate failure.

---

[2] Gustavo Gorriti Ellenbogen, *Sendero: Historia de la guerra milenaria en el Perú* (Lima:
Editorial Apoyo, 1990), pp. 60 ff.
[3] Abimael Guzmán, "Exclusive Comments by Abimael Guzmán," *World Affairs* 156.1
(Summer 1993), pp. 53–54. From *Sí* (Lima), February 8, 1993, reprinted from
Foreign Broadcast Information Service, Latin America, February 25, 1993.
[4] Carlos Iván Degregori, *Ayacucho 1969–1979: El surgimiento de Sendero Luminoso* (Lima:
Instituto de Estudios Peruanos, 1990), pp. 69–79.

Explaining Shining Path's emergence

Shining Path was born and evolved in Peru in a context that was more often than not favorable to the development of Marxist groups generally, and Maoism in particular. In fact, between the Sino-Soviet split in early 1963 and the development of a full-blown people's war led by Shining Path in the 1980s, Peru became the Latin American country with the largest Maoist-oriented communist movement.[5]

A variety of factors, some more general and some Peru-specific, help to explain this rather fascinating phenomenon. One of the regional influences was a particularly receptive context for Marxist alternatives in the aftermath of the success of the Cuban revolution in 1959 and Fidel Castro's post-Bay of Pigs declaration in 1961 that he was a Marxist–Leninist and always would be. A second important contributing element was the formulation of both Marxist and non-Marxist dependency theory within Latin American intellectual circles in the 1960s and 1970s as a comprehensive explanation for capitalist under-development in the region.[6] Although Maoism was not explicitly linked to these dependency theories, it did come to be seen as a left ideological alternative that was also capable of bringing to an end the longstanding externally imposed capitalist dominance in Latin America and the Third World.

As for considerations favorable to the rise of Maoism in Peru itself, one was a socioeconomic reality of a large rural peasantry which comprised over 40 percent of the country's total population. It was overwhelmingly indigenous, lived in extreme poverty, and was concentrated in the Andean highlands, or sierra.[7] Another was the presence of a large and longstanding non-Marxist left party dating from the 1920s, the American Popular Revolutionary Alliance (APRA, Alianza Popular Revolucionaria Americana), which had moved to the right in the late 1950s in a bid to come to power, thereby leaving open significant political space on the left for others to occupy.[8] In addition, the first democratically elected

---

[5] Gorriti, "Shining Path's Stalin and Trotsky," p. 175; Maritza Paredes, "Indigenous Politics and the Legacy of the Left," in John Crabtree, ed., *Fractured Politics: Peruvian Democracy Past and Present* (London: Institute for the Study of the Americas, University of London, 2011), p. 137.

[6] A major example of Marxist dependency analysis is André Gunder Frank, *Capitalism and Underdevelopment in Latin America* (New York: Monthly Review Press, 1969); for a non-Marxist alternative, see Fernando Henrique Cardoso and Enzo Faletto, *Dependency and Development in Latin America* (Berkeley: University of California Press, 1979).

[7] José Matos Mar and José Manuel Mejía, *La Reforma Agraria en el Perú*, Perú Problema 19 (Lima: Instituto de Estudios Peruanos, 1980), pp. 16–50.

[8] Carol Graham, *Peru's APRA: Parties, Politics, and the Elusive Quest for Democracy* (Boulder: Lynne Rienner, 1992), pp. 34–35.

government of President Fernando Belaúnde Terry (1963–68) was a left-tolerant one which enabled a variety of Marxist parties, Moscow-, Peking-, and Havana-oriented, to organize and expand during his years in office.[9]

The most important Peru-specific factor, however, was the self-titled Revolutionary Military Government (RMG – 1968–80) which deposed President Belaúnde in a bloodless coup and attempted to transform the country through a set of major social, political, and economic reforms.[10] Over the course of its twelve years in power, but particularly until 1975, it pursued significant structural changes which reduced the power of traditional actors, including large landowners, foreign corporations, and APRA, while actively encouraging Marxist organizations and individual leaders to become involved in its reformist project.[11]

Rise of the Marxist left as a major electoral and union force

Although the RMG failed rather spectacularly in its goals of effecting transformative change and stimulating grassroots participation while simultaneously controlling both from above, it also served to legitimize a large, diverse, and predominantly Marxist left. When the military decided to get out of power and agreed to allow elections in 1978 for a constitutional assembly, a variety of Marxist–Leninist and Maoist parties, along with two non-Marxist left groups, won 33 percent of the vote between them (Marxists 23 percent, others 10 percent), second only to APRA with 35 percent.[12]

The resulting constitution of 1979, which included universal suffrage for the first time, brought forth a full return to democracy at the national level in July 1980. Beginning with the November 1980 municipal elections, and continuing through elections at both the national and local levels for the rest of the decade, most of these moderate and far-left parties formed a loose coalition, the United Left (IU, Izquierda Unida), and achieved significant electoral success. In fact, until breaking apart over ideological and tactical differences in 1989, just as the IU appeared

---

[9] Jane Jaquette, *The Politics of Development in Peru*, Dissertation Series 33 (Ithaca: Latin American Studies Program, Cornell University, 1971).

[10] Abraham Lowenthal, ed., *The Peruvian Experiment: Continuity and Change under Military Rule* (Princeton: Princeton University Press, 1975).

[11] David Scott Palmer, *Peru: The Authoritarian Tradition* (New York: Praeger, 1980).

[12] Howard Handelman, "Peru: The March to Civilian Rule," *American Universities Field Staff Reports*, South America 2 (1980), p. 12.

to be in the best position to win the presidential elections of 1990, it was the second most popular electoral force in Peru.[13]

What such apparent unity and demonstrated electoral capacity had disguised in hindsight were the large number of ideological perspectives, leadership disputes, and different sources of outside support among the Marxist parties and factions. These issues made the IU a very fragile coalition in practice that could not be sustained at a critical juncture in its history. The challenge the IU faced is demonstrated by the variety of political groups it comprised. One was Peru's Soviet Union-oriented Communist Party, established in the 1930s. Another was a Trotskyist movement dating from farm invasions in the late 1950s and early 1960s led by Hugo Blanco.[14] A third was a loose coalition of Maoist and Cuba-oriented parties that had blossomed in the 1960s and early 1970s.[15] Whenever they were established, however, this wide array of Marxist left parties and factions grew substantially over the course of the reformist military government after it took power in 1968.

The labor movement also expanded at a rapid rate during the military regime, with RMG-favored Marxist organizations significantly increasing their numbers at the expense of the unions historically under APRA's control. By 1977, the Communist Party-affiliated union had three times the number of members as APRA's previously dominant workers' confederation, mostly drawn from the manufacturing sector.[16] In addition, the influential miners' union, in a sector accounting for over half of Peru's exports, shifted from APRA to Maoist control over the course of the 1970s. During the same period, about a third of Peru's 360,000 teachers affiliated with a Maoist union, a group which became closely identified with Shining Path.[17] In the countryside, a military-government-founded and -supported peasant federation increasingly competed with a Maoist alternative as well.[18] One result of the growing

---

[13] William A. Hazleton and Sandra Woy-Hazleton, "Terrorism and the Marxist Left: Peru's Struggle against Sendero Luminoso," *Terrorism* 11 (1988), p. 471.

[14] Hugo Blanco, *Luchas campesinas de la Convención y Lares – Chaupimayo – Quillabamba* (Lima: n.p., 1987).

[15] Hazleton and Woy-Hazleton, "Terrorism," pp. 472–75, 477–80; Lewis Taylor, *Maoism in the Andes: Sendero Luminoso and the Contemporary Guerrilla Movement in Peru*, Working Paper 2, Centre for Latin American Studies (Liverpool: University of Liverpool, 1983), p. 7.

[16] Evelyne Huber Stephens, "The Peruvian Military Government, Labor Mobilization, and the Political Strength of the Left," *Latin American Research Review* 18:2 (1983), p. 72.

[17] The origins of SUTEP (Sindicato Único de Trabajadores Educativos del Perú [Sole Union of Education Workers of Peru]) in teacher protests in Ayacucho in the late 1960s and early 1970s are described in detail in Degregori, *Ayacucho 1969–1979*, pp. 49–79.

[18] Handelman, "March to Civilian Rule," p. 8; Susan Bourque and David Scott Palmer, "Transforming the Rural Sector: Government Policy and Peasant Response," in Lowenthal, ed., *Peruvian Experiment*, pp. 179–219.

influence of Marxist and Maoist leaders, in combination with worsening economic conditions during the final years of military rule, was a dramatic increase in worker strikes in 1977 and 1978.[19]

The growing numbers, organizational capacity, and mobilization of the Marxist and Maoist left during the 1970s, in combination with increasing discontent over economic problems, led the most militant among them to conclude that Peru was experiencing a "pre-revolutionary" situation.[20] At the same time, however, such relative successes masked a fundamental underlying ideological disagreement among the various left parties and factions, dating back to the 1960s, over whether or not objective conditions in Peru were favorable for revolution or people's war. This disagreement, combined with differences related to doctrinal origins across the left ideological spectrum – ranging from traditional Marxism–Leninism to Trotskyism to Maoism, disputes over whether control should be centralized or localized, and to personality conflicts among leadership, provoked multiple fissures and party splits. They generated over time a veritable alphabet soup of parties, factions, and sub-groups.[21]

Even so, when an electoral opportunity finally presented itself in 1978 with the constitutional convention, fully fifteen years after the last national elections, virtually all of the left parties and factions opted to participate in the process – and achieved unexpected success. Even though their multiple differences remained, they were able to form a working electoral coalition under the banner of the IU and to maintain their status as a major political force at both the national and local levels for more than a decade.[22] Only in 1989, in the midst of Peru's worst economic crisis in over a century and growing political violence, did the longstanding differences over the role of force and guerrilla warfare provoke a breakup of the IU left coalition.[23] This marked the beginning of a decline in the electoral capacity of the left that has continued to the present, most particularly at the national level.

Shining Path's shift from organization to action

One faction of the far left, however, rejected from the outset an electoral route to power. After the 1963–64 Sino-Soviet split, the pro-Chinese offshoot had defined Peruvian society as "semi-feudal" and

---

[19] Stephens, "Peruvian Military," p. 75.   [20] Taylor, *Maoism in the Andes*, p. 6.
[21] Ibid.   [22] Hazleton and Woy-Hazleton, "Terrorism."
[23] Sandra Woy-Hazleton and William A. Hazleton, "Sendero Luminoso and the Future of Peruvian Democracy," *Third World Quarterly* 12.2 (April 1990), pp. 25–26.

"neo-colonial" in line with both Mao's characterization of pre-1949 China and Peruvian Marxist José Carlos Mariátegui's depiction of his country in similar terms in the 1920s.[24] It followed, then, their members argued, that Peru's own revolution would originate in the countryside, gain control there, and eventually encircle the cities and cause their collapse.[25]

A dispute between the pro-Chinese offshoot leader Saturnino Paredes, former legal advisor to the Maoist peasant confederation, and several of his lieutenants in the sierra over how best to build a capacity to wage revolutionary warfare provoked the first schism in Peruvian Maoism in 1967, followed three years later by the departure of the group's most radical elements, led by Professor Guzmán in Ayacucho.[26] Already well known in Maoist circles as an adherent of Mao's "Gang of Four," Guzmán organized Shining Path, named in homage to Mariátegui's shining path of revolution statement,[27] to prepare for a people's war in Peru. Over time, after well over a decade of preparation, Shining Path was to become the dominant and most consistently radical organization on the left, pursuing a defiantly Maoist path to guerrilla war that was based on its leader's interpretation of Mao's ideology, strategy, and tactics.

By virtue of his teaching position at the University of Huamanga in Ayacucho, one of Peru's poorest and most indigenous departments, Guzmán built an organization there to respond to what he perceived as conditions replicating those of pre-revolutionary rural China.[28] In his positions at the university as director of the teacher training school in the 1960s and as general secretary in the early 1970s, he slowly built up a cadre of supporters among rural teachers, university faculty, and a university student movement.

In this first phase of his revolutionary strategy, agitation and propaganda, Guzmán also developed a base of student and faculty support in several other Peruvian public universities in Lima and a number of sierra

---

[24] Alexander Cook, "Third World Maoism," in Timothy Cheek, ed., *Critical Introduction to Mao* (New York: Cambridge University Press, 2010), p. 305.

[25] Thomas A. Marks, "Making Revolution with Shining Path," in Palmer, ed., *Shining Path*, p. 211.

[26] Mario Fumerton, *From Victims to Heroes: Peasant Counter-Rebellion and Civil War in Ayacucho, Peru, 1980–2000* (Amsterdam: Thela Publishers, 2002), p. 37.

[27] José Carlos Mariátegui, *Seven Interpretive Essays on Peruvian Reality* (Austin: University of Texas Press, 1971), translated from *Siete ensayos de interpretación de la realidad peruana* (Lima: Amauta, 1928).

[28] Antonio Díaz Martínez, *Ayacucho: Hambre y esperanza* (Ayacucho: Ediciones Waman Puma, 1974). Díaz Martínez, a colleague of Guzmán's at the University of Huamanga, built much of his Maoist-focused analysis around the undergraduate theses of his students, whom he sent out for field research across the rural sierra of Ayacucho and then helped to recruit for Shining Path.

department cities, including Huancayo and Cajamarca. Between 1970 and 1977, Shining Path had considerable success in constructing a student organization and regional committee-based party in the central sierra and Lima through intensive indoctrination. The most charismatic central committee members of his party, including Guzmán (now known as Comrade or President Gonzalo or Puka Inti: "Red Sun" in Quechua) and then-key lieutenant Luis Kawata Macabe, assumed the task of indoctrination of potential supporters.[29]

From 1977 to 1980, when it was clear that Shining Path's separation from China was complete, Guzmán concentrated on preparations for revolution in Peru under his direction. As he moved forward with the second phase, building a political and military organization to initiate the armed struggle, he focused on setting up training-camps in Ayacucho and recruiting from other Marxist parties and factions members who favored his more radical approach.[30] Between March and May 1980, an extended debate at the meeting of the central committee concluded that the party and its military apparatus had been sufficiently reconstructed. The revolutionary Rubicon was crossed with the decision to carry out intensive ideological indoctrination at Shining Path's first military school in final preparation for the people's war.[31]

The first armed actions of Shining Path took place on May 17, 1980, the evening before Peru's first presidential elections in seventeen years, with the burning of ballot boxes in the remote sierra district capital of Chuschi, Ayacucho.[32] This did not appear to be a propitious moment to begin the people's war, since it occurred just as illiterates had been given the right to vote and at a historic political juncture when Marxist and Maoist parties could freely participate in electoral politics for the first time. Nevertheless, over the course of the next decade, a combination of Shining Path's systematic campaign of violence, terror, and destruction and Peruvian government ineptitude in both counterinsurgency and governance brought the country to its knees.[33]

The result was the progressive creation of the objective conditions favorable for revolution that had not been present at the outset of the

---

[29] Taylor, *Maoism in the Andes*, pp. 9–10; Gorriti, "Shining Path's Stalin and Trotsky," pp. 176–78.
[30] Taylor, *Maoism in the Andes*, pp. 10–13.   [31] Gorriti Ellenbogen, *Sendero*, pp. 49–68.
[32] David Scott Palmer, "Rebellion in Rural Peru: The Origins and Evolution of Sendero Luminoso," *Comparative Politics* 18.2 (January 1986), p. 129; Gorriti Ellenbogen, *Sendero*, pp. 43–47.
[33] David Scott Palmer, "Terror in the Name of Mao: Revolution and Response in Peru," in Robert J. Art and Linda Richardson, eds., *Democracy and Counterterrorism: Lessons from the Past* (Washington, D.C.: US Institute of Peace Press, 2007), pp. 195–219.

people's war. These served to justify Guzmán's decision to launch Shining Path on its people's war when he did, and to bolster his confidence that he was pursuing the correct interpretation of Maoist ideology, strategy, and tactics in the quest for power and creation of the so-called "New Democracy." By the early 1990s, over 50,000 Peruvians had been killed and some 600,000 internal refugees had been created, along with over a million émigrés as a result of what had become generalized political violence, with more than $14 billion in infrastructure destroyed as well.[34] The insurgents, following Mao's guerrilla war progression, claimed that their struggle had passed from the defensive "war of guerrillas" during the 1980s to a "strategic equilibrium" by 1991[35] and to the "final offensive" stage by mid-1992.

Explaining Shining Path's failure on the brink of success

Yet just as Shining Path was poised for victory, the people's war failed in dramatic fashion. Much of the explanation for this outcome may be attributed to the ability of the Peruvian government, beginning in 1989, to make significant adjustments in its counterrevolutionary strategy and tactics. These included the creation of a special police task force to track Shining Path leadership and a new approach by the military to reduce indiscriminate violence and to pursue "hearts and minds" tactics to regain popular support.[36] Another component of the significant alteration in the army's approach to the guerrilla war, after years of resistance, was the beginning in 1991 of a program to train and provide some weapons to local peasant militias, or *rondas campesinas*, which had been struggling for several years on their own to resist Sendero incursions with spears, stones from slingshots, and a few old muskets and shotguns.[37] Central government's changed approach in the early 1990s also included a major micro-development program to reduce poverty and increase central government presence in Peru's poorest districts, most of which had been profoundly affected by the

---

[34] Ibid., p. 211.

[35] Abimael Guzmán Reynoso, "¡Que el equilibrio estratégico remezca más el país! (Gran culminación de la III campaña de impulsar)," unpublished typescript, November 1991.

[36] Benigno Jiménez Bacca, *Inicio, desarrollo, y ocaso del terrorismo en el Perú*, vols. I–III (Lima: Editorial SANKI, 2000); Carlos Tapia, *Las Fuerzas Armadas y Sendero Luminoso: Dos estrategias y un final* (Lima: Instituto de Estudios Peruanos, 1997).

[37] Carlos Iván Degregori, "Harvesting Storms: Peasant Rondas and the Defeat of Sendero Luminoso in Ayacucho," in Steve J. Stern, ed., *Shining and Other Paths: War and Society in Peru, 1980–1995* (Durham: Duke University Press, 1998), pp. 131–40; Orin Starn, ed., *Hablan los ronderos: La búsqueda por la paz en los Andes*, Documento de Trabajo 45 (Lima: Instituto de Estudios Peruanos, 1993), pp. 11–28.

violence.[38] Along with these significant measures, a 1993 "repentance law" aimed with considerable success to encourage guerrilla defections with the promise of reincorporation into society.[39]

Shining Path's collapse also resulted from its own mistakes. One was the increasing employment by its cadres of intimidation and terrorism as they attempted to maintain control over the peasantry in the name of imposing the new "generated organisms" of democratic centralism at the core of the New Democracy. In the quest for purity, Guzmán and his central committee pursued ideological correctness over adaptation to local circumstances and practices, including indigenous customs and traditions. Illustrative of such ideological blindness is the complete absence in any of Guzmán's statements or Shining Path tracts of references to ethnicity, such as indigenous or Indian, and an insistence on using the class-based term peasants. Other examples include prohibiting such longstanding indigenous practices as community markets, communal administrative divisions, or *ayllu*s, and selection of traditional authorities, known as *varayoq*s. In so doing, they completely disregarded a core principle of Mao's revolutionary tactics to win and retain peasant support.[40] As the military shifted its counterinsurgency approach though, however belatedly, peasants previously under the repressive thumb of Shining Path began once again to turn to the government for protection and support.

A second error derived from Guzmán's creation of a cult of personality around himself almost from the beginning as the founder, organizer, and purveyor of the correct ideological line of the party, as he followed what he erroneously interpreted to have been Mao's own approach to leadership.[41] Unlike Mao, who built a cult of personality through the Little Red Book and official propaganda to consolidate his control only after the armed revolution had succeeded, Guzmán pursued his own cult from the beginning of the guerrilla struggle itself. Among the devices he used to promote his own central role were posters portraying him as a

---

[38] David Scott Palmer, "FONCODES y su impacto en la pacificación en el Perú: Observaciones generales y el caso de Ayacucho," in Fondo Nacional de Compensación y Desarrollo Nacional (FONCODES), *Concertando para el desarrollo: Lecciones aprendidas del FONCODES en sus estrategias de intervención* (Lima: Gráfica Medelius, 2001), pp. 147–77.

[39] Tapia, *Fuerzas Armadas*, pp. 133–52.

[40] "To link oneself with the masses, one must act in accordance with the needs and wishes of the masses": Mao Tse-Tung, *Quotations from Chairman Mao Tse-Tung* (Peking: Foreign Languages Press, 1966), p. 124.

[41] Guzmán articulated his rationale for a cult of personality in an interview reported verbatim by Luis Borja Arce and Janet Talavera Sánchez, "La entrevista del siglo: El Presidente Gonzalo rompe el silencio," *El Diario* (Lima) (July 24, 1988), pp. 2–48.

bespectacled academic above scenes of violence holding a book of Gonzalo thought. Others showed armed villagers with red armbands amidst indigenous sacred symbols of high mountain peaks and the red sun. And wall graffiti portraying the hammer and sickle and slogans such as "Long live President Gonzalo" became ubiquitous across the communities of the sierra and in many urban areas as well. It is clear that Guzmán concluded that only he was ultimately capable of leading the guerrilla struggle, and that it was important to use every device possible to convey an image of the inevitability of revolutionary success under his direct control. At the same time, for years he remained an elusive figure, rarely seen in public or heard from directly, but with the symbols of his presence in posters and graffiti visible throughout the region. Such personal image cultivation, which acquired almost mythological proportions, helped Guzmán to achieve a variety of goals, including the mobilization of popular support, demonstration of superiority over rivals in the party, and solidification of his role as the sole legitimate interpreter and synthesizer of what he called "Marxist–Leninist–Maoist–Mariateguist–Gonzalo Thought." It is also the case, however, that such patterns of messianic political leadership are common features of Latin American politics, making Guzmán one more example of such a tendency. By making himself indispensable, he created over the course of almost three decades a hydrocephalic revolutionary organization which he justified on the grounds that he was following Mao's own approach – mistaken as that was. The top-heavy guerrilla organization dominated by a single leader is a major reason why Peru's people's war could not survive Guzmán's capture by the specialized leadership-tracking police unit on September 12, 1992 (along with several other members of Shining Path's central committee).[42]

Third, Guzmán's decision to take the people's war to the cities in 1989, particularly the capital city, Lima, turned out to be a major strategic error, even though it sowed havoc for a time with bombings of banks, hotels, embassies, and other targets in the middle- and upper-class suburbs. Food supplies, electricity, and water from the sierra were regularly cut off. Early successes in this application of the Maoist model created a growing sense of confidence, bordering on hubris, that victory was at hand, and contributed to an acceleration of the timetable for the "final offensive" that was to begin in October 1992 and culminate with victory by the anniversary of Mao's birthday on December 26.[43]

[42] Jiménez Bacca, *Terrorismo en el Perú*, vol. I.

[43] Carlos Iván Degregori, "After the Fall of Abimael Guzmán: The Limits of Sendero Luminoso," in Maxwell A. Cameron and Philip Mauceri, eds., *The Peruvian*

What Guzmán failed to consider, however, was that bringing the war to the cities, where the government intelligence apparatus was on much more familiar territory and where popular support was much more limited, served to galvanize citizenry and government alike, and to redouble official efforts to thwart Shining Path's further advance.[44] His commitment to the Maoist model and sequencing for revolutionary success appears to have blinded him to the differences between Chinese and Peruvian realities, where there was no foreign enemy to make common cause and where Shining Path lacked the logistical capacity it had shown in the sierra. For all intents and purposes, in bringing the guerrilla war to Lima, Shining Path became a fish out of water, violating one of Mao's basic tenets.[45]

A final factor in Shining Path's defeat was President Gonzalo's obsession with ensuring that the people's war in Peru follow the same Maoist ideology, strategy, and tactics that had produced success in the Chinese revolution. Guzmán had an extraordinary capacity throughout his career to see all reality through ideological lenses, from Stalinism as a university student,[46] which he still revered, even after his capture,[47] to Marxism–Leninism, Maoism, and so-called Gonzalo thought drawn from Peruvian Communist Party founder José Carlos Mariátegui. Even though Peru in the 1970s and 1980s bore little resemblance either to China in the 1930s or to Peru as described by Mariátegui in the 1920s, Guzmán insisted on a literal extrapolation of Marxism–Leninism–Maoism–Gonzalo thought to justify his people's war.

As a teacher and interpreter of such ideological dogma, he determined through extended and turgid written analyses that the people's war in Peru was advancing through the phases originally articulated by Mao, and that these interpretations were, therefore, scientific and inevitable. His 1988 interview,[48] 1991 typescript,[49] and 2009 book-length musings from prison[50] all reflect his obsession with ideological purity and its applicability to Peruvian reality, however at variance his interpretation of that reality was from Peru's actual social, economic, and political situation at the time.

Labyrinth: Polity, Society, Economy (University Park: Pennsylvania State University Press, 1997), pp. 179–91.

[44] Tapia, *Fuerzas Armadas*, pp. 133–52.

[45] This insight is drawn from comments by Alexander Cook on an earlier version of this chapter.

[46] Gorriti, "Shining Path's Stalin and Trotsky," pp. 167–88.

[47] Guzmán Reynoso, "Exclusive Comments."

[48] Borje Arce and Talavera Sánchez, "Entrevista del siglo."

[49] Guzmán Reynoso, "Equilibrio estratégico."

[50] Abimael Guzmán Reynoso, *De puño y letra* (Lima: Manoalzada, 2009).

Unlike China from the 1920s through the 1940s, Peru's agrarian reform in the late 1960s and early 1970s had already all but eliminated large landlords. Indigenous communities of various ethnic and historical origins rather than private holdings predominated in most of the Peruvian sierra. There was no foreign occupation or devastation from war in Peru; on the contrary, rapid economic growth and social change from the 1940s forward contributed to significant urbanization, education, and expanded communications. In addition, political repression was uncommon; on the contrary, political parties and unions spanned the left–right spectrum and participated in a context of universal suffrage and full democracy at both the national and local levels beginning in 1980. Ideology drove the people's war in Peru irrespective of reality, and in so doing made a mockery of Mao's conceptualization and practice.

After so much violence and destruction over more than a decade (final revised estimates drawn from more detailed research in the most isolated parts of the sierra, especially in Ayacucho, put total deaths at over 69,000 and destroyed infrastructure at $24 billion),[51] Guzmán's capture produced a popular euphoria unmatched in Peru's modern history.[52] One can only speculate as to whether or not the outcome might have been different had Shining Path's leader paid more attention to the broad strokes of the Little Red Book and adapted some of its ideas and approaches to the specific reality of highland Peru rather than insisting on ideological purity in conducting his guerrilla campaign. While appealing to the educated Spanish speakers who made up the entire central committee and most of the mid-level cadre of Shining Path, such doctrinal-based appeals and applications failed to retain popular support among the largely indigenous peasantry of the sierra, in large measure because they were so at odds with their own traditions and experiences. In the final analysis, as Mao noted, "The revolutionary war is a war of the masses; only mobilizing the masses and relying on them can wage it."[53]

Shining Path's legacy in Peru

Since the dismantling of Shining Path during the years immediately following the capture of its founder and dominant leader, Peru has

---

[51] Comisión de la Verdad y Reconciliación (CVR), *Informe final, Tomo I, Primera parte: El proceso, los hechos, las víctimas* (Lima: Editorial Navarrete, 2003).

[52] The author was in Lima on several occasions in 1992 and can confirm from personal observation the popular transformation from general despair in July, when explosions, blackouts, and significant civilian casualties were rocking the city and demoralizing its six million inhabitants, and October, when everyone was celebrating, if somewhat prematurely, the end of Shining Path and the violence Guzmán had spawned.

[53] Mao, *Quotations*, p. 88.

recovered in many ways from the generalized violence produced by Guzmán's mechanical application of Maoism. There has been sustained economic growth for several years, and democratic procedures and practices appear to be well ensconced at both the national and local levels. However, the human cost of Shining Path's systematic destruction of local traditions and ways of life, especially in the Ayacucho sierra where indigenous communities continue to dominate the countryside, remains the principal legacy of his Maoist-inspired people's war. Given this continuing challenge in the sierra, especially in Ayacucho, it is disappointing that central government has remained reluctant until recently to respond more effectively to the need there to foster reconciliation through individual reparations and exhumation of the hundreds of mass graves to help to bring closure to family members still grieving the loss of their loved ones.[54]

In addition, the Peruvian army has to date been ineffective in dealing with a residual group of Shining Path militants, perhaps 450 strong, which continues to operate in the isolated jungle valleys of the Apurímac, Ene, and Mantaro rivers in south–central Peru and continues to proclaim the legitimacy of the armed struggle in Mao's name. Also present is a totally separate organization which continues to identify with Maoist and Gonzalo thought, the Amnesty and Fundamental Rights Movement (MOVADEF, Movimiento de Amnestía y Derechos Fundamentales), which is attempting to insert itself into Peru's political system through popular protest and signature gathering to become a recognized political party.[55] It is supported by the Maoist-dominated teachers' union SUTEP, long known for its militancy and opposition to Peruvian education ministry efforts to carry out moderate public education reforms.

These groups that continue to identify with Maoism, one continuing to engage in violence and one trying to operate openly in the political arena, do not represent a threat to the Peruvian state today. However, their actions do have ongoing effects on the government's ability to manage public policy in such critical areas as foreign investment, education, and cocaine production and trafficking. Furthermore, central

---

[54] Enrique Chávez, "Las fosas que no cicatrizan," *Caretas* (Lima) (July 10, 2008), pp. 34–37; José Coronel, UNICEF regional representative and former regional director, Peruvian Truth and Reconciliation Commission, interview by the author, Ayacucho, Peru, August 16 and 17, 2010. He estimates that there were as of mid 2010 at least 15,000 individuals in this situation in the Department of Ayacucho alone, and quite likely many more who had not yet come forward.

[55] David Scott Palmer and Alberto Bolívar, "Peru's Shining Path: Recent Dynamics and Future Prospects," Western Hemisphere Security Analysis Center –WHEMSAC (Miami: Applied Research Center, Florida International University, May 2011).

authorities do not yet appear to have either a clear strategy for putting together an effective response to their presence or a willingness to assist the thousands of humble sierra survivors to overcome their loss. Guzmán himself is gone, serving a life term in jail, but the Maoist legacy he inspired lives on.

BIBLIOGRAPHY

Blanco, Hugo, *Luchas campesinas de la Convención y Lares – Chaupimayo – Quillabamba* (Lima: n.p., 1987)

Borja Arce, Luis, and Janet Talavera Sánchez, "La entrevista del siglo: El Presidente Gonzalo rompe el silencio," *El Diario* (Lima) (July 24, 1988), pp. 2–48

Bourque, Susan, and David Scott Palmer, "Transforming the Rural Sector: Government Policy and Peasant Response," in Lowenthal, ed., *Peruvian Experiment*, pp. 179–219

Cardoso, Fernando Henrique, and Enzo Faletto, *Dependency and Development in Latin America* (Berkeley: University of California Press, 1979)

Comisión de la Verdad y Reconciliación (CVR), *Informe final, Tomo I, Primera parte: El proceso, los hechos, las víctimas* (Lima: Editorial Navarrete, 2003)

Cook, Alexander, "Third World Maoism," in Timothy Cheek, ed., *Critical Introduction to Mao* (New York: Cambridge University Press, 2010), pp. 288–312

Degregori, Carlos Iván, "After the Fall of Abimael Guzmán: The Limits of Sendero Luminoso," in Maxwell A. Cameron and Philip Mauceri, eds., *The Peruvian Labyrinth: Polity, Society, Economy* (University Park: Pennsylvania State University Press, 1997), pp. 179–91

Ayacucho 1969–1979: El surgimiento de Sendero Luminoso (Lima: Instituto de Estudios Peruanos, 1990)

"Harvesting Storms: Peasant Rondas and the Defeat of Sendero Luminoso in Ayacucho," in Steve J. Stern, ed., *Shining and Other Paths: War and Society in Peru, 1980–1995* (Durham: Duke University Press, 1998), pp. 131–40

Díaz Martínez, Antonio, *Ayacucho: Hambre y esperanza* (Ayacucho: Ediciones Waman Puma, 1974)

Fumerton, Mario, *From Victims to Heroes: Peasant Counter-Rebellion and Civil War in Ayacucho, Peru, 1980–2000* (Amsterdam: Thela Publishers, 2002)

Gorriti Ellenbogen, Gustavo, "Shining Path's Stalin and Trotsky," in Palmer, ed., *Shining Path*, pp. 167–88

Sendero: Historia de la guerra milenaria en el Perú (Lima: Editorial Apoyo, 1990)

Graham, Carol, *Peru's APRA: Parties, Politics, and the Elusive Quest for Democracy* (Boulder: Lynne Rienner, 1992)

Gunder Frank, André, *Capitalism and Underdevelopment in Latin America* (New York: Monthly Review Press, 1969)

Guzmán Reynoso, Abimael, "Exclusive Comments by Abimael Guzmán," *World Affairs* 156.1 (Summer 1993), pp. 52–57

De puño y letra (Lima: Manoalzada, 2009)

"¡Que el equilibrio estratégico remezca más el país! (Gran culminación de la III campaña de impulsar)," unpublished typescript, November 1991

Handelman, Howard, "Peru: The March to Civilian Rule," *American Universities Field Staff Reports*, South America 2 (1980), 24 pp.

Hazleton, William A., and Sandra Woy-Hazleton, "Terrorism and the Marxist Left: Peru's Struggle against Sendero Luminoso," *Terrorism* 11 (1988), pp. 471–90

Jaquette, Jane, *The Politics of Development in Peru*, Dissertation Series 33 (Ithaca: Latin American Studies Program, Cornell University, 1971)

Jiménez Bacca, Benigno, *Inicio, desarrollo, y ocaso del terrorismo en el Perú*, vols. I–III (Lima: Editorial SANKI, 2000)

Lowenthal, Abraham, ed., *The Peruvian Experiment: Continuity and Change under Military Rule* (Princeton: Princeton University Press, 1975)

Mao Tse-Tung, *Quotations from Chairman Mao Tse-Tung* (Peking: Foreign Languages Press, 1966)

Mar, José Matos, and José Manuel Mejía, *La Reforma Agraria en el Perú*, Perú Problema 19 (Lima: Instituto de Estudios Peruanos, 1980)

Mariátegui, José Carlos, *Seven Interpretive Essays on Peruvian Reality* (Austin: University of Texas Press, 1971); translated from *Siete ensayos de interpretación de la realidad peruana* (Lima: Amauta, 1928)

Marks, Thomas A., "Making Revolution with Shining Path," in Palmer, ed., *Shining Path*, pp. 209–23

Palmer, David Scott, "FONCODES y su impacto en la pacificación en el Perú: Observaciones generales y el caso de Ayacucho," in Fondo Nacional de Compensación y Desarrollo Nacional (FONCODES), *Concertando para el desarrollo: Lecciones aprendidas del FONCODES en sus estrategias de intervención* (Lima: Gráfica Medelius, 2001), pp. 147–77

Peru: The Authoritarian Tradition (New York: Praeger, 1980)

"Rebellion in Rural Peru: The Origins and Evolution of Sendero Luminoso," *Comparative Politics* 18.2 (January 1986), pp. 127–46

"Terror in the Name of Mao: Revolution and Response in Peru," in Robert J. Art and Linda Richardson, eds., *Democracy and Counterterrorism: Lessons from the Past* (Washington, D.C.: US Institute of Peace Press, 2007), pp. 195–219

ed., *Shining Path of Peru*, 2nd edn. (New York: St. Martin's Press, 1994)

Palmer, David Scott, and Alberto Bolívar, "Peru's Shining Path: Recent Dynamics and Future Prospects," Western Hemisphere Security Analysis Center – WHEMSAC (Miami: Applied Research Center, Florida International University, May 2011)

Paredes, Maritza, "Indigenous Politics and the Legacy of the Left," in John Crabtree, ed., *Fractured Politics: Peruvian Democracy Past and Present* (London: Institute for the Study of the Americas, University of London, 2011), pp. 129–57

Starn, Orin, ed., *Hablan los ronderos: La búsqueda por la paz en los Andes*, Documento de Trabajo 45 (Lima: Instituto de Estudios Peruanos, 1993)

Stephens, Evelyne Huber, "The Peruvian Military Government, Labor
    Mobilization, and the Political Strength of the Left," *Latin American Research
    Review* 18.2 (1983), pp. 57–93

Tapia, Carlos, *Las Fuerzas Armadas y Sendero Luminoso: Dos estrategias y un final*
    (Lima: Instituto de Estudios Peruanos, 1997)

Taylor, Lewis, *Maoism in the Andes: Sendero Luminoso and the Contemporary
    Guerrilla Movement in Peru*, Working Paper 2, Centre for Latin American
    Studies (Liverpool: University of Liverpool, 1983)

Woy-Hazleton, Sandra, and William A. Hazleton, "Sendero Luminoso and the
    Future of Peruvian Democracy," *Third World Quarterly* 12.2 (April 1990),
    pp. 21–35

9   The book that bombed

Mao's Little Red Thing in the Soviet Union

Elizabeth McGuire

In early February 1967, the Soviet Union evacuated women and children from its embassy in Beijing. When the evacuees got off the plane at Moscow's Sheremetyevo airport, hundreds of Muscovites were gathered to greet them. The arriving women gave their names – Olga, Natasha, Marina – and brief accounts of their departure from China. Babies in their arms, they told of running a gauntlet of hostile Red Guards to board their plane. At least one Chinese hurled a copy of the Little Red Book at the Russians, and it hit an eight-month-old girl on the head. Or so the Soviet press reported.[1] Whereas for communists in many parts of the world, the Little Red Book functioned as a physical manifestation of the rejuvenation of leftism, for the Soviet Union it was anything but. While radicals from Berkeley to Bengal may have pocketed their books with hope and pride, nobody – really, absolutely nobody – in the Soviet Union would have been caught dead with one.

On the contrary, the book was universally perceived as a weapon. Its symbolism operated on several levels intellectually, politically, and socially, and had different implications in different contexts. Orthodox party members saw a rival ideology to refute; dissidents found an example of communism at its worst to brandish in their battle with the regime; ordinary people sensed a more concrete, literal threat. But all interpretations began from the same place: the Little Red Book and the Maoism it embodied were an assault, one that began rhetorically but could end physically.

The attack demanded an answer, a defense, a counterattack. In formulating it, Soviet people across the political and social spectrum were forced to articulate exactly what it was about their system that was (or wasn't) worth defending. As dissidents, ordinary people, and party propagandists thought through events in China, they made explicit

---

[1] Iu. Kosyukov and A. Aleksandrov, "They have returned from Peking," *Izvestiia* (February 6, 1966).

comparisons to their own experiences, and expressed a sense of responsibility for China's crisis, even as they attempted to distance themselves from it.

While it is common to think of the effect of the Chinese Cultural Revolution on the Soviet Union in terms of international politics, perhaps less known and more fascinating is the way in which Mao and his book intervened in Soviet domestic politics. By providing an alternate version of socialism that the Soviet Union as both a state and a society had no choice but to counter, Mao unwittingly opened the way for unprecedented critique and mockery of socialism itself – an erosion of universalism that was just as critical for the Soviet Union at home as abroad.

The attack

Seen from a distance in space and time, today in the West the Sino-Soviet split is remembered as an ideological and geopolitical battle for leadership of the communist bloc. But judging from contemporary sources, Soviet people absolutely experienced China's rhetorical invasion literally, and the Little Red Book was the object that transformed words into weapons. These attacks occurred all over the place – inside the Soviet Union, at the border, at embassies, on boats, in China – anywhere where Soviet and Chinese people came into contact.

Perhaps the most symbolic attack occurred in January 1967, when a group of Chinese tourists in Moscow brought the war of rhetoric to the symbolic heart of Soviet socialism. In an incident that made the papers for days afterward, Chinese tourists "began rudely to violate the established and commonly known rules for visiting the V. I. Lenin Mausoleum." They jumped over a barrier and began chanting Mao quotes, holding up their Little Red Books. Soviet citizens in line "waited patiently" and guards asked the Chinese to move on, but the Chinese just kept singing and even demanded that Soviet onlookers join them. Then one Chinese tourist allegedly hit a Soviet woman, and the rest began attacking other onlookers. This lasted a few minutes, until, according to the party newspaper *Izvestiia*, several Soviet citizens "locked arms, formed a human chain, and forced the Chinese group several meters away from the Mausoleum."[2]

Similar physical confrontations occurred in a wide variety of places on the Sino-Soviet periphery and on Chinese territory. In August 1967, Chinese authorities in the northeastern port of Dalian arbitrarily detained

---

[2] I. Ivanov, "Insolent sally by *Khunveibin*," *Izvestiia* (January 28, 1967).

the Soviet steamship *Svirsk*. When a Soviet seaman refused to put on a Mao button, the Chinese became very angry. The ship's captain refused to surrender the seaman to the Chinese, at which point the captain was taken into Chinese custody, beaten, and paraded around the city with his hands tied behind his back and his head down. When the Red Guards finally found the guilty sailor, they dragged him and the captain to a stadium, where the two were subjected to verbal attacks by a mob. But none of this bothered anyone as much as the Chinese attack on the ship itself: they overran it and draped it with slogans and curses.[3] It seems to have taken a note from Soviet prime minister Kosygin to Chinese prime minister Zhou Enlai to end the incident.[4]

Embassies were another battleground in the war of words, and here more than elsewhere the attack threatened to become physical. In August 1966, the Soviet Ministry of Foreign Affairs sent the first of several notes to the Chinese embassy in Moscow protesting aggressive Chinese behavior outside the Beijing embassy.[5] In perhaps their most successful raid, on August 14, 1969 Mao enthusiasts climbed over the embassy gate, dealt minor injuries to several staff members, ransacked the embassy, and put a portrait of Mao up in front of it. The next day they brought loudspeakers, began shouting obscenities, and beat up an embassy official as he left the building.[6]

Delegations and individual travelers were just as vulnerable. Accounts of travel to China during this period often included reports of being inundated with propaganda in a Chinese train station or airport, or even in the plane on the way. The writer Vladimir Turkin traveled to China by train and reported that he was overwhelmed by propaganda the minute he crossed the border.[7] Similarly, for I. P. Kozhar, a decorated Hero of the Soviet Union, the rhetorical assault began when the Chinese–American Friendship Society delegation with which he was traveling transferred to a Chinese plane in Irkutsk. A portrait of Mao and several posters of quotations hung on the cabin walls, the in-flight magazines were filled with Mao quotes, and the stewardesses sang Mao songs and played radio broadcasts praising Mao.[8] Once in China, the delegation

---

[3] P. Demidov, "The *Svirsk* arrives in Vladivostok," *Izvestiia* (August 18, 1967).

[4] "Stop Lawlessness and Highhandedness ..." *Pravda* (August 13, 1967); "Vandalism of the *Khunveibin*," *Izvestiia* (August 14, 1967).

[5] "USSR Ministry of Foreign Affairs," *Pravda* (August 28, 1966); "In the USSR Ministry of Foreign Affairs," *Pravda* (February 10, 1967).

[6] "'Kul'turnaia revoliutsii v kitae prodolzhaetsia," *Pravda* (September 3, 1966). See also "Porochnyi kurs." *Pravda* (October 23, 1966).

[7] "Revoliutsiia vo imia kul'tury ili vo imia kul'ta," *Literaturnaia Rossiia* (February 24, 1967).

[8] "Why our trip to the PRC was interrupted," *Izvestiia* (November 22, 1966).

attended an ostensibly "friendly" meeting that took a predictable turn for the worse. When they got up to leave they found their exit blocked by an angry crowd. Uncertain how to respond, in desperation they began to sing "The Internationale." But the universal music of proletarian unity didn't calm the crowd, which answered by striking up the anthem of the Chinese Cultural Revolution, "The East is Red." The Soviets barely escaped.[9]

Another traveler reported how, exasperated with the Maoist sloganeering of his tour guide, he asked her to "tell us, please, some specifics, about interesting buildings, interesting places ... Tell us about what we are seeing directly outside the window of our bus." But she answered coolly, "OK. Here on the right you will see a big warehouse. On the walls of that warehouse you see big characters. They say, 'The light of Mao's ideas is in the hearts of peoples of the whole world.'"[10] Another visitor portrayed himself as querying the Red Guards: "'Why are you acting so inhumanely?' The answer was guffaws."[11]

In the late 1960s, one of the most internationally renowned Soviet directors, Andrei Tarkovskii, made an autobiographical film that featured an iconic scene from the Chinese Cultural Revolution. The film was called *The Mirror*, and it juxtaposed personal memories, news footage, and the poetry of Tarkovskii's father to create a complex evocation of the personal past, of Tarkovskii, and implicitly others of his generation. In a black-and-white sequence devoted to images of the Cultural Revolution, Tarkovskii shows Chinese men rushing toward a human chain of Soviet border guards in the snow. They wave Little Red Books and shout, pressing unsuccessfully to break through the unified Soviet defense. The Soviet guards maintain a blank, business-as-usual expression. The attack is repelled.

This scene – iconic in the Soviet context – captures the moment when rhetoric as physical weapon began its metamorphosis to threatening military offensive. In real life, border scuffles began like many of the incidents described above. A year before serious incursions began, a Soviet border guard explained his encounters with Chinese:

This is the situation: A fisherman comes, sticks a pole with Mao's portrait on it in the snow and begins to dig a hole. We explain that it is forbidden to cross the border. We escort him back. The next day 20 fishermen come. They only have three nets, but each one has a Little Red Book. They wave them around so that

[9] Ibid.
[10] "Revoliutsiia vo imia kul'tury ili vo imia kul'ta," *Literaturnaia Rossiia* (February 24, 1967).
[11] "V tsarstve krivykh zerkal," *Sovetskaia kul'tura* (February 25, 1967).

the fishing will be better. We escort them back to the border. About 500 people are brought to the border. There are women and children among them. They organize a rally and beat drums. They are loaded on trucks and head for the Soviet shore. Our fellows stand in a chain. The trucks race at them, intending to frighten them. Nothing happens, and they go away.[12]

However, these relatively harmless forays gradually gave way to a serious military conflict, the most infamous of which occurred on Zhenbao (Russian, Damanskii) Island in 1969. On March 1 of that year several hundred camouflaged Chinese border guards crossed the Ussuri River to an island in the middle, burrowed into foxholes, and strung a telephone wire back to the Chinese side of the border. In the morning, several dozen Chinese marched over the ice toward the Russian side of the river, yelling slogans.

The Soviets took this for a routine, symbolic gesture and responded as usual, linking arms to block the Chinese – until the first wave of Chinese dove aside, revealing a second row, who opened fire on the Soviets with submachine guns, killing six immediately. Ultimately, three hundred Chinese managed to overrun their Soviet counterparts. Although this incident was the most well known, in fact it was one of several border skirmishes in 1969, and these ultimately led to a major Soviet buildup along what was the longest border between two states in the world. Only with the accession of Gorbachev did demilitarization of the border occur.[13]

The Damanskii Island incident crystallized and fueled anxiety about a Chinese attack, anxiety centered on the size of the Chinese population and China's potential as a nuclear power. The large number of jokes on the subject suggests that Chinese numerical superiority was, in fact, threatening to many ordinary Soviet citizens. "How will the war between the USSR and China end? With the unconditional surrender of the USSR after it has taken 400 million Chinese as prisoners of war." Or, "Is it possible to destroy the Chinese by putting them in columns and machine-gunning them? Yes, if they multiply slower than you shoot." Judging from the jokes, war with China seemed imminent, and the Chinese seemed likely to win. Many played on the idea that China would swallow the Soviet Union, including jokes about a not-so-distant future in which Polish streets have Chinese names, Finland shares a border with

---

[12] Iu. Apenchenko and Iu. Mokeyev, "That's how it is on the border," *Pravda* (March 12, 1969).

[13] Nikolai Lobodiuk, *Ostrov Damanskii: dopolnitel'nye shtrikhi k sobytiiam v marte 1969 goda, interviu, vospominaniia, fotografii* (Moscow: Granitsa, 2009).

China, and the price of vodka is calculated in yuan. Several jokes suggested that Russian speakers had best learn Chinese.[14]

It was the famous dissident Andrei Amalrik who articulated the most thorough vision of war with China in his well-known polemic, *Will the Soviet Union Survive Until 1984?* Writing in the aftermath of Damanskii, Amalrik argued that just as the Soviet Union had sought to expand westward, so China had its eye on the lands of Siberia and the Soviet Far East. Seeking to become the "supreme controller of the fate of the world," China would start a war using a combination of nuclear and guerrilla tactics (to take advantage of its numerical superiority) to solve its economic problems and gain its rightful place of dominance in the world. Furthermore, it might be difficult to tell when the war had actually begun, because China would escalate conflict simply by intensifying border skirmishes. "These skirmishes will be escalated into total war at the moment most suitable to China."[15]

The war with China, according to Amalrik, would cause the collapse of the Soviet Union. The Soviet military was overextended, so Germany would take advantage of the war to reunite, and Eastern Europe would slip away from the USSR and assert various territorial demands. The nationalist tendencies of non-Russian Soviet peoples would grow under wartime tensions, and new states would emerge in the borderlands. The only way to avoid this fate would be to democratize and forge a lasting alliance with the United States, an unlikely scenario. Amalrik predicted that the war with China would begin within five or ten years, at the most – between 1975 and 1980. Hence the title of his landmark essay, "Will the Soviet Union Survive Until 1984?" Amalrik's prediction regarding the eventual collapse of the Soviet Union proved oddly prescient – except for his belief that China would be the catalyst. His book suggests that astute Soviet observers saw more clearly when they faced west than when they faced east.

The counterattack

Although subsequent scholarship has emphasized the reaction of Soviet elites, in fact the Soviet people had a visceral, negative reaction to events in China that had little to do with communism per se. There was something deeply repelling about what was happening in China, a

---

[14] Dora Shturman and Sergei Tiktin, *Sovetskii Soiuz v zerkale politicheskogo anekdota* (Jerusalem: Express, 1987), pp. 431–49.
[15] Other dissidents expressed similar fears. See, for example, Andrei Sakharov, *Memoirs*, trans. Richard Lourie (New York: Alfred Knopf, 1990), pp. 321 and 366; Andrei Amalrik, *Will the Soviet Union Survive Until 1984?* (New York: Harper Colophon Books, 1970), pp. 46, 50–51.

sentiment that Vladimir Vysotskii once again captured perfectly in a vaguely dirty song about the Red Guards. In fact, the Russian term for "Red Guards" was rarely used in reference to the Chinese – in all likelihood it was simply unacceptable to use a term so central to Soviet history. Various Russian terms were used instead, but the vast majority of commentators eschewed Russian words altogether in favor of a transliteration of the word for Red Guard in Chinese (*hong wei bing*): *khunveibin* or *khunveibiny* in the plural.[16]

In Russian this exotic name provided no end of amusement, since its first syllable sounded very much like one of the most common and dirty Russian curse words, generally referring to the male anatomy and used in any number of combinations. The refrain Vysotskii penned for his song, "Khunveibiny," played on the name: "And really, the key thing is that I know perfectly / how they pronounce their name / But something highly indecent / is on the tip of my tongue: / Khuuuu....nveibiny."[17] Various *chastushki* (rhymed poems expressing popular humor) riffed on the sound of it as well. "I fell in love with a khunveibin / And hung up his picture / But when I woke up early this morning / The khun was hanging and the bina was gone."[18] This moniker might have been preferable to the Russian alternatives not only for its hilarious pronunciation but also because it precluded any Soviet connotation.

Perhaps the regime might have picked up on popular sentiment – Vysotskii was wildly popular – and left well enough alone. But Soviet ideologues were nothing if not earnest, and for them, Chinese propaganda posed a serious dilemma. As the numerous stories about Soviet people being literally struck by the Little Red Book suggest, Maoism hit hard. China had been one of the most important members of the worldwide socialist family, and the alliance was steeped in the Marxist–Leninist rhetoric so central to each country's domestic claims to power.[19] The Soviet Union somehow had to publicly extricate itself, and defend

---

[16] For a good selection of terms see I. Gavrilov, "Za fasadom 'kul'turnoi revoliutsii' v Kitae," *Dal'nii vostok* 2 (1967). For an explicit definition of *khunveibiny* see "'Khunveibiny,' i kto imi komanduet," *Agitator* (1966), pp. 51–53. *Agitator* did explain that "*khunveibiny* in translation means *krasnaia okhrana* [red guard]." Soviet commentary on China could substitute for direct expression on the Soviet Union. See Gilbert Rozman, *A Mirror for Socialism: Soviet Criticisms of China* (Princeton: Princeton University Press, 1985).

[17] Vladimir Vysotskii, "Khunveibiny," in *Sobranie Stikhov i pesen v trekh tomakh*, vol. I (New York: Apollon Foundation and Russica Publisher, 1988), pp. 158–59.

[18] "On the clothesline is hanging / a yellow kerchief / My darling is a khunveibin / And I am a khunveibinochka": I. Borev, *XX vek v predaniiakh i anekdotakh b shesti knigakh*, vol. IV: *1953–1984: kholodnaia voina za pravo uluchshat' mir, ukhudshaia ego po-svoemu* (Khar'kov and Rostov-na-donu: Folio and Feniks, 1996), p. 451.

[19] Odd Arne Westad, ed., *Brothers in Arms: The Rise and Fall of the Sino-Soviet Alliance, 1945–1963* (Washington, D.C.: Woodrow Wilson Center Press, 1998), pp. 2–3.

itself from China's assaults, without repudiating the very rhetoric that China was using for its attacks. Hence the attempt to distinguish Soviet and Chinese socialism was a key part of the Soviet reaction to the Cultural Revolution, perhaps more important to the ultimate integrity of the Soviet state than border defense.

Brezhnev and his cronies, who had been in power less than two years in 1966, were seeking to reverse at least some elements of the Khrushchev thaw. For conservative Brezhnev, the Chinese attack on de-Stalinization ("revisionism") came at a most inauspicious moment, for it placed any attempt to *reverse* liberalization in the Soviet Union right in line with the obviously anti-Soviet attitudes of the Chinese. The regime also faced an incipient dissident movement, which naturally seized upon the Cultural Revolution as a weapon against what they feared to be re-Stalinization. China during the Cultural Revolution presented a picture of the sort of extreme material and cultural poverty that the Soviet Union had once experienced under Stalin and that many feared could yet reemerge. The challenge, then, for the Soviet ruling elite, was to work out the differences between Chinese and Soviet concepts of revolution, culture, and socialism.

The formula they came up with boiled down to a few basic points: communist revolutions were led by workers; once workers were in power, revolution gave way to evolution; under socialism the cultural level of the masses was supposed to rise not fall, along with the standard of living for average citizens.

Whereas the other elements of the Soviet ideological defense wavered, commitment to workers, represented by the Communist Party, was staunch. *Pravda* pondered, "Questions arise: Why are non-Party youths and school children called upon to criticize communists and to judge the work of Party bodies? Why is this 'proletarian' movement proceeding without any participation of the working class of China?"[20] And, a week later, it rephrased the question: "Where is the working class? Where in this thing are the party and government organs, the professional societies, and other social organizations?"[21] Similarly, "It is worthy of note that to carry out a cultural revolution it was necessary to create a special youth organization based on the personal loyalty of its members to Mao, standing outside of the Party and the Communist Youth League (Komsomol)."[22] Similarly, Hero of the Soviet Union and Soviet–Chinese

---

[20] "The *Khunveibiny* continue the 'cultural revolution'," *Pravda* (September 16, 1966).

[21] "Porochnyi Kurs," *Pravda* (October 23, 1966).

[22] "Kul'turnaia revoliutsiia' prodolzhaetsia," *Literaturnaia gazeta* (September 22, 1966). The idea that good workers and party members could fall victim to outside forces acting on behalf of a despotic leader was not new; it had been a key element of Khrushchev's criticism of Stalin in his famous secret speech.

Friendship Society delegate Kozhar commented, "The working class overthrows the capitalists and wins power seemingly only to perpetuate its poverty. Isn't this a caricature of Marxism?"[23]

The Soviet press repeatedly reported on working-class opposition to the Cultural Revolution in China.[24] *Pravda* claimed that when Red Guards tried to burn the Municipal Party Committee building in Nanjing, they were met by thousands of workers. "Workers came out in defense of their vanguard – the Party."[25] Similar clashes were reported in Sichuan and Hunan, the latter with thousands of casualties.[26] If a revolution is led by workers, and workers oppose the Chinese Cultural Revolution, it can't possibly be a genuine revolution.

The other problem with the Chinese Cultural Revolution for Soviet commentators in the 1960s was its violence. Apparently forgetting that the Soviet Union had experienced a rather violent and regressive cultural movement in the late 1920s (never mind the purge of the 1930s), now ideologues claimed that revolution was a long process; that the only phase that may require sudden change or violence is the seizure of power by the working class; that even this may occur slowly and preferably without violence; and that no sudden, radical change can be effective if it is not preceded by gradual evolutionary change.[27] According to this scheme, China had already experienced all the radical change and violence warranted during the communist seizure of power in 1949. *Pravda* asked: "How to explain the fact that in a socialist country, led by a communist party, a major rebellion is required to realize a cultural revolution?"[28] Violent rebellion has no place in a socialist context.

While *Pravda* had to trot out professional ideologues to explicate Chinese "revolution," more creative minds were ruminating on Chinese "culture." Nothing, apparently, was more anathema to cultural sensibilities of all persuasions than the destruction of ancient Chinese, Soviet, and particularly Western culture that was a key feature of the Chinese Cultural Revolution. The famous dissident poet Evgenii Evtushenko scolded the Chinese: "How disgusting, how stupid / To burn reproductions

---

[23] "Why our trip to the PRC was interrupted."

[24] "Khunveibiny deistvuiut," *Pravda* (September 23, 1966); "Clash between workers and the *hungweiping*," *Pravda* (December 9, 1966).

[25] "Stolknoveniia prodolzhaiutsia," *Pravda* (October 9, 1966).

[26] "Zalpy po khunveibinam," *Izvestiia* (June 28, 1967). See also "New clashes in China," *Pravda* (January 15, 1967).

[27] M. Rozental, "Questions of Theory: Evolutional and Revolutionary Forms of Development of Society," *Pravda* (September 30, 1966).

[28] "Nichego obshchego s revoliutsiei," *Pravda* (September 17, 1966).

of Goya, El Greco!"[29] Less earnestly, Vysotskii's ode to the Red Guards opened with the image of Red Guards ransacking Beijing for old paintings and statues: "Instead of statues there will be trashcans for the Cultural Revolution."[30] The most passionate condemnation of the Chinese destruction of culture came from Andrei Voznesenskii:

> Will Shakespeare be forced to make public confession of ignorance
>   of "isms"
> Will Stravinsky be dragged through warring streets with a garbage
>   pail on his gray head?
> I think –
> Question: Is the majority always right?
> Was the Florentine flood right, cracking palazzos like big pistachios?
> Yet Cellini will win, and not the tide.
> I think – crowd or individual?
> Which lasts longer – the century or the instant
> That Michelangelo achieved?
> The century died, but the instant lives on.[31]

For Voznesenskii, the Chinese Cultural Revolution was the triumph of mass ignorance over individual creativity, a triumph that history had proven can only be temporary.

Given the potentially subversive nature of Voznesenskii's verses in the Soviet context, it may come as a bit of a surprise that they were published in the pages of *Literaturnaia Rossiia* in early 1967. Evtushenko's poem was featured two years later in *Literaturnaia gazeta*.[32] Both poems dovetailed nicely with a message that had been appearing regularly in the press at least since the beginning of the Cultural Revolution: socialist culture is cumulative and inclusive, not only of a revolutionary country's pre-socialist heritage, but also of the Western cultural legacy. "In the history of culture were not the creations of Beethoven, Leonardo da Vinci, or Shakespeare a disclosure of man's spiritual potentialities?" asked one professor in the pages of *Izvestiia*. He reminded readers of Lenin's instructions to draw upon capitalist achievements to reach socialist goals.[33] For another Soviet Sinologist, the Chinese Red Guards were

---

[29] Evgenii Evtushenko, "Na krasnom snegu ussuriiskom," *Literaturnaia gazeta* (March 19, 1969).

[30] Vysotskii, "Khunveibiny," pp. 158–59.

[31] Andrei Voznesenskii, "From the Walkie-Talkie Cycle: Prologue to a Poem," *Literaturnaia Rossiia* (March 24, 1967); translation from the *Current Digest of the Soviet Press* 19, 3 (1967), p. 17.

[32] Evtushenko, "Na krasnom snegu ussuriiskom."

[33] I. Frantsev. "Talks with readers: revolution and culture," *Izvestiia* (September 27, 1966). See also "Kul'turnaia revoliutsiia – zakonomernost' razvitiia sotsializma," *Pravda* (September 26, 1966); S. Kovalev, "Questions of Theory: Socialism and

reminiscent of the Soviet Proletcult, whose extreme ideas about revolutionary culture had been repudiated by Lenin.[34]

This mention of the Proletcult, a group dedicated to the creation of a "working class culture" pointed to an irony in the indignant reaction to Chinese destruction of the material manifestations of traditional culture. On the one hand, some of these experiments themselves are widely recognized even today as major contributions to world culture: the movies of Eisenstein, the short stories of Isaac Babel, the paintings of Kandinsky and Lissitsky. On the other, the wanton destruction or theft of the most treasured elements of pre-revolutionary culture – its churches, their all-important bells which had modulated village life for hundreds of years, and the beautiful icons found inside them – seem to have been entirely forgotten by Soviet detractors of cultural destruction in China. Perhaps this was because after an initial period of radicalism, Soviet society fell in line with a new emphasis on traditional, even bourgeois, standards of global culture. A socialist society was supposed to begin by increasing literacy rates, so that workers and peasants alike could enjoy the poems of Pushkin and the paintings of Michelangelo.[35] This gradual "upward" cultural mobility was how Soviet thinkers of the 1960s defined "cultural revolution."

China could not possibly be experiencing a cultural revolution because the opposite was occurring there: books were being destroyed, cultural production had come to a standstill, learned people were being persecuted. Hence the quotation marks that surround every mention of the Chinese Cultural Revolution in every article on the subject. The fact that Chinese schools were closing so that students could participate in the Cultural Revolution was, to Soviet observers, the ultimate irony.[36]

Even Vysotskii – hardly a buttoned-up representative of high culture himself – highlighted Maoist school closings in his ode to the Red Guards: "Now their leader comrade Mao / Thought up a game for them / Don't go, children, to school! / Help fight sedition!"[37] Whatever

Cultural Heritage," *Pravda* (September 16, 1966); "Komu meshaet kul'tura?" *Izvestiia* (February 21, 1967); "Kitai, 'kul'turnaia revoliutsiia': programma unichtozheniia iskusstva," *Literaturnaia gazeta* (June 11, 1967).

[34] "Why our trip to the PRC was interrupted," *Izvestiia* (November 22, 1966). Leading Soviet historian Sheila Fitzpatrick has argued that the Soviet cultural revolution was a clear precedent for the Chinese Cultural Revolution. See Sheila Fitzpatrick, ed., *Cultural Revolution in Russia, 1928–1931* (Bloomington and London: Indiana University Press, 1978), pp. 1–40.

[35] "Contrary to the Interests of the Chinese People," *Pravda* (August 16, 1967).

[36] "Why our trip to the PRC was interrupted"; K. Dashev, "Voluntaristic challenge to socialism," *Izvestiia* (October 3, 1967).

[37] Vysotskii, "Khunveibiny," pp. 158–59.

education was still occurring clearly was compromised. *Asia and Africa Today* published a list of quotes from Mao on education, which – bordering on the satirical – revealed that even before the Cultural Revolution began, he had wanted to cut down dramatically the number of subjects taught in school, give children the questions that would appear on their exams in advance, and allow cheating. "They have to read so many books ... It's a terrible torment. It must be stopped."[38]

Mao's deemphasis of education was connected in Soviet minds with his failure to grasp the necessity of increasing standards of living for socialist states. If education has a purpose beyond providing citizens with the means of accessing bourgeois culture, the Soviet press coverage of the Cultural Revolution made clear, it lies in improving their material well-being. "[Mao] removes from the agenda the chief, prime task confronting every people who embark on the road to socialism – comprehensive, proportional development of the productive forces of the country and, on this foundation, a steady rise in the material and cultural level of the popular masses."[39]

Unlike their Soviet counterparts, it was pointed out, Chinese workers did not receive paid vacations and had access only to the most rudimentary health care. Not only China's poverty, but also, more importantly, Mao's glorification of that poverty was evidence that China was not on the road to socialism.[40] Economically, Soviet socialism represented specialization of labor; Maoism advocated a return to an undifferentiated economy in which communes engaged in industry, trade, agriculture, and education simultaneously.[41] To the Soviets, socialism also meant collective farming, but peasants in China were engaging in spontaneous decollectivization as a protest against the Cultural Revolution.[42] Overall, the contrast between Soviet economic success and Chinese economic failure was a threat to the legitimacy of Maoism.[43] In fact, it appeared

---

[38] "Mao Tsze-Dun o reforme obrazovaniia," *Aziia i Afrika segodnia* 2 (1968), p. 27. *Aziia i Afrika segodnia* was, like *Narody Azii i Afriki*, issued by the USSR Academy of Science's Institut Narodov Azii and Institut Afriki, but seems to have been geared toward a less specialized audience; from 1957 to 1961 it was called *Sovremennyi vostok*.

[39] L. Deliusin and L. Kyuzadzhian, "A threat to socialism in China," *Izvestiia* (July 4, 1967). See also "What lies behind the struggle against 'economism'," *Krasnaia zvezda* (February 28, 1967); V. G. Gel'bras, "K voprosu o stanovlenii voenno-biurokraticheskoi diktatury v Kitae," *Narody Azii i Afriki* 1 (1968), p. 21.

[40] "Aggravation of Situation in China," *Pravda* (January 28, 1967), translated in *Current Digest of the Soviet Press* 19.4 (1967), p. 8.

[41] Deliusin and Kyuzadzhian, "A threat to socialism in China."

[42] "'Kul'turnaia revoliutsiia' v Kitae i krest'iane," *Sel'skaia zhizn'* (April 12, 1968).

[43] "On the anti-Soviet policy of Mao Tse-Tung and his group," *Pravda* (February 16, 1967).

that China had so completely violated the principles of socialism that it was possible to deduce a model socialist country by simply taking the opposite of Chinese behavior. China, then, was a perfect negative image of the Soviet Union.

Confusion

A negative image is an image nonetheless, and the problem with so many attacks that referred to Chinese socialism as a caricature of the Soviet experience, or of true Marxism–Leninism, is that they implied some sort of fundamental similarity. Caricature, of course, is an exaggeration through ludicrous distortion of parts of the whole. And often the funniest visual caricatures are those that, in their exaggeration, somehow reflect our true opinion of the person or object in question. The author of this joke erased the line between distortion and reflection: "Who are the Chinese? Russians, squinting and yellowed from an excess of Marxism."[44] And where some saw caricature, others saw straight resemblance. "How are relations between the USSR and China defined?" another joke went. "As hostile coexistence of great powers with similar socio-political systems."[45]

The famous dissident Sakharov expressed similar sentiments more ceremoniously in his well-known *Thoughts on Progress, Peaceful Coexistence, and Intellectual Freedom*:

In recent years an element of demagoguery, force, cruelty and baseness has once again gripped a great country, set on the path to socialist development. I am speaking, of course, about China. It is impossible to read without horror and pain about the mass infection of anti-humanism, which the great helmsman and his colleagues are spreading ... The idiocy of the cult of personality in China has taken monstrous, grotesque, tragicomic forms, taking to the absurd many characteristics of Stalinism and Hitlerism.[46]

In a similar vein, Andrei Amalrik wrote: "It seems to me that the Chinese revolution is passing through the same stages [as the Soviet revolution]: the international period has been followed by a nationalist period (borrowing from us even its terminology.)"[47]

---

[44] Shturman and Tiktin, *Sovetskii Soiuz*, p. 431. This joke is not dated.
[45] Ibid. This joke dates from the late 1960s.
[46] Andrei Sakharov, "Razmyshleniia o progresse, mirnom sosushchestvovanii i intellektual'noi svobode," in *A. Sakharov v bor'be za mir*, comp. I. Trushnovich (Frankfurt: Possev-Verlag, 1973), p. 36.
[47] Amalrik, *Will the Soviet Union Survive Until 1984?*, p. 45.

What is remarkable is that while prominent Soviet dissidents tended to be earnest and outraged about the similarities between Soviet and Chinese socialism, the writers who filled the pages of some of the Soviet Union's most orthodox publications joined in the general comedy that anonymous jokes made at the Soviet Union's own expense. Their humor was more subtle, of course, but perhaps even funnier. They got away with it by producing articles that were supposedly translations from the Chinese press. The tip-off that something funny was in store was the use of direct quotations with minimal or no commentary, even extending to the reprinting of entire Chinese articles with little or no introduction.

Hence, in early 1966, before the true dimensions of the Cultural Revolution were even clear, *Literaturnaia gazeta* was carrying articles such as "Let's talk about the philosophical aspects of the sale of water-melons in large cities." Reprinted from a Chinese paper, this article was apparently written by a Chinese salesman of watermelons who claimed to have overcome the number one enemy in the watermelon business – the rotting of watermelons – by applying Maoist ideology to his work.[48] Two months later, *Literaturnaia* ran a similar but even more hilarious article, "Let's talk about the dialectic in the hairdressing business." Here the author proclaimed, "I realized more and more that to cut hair is to make revolution." He decided to use the time with his clients to inundate them with Maoist propaganda, and claimed that Maoist thought had helped him to overcome the devilish contradiction between cutting hair well and cutting it quickly.[49]

The fact that such articles included no commentary by *Literaturnaia gazeta* suggests that their subject – the cult of personality – required no introduction at all, as readers were well familiar with it. Coming a decade after Khrushchev's attacks on the Stalinist personality cult, but before Brezhnev attempted to resuscitate it, these stories were little caricatures of the Stalin cult, and funny ones at that. They were the journalist's answer to popular jokes that played on the theme more directly: "When will Mao Tzse-Dun's cult of personality end? When they lay him in the Mao Zo Leum."[50]

Sometimes humorous caricature could pop up in the middle of an otherwise serious piece. In May 1967, *Izvestiia* featured an exposé of the

---

[48] "Pogovorim o filosofskikh voprosakh prodazhi arbuzov v krupnykh gorodakh," *Literaturnaia gazeta* (May 24, 1966).

[49] "Pogovorim o dialektike v parikhmakherskom dele," *Literaturnaia gazeta* (July 30, 1966).

[50] Shturman and Tiktin, *Sovetskii Soiuz*, p. 432. The compilers date this joke to 1966.

Chinese model oilfield in Daqing, charging that the supposedly high levels of production achieved there were the result of horrendous exploitation of workers. The article was one of many, as noted above, that decried the poverty of Chinese socialism. But midway through, its tone of indignation gave way, momentarily, to one of pure comedy:

"The model worker," "the hero of our era," "the knight of socialist construction," Chinese propaganda claims, is to be found right here in Tatsing [Daqing]. The person meant is one "Iron Wang," the leader of a driller's brigade. Whereas the semi-mythical Lei Feng (a soldier in the People's Liberation Army) dreamed of becoming "a little rust-proof screw," the ideal of "Iron Wang" is the humble buffalo. "All my life I have wanted to be a buffalo," he is supposed to have said ... "to achieve a high level of production and to keep my personal life to a low level."[51]

Immediately after this passage, the article reverted to its original, more didactic tone. Even the most righteous indignation could, it seems, dissolve momentarily in a fit of giggles. Yet there is something ambiguous about the humor. Who is the subject of it? What better caricature of the Soviet Stakhanovite (the shock workers lauded during the early years of the five-year plans), could there be than "Iron Wang?" Less humorous were implicit comparisons between the Chinese youths who denounced their parents or other authority figures and the infamous Pavlik Morozov, a Soviet boy who had done something similar in the 1930s. *Pravda* told of a six-year-old girl, Tsiu Khun, who studied the works of Mao at the age of five and could recite them by six. This child was paraded through various enterprises and military units, and when asked whether she missed her family, answered, "To think of one's family is dogmatism."[52] Other commentators told of Chinese children spying on and denouncing their parents.[53] One Sinologist indicted Chinese adults for warping children. "These young people have grown up in an upside-down world, in the reign of fun-house mirrors," he wrote.[54] At the same time, however, many press reports showed children as happily taking advantage of the Cultural Revolution to usurp the adults who were normally supposed to care for and control them. Several accounts related how students were taking control of schools, determining which subjects should be taught, and disciplining their teachers.[55]

---

[51] "What is the Spirit of Tatsing?" *Izvestiia* (May 18, 1967).

[52] "What Chinese young people are being taught," *Pravda* (March 11, 1967).

[53] Gavrilov, "Za fasadom 'kul'turnoi revoliutsii' v Kitae," p. 152.

[54] "V tsarstve krivykh zerkal," *Sovetskaia kul'tura* (February 25, 1967).

[55] Ovcharenko, "Tragicheskii Kitai," p. 217. Gavrilov, "Za fasadom 'kul'turnoi revoliutsii' v Kitae," p. 154.

The consequences of childish insubordination could be frightening. Unlike newspapers in other parts of the world, the Soviet press did not hesitate to report fully on the violence of the Cultural Revolution. A particularly gruesome example was an article that appeared in *Litera-turnaia gazeta* in June 1967, titled "Blood on the school walls." In a tone that can only be described as morbid sensationalism, its author described how the Red Guards at School Number Six in Beijing built a chamber where they tortured people to death at night, ringing the school bell to drown their victims' cries. The article included many graphic descriptions of their methods. The journalist vowed that his story was "documented from beginning to end" and quoted directly from victims' testimony, saying that their names had not been revealed to protect them.[56]

Such tales of the most extreme aspects of the Cultural Revolution probably repelled readers and reminded them of the difference between themselves and the objects of their voyeurism. The alienation of Soviet people from the Chinese found its most complete (and hence perhaps ironic) expression in a Vladimir Vysotskii song called "Tau Kita" (1966). "Tau Kita" is a play on the Russian word for China, *kitai*, or Chinese, *kitaiskii*. Vysotskii sang of a trip to the "faraway planet of Tau Kita" where "our comrades in conscience," the "*taukitaiskii* brotherhood has lost its wits." When a signal sent to Tau Kita to ask what is going on there provokes only obscenities in response, the singer, like the Soviet–Chinese Friendship Society delegation, decides to fly to Tau Kita "to sort it out on the spot." But once he arrives there, he can't find anyone to explain to him the incomprehensible situation he finds, in which even sex has been abandoned in favor of asexual reproduction. He tries to tell inhabitants of Tau Kita that the galaxy is ashamed for them, but the only answer he receives is some kind of inscrutable flashing. The *taukitaiskii* brother-hood seems perfectly happy with its situation. In frustration the singer yells out some obscenities. It is unclear whether the bard is using refer-ences to aliens to describe the Chinese or the reverse.

Either way, there was something of a vicious circle at work, for it is unlikely that the idea of caricature was ever far from the minds of attentive observers. Absorbing the accounts of Chinese children spying on their parents, could Soviet readers have forgotten about Pavlik Morozov? How different were the Chinese torture chambers from the basement of the infamous Moscow prison, the Lubianka? Wasn't the difference one of degree, rather than one of essence? Stories that

---

[56] V. Georgiev, "Krov' na shkol'noi stene," *Literaturnaia gazeta* (June 7, 1967).

alienated readers from the Chinese could not help but simultaneously recall Soviet analogs, obliterating the space they were trying to create.

Furthermore, if Chinese adults bore some responsibility for the behavior of their children, didn't the Soviet Union face a similar responsibility for its protégés? Commentators have since suggested that Soviet humor about the Cultural Revolution betrayed not only embarrassment regarding the similarities between Chinese and Soviet communism, but also a sense of responsibility for having inspired such horrors. Dora Shturman and Sergei Tiktin, compilers of a comprehensive collection of jokes about China, suggested, "It's very symptomatic that, while playing on various aspects of life in Communist China, anecdotists didn't forget the USSR's responsibility for everything that happened in China."[57] Similarly, in their book on the 1960s Petr Vail' and Aleksandr Genis wrote that the Soviet person of the late 1960s "felt his own responsibility for the Beijing *khunveibiny*. You see, China was a threatening caricature of the Soviet Union." To support this view, they related what was apparently a well-known joke: "How can we tell that the earth is round? Because all the trash that we send west comes back to us from the east."[58] Vail' and Genis also noted Sakharov's formulation of Soviet responsibility for the Cultural Revolution: "Sakharov, hoisting the Frankenstein complex onto his own shoulders (which were accustomed to the weight), wrote that the Chinese tragedy is the result of the 'incomplete and belated character of the war with Stalinism in the USSR'."[59]

Conclusion

The Little Red Book embodied the radical Maoist assault on Soviet socialism: revolutionary and countercultural. Meanwhile, the Soviet press presented a very different vision of socialism, emphasizing evolutionary change and cultural freedom. Underlying this difference, however, was implicit agreement that the Soviet revolution was basically over. It is striking, then, how little these Soviet authors seem to have considered the potential significance of their rhetoric. Ideologues who questioned China's legitimacy as a socialist country because it was poor, undemocratic, and repressive did not know that these categories would be applied in the future with fatal force to the Soviet Union. Those who expressed loss over the breakdown of socialist unity could not have

---

[57] Shturman and Tiktin, *Sovetskii Soiuz*, p. 429.
[58] Petr Vail' and Aleksandr Genis, *60-e: Mir Sovetskogo cheloveka* (Moscow: Novoe literaturnoe obozrenie, 1998), p. 281.
[59] Ibid., p. 281.

realized the magnitude of the loss that was to come. Even satirists, who were no doubt aware of the double entendre in their humor, could not have foreseen how thoroughly pervasive mockery of Soviet socialism would become in the Brezhnev era. And whereas in the case of China tensions could be released by externalizing the enemy and fearing an invasion, once the criticism and the laughter were aimed directly inward, release was more difficult to achieve. Indeed, while the Cultural Revolution may have unified some segments of the Soviet population, the precedent set by the Soviet reaction to it was decidedly dangerous. The lambasting and lampooning of China was an unwitting dress rehearsal for the critique and mockery that would eventually help to bring Soviet socialism to its knees.

BIBLIOGRAPHY

Amalrik, Andrei, *Will the Soviet Union Survive Until 1984?* (New York: Harper Colophon Books, 1970)

Borev, I., *XX vek v predaniiakh i anekdotakh b shesti knigakh*, vol. IV: *1953–1984: kholodnaia voina za pravo uluchshat' mir, ukhudshaia ego po-svoemu* (Khar'kov and Rostov-na-donu: Folio and Feniks, 1996)

Current Digest of the Soviet Press (Columbus, OH: American Association for the Advancement of Slavic Studies)

Fitzpatrick, Sheila, ed., *Cultural Revolution in Russia, 1928–1931* (Bloomington and London: Indiana University Press, 1978)

Gavrilov, I., "Za fasadom 'kul'turnoi revoliutsii' v Kitae," *Dal'nii vostok* 2 (1967), pp. 152–60

Gel'bras, V. G., "K voprosu o stanovlenii voenno-biurokraticheskoi diktatury v Kitae," *Narody Azii i Afriki* 1 (1968), pp. 21–35

"'Khunveibiny,' i kto imi komanduet," *Agitator* 24 (1966), pp. 51–53

Lobodiuk, Nikolai, *Ostrov Damanskii: dopolnitel'nye shtrikhi k sobytiiam v marte 1969 goda, interviu, vospominaniia, fotografii* (Moscow: Granitsa, 2009)

"Mao Tsze-Dun o reforme obrazovaniia," *Aziia i Afrika segodnia* 2 (1968), p. 27

Rozman, Gilbert, *A Mirror for Socialism: Soviet Criticisms of China* (Princeton: Princeton University Press, 1985)

Sakharov, Andrei, *Memoirs*, trans. Richard Lourie (New York: Alfred Knopf, 1990) "Razmyshleniia o progresse, mirnom sosushchestvovanii i intellektual'noi svobode," in *A. Sakharov v bor'be za mir*, comp. I. Trushnovich (Frankfurt: Possev-Verlag, 1973), pp. 9–65

Shturman, Dora, and Sergei Tiktin, *Sovetskii Soiuz v zerkale politicheskogo anekdota* (Jerusalem: Express, 1987)

Vail', Petr, and Aleksandr Genis, *60-e: Mir Sovetskogo cheloveka* (Moscow: Novoe literaturnoe obozrenie, 1998)

Vysotskii, Vladimir, "Khunveibiny," *Sobranie Stikhov i pesen v trekh tomakh*, vol. I (New York: Apollon Foundation and Russica Publisher, 1988), pp. 158–9

Westad, Odd Arne, ed., *Brothers in Arms: The Rise and Fall of the Sino-Soviet Alliance, 1945–1963* (Washington, D.C.: Woodrow Wilson Center Press, 1998)

10   Mao and the Albanians

Elidor Mëhilli

A bosom friend afar brings a distant land near.[1]
Greeting in the Albanian edition

The meeting with Mao was arranged in secret, late in the summer of 1967. The two guests, who had come all the way from Albania, explained their mission to the Chairman: editing his Little Red Book of quotations, which the Chinese had recently translated into the Albanian language.[2] With the Cultural Revolution underway, Mao had left Beijing for Shanghai in great secrecy. No one was supposed to know his exact location, including high-ranking Chinese Communist Party (CCP) Central Committee members. The Chairman agreed to the meeting anyway – evidence, Kang Sheng explained to the visitors, that Mao cared deeply about the tiny Balkan ally.[3] But what Mao had to say on account

---

[1] From Mao Zedong's greeting to the Fifth Congress of the PPSH (October 25, 1966). It was published as "Comrade Mao Tse-tung's Message of Greetings to the Fifth Congress of the Albanian Party of Labour," *Peking Review* 9.46 (November 11, 1966), p. 5.

[2] Work on the Albanian edition of Mao's quotations had been going on for months. Kang Sheng claimed that he had promised Albanian prime minister Mehmet Shehu, during the latter's visit to China in April–May 1966, that the quotations would be completed by May 1967. See Albanian embassy in Beijing to Tirana (Top Secret), 2 May 1967, in Arkivi i Ministrisë së Punëve të Jashtme (Archive of the Ministry of Foreign Affairs), Tirana (AMPJ), V. 1967, Dos. 61, Fl. 40–1. The two specialists in question were Vangjel Moisiu and Myfit Mushi, and they stayed in China from April 18 to August 22, 1967. In addition to taking detailed notes during meetings with Chinese officials, Mushi also recorded his impressions of the Cultural Revolution, as witnessed in Beijing, Shanghai, and Jinan. See "Shënime mbi revolucionin e madh kulturor proletar në RPK," September 1967, in Arkivi Qendror Shtetëror (Central State Archives), Tirana (AQSH), F. 14/AP, Sektori i Jashtëm (Foreign Department), V. 1967, Dos. 265/2. See also Ministry of Foreign Affairs memorandum on relations with China in 1967, February 1968, in AMPJ, V. 1967, Dos. 64, Fl. 102–03. More recently, Mushi has recounted the details of his meeting with Mao in the Albanian press: "Një takim misterioz me Kryetarin Mao" [A mysterious meeting with Chairman Mao] *MAPO*, September 2009.

[3] Kang, who had recently been appointed advisor to the Central Cultural Revolution Group, did not even notify the Albanian ambassador in Beijing about the meeting. The others in attendance were Yao Wenyuan, who had also been present at the congress of the Albanian Union of Working Youth, and the Chinese translator, who was summoned in secret and sent to Shanghai with Mao's Little Red Book. See memorandum of

of the Little Red Book came as a shocking surprise to the guests. His quotations were "worthless," he told them, and they could not possibly be of any value to the Albanians. The book was "nothing more than a collection of materials with historical insights into China." Mao went on to explain that he had given instructions to publish Marx's quotations, as well as Engels', Lenin's, and Stalin's. But his inferiors had neglected the classics. "Now we ought to do this," the Chairman added. "Marx, Engels, Lenin, and Stalin have authored a lot of works and, in order to popularize them, we must publish their quotations."[4] Utterly baffled, the Albanians rushed to affirm that Mao's quotations were of utmost political importance for their country. Comrade Enver Hoxha, head of the Party of Labor of Albania (PPSH), had entrusted them personally with this important task. "See if you find them useful," Mao responded. "China's experience may serve other countries, but they must judge this for themselves."[5]

Later that fall, Beijing's Foreign Languages Press published the Albanian edition of the Little Red Book.[6] Officials in Tirana asked for 100,000 copies and the CCP Central Committee decided to present them as a gift.[7] The Albanian party newspaper, *Zëri i popullit*, praised the book as an indispensable revolutionary text in an editorial titled "In Albanian – Chairman Mao's quotations – A Great and Precious Gift from the Fraternal Chinese People."[8] As Albanian party officials had requested, this edition included Mao's greeting to the Fifth Congress of the Party of Labor, in which he called Albania "a beacon of socialism in Europe." Proclaiming the ironclad brotherly love binding Albania and China, the party newspaper called the two countries "shock brigades of

conversation between Kang Sheng, Vasil Nathanaili, Vangjel Moisiu, and Myfit Mushi (Top Secret), August 18, 1967, in AQSH, F. 14/AP, M-PKK, V. 1967, Dos. 48, Fl. 1–6. Mushi believes that the meeting was held precisely so that Chinese authorities could publish a notice showing that Mao was alive and well. The fact that the notice (as well as the photograph from the meeting) was published so widely lends support to this idea. However, the Chinese reports published in *People's Daily and Peking Review* later that month claimed that the meeting had taken place on 21 August, five days later than the actual day of the meeting. See "Chairman Mao Receives Albanian Comrades," *Peking Review*, Vol. 10, Nr. 35 (25 August 1967), p. 5.

4   Memorandum of conversation between Chairman Mao Zedong, Vangjel Moisiu, and Myfit Mushi in Shanghai (Top Secret), 16 August 1967, in AQSH, F. 14/AP, M-PKK, V. 1967, Dos. 47, Fl. 1.

5   Ibid.

6   *Citate të Kryetarit Mao Ce-Dun* [Quotations of Chairman Mao Zedong] (Pekin [Beijing]: Shtëpia botonjëse e gjuhëve të huaja, 1967).

7   The first 5,000 copies were rushed to Albania via plane in early October. See "Informacion," October 4, 1967, in AQSH, F. 14/AP, M-PKK, V. 1967, Dos. 53, Fl. 4.

8   *Zëri i popullit* (October 8, 1967). A translation of the editorial also appeared in *Peking Review* 10.44 (October 27, 1967), pp. 29–31.

world revolution." The Albanian communists and working people, the paper concluded, "will study the book *Quotations from Chairman Mao Zedong* with great diligence and attention" alongside "the teachings of Comrade Enver Hoxha."[9] A week later, East German diplomats in Tirana reported that a Chinese professor was teaching Mao's quotations at the university.[10]

But the mutual praise and the colorful metaphors concealed periods of profound uncertainty and tension between the two parties. Mao seemed to suggest that Albania could not possibly imitate far-away China. A decade later, following Mao's death and after the PPSH had severed ties with Beijing, Hoxha blamed the Chinese precisely for seeking to force their Cultural Revolution and Mao's cult on the Albanians. Published in 1979, Hoxha's *Reflections on China* was allegedly based on a political diary that he kept during the 1960s and 1970s.[11] So far, no original version of this diary has surfaced in the party archives. Still, Hoxha's recollections, though filled with paranoid stories of traitors and spies, are not a total fabrication either. Party records show that he initially had serious misgivings about Mao's gamble and sought to control propaganda for the Chairman. Two versions, then, emerge on the reception of Mao's teachings in 1960s Albania: party records reveal that Hoxha embraced the Cultural Revolution only once he had obtained political reassurances, whereas his published "diary" makes it seem as if he maintained a principled opposition against Mao all along. A systematic comparison of these sources is in order. That hastily organized meeting with Mao in Shanghai offers the opportunity to begin to untangle the Sino-Albanian relationship, to revisit a puzzling Cold War alliance that only a handful of scholars have addressed in over forty years.[12]

---

[9] Ibid.

[10] Botschaft Tirana, "Informationsbericht 6/1967," 18 October 1967, in Politisches Archiv des Auswärtigen Amtes – Ministerium für Auswärtige Angelegenheiten (Political Archive of the Foreign Office – Ministry for Foreign Affairs), Berlin (PA AA, MfAA), C 1.418/70, p. 36.

[11] Enver Hoxha, *Reflections on China (1962–1972): Extracts from the Political Diary*, vol. I (Tirana: "8 Nëntori," 1979). In addition to Albanian and English, Hoxha's reflections on Mao's China were simultaneously published in French, German, Spanish, Italian, and a number of other languages, thus mimicking the kind of work that had gone into translating and widely disseminating Mao's writings over the previous decade. Excerpts from Hoxha's numerous books were also compiled in a valuable English-language volume: Jon Halliday, *The Artful Albanian: The Memoirs of Enver Hoxha* (London: Chatto & Windus, 1986).

[12] The last substantial account of the Sino-Albanian relationship is Elez Biberaj, *Albania and China, 1962–1978: A Study of an Unequal Alliance* (Boulder: Westview Press, 1986). See also Daniel Tretiak, "The Founding of the Sino-Albanian Entente," *China Quarterly*

The chapter begins with a broad overview of Tirana's relations with Moscow and Beijing, focusing on Hoxha's handling of two central challenges introduced by Soviet leader Nikita Khrushchev in the late 1950s: de-Stalinization and *rapprochement* with Yugoslavia. Grasping these dynamics is crucial for understanding Hoxha's motivations vis-à-vis Beijing, as well as the trajectory of that contentious relationship in the 1960s. The chapter then outlines the discrepancies between Hoxha's "political diary" and high-level party records – almost all of them surveyed here for the first time. It shows that the Albanian party boss initially panicked that the Cultural Revolution would liquidate the Chinese party leadership; that Albania would lose China. The party was Hoxha's strongest weapon forged in war; he could not fathom how Mao could sacrifice his own party. Once the Chinese provided reassurances in late 1966, however, Hoxha revised his position. Over the course of 1967, the Albanians expressed wild enthusiasm for the Cultural Revolution. They hailed Mao as a great Marxist–Leninist thinker. But even as the Albanian leader kept sending delegations to China to "learn" from the Chinese, he carefully kept propaganda for Mao under control.

From Moscow to Mao

Founded in 1941, the Communist Party of Albania (renamed Party of Labor in 1948) was initially under Yugoslav influence. Belgrade played a central role in shaping the party's internal structures and, once the country was liberated from Nazi occupation in late 1944, Yugoslav advisors were heavily involved in virtually all state matters. Indeed, for many outside observers in the immediate postwar period, the fact that Albania would eventually become a Yugoslav republic seemed a foregone conclusion. At this time, Hoxha and his comrades were keenly aware of their inferior hand in relation to Belgrade. Still, the Albanian leader went along with Belgrade's wishes. Stalin also initially supported Yugoslavia's "handling" of Albania, but became increasingly anxious with Tito's regional ambitions. At the height of conflict between Moscow and Belgrade in 1948, Hoxha saw a political opportunity and proclaimed

10 (April–June 1962), pp. 123–43; Harry Hamm, *Albania: China's Beachhead in Europe* (New York: Praeger, 1963); William Griffith, *Albania and the Sino-Soviet Rift* (Cambridge, Mass.: MIT Press, 1963); Nicholas C. Pano, *The People's Republic of Albania* (Baltimore: Johns Hopkins University Press, 1968); Peter R. Prifti, "Albania and the Sino-Soviet Conflict," *Studies in Comparative Communism*, 6.3 (Autumn 1973), pp. 241–79.

loyalty to Stalin.[13] His main opponent at home, interior minister and security police chief Koçi Xoxe, was labeled a pro-Yugoslav conspirator and shot. Stalin's intervention, then, did not just incidentally keep Hoxha in power; the tiny Balkan country became, as one scholar has put it, "the Stalinist avant-garde" in Soviet-dominated Eastern Europe.[14]

Soviet support proved crucial for a predominantly rural and poverty-stricken country. By the middle of the 1950s, Albania had received substantial loans from Moscow and other socialist countries, in addition to military aid. Its entire industrialization campaign depended on Soviet technical assistance, expertise, and the provision of blueprints for cement factories, textile mills, and sugar-processing plants. Qualified local personnel were in short supply, and communist functionaries distrusted older technical elites. Soviet engineers and managers, therefore, were in high demand. At the request of Albanian party apparatchiks, Soviet advisors came to organize state agencies, dispense advice, and train the local workforce.[15] The country's first university was modeled after a Soviet example. Russian became widely taught in schools. Stalin, in turn, became a fixture in daily newspapers, magazines, and textbooks. Having joined the Council for Mutual Economic Aid (Comecon) in 1949, Albania also became a founding member of the Warsaw Pact in 1955. Throughout all of this, the Soviets were keen to showcase the Mediterranean country as an example of successful Soviet-financed modernization to the Third World.[16] Aid to Albania, Khrushchev would claim, was proof of disinterested socialist solidarity.[17]

Khrushchev's attack against Stalin in 1956, however, and especially his efforts to restore relations with Belgrade, provoked great anxiety among the PPSH leaders. For years Hoxha had accused Tito of planning to annex Albania. The central party apparatus had mounted a vigorous campaign casting the Yugoslav leader as a scheming aggressor and his brand of socialism as profoundly corrupt. Rapprochement would require

---

[13] For an overview of these developments, see Leonid Gibianskii, "The Soviet–Yugoslav Split and the Cominform," in Norman Naimark and Leonid Gibianskii, eds., *The Establishment of Communist Regimes in Eastern Europe, 1944–1949* (Boulder: Westview Press, 1997), pp. 291–312; and Jeronim Perović, "The Tito–Stalin Split: A Reassessment in Light of New Evidence," *Journal of Cold War Studies* 9.2 (Spring 2007), pp. 32–63.

[14] François Fejtö, "La Deviazione albanese," *Comunità* 107 (1963), pp. 18–32, at p. 25.

[15] "O polozhenii s ispol'zovaniem kreditov, predostavlyaemykh Albanii Sovetskim Soyuzom i stranami narodnov demokratii" (Secret), September 24, 1956, in Rossiiskii Gosudarstvennyi Arkhiv Noveishei Istorii (Russian State Archive of Contemporary History), Moscow (RGANI), F. 5, Op. 28, D. 391, Ll. 194–95.

[16] Ibid.

[17] Khrushchev's speech at a lunch reception in honor of the Albanian party and government delegation, n.d. (1957), in AQSH, F. 14/AP, M-PK(b)BS, V. 1957, Dos. 2.

an embarrassing revision of this narrative. The Soviet handling of the uprising in Hungary in late 1956, moreover, further estranged the Albanian party chief. Still, Tirana was completely dependent on the Soviets – for loans, security, and much-needed imports – so Albanian objections were downplayed in public. On important issues such as relations with Belgrade and de-Stalinization, however, the Soviets and the Albanians continued to have serious disagreements. Hoxha's tactic was to promise compliance in Moscow, but revert to a hardline position back at home, including no rehabilitation of the slain Xoxe, no concessions on Yugoslavia, and an aggressive campaign against those who sought reforms or complained about the country's poor economic performance.[18] Like North Korea, Albania ultimately refused de-Stalinization. But in addition to ideological disagreements (Stalin's legacy) and geopolitical considerations (Yugoslavia), Soviet aid also emerged as a point of contention. Over the years, Soviet functionaries consistently criticized their Albanian counterparts for planning errors and for relying too heavily on Moscow's subsidies. When Khrushchev visited Albania in 1959, his view of the country's future (as an agricultural supplier to the Eastern bloc) departed sharply from Hoxha's visions of expanding heavy industries and constructing oil refineries.[19]

Relations between Tirana and Beijing were limited during these years. The two countries exchanged ambassadors in 1954 and the first high-level Chinese delegation came to Tirana in late 1956. Headed by Peng Zhen, a Politburo member and vice chairman of the Central Committee of the National People's Congress, the parliamentary delegation was treated to lengthy diatribes directed at the Yugoslavs. The Chinese, who were still attempting to act as mediators in Eastern Europe at the time, reacted coolly. But by 1960 Sino-Soviet relations had deteriorated considerably. When Communist Party leaders gathered in Bucharest in June that year, the Soviets attempted to bring the Chinese under control. Hoxha, who had sensed this impending escalation, decided not to travel to Bucharest. Faced with mounting Soviet pressure, the Albanian delegation refused to fall in line. As Chinese officials expressed admiration for Hoxha's stance, the Albanian leader became even more vocal in his opposition to Moscow. Disgruntlement over Soviet tactics and profound anxieties about the implications of de-Stalinization suddenly resurfaced,

---

[18] For an extended analysis of these developments, see Elidor Mëhilli, "Defying De-Stalinization: Albania's 1956," *Journal of Cold War Studies* 13.4 (Fall 2011).

[19] Notes from meetings between the Soviet delegation and Albanian party and government officials (Top Secret), May 25–29 and June 3, 1959, in AQSH, F.14/AP, M-PK(b)BS, V. 1959, Dos. 23, Fl. 1–18.

as Hoxha catalogued Soviet ideological mistakes at a party plenum in July 1960.[20] The Albanians also refused Moscow's invitation later that year to mend relations. Calling the Soviet ambassador in Tirana a "saboteur," Hoxha angrily denounced the Soviet leadership (after consultations with the Chinese) at the meeting of the eighty-one communist parties in Moscow in November.[21] The following year, party disagreements turned into a full-blown conflict in state relations, as Tirana and Moscow quarreled over Soviet-manned submarines stationed in Vlorë. Notably, even as the Chinese urged Hoxha to consider revising relations with Moscow in early 1961, he refused.[22] The Soviets finally withdrew their advisors and suspended diplomatic relations. Khrushchev went on an angry tirade against the Albanians at the Twenty-Second Congress of the Communist Party of the Soviet Union. Hoxha, in turn, famously declared in November that the Albanians would "eat grass – if necessary – rather than sell themselves for thirty silverlings."[23]

This loss of Soviet credit and technical personnel threatened to spell disaster for Albania's economic plans, especially the third Five Year Plan (1961–65). China was expected to step in. "One good friend," Mao reportedly told the Albanians, "is just enough."[24] Praising Tirana's political courage in standing up to Khrushchev, Beijing quickly promised 50,000 tons of grain. In August 1960, Chinese officials also affirmed that their party "as in the past, today, and in the future, has recognized, entrusted, and admired the unwavering position of the Party of Labor of Albania in the battle to defend the principles of Marxism Leninism."[25] But the Chinese were simply not able to provide all of the requested industrial aid, though this did not deter the Albanians from issuing exorbitant requests for full industrial plants, massive amounts of equipment, and military aid. And though they often complained, Chinese officials typically

---

[20] Transcript of the Seventeenth Plenum of the Third Congress of the PPSH, July 11–12, 1960, in AQSH, F. 14/AP, OU, V. 1960, Dos. 2, Fl. 33.

[21] Extensive records from these meetings have been published in translation: Ana Lalaj, Christian F. Ostermann, and Ryan Gage, "'Albania is not Cuba': Sino-Albanian Summits and the Sino-Soviet Split," *Cold War International History Project Bulletin* 16 (Fall 2007/Winter 2008), pp. 183–337. Some excerpts from Albanian archival sources related to the Warsaw Pact have also been published in Italian translation: See Antonella Ercolani, *L'Albania di fronte all'Unione Sovietica nel patto di Varsavia, 1955–1961* (Viterbo: Sette città, 2007).

[22] Transcript of conversation with Chinese delegation headed by Li Xiannian, February 9, 1961, in AQSH, F. 14/AP, M-PKK, V. 1961, Dos. 2, Fl. 1–28.

[23] *Zëri i popullit* (8 November 1961).

[24] Quoted in Lorenz Lüthi, *The Sino-Soviet Split: Cold War in the Communist World* (Princeton: Princeton University Press, 2008), p. 173.

[25] Notes from meeting between Mehmet Shehu and Van Dun, August 1, 1960, in AQSH, F.14/AP, M-PKK, V. 1960, Dos. 5, Fl. 1.

followed through. They agreed, for example, to buy wheat in France and Canada and ship it to Albania.[26] Politically, too, Albania's role in this alliance was far more significant than it had been with the Soviets. In the early 1960s, Beijing was still pursuing improved relations with Moscow, but Tirana was not. Hoxha dismissed these Chinese overtures and objected to any suggestion of concessions. Albania served as an advocate, finally, for China's membership in the United Nations. And because Tirana often served as a proxy for Soviet attacks against Beijing, Hoxha quickly learned to exploit this position when seeking assistance from the Chinese as well. He kept suspicions about Chinese foreign policy private, as Tirana continued to plead with the Chinese for everything from fully equipped industrial plants to artillery and army gear.[27] Party propaganda, in turn, lauded China as the crucial factor in the building of socialism.

While presenting a number of economic problems, then, the shift from Moscow to Mao solved a number of domestic problems for Hoxha. Chinese premier Zhou Enlai's visits to Albania in 1963/64, 1965, and 1966 lent the impression of crucial external support for the party establishment, even as the guest often warned that the Albanians expected too much from China (by contrast, Hoxha had pleaded with Khrushchev for years for an official visit). Politburo member Kang Sheng, deputy premier Li Xiannian, and leading Cultural Revolution activist Yao Wenyuan made similarly highly publicized visits to the country. After the Soviet invasion of Prague in 1968, a time of great panic about a possible military confrontation, the Chinese sent a delegation headed by Chief of the General Staff of the People's Liberation Army Huang Yongsheng to Tirana – a remarkable display of support. During Mao's Cultural Revolution, too, an endless procession of Chinese workers, engineers, scientists, athletes, agricultural specialists, women activists, and youths showed up in Tirana, on highly choreographed official visits. From the outside, the Sino-Albanian bond seemed strong.

Brothers in revolution?

Hoxha was initially very nervous about the Cultural Revolution's destructive potential. He could not fathom how a communist leader

---

[26] See, for example, "Memorandum of Conversation with Zhou Enlai," February 2, 1961, and "Report on the Second Meeting with the CCP Delegation to the Fourth Congress of the Albanian Labor Party," February 25, 1961, published in *Cold War International History Project Bulletin* 16 (Fall 2007/Winter 2008), pp. 197–200, 200–16.

[27] Elsewhere, I have analyzed these developments more extensively: Elidor Mëhilli, "Building the Second World: Postwar Socialism in Albania and the Eastern Bloc,"(Ph.D. thesis, Princeton University, 2011.

could intentionally destroy his own communist party. By the end of 1966, however, Hoxha threw his support behind Mao. The following year, the Albanians energetically defended Mao's ideological war. *Reflections on China* offers another version of this story. According to this account, Hoxha was consistently critical of the Chinese party higher-ups in general, and Mao's cult of personality in particular. His "political diary" is filled with angry tirades about the "catastrophic" mistakes of the Chinese. On the one hand, then, party records show that Hoxha praised Mao effusively in 1967. On the other, his "political diary," supposedly written at the same time, has him viciously attacking Mao's cult of personality. To be sure, such an ambiguous reaction to Mao and Chinese policies predated the Cultural Revolution. In the early 1960s, Hoxha had warned his colleagues not to exaggerate Mao's significance, as he feared that the Chinese would eventually manage to rebuild relations with the Soviet Union.[28] The Sino-Albanian relationship during these years was marked by ups and downs. Public pronouncements of unity went hand in hand with private expressions of caution in the Politburo.

But a number of developments in 1966 brought the two parties in closer alignment: the collapse of Sino-Soviet relations in the spring of that year and Mao's Cultural Revolution. The former temporarily reassured Hoxha that Beijing would not succumb to "Soviet revisionism." The effect of the Cultural Revolution, however, was more complicated. To outside observers at the time, it seemed that the Albanians merely imported Mao's revolution – if not wholesale, then in spirit.[29] Throughout 1967, Tirana and Beijing made similar revolutionary pronouncements, which lent credence to this idea. True, Chinese officials sought to familiarize the Albanians with their revolutionary tactics. Albanian delegations, moreover, were given privileged access to China at a time when it was virtually closed to the outside world. But there is no evidence that the Chinese sought to impose their Cultural Revolution on the Albanians, as Hoxha accused them in his later published accounts. Quite the opposite, in fact: Mao was not the only one who argued that Albania could not merely copy China. Albanian party higher-ups themselves, such as prime minister Mehmet Shehu, often pointed out in conversations with their Chinese counterparts that conditions in Albania were radically different from China's. This period of apparent revolutionary harmony in 1967, therefore, did not come about through Chinese pressure. Nor was it inevitable; Hoxha had to be reassured that China's

---

[28] Ibid.   [29] "Albania: Mediterranean Maoists," *Newsweek* (August 14, 1967), p. 49.

leadership would not unravel and that *his* party was completely under control before embracing the Chinese Cultural Revolution.

Ideological arguments between the two parties resurfaced in the summer of 1966. During a visit by Mehmet Shehu to Beijing earlier that year, the issue of existing class antagonism under socialism had come up – an idea that the Albanians rejected. At that time, Hoxha argued that China's domestic struggles did not concern Albania, where the Party of Labor was robust and where "enemies" had been wiped out. When Zhou Enlai returned the visit later that June, he sought to clarify the Chinese position on class antagonism.[30] This visit, however, does not appear to have appeased Hoxha. With little information forthcoming from Beijing later that fall, he worried about what a sudden reversal in Chinese leadership might mean for his regime. Albania was fully reliant on the Chinese for credit, technology, and military support. But Mao's gamble could also do great political damage. Hoxha's notes from this period betray a sense of deep anxiety: Events in China seemed like a disturbing déjà vu of the damage done by Khrushchev's assault against Stalin in 1956.[31] Back then, the Soviet leader's decision to rekindle relations with Belgrade had thrown Hoxha into a similar panic. What if Mao lost control of the party and the Chinese changed course?

In this context, Hoxha quickly prepared the groundwork in case this reversal took place in Beijing. He warned Central Committee officials about the destructive nature of Mao's Cultural Revolution, which he deemed inexplicably chaotic. In October, during a meeting of the Politburo, he defended the idea of a proletarian cultural revolution but insisted that "it ought to be in great seriousness led by the party."[32] At the party plenum held shortly thereafter, he repeated his warnings that the loss of party control was unacceptable. In a clever tactical move, moreover, he argued that the exaggerated emphasis on Mao's "genius" was antithetical to Marxism. (The implication, of course, was that Hoxha was firmly against a similar cult of personality around *him* in Albania.)

These initial misgivings also appear in *Reflections on China*, although the tone of entries there is much more severe than in the party records. In one entry bearing the date August 9, 1966, for example, Hoxha

---

[30] Memorandum of conversation between the Chinese and Albanian party leaders, June 27, 1966, published in *Cold War International History Project Bulletin* 16 (Fall 2007/ Winter 2008), pp. 311–28.

[31] Hoxha's remarks on the Cultural Revolution to the PPSH Politburo, October 10–11, 1966, in AQSH, F. 14/AP, V. 1966, Dos. 21, Fl. 376–408.

[32] Hoxha's speech on the Cultural Revolution in China held at the Eighteenth party Plenum of the Fourth Congress of the PPSH, 14 October 1966, in AQSH, F. 14/AP, V. 1966, Dos. 4.

admonishes the Chinese for turning the cult of Mao "almost into a religion, exalting him in a sickening way."[33] He wonders: "Are we dealing with Marxists or with religious fanatics? Because truly, from what we are seeing with our eyes and hearing with our ears, in China they are treating Mao as the Christians treat Christ."[34] Hoxha's published entries also accuse the Chinese of seeking to promote Mao's cult in Albania, for portraying him "as a 'God,' as 'infallible,' the lone 'Pole Star'."[35] Were these assessments actually made in a personal diary? Were they, instead, produced retroactively as a form of political retribution against the Chinese, after Mao's death? Or are they a combination of both? It is not possible to say with certainty. Past episodes with Xoxe and other purged party officials had shown that Hoxha could be cunning and ruthlessly vindictive. Albanian party leaders were bound together by a shared history of intra-party violence and fabrications. The task is further complicated by the fact that *Reflections on China*, like numerous other volumes that appeared under Hoxha's name, seems to have been based on careful and selective readings of party records. As a result, Hoxha's entries correspond to actual events and refer accurately to some conversations, while leaving others out, or manipulating context and timing.

It clearly emerges, in any case, that in the fall of 1966 Hoxha called for vigilance within the Albanian party ranks. At the Politburo and party plenum, he admitted that he did not have enough information about events in China but nevertheless recommended that party functionaries be put on alert. The Albanians would follow Chinese developments closely, hoping that the CCP would retain control. In the meantime, Hoxha advised, they would refer to Mao only by following standard party protocols, avoiding exaggerations and euphoria. The Albanian press, similarly, was supposed to avoid lengthy coverage of the revolutionary texts being published in China. Even if "demanded by the Chinese comrades," Hoxha instructed, propaganda for China was supposed to be controlled from above. These warnings made it clear – if it was at all necessary – that Hoxha was fully in control of the party apparatus. They also established that the PPSH would not tolerate any Chinese-style chaos "from below." To soften his assessment somewhat, Hoxha reassured party functionaries that relations with China would remain strong.[36]

---

[33] Hoxha, *Reflections on China*, p. 223.   [34] Ibid., p. 224.   [35] Ibid., p. 282.

[36] Hoxha's remarks on the Cultural Revolution, in AQSH, F. 14/AP, OU, V. 1966, Dos. 21, Fl. 376–408; Hoxha's speech on the Cultural Revolution in China is contained in AQSH, F. 14/AP, OU, V. 1966, Dos. 4.

Then, in early November, the Albanian party chief suddenly revised his position on Mao's revolutionary experiment. This reversal coincided with the Fifth Congress of the PPSH. Kang Sheng, who headed the Chinese delegation to the Congress, ceremoniously presented a message from Mao, which hailed Albania as the vanguard of Marxism–Leninism:

China and Albania are separated by thousands of mountains and rivers but our hearts are closely linked. We are your true friends and comrades. And you are ours. You are not like those false friends and double-dealers who have "honey on their lips and murder in their hearts," and neither are we. Our militant revolutionary friendship has stood the test of violent storms.[37]

The Chairman's flattery dispelled concerns that the Chinese might abandon the Albanians.[38] His greeting received frantic applause at the congress and a red flag adorned with the embroidered message was displayed in front of the delegates. So intense was the euphoria around Mao's greeting, in fact, that when the Chinese leader was told about it the following year, he expressed disbelief.[39] Crucially, Kang Sheng provided a detailed account of the Cultural Revolution's aims in meetings with Hoxha and his associates. His explanations offered some reassurance to the Albanian leader (who admits as much in *Reflections on China*).[40] He was told that the CCP was seriously endangered by a group of enemies and revisionists who were to blame for past errors in China's policies. Peng Zhen, Liu Shaoqi, Deng Xiaoping, and others, this explanation went, had embarked on a capitalist path, hoping to steer China along Khrushchev's path. China had made many mistakes, including in relations with Albania. More assured of the position of the CCP, Hoxha praised Mao during receptions for the Chinese delegation. Quickly thereafter, the Ministry of Foreign Affairs instructed diplomats abroad to study Hoxha's speeches so as to understand Mao's Revolution. "The aim of the Cultural Revolution," these officials instructed, "is to wage a merciless battle against bourgeois and revisionist ideology and leftovers in the consciousness of people, to uproot any possibility for the eruption of revisionism and the restoration of capitalism, and to ensure the final victory of the socialist path and the general strengthening of the People's Republic of China."[41]

---

[37] "Comrade Mao Tse-tung's Message of Greetings to the Fifth Congress of the Albanian Party of Labour," *Peking Review* 9.46 (November 11, 1966), p. 5.

[38] Contemporary film sequences show how vigorously the Albanians promoted Mao's message. One good example is *Kongresi i luftëtarëve revolucionarë* (Shqipëria e Re, 1966).

[39] Memorandum of conversation between Mao, Hysni Kapo, and Beqir Balluku (Top Secret), February 3, 1967, in AQSH, F. 14/AP, V. 1967, Dos. 6, Fl. 15.

[40] Hoxha, *Reflections on China*, pp. 308–10.

[41] Tirana to all missions abroad, except New York (Top Secret), November 19, 1966, in AMPJ, V. 1966, Dos. 72, Fl. 78.

The Albanian response to the Cultural Revolution was fully formed during the early months of 1967. In January, a military delegation arrived in China to request more aid. Hysni Kapo, officially in Beijing for medical reasons, also met with high-level Chinese functionaries, including Mao.[42] During these meetings, the Chinese admitted to past mistakes and acknowledged that the CCP was under siege. They also provided the Albanians with a list of "enemies" who had been unmasked. Mao, notably, criticized the cult created around him and insisted that he was to blame for much of the chaos around China. The visitors were also sent to local organizations to witness the Cultural Revolution in action. It is difficult to say precisely how much these forthcoming details from China relieved Hoxha's concerns. At a meeting of the Politburo in February, he admitted that the chaos in China was real and the fact that the party there had allowed this to happen was astonishing. Still, Hoxha argued that the aims of the Cultural Revolution – and Mao's line – were politically correct. Without China, he told his associates, Albania would be lost.[43] At the party plenum later that summer, he continued to endorse the Cultural Revolution.[44] It also helped that the Chinese admitted to their political mistakes and that they publicly attacked "China's Khrushchev" and "capitalist roaders." But Hoxha's growing sympathy for the Cultural Revolution was also underlined by a streak of pragmatism: caught in the middle of the havoc of the Cultural Revolution, Chinese officials nevertheless appeared extremely eager in 1967 to provide substantial amounts of technical and military aid. "Sometimes our Albanian friends had too big an appetite for Chinese assistance," one of these Chinese officials later recalled.[45] Regardless, Beijing fulfilled most of the requests and agreed to fully equip the Albanian army. By the middle of 1967, then, Sino-Albanian relations seemed to have reached a peak. That October, prime minister Mehmet Shehu was back in China with the explicit task of expressing public support for Mao's

---

[42] Memorandum of meeting between Mao, Kapo, and Balluku, in AQSH, F. 14/AP, M-PKK, V. 1967, Dos. 6, Fl. 12–32.

[43] Transcript of the meeting of the PPSH Politburo, February 15, 1967, in AQSH, F. 14/AP, OU, V. 1967, Dos. 5.

[44] Hoxha's speech on the Chinese Cultural Revolution at the Second Plenum of the Fifth Congress of the PLA, June 15–16, 1967, in AQSH, F. 14/AP, OU, V. 1967, Dos. 1, Fl. 523–48.

[45] Fan Chengzuo's recollections are contained in Xiaoyuan Liu and Vojtech Mastny, eds., *China and Eastern Europe, 1960s–1980s: Proceedings of the International Symposium: Reviewing the History of Chinese–East European Relations from the 1960s to the 1980s* (Zurich: Center for Security Studies, 2004), p. 184.

Cultural Revolution. Chinese functionaries, in turn, referred to Hoxha as "a great Marxist–Leninist."[46]

Reflections on China presents a wildly different picture of this period. Hoxha's "political diary" skips over five whole months between August 1967 and January 1968 – a period in which Tirana feverishly supported Mao's Cultural Revolution. His 1967 entries are consistently negative vis-à-vis the Chinese. He lambasts them for challenging Stalin's legacy, among other things. He catalogues Mao's failures of leadership. And in an April 1967 entry, he takes the Chinese to task for launching a revolution "without the party."[47] The Chinese had made "a mistake of catastrophic proportions" in leaving their party uninformed of developments and agitating the masses against it. Long and angry, these entries also condemn the Chinese for pushing other countries to adopt the Cultural Revolution and for presenting Mao's philosophy as universal. They conclude with Hoxha's ruminations in the summer of 1967 about Beijing's self-inflicted isolation in foreign policy. The Chinese had relinquished their responsibilities in the Third World. They kept hailing Mao's thoughts as "the culmination of Marxism." But how could they try to teach the rest of the world how to conduct a revolution when they decided to liquidate their own party and threw themselves wholeheartedly into total chaos?[48]

Here the discrepancies between party records and Hoxha's later recollections are clearer. At the same time that he was allegedly denouncing Mao's cult of personality in his diary, the Albanian leader was recorded praising Mao's ideas as significant for the entire world.[49] By June 1967, in fact, Hoxha explained to party cadres that Mao himself was *against* the cult of personality, referring to Mao's comments made to the Albanian delegation earlier that year. "Our opinion is that Mao Zedong's line is, in general, correct," he said at the party plenum, adding that it was "Marxist–Leninist, internationalist, and in opposition to modern revisionism inside China and abroad."[50] He admitted that he might have had some misgivings about Mao before, but that the Albanians had come around to understand the Chinese comrades and their internal struggles. There is no trace of this defense of Mao in *Reflections on China*. Hoxha's

---

[46] See, for example, Shehu's report on his visit to China, October 18, 1967, in AQSH, F. 14/AP, OU, V. 1967, Dos. 15, Fl. 24.

[47] Hoxha, *Reflections on China*, p. 353.   [48] Ibid., pp. 370–72.

[49] Memorandum of conversation between Enver Hoxha and Chinese delegation, May 6, 1967, in AQSH, F. 14/AP, M-PKK, V. 1967, Dos. 42, Fl. 7.

[50] Hoxha's speech on China's Cultural Revolution delivered to the Second Plenum of the Fifth Congress of the PPSH, June 15–16, 1967, in AQSH, F. 14/AP, OU, V. 1967, Dos. 1.

book also complains that Chinese functionaries routinely ignored the Albanians, but at the plenum he insisted that the Chinese comrades valued Albanian opinions and took them seriously. On July 8, in fact, he received a delegation of Red Guards and showered them with praise. "Like our great classics of Marxism–Leninism teach us and like it is also written in Mao Zedong's Little Red Book," Hoxha told them, "the party stands above everything; without the party there can be no victory."[51] Hoxha also told the Red Guards that Mao was "a shining ideological and political beacon" for the international communist world.[52] Albanian youths, he reassured them, "love you and admire you."[53] *Reflections on China* contains an entry allegedly written barely a week after that meeting, on July 14. Hoxha's position there is radically different. "If we observe the official state policy of the Chinese comrades," that entry states, "we shall see that it is not at all balanced, can say that it is non-existent, or when it is expressed, it is wrong."[54]

That same entry takes the Chinese to task for their extremism in promoting Mao's philosophy: "He who is with the ideas of Mao Tsetung is a Marxist-Leninist; he who allows himself to ask certain natural, fair questions is suspect and can even be considered an anti-Marxist."[55] Party records show, however, that this was *the Albanian* position, not the Chinese. When Shehu visited China later that fall, he explicitly submitted that Mao's Cultural Revolution was the ultimate ideological test for a communist: Those who defended it were Marxist–Leninists; those who went against it were not.[56] The Chinese, needless to say, were immensely flattered. Shehu made the same remark in his public speech in Shanghai: "We hold that one's attitude towards China's great proletarian cultural revolution is the touchstone for distinguishing between Marxist–Leninists and revisionists and opportunists, and between genuine revolutionaries and counter-revolutionaries." The Albanian party and people, he concluded, had "consistently supported the great proletarian Cultural Revolution and will support it to the end."[57] In reality, they had not. Hoxha's "diary" takes a position that he advocated, and Shehu publicly held, and blames the Chinese for it. We are presented, then, with two images of the Albanian leader: one is furious at Mao and

---

[51] Transcript of meeting between Enver Hoxha and a delegation of the Red Guards headed by Yao Wenyuan, July 8, 1967, in AQSH, F. 14/AP, M-PKK, V. 1967, Dos. 43, Fl. 4.

[52] Ibid., Fl. 14.   [53] Ibid., Fl. 15.

[54] Hoxha, *Reflections on China*, p. 375.   [55] Ibid., p. 370.

[56] Memorandum of conversation between Mehmet Shehu and Zhou Enlai, September 30, 1967, in AQSH, F. 14/AP, M-PKK, Dos. 19, Fl. 28.

[57] "Comrade Shehu's Speech – At the October 11 Shanghai Rally Welcoming the Albanian Party and Government Delegation," *Peking Review* 10.44 (October 27, 1967), p. 18.

bewildered by the Chinese Cultural Revolution, the other asks for 100,000 volumes of the Little Red Book and embraces the Red Guards in Tirana.

One way of making sense of these discrepancies in sources is to read them as part of a later effort to write a particular version of history. But they also begin to tell us something significant about the political uses of Mao's cult halfway across the world. In late 1967, Mao's quotations made their way into speeches and textbooks.[58] The plastic jacket of the pocket-size book became very popular (many appeared to find alternative uses for it as a wallet).[59] True, not everyone was immediately taken with the Chairman. According to one account, Mao seemed like a disastrous choice to those intellectuals and youths entertaining hopes that Albania might open up to the West instead: "All of our resentment was aimed at Mao," recalled one such individual, "and we only had bad things to say about him, only ridicule; Tirana's elite circles nurtured great antipathy towards him. Then, two years later, when we saw the kind of support he generated among Western youths, this surprised and upset us."[60] Hoxha's own ambivalent reaction to Mao's cult, in other words, was amplified throughout party ranks and intellectuals, even as the party continued daily to hail the Chairman.

When compared to the propaganda for Stalin in 1950s Albania, the promotion of Mao's teachings was significantly more subdued. The Chinese embassy in Tirana issued his "paper tiger" speech in 1956. The following year, Tirana's state publishing house published his essays "On Practice" and "On Contradiction."[61] In 1961, Albanians added Mao's excerpts to the standard roster of Marx and Engels; his selected works, printed in China, were published over several years, with the last volume appearing in 1965.[62] But translation and editing posed serious problems. For one thing, there were not enough qualified individuals with a working knowledge of Chinese. The limited translations from

---

[58] See, for example, *Buletin i universitetit shtetëror të Tiranës* (Tirana, 1967), p. 19.

[59] "Miqësia shqiptaro-kineze" [Albanian–Chinese friendship], *Klan* (May 15, 2009).

[60] Spartak Ngjela, *Përkulja dhe rënia e tiranisë shqiptare: 1957–2010* [The decline and fall of Albanian tyranny: 1957–2010] (Tirana: UET Press, 2011), p. 337. The author's father served as minister of foreign trade at the time. He suggests that, after the break with the Soviet Union, some of the children of high-ranking officials had also hoped for an opening to the West.

[61] Mao Zedong, *Në lidhje me praktikën; Në lidhje me kontradiktën* [On practice; On contradiction] (Tirana: Ndërmarrja Shtetërore e Botimeve, 1956).

[62] Memorandum on translations of Marx and Engels, dated by hand July15, 1961, in AQSH, F. 14/AP, OU, V. 1961, Dos. 55, Fl. 135–39; "Letërsia kineze në gjuhën shqipe," [Chinese literature in the Albanian language] *Miqësia* 10 (October 1965), p. 6.

Chinese materials, therefore, came from Russian-language versions. Then, suddenly, in 1967, after Hoxha had declared that the Cultural Revolution was ideologically correct, a flurry of books came out. Sporting shiny red covers, these books included hundreds of quotations from Marx, Engels, Lenin, Stalin, and Mao on subjects such as the dictatorship of the proletariat, class war, self-reliance, democratic centralization, patriotism and self-reliance, youth, women, and religion.[63] A few separate volumes devoted entirely to Mao also appeared, but it is noteworthy that the Albanians took care to showcase Mao as one thinker alongside the other classics.[64] Albanian authorities were also hesitant to become involved with Beijing's promotion of the quotations abroad. In the summer of 1967, the Chinese representative in Prague asked the Albanians for help in finding a person who could help edit the translations of Mao's quotations into the Czech language. Such work could not be carried out at the Chinese embassy, this official explained, for fear of controls placed by the local Czechoslovak police.[65] The following year, Chinese officials asked if the Albanians could secure them translators in Turkey so as to be able to publish Mao's quotations there. Officials in Tirana, however, were reluctant to risk annoying the Turkish government.[66]

Precisely because the Albanian communist leaders did not intend to copy Mao's Cultural Revolution wholesale, Sino-Albanian exchanges at this period also produced great confusion. When an Albanian volleyball team visited China in September 1967, they were handed Mao's quotations and instructed to read them during training sessions. The local authorities demanded that Chinese players read the quotations aloud

---

[63] *Mbi diktaturën e proletariatit* [On the dictatorship of the proletariat] (Tirana: Naim Frashëri, 1967); *Mbi luftën e klasave* [On class war] (Tirana: Naim Frashëri, 1967); *Mbi mbështetjen në forcat e veta* [On self-reliance] (Tirana: Naim Frashëri, 1967); *Mbi centralizmin demokratik në parti* [On democratic centralization within the party] (Tirana: Naim Frashëri, 1967); *Mbi patriotizmin dhe internacionalizmin proletar* [On proletarian patriotism and internationalism] (Tirana: Naim Frashëri, 1967); *Mbi fenë: pjesë të nxjerra nga veprat e K. Marksit, F. Engelsit, V. I. Leninit, J. V. Stalinit dhe të Mao Ce-dunit* [On religion: selections from the works of Marx, Engels, Lenin, Stalin and Mao Zedong] (Tirana: Naim Frashëri, 1967).

[64] See, for example, Mao Ce-dun [Mao Zedong], *T'i shërbejmë popullit! Përmbledhje artikujsh e fjalimesh* [Let us serve the people! Articles and speeches] (Tirana: Instituti i Studimeve Marksiste-Leniniste pranë KQ të PPSH, 1968); *Mbi partinë (përmbledhje me pjesë nga veprat e zgjedhura)* [On the party: excerpts from selected works] (Tirana: Shkolla e Partisë "V. I. Lenin," 1971).

[65] Albanian embassy in Prague to Tirana (Top Secret), August 10, 1967, in AMPJ, V. 1967, Dos. 64, Fl. 66.

[66] Memorandum on relations with the PRC during 1968, in AMPJ, V. 1968, Dos. 64, Fl. 128; Ministry of Foreign Affairs report to Enver Hoxha, Mehmet Shehu, Hysni Kapo, and Ramiz Alia, n.d., in AMPJ, V. 1968, Dos. 17/1, Fl. 54.

immediately before the match. They also encouraged the Albanian athletes to do so.[67] Shortly thereafter, ministry officials sent an explanatory
missive to Beijing stating, "Each of our delegations that visit China ought
to study the quotations of comrade Mao and draw lessons from them.
This kind of reading and studying should be done according to the
educational methods used by our party. We are not used to and do not
practice the reading of party materials and quotations aloud or in unison,
as a group."[68] Indeed, even the practice of having Mao's quotations
distributed upon a delegation's arrival at the airport in Beijing seemed
peculiar, and the Albanian embassy sent a special note warning incoming
visitors that they might have to read quotes aloud in front of welcoming
crowds.[69]

Intent on not following Mao's example in liquidating the party,
Hoxha nevertheless saw an opportunity in the upheaval of 1967 to
escalate his own "uninterrupted revolution" at home. Since 1965, he
had waged a so-called campaign against bureaucracy, which escalated
after February 1967 – a crucial and neglected episode that demands
further research.[70] But this chapter has shown that this was hardly a
matter of faithfully following Mao's example. The discrepancies
between high-level party records and Hoxha's later published recollections point to the importance of untangling the Sino-Albanian relationship and the crucial links between ideology, geopolitics, external
factors, and domestic constraints. The Albanian party had not, as
Shehu claimed in Shanghai, supported Mao's Cultural Revolution
from the very beginning. But the version presented in Hoxha's *Reflections* is also manipulative – a 1979 act of literary retribution against
the Chinese. Given that Mao's Little Red Book was itself seen as a
kind of weapon in the 1960s, it is hardly surprising that Hoxha, in his
later years of ill health and paranoia, sought to fight back with a book
of his own. By the late 1970s, however, Mao was gone and the Chinese
had moved on.

---

[67] Albanian embassy in Beijing to Tirana (Top Secret), September 19, 1967, in AMPJ,
V. 1967, Dos. 64, Fl. 67. The details about the team are contained in a separate file. See
Ministry of Foreign Affairs memorandum on relations with China in 1967, February
1968, in AMPJ, V. 1967, Dos. 64, Fl. 89.
[68] Tirana to Albanian embassy in Beijing (Top Secret), September 23, 1967, in AMPJ,
V. 1967, Dos. 64, Fl. 70.
[69] Albanian embassy in Beijing to Tirana (Top Secret), September 25, 1967, in AMPJ,
V. 1967, Dos. 64, Fl. 71.
[70] For an overview of Hoxha's revolutionary campaign, see Nicholas Pano, "The Albanian
Cultural Revolution," *Problems of Communism* 23.4 (July–August 1974), pp. 44–57.

BIBLIOGRAPHY

ARCHIVAL SOURCES

Arkivi i Ministrisë së Punëve të Jashtme (Archive of the Ministry of Foreign Affairs), Tirana

Arkivi Qendror Shtetëror (Central State Archives), Tirana

Fondi 14/AP (formerly the Archive of the Central Committee of the Party of Labour of Albania)

Politisches Archiv des Auswärtigen Amtes – Ministerium für Auswärtige Angelegenheiten (Political Archive of the Foreign Office – Ministry for Foreign Affairs), Berlin

Rossiskii Gosudarstvennyi Arkhiv Noveishei Istorii (Russian State Archive of Contemporary History), Moscow

GENERAL SOURCES

Biberaj, Elez, *Albania and China, 1962–1978: A Study of an Unequal Alliance* (Boulder: Westview Press, 1986)

Citate të Kryetarit Mao Ce-Dun [Quotations of Chairman Mao Zedong] (Beijing: Shtëpia botonjëse e gjuhëve të huaja, 1967)

Ercolani, Antonella, *L'Albania di fronte all'Unione Sovietica nel patto di Varsavia, 1955–1961* (Viterbo: Sette città, 2007)

Fejtö, François, "La Deviazione albanese," *Comunità* 107 (1963), pp. 18–32

Gibianskii, Leonid, "The Soviet–Yugoslav Split and the Cominform," in Norman Naimark and Leonid Gibianskii, eds., *The Establishment of Communist Regimes in Eastern Europe, 1944–1949* (Boulder: Westview Press, 1997), pp. 291–312

Griffith, William, *Albania and the Sino-Soviet Rift* (Cambridge, Mass.: MIT Press, 1963)

Halliday, Jon, *The Artful Albanian: The Memoirs of Enver Hoxha* (London: Chatto & Windus, 1986)

Hamm, Harry, *Albania: China's Beachhead in Europe* (New York: Praeger, 1963)

Hoxha, Enver, *Reflections on China (1962–1972): Extracts from the Political Diary*, vol. I (Tirana: "8 Nëntori," 1979)

Lalaj, Ana, Christian F. Ostermann, and Ryan Gage, "'Albania is not Cuba': Sino-Albanian Summits and the Sino-Soviet Split," *Cold War International History Project Bulletin* 16 (Fall 2007/Winter 2008), pp. 183–337

Liu, Xiaoyuan, and Vojtech Mastny, eds., *China and Eastern Europe, 1960s–1980s: Proceedings of the International Symposium: Reviewing the History of Chinese–East European Relations from the 1960s to the 1980s* (Zurich: Center for Security Studies, 2004)

Lüthi, Lorenz, *The Sino-Soviet Split: Cold War in the Communist World* (Princeton: Princeton University Press, 2008)

Mao Zedong, *Në lidhje me praktikën; Në lidhje me kontradiktën* [On practice; On contradiction] (Tirana: Ndërmarrja Shtetërore e Botimeve, 1956)

T'i shërbejmë popullit! Përmbledhje artikujsh e fjalimesh [Let us serve the people! Articles and speeches] (Tirana: Instituti i Studimeve Marksiste-Leniniste pranë KQ të PPSH, 1968)

Mbi partinë (përmbledhje me pjesë nga veprat e zgjedhura) [On the party: excerpts from selected works] (Tirana: Shkolla e Partisë "V. I. Lenin," 1971)

Mëhilli, Elidor, "Building the Second World: Postwar Socialism in Albania and the Eastern Bloc," Ph.D. thesis, Princeton University, 2011

"Defying De-Stalinization: Albania's 1956," *Journal of Cold War Studies* 13.4 (Fall 2011), pp. 4–56

Ngjela, Spartak, *Përkulja dhe rënia e tiranisë shqiptare: 1957–2010* [The decline and fall of Albanian tyranny: 1957–2010] (Tirana: UET Press, 2011)

Pano, Nicholas, "The Albanian Cultural Revolution," *Problems of Communism* 23.4 (July–August 1974), pp. 44–57

The People's Republic of Albania (Baltimore: Johns Hopkins University Press, 1968)

Perović, Jeronim, "The Tito–Stalin Split: A Reassessment in Light of New Evidence," *Journal of Cold War Studies* 9.2 (Spring 2007), pp. 32–63

Prifti, Peter R., "Albania and the Sino-Soviet Conflict," *Studies in Comparative Communism* 6.3 (Autumn 1973), pp. 241–79

Tretiak, Daniel, "The Founding of the Sino-Albanian Entente," *China Quarterly* 10 (April–June 1962), pp. 123–43

11 Partisan legacies and anti-imperialist ambitions
The Little Red Book in Italy and Yugoslavia

Dominique Kirchner Reill

> We should support whatever the enemy opposes and oppose whatever the enemy supports.
>
> Classes and Class Struggle

You've got (Chinese) mail: Italy and Yugoslavia

In early 1971, a university student in Venice, Italy, wrote to the Chinese embassy in Rome expressing interest in receiving an Italian-language copy of the Little Red Book. At more or less the same time, a high-school student in Pakrac, Yugoslavia, wrote to the Chinese embassy in Belgrade expressing interest in receiving a Serbo-Croatian-language copy of the Little Red Book. Each Chinese embassy complied and sent free of charge "exotically packaged" bundles to their respective applicants containing a little red book with a gold star, a plastic covering, and Mao's portrait inside. But with one difference: intent.

The university student in Venice was called into the Central Post Office to receive his mail from the Chinese embassy. And once he saw what awaited him, he was perplexed by the fact that the Chinese embassy had sent well over a hundred copies of the Little Red Book. With no way to carry such a quantity in a city with many bridges and no cars, the student corralled his friends to help him carry the books home. And once home, he opened a letter from the People's Republic of China inviting him to distribute the books.[1] The high-school student in Pakrac received no such surprises. Instead, he strolled along the busy provincial streets of his town in northern Yugoslavia to pick up, at the local post office, the single copy of the Little Red Book he had requested. To his delight, he also received a letter, but this one only expressed the guarded compliments of the People's Republic of China.[2]

---

[1] Interview with Roberto D'Agostino, Friday, June 24, 2011, Venice.
[2] Blog from Zdenko Čoban, zdenko-coban.bloger.hr/default.aspx?date=1.7.2010, accessed July 16, 2011.

The Little Red Book arrived through the state postal systems of Italy and Yugoslavia into the hands of two students on either side of the Iron Curtain. Both students independently sought out the book. And each student directly contacted the Chinese embassy in his country to obtain it. In response, both received letters from their Chinese embassies, and both were excited to collect packages that had been clearly produced and prepared in China, bundled together in a fashion and with materials that spoke of faraway Chinese practices. But what the Chinese embassies expected from the reception of the books was very different. One bundle was sent to help proselytize; the other was sent to inform. This chapter will highlight the commonalities and differences in how the Little Red Book was received in both contexts, commonalities and differences that both coaligned with and diverged from what Chinese embassy officials probably would have expected.

Italy: *La Cina è vicina* (China is near)

In similar vein to the French and German cases discussed by Julian Bourg (chapter 13) and Quinn Slobodian (chapter 12) in this volume, how and why Italians sought out, read, quoted, and ceremonially flaunted the Little Red Book varied enormously, and ran the gamut from hard-headed communists immersed in untangling intellectual dialectics, to heady youths seeking pop liberation from their conventional surroundings, to Mussolini-loving neo-fascists who believed Mao held the key to national liberation from the Americans. Even chronologically, the drive to read the words that fed China's Cultural Revolution was uneven, beginning in the mid-1960s and still attracting a reading public well into the late 1970s, if not longer. Contact with the Chinese communists and distribution of the book itself did not follow the top-down approach of the Albanian case described here by Elidor Mëhilli (chapter 10). No state or party, no centralized organization spearheaded the introduction of Maoist thought and Maoist propaganda into the lives of Italians. And unlike the West German or Soviet cases, no state initiatives worked to "attack" or "block" the book itself. The Little Red Book was first trans-lated in China and distributed in Italy through communist and socialist centers, student centers, and individuals with direct connections to China. But as was true in the West German, Austrian, and French cases, for-profit domestic editions of the book were also produced and sold by booksellers, most notably the communist publisher Giangiacomo Feltrinelli.

So, why this multifaceted, multi-temporal, and multi-sited distribution of the Little Red Book? To even begin to answer that question a much more simple one needs to be posed: why would Italians want to read it in the first place? What did they hope to learn from the Little Red Book? Having the largest Communist Party in Western Europe, Italians were not ignorant of the teachings of Marx and Lenin. Also, living in one of the richest and most industrialized countries in the world with an astoundingly religiously and linguistically homogeneous population, what could they really learn from a book written for a largely agricultural, largely industrially undeveloped, and incredibly ethnically diverse country so far away? To people who experienced the thirst for Mao in the 1960s and 1970s, perhaps this question seems naïve, but it is a useful one to ask when considering that until the mid-1960s only a select few could have talked at length about the current political situation in China; and almost no one could have quoted Mao at a rally, let alone across a dinner table. By the early 1970s, few did not talk at length about the current political situation in China, and if they didn't quote Mao to each other, they certainly would hear him quoted *at* them often enough.

To understand why Italians wanted to read the Little Red Book, two timelines are necessary: before and after August 1966. That is to say, before and after the dramatic pictures of China's Red Guards were splashed on the front page of almost every newspaper. The first sparks of interest in studying Mao's thought were not a natural consequence of the well-received and widely read 1965 Italian translation of Egdar Snow's 1937 *Red Star Over China*. Though inspiring and sympathetic, Snow's account was interpreted as depicting a China that was coming closer to the developed world through communism, not one that was formulating a new kind of communism that would teach the developed world how to do it. Before 1966, interest was spurred by a 1963 book titled *Le Divergenze tra il compagno Togliatti e noi* (Divergences between Comrade Togliatti and us).[3] Written and published in China and then sent to communist activists in Italy, *Divergenze* was an extension of the Sino-Soviet conflict set on Italian soil. It was published in response to the Tenth Annual Italian Communist Party Congress, where the leader of the Italian Communist Party, Palmiro Togliatti, directly upbraided Mao's stance against de-Stalinization. *Divergenze* was a pointed Chinese response to Togliatti's criticisms.

So, what was in *Divergenze* to spur committed Italian communists to seek out the Little Red Book? Well, much that one would suspect.

---

[3] As a side note, the recognized influence of this book in communist circles was so widespread that a 1980s–1990s Italian punk group, CCCP, named one of their albums after it. See CCCP, *Affinità-divergenze fra il compagno Togliatti e noi*, distributed by *Attack punk records*, 1986.

The *noi* (aka Chinese communists) criticized the ideological and political corruption of their sister Italian party for falling into line with the "revisionist" policies that defined the field of action for communism within the halls of Rome's parliament and local election booths, instead of preparing a mass party capable *also* of fighting capitalist–imperialism through revolutionary means. Fine and good. But what about this book inspired Italians to believe that the Chinese promoted a type of communism to be learned from instead of just to be criticized by? Well, to answer that I first must commit a crime for the sake of space and simplify to the point of absurdity a book that is over two hundred pages long and includes sections on the history of communism, the history of China, the Cuban Missile Crisis, the Congo Crisis, Vietnam, decolonization throughout the world, Tito's socialism, the Sino-Indian War, the Cold War, the history of Italy, the history of the Soviet Union, analysis of Marxist, Leninist, and Stalinist thought, and the future of international communism. So, short but sweet, here it goes: *Divergenze* asked the accusatory question: "Italian communists, what have you done *since* the war?"

To sharpen the punch of this question *Divergenze* interwove a comparative history of China's successful communist seizure of power against local "capitalists" and aggressive American imperialism vis-à-vis Italian communists' history of cooperation and peaceful coexistence with unrepentant (ex?) fascists and American imperialists. Essential throughout the book is Mao's famous line "Imperialism and all Reactionaries are Paper Tigers," the argument being that sphere-of-influence, Cold War, atomic-bomb excuses for why Italian communists had no choice but to work purely within a bourgeois–imperialist parliamentary system were false, as could be seen by the example of China and, more recently, Cuba. Also false, according to *Divergenze*, were recent arguments that Italian socialism could be achieved through the proletariat being *elected* into controlling the state. The Italian state, according to *Divergenze*, was no socialist utopia ripe for Italian communist takeover. Instead, it was a bureaucratic octopus where the political party could never hope to control the state through elections. As *Divergenze* stated: "with a population of 50 million ... in times of peace it [Italy] has hundreds of thousands of functionaries, plus 400,000 men permanently assigned to the military, around 80,000 military police, around 100,000 regular police, over 1,200 courts and circa 1,000 prisons, if you don't count the secret services of repression and their armed personnel."[4] With that kind of manpower,

---

[4] *Le Divergenze tra il compagno Togliatti e noi: Ancora sulle divergenze tra il compagno Togliatti e noi* (Beijing: Casa Editrice in Lingue Estere, 1963), p. 98.

who was controlling whom? The state, the electorate, or the proletariat? *Divergenze* argued it was the state, and to prove this it listed off statistics for the period covering 1948–62 showing how many workers and political protesters were either imprisoned, injured, or killed for disrupting the state's "peace."[5]

So, what did *Divergenze* require? It called on Italian communists to recover their "glorious history of struggle within the ranks of the International Communist movement" and give up bourgeois delusions of changing social structures primarily through liberal politics.[6] *Divergenze* repeatedly voiced its own admiration for Italy's propensity for revolutionary communist action, and invited its members to shed the corruption of revisionism and return to their Marxist–Leninist roots, the same roots that had led them to triumph over Nazi occupiers and Fascist sympathizers in World War II, and which now could be channeled to combat the American imperialist occupiers and their capitalist sympathizers who were working to re-enslave the Third World just as they were oppressing the First.

Divergenze sent shockwaves through communist circles. Sections of the text were published in mainline communist journals, such as *Avanti!*, with Togliatti's dismissive replies. But where *Divergenze* really took off was in the splinter groups of Padua, Venice, Milan, Turin, Rome, and Naples that had been suspected of displaying "Trotskyist" sympathies. *Divergenze* argued that fighting capitalism in the West was tantamount to fighting imperialism in the Third World: they were one and the same enemy. *Divergenze* also insisted that voting is not fighting, that revolutionary activity needed to be prioritized, and that communism had as its goal the downfall of the bourgeois state through the overthrow of the bourgeoisie by the proletariat. These were exciting words for those who reviled the Italian Communist Party's daily deal-making with the ruling Christian Democratic Party and abhorred what they viewed as a party apparatus ever more vulnerable to cronyism.

One thing must be made explicit: The excitement over *Divergenze* was not limited to Italy's youth. Instead, it reverberated amongst an older group as well: the veterans of Italy's World War II Partisan movement. Figures such as Giuseppe Regis and Luciano Raimondi, who had fought during the Communist Party's battle with Fascism and then the Nazi occupation, recognized in the Chinese example a continuity with the Partisan movement that had brought communism to the greater Italian consciousness in the first place. Communism for them was the fight, was

---

[5] Ibid., p. 99.   [6] Ibid., p. 1.

taking sides, was against the occupier, and was unafraid of upsetting unjust orders or using violence to promote social justice. Mao's hardline communism seemed exactly what they needed to recover the fight. Within a few months the first Mao-inspired party was founded in Padua, with their own journal, *Viva il Leninismo!* In Milan a few months later, the ex-Partisan Giuseppe Regis – who had joined his wife in China between 1957 and 1961 while she worked with the circle of Beijing translators described by Xu Lanjun (chapter 5) – founded the publishing house Edizioni Oriente (Eastern editions), which translated and distributed Maoist texts (including the Little Red Book).[7] In early 1964, various Maoist activists got together and founded their own newspaper, *Nuova Unità* (New unity), in direct opposition to Antonio Gramsci's historic journal *L'Unità*. The Maoist *Nuova Unità* proclaimed the need for Italian communists to drop the official Italian Communist Party (PCI) and unite their efforts – among themselves and with the rest of the socialist world – to battle American imperialism. And so began the local grassroots drive throughout the peninsula to convince Italians that "Imperialism and all Reactionaries are Paper Tigers." And so began, also, the first spurts of Italian interest in reading and disseminating Maoist texts.

As mentioned earlier, the origin of Italians' interest in reading the Little Red Book follows two timelines: one before August 1966 and one thereafter. Before August 1966, the only people interested in reading a copy of the Little Red Book would have already been firmly entrenched within activist communist circles. And within these circles, interest was not generational. Old and young Communists proved receptive to a return to the "revolutionary." Old and young hoped to reinvigorate Italian Communism with the "Chinese turn" to recapture the energy and success that Partisan-Communism had embodied just fifteen years earlier. Nevertheless, on the streets of Bologna, Florence, Rome, Palermo, or Milan few would have noted this transformation. By 1967, however, few people could ignore it. And mainline center-right newspapers such as the Milanese *Corriere della Sera* dedicated bylines to explaining its appeal.[8] The reason for the change? China's Red Guard student movement and Italian youths' interest in replicating it.

---

[7] Giuseppe Regis explained his and his wife's interest in China as a direct consequence of their experience in Italy's Resistance movement and their disillusion with Cold War European socialism in Roberto Niccolai, "Intervista a Giuseppe Regis, Cofondatore delle Edizioni Oriente," *Parlando di rivoluzioni* (Pistoia: Centro di Documentazione di Pistoia, 1998), pp. 70–76.

[8] For example, see "Chi sono, come nascono e cosa vogliono i terroristi di Mao," *Corriere della Sera* (January 13, 1967), p. 3.

It is easy to understand the appeal Italian teenagers and college students felt for the daily news stories reporting how China's youth had become the political protagonists of the country. "Bourgeois" teaching practices – the target of Red Guard scorn – were also something that Italian students were already beginning to rebel against. When flipping through a newspaper and reading how Beijing Red Guards, with Little Red Books in hand, humiliated their teachers for promoting reactionary value systems, Italians felt that China was near, that their trials were similar. Italians, like the Chinese, needed to rise up to lead their country to transformation. All of a sudden, interest in Mao's thought exploded from the relatively limited meetings of the Maoist political parties, and now included a myriad of participants, mostly under the age of thirty, who responded to the idea of "liberation" from old hierarchies, old injustices, and old hypocrisies. From being a message for some, the Little Red Book became a symbol for many. From being a book that encapsulated the question: "Italian Communists, what have you done *since* the war?" it became a quick and visible means for baby boomers to bark against their elders, "Daddy, what did you do *during* the war and why are you trying to teach us to keep doing it?"

While in West Germany these questions focused on Nazi participation in the Holocaust, à la Kommune 1, in Italy they focused on the country's over twenty-year-long idolatry of Mussolini. Though scholars agree that the de-Nazification of West Germany's infrastructures proved wanting, Italy's process of de-Fascistization was even more of a joke. After World War II, only 1,580 government employees were dismissed for their Fascist activities. This in a country of 50 million that had participated in and been controlled by a fascist state for over twenty years. As such, by the mid-1960s, radical youths throughout the Italian peninsula rallied to "oust their fascist functionaries."[9] The temerity of China's Red Guards in opposing their "bourgeois" elders was something Italians could identify with, and they carried their Little Red Books and quoted Mao at rallies to show their common cause. Overtly, with Little Red Books held high, they were the Red Shirts fighting their Black Shirt elders. They were the next generation of Partisans – the fighters – taking up a battle the official Italian Communist Party had set aside and most of their parents hadn't ever fought.

By 1968, so many different groups of people waved the Little Red Book that identifying the movement as "Maoist" per se would be foolhardy. Some joined the growing Maoist branch of communism begun

---

[9] For a succinct comparison of postwar de-Nazification and de-Fascistization policies in Europe see chapter 2 in Tony Judt, *Postwar: A History of Europe since 1945* (New York: Penguin, 2005), pp. 41–63.

after the publication of *Divergenze*. Others waved their Little Red Books alongside pictures of Che Guevara, Black Power fists, and Peace doves, while singing the Resistance-era Partisan song *Bella ciao*. But there were new hard-core Maoists around, as well. Perhaps the most visible faction to plaster images of Mao on every flyer, wall, newsletter, and party program was the ur-Maoist group Servire il Popolo (Serve the people), which not only took up Mao's message of reigniting Italian socialism with a revolutionary spirit, but actually fashioned themselves as members of China's Red Guard: they practiced "self-criticism" sessions; they marched into the countryside intent on "serving and teaching the peasants"; they instilled in their members a strict observance of party hierarchy and order; and they concentrated their efforts on educating "pioneers" by introducing Maoist teachings into daycare centers and afterschool programs.

Interestingly enough, in Italy Mao-mania was not purely a left-wing phenomenon. Some ultra-right-wing groups, too, quoted their Little Red Books to bolster their arguments. For example, the 1968–73 neo-fascist party Lotta di Popolo (The people's fight) characterized Mao as a brilliant nationalist who correctly identified the United States as a global colonizer intent on controlling and weakening Europe's nations in tandem with similar activities in Asia, Africa, and South America.[10] Just as Mao pushed for China's national liberation against American imperial aims, so too, Lotta di Popolo argued, Italians needed to fight the Americans to reinvigorate their own nation.

But of all the groups that cited Mao, the most famous Little-Red-Book wavers were the terrorist cells that began their activities in 1967, planting bombs in police stations and American military bases, robbing banks, and kidnapping "enemy" political figures. The Brigate Rosse (Red brigades) were the most notorious of these cells, but other groups such as Lotta Continua (Continuous fight) identified themselves with Maoism as well. Some of these terrorist cells had grown out of the original post-*Divergenze* Maoist parties, others from the mishmash of liberation movements infusing themselves within the Italian political scene. One way or another center- and right-wing newspapers and politicians in Italy began a campaign to equate the Little Red Book with Molotov cocktails, indelibly placing within the Italian imagination the idea that "Mao Means Murder." When some of the more chilling facts about the Cultural Revolution were unveiled, this impression was only strengthened.

[10] For those interested in the so called "Nazi-Maoist" movement in Italy, which included many other figures and groups besides the aforementioned Lotta di Popolo, see the new documentary: Gaudenzi, Ugo, *Ci chiamavano Nazi-Mao* [They called us Nazi-Maos], distributed by Rinastica, 2010.

Except for the neo-fascist Lotta di Popolo, most interest in the Little Red Book combined a yearning for the exotic with a seemingly contradictory desire for continuity. Third-Worldism was evident throughout. This can be seen in part by which Mao Zedong "citations" were most often quoted. Though the Little Red Book is filled with political arguments that read far from Orientalist, Mao-quoters in Italy preferred (alongside the all-time favorite "Political power grows out of the barrel of a gun") the un-Western-sounding sayings such as "Women hold up half the sky," "Let one thousand flowers bloom," and "The guerrilla must move amongst the people as a fish swims in the sea." The journalist Stefano Ferrante described his baby-boomer cohort's fascination with Mao in these terms: "with his armory of analysis and his maxims soaked with Confucianism, the *Little Red Book* and the athletic swims in the Yellow River, a prophet who speaks of a faraway, misunderstood, and mysterious Orient."[11]

Critics of the Little Red Book craze took special aim at Maoists' desire to be "different," to insert themselves in a world as far away as possible from the daily expectations of "comfortable" Italy. In Marco Bellocchio's 1967 film *La Cina è vicina* (China is near) – a searing satire of Italian socialism in a provincial town – a young boy points out another fellow student to his grandmother, saying:

(BOY):	"That one's Chinese."
(GRANDMOTHER):	"Chinese? What are you talking about? He's a European, of the Aryan race."
(BOY):	"Hm. I don't know."
(GRANDMOTHER):	"What do they say about him at school?"
(BOY):	"That he's a Chinese Communist."
(GRANDMOTHER):	"A Communist? In such a respectable school? That's something from another world."[12]

Being from "another world," upsetting expectations of class and environment, strengthened readers' interest in the Little Red Book. And this was exactly what anti-Maoists pounced upon to brush it off. By 1969, when Chinese-mania was at an all-time high, the top-selling singer Bruno Lauzi – a liberal and anti-Maoist – released a song that used the humor of racism to jab at the growing number of Italians professing themselves "Chinese." The song "*Arrivano i cinesi*" (The Chinese are coming) became a radio favorite that year:

---

[11] Stefano Ferrante, *La Cina non era vicina: Servire il popolo e il maoismo all'italiana* (Milan: Sperling & Kupfer, 2008), p. 20.
[12] Marco Bellocchio, *La Cina è vicina*, Vides Cinematografica, 1967.

The Chinese are coming / They'll get here by swimming / Ruggero Orlando [famous Italian newscaster] says / That they'll be here tomorrow.

The Chinese are coming / They're coming by the millions / Yellower than the lemons / That I put in my tea. Why? Why? / I'm asking you why.

The Chinese are coming / And they happily eat / The Quails and partridges / That you got.

The Chinese are coming / A real 1848 / They plant themselves in the living room / And they won't go away. Why? Why? / I'm asking you why.

I only eat boiled rice / I dress in silk / I've gotten all yellow / And if I have an idea / I write it, if I can, / In a special book / A little red book.

The Chinese are coming. / They're small and fast / They pass you / When crossing the street / With their heads bowed low.

The Chinese are coming / They'll teach you the greeting / With their mute alphabet / That way you won't talk anymore. Why? Why?/I'm asking you why.[13]

Reminiscent of the anti-Maoist Russian songs discussed by Elizabeth McGuire (chapter 9), communists and non-communists alike sang along to Lauzi's racist slurs, belittling their "Aryan-race" Little-Red-Book-reading co-nationals by intimating that they were "getting all yellow" and would soon turn "small, fast, and mute" if they kept up this obsession with their "special book." As can be imagined, to most Italian "Chinese" these shows of racism only strengthened their conviction that Italy was steeped in cultural degeneracy and that it was their job to fight in the name of the "faraway, misunderstood, and mysterious Orient."[14] The more racist the attacks became, the more readers of the Little Red Book proudly presented themselves as "Third-worldly."

As mentioned earlier, rupture with norms was not the only thing that drew followers to Maoist teachings. Continuity with prior Italian models also appealed. Just as "Old Guard" Partisans responded with interest to *Divergenze*'s call to reinstill Italian communism with the revolutionary values they had fought for during World War II, baby boomers framed their Maoism within the rites and rituals of their spiritual parents, the Partisans. Perhaps the clearest expression of this can be seen in the Maoist marriage ceremonies conducted in the early 1970s. "Maoist marriages" were not one of the practices that Italians copied from their

---

[13] Lauzi, Bruno, "Arrivano i cinesi," 1969.
[14] Ferrante, *La Cina non era vicina*, p. 20.

Fig. 7. Album cover for Bruno Lauzi's "Arrivano i cinesi" (1969),
Ariston LUV 0088 7" sleeve. Note the slant-eyed lemon in Chinese
scholar's cap.

comrades-in-arms in China. Instead, they were a conscious "Italian"
invention, one that even merited the publication of a handbook to teach
Italian Maoists throughout the peninsula how to do it.[15] As described in
memoirs, newspaper reports, and the aforementioned handbook, a
Maoist marriage was one conducted within the Communist Party (the
Servire il Popolo Party, to be exact) without the presence of Catholic
priests or Italian state officials. The services were organized around the
rites of a loyalty oath to party and spouse, where young heterosexual
couples stood in front of a leading party member who asked them "Do
you, comrade [insert name], want to unite yourself to comrade [insert

---

[15] *Un Matrimonio Comunista* (Milan: Edizioni "Servire il Popolo," 1972).

name] so as to constitute a communist family, to serve the people of Italy in its march towards a popular insurrection and the instauration of a revolutionary government?"[16]

These ceremonies were "Maoist" in that they emphasized the inter-penetration between "political" space and "family" space. And, of course, the walls of the marriage hall were covered with pictures of Lenin, Stalin, Mao, hammer-and-sickle flags, and a big banner proclaiming "the unity of the Communist family for the people's unity on their way to socialist revolution." But how the marriage itself was celebrated, both in vows and banquet style, was a direct copy of the "Partisan" marriages that had been conducted in the hillsides of northern and central Italy during World War II. According to tales told by former Partisans, couples eager to marry during the war received permission from the Partisan Command to be married "in the Partisan way." Few knew exactly what the guidelines for the "Partisan way" were, but as a whole it seems to have included the highest-ranking Partisan officer conducting the service, with wedding guests consisting primarily of fellow comrades-in-arms. Marriage vows did not make reference to Church or state, but instead to the "people of Italy," and once married the Partisan com-mander expressed the wish that from the new union "little Garibaldini [Partisan] militants" would be born. Festivities were brought to a close with a wedding banquet potluck, where everyone would make whatever music they could until the wine ran out.[17] Italian communists who conducted Maoist marriages made explicit reference to these Partisan marriages when inventing the rites to be followed, imagining it as a "revival of the marriages celebrated by Partisans in the mountains."[18]

The first of the approximately one hundred Maoist couples to conduct such a marriage rite were convinced to do so with the Servire il Popolo party secretary explaining that "the communist marriage is like the marriage celebrated between Partisans in the mountains during the war

---

[16] Ferrante, *La Cina non era vicina*, p. 214. I emphasize "heterosexual" couples for two reasons. First, these Maoist marriages were never intended to upset sexual norms. Families were defined as being made by a man and woman. Though gender norms regarding female orgasm and gender roles in political and household activity were challenged in Marxist–Leninist circles, sex as a positive "revolutionary" activity was imagined in particularly hetero-normative terms. Second, today political groups pushing for the acceptance of gay marriage in Italy have made direct reference to Maoist marriages, indicating that if state and Church will not accept single-sex unions, then perhaps everyone (even non-gays) should make use of extra-state marriages until the laws are changed.

[17] For more on the ritual and symbolism of marriages conducted by Italian World War II Partisan groups see Filippo Colombara, *Vesti la giubba di battaglia: Miti, riti e simboli della guerra partigiana* (Rome: DeriveApprodi, 2009).

[18] Ferrante, *La Cina non era vicina*, p. 208.

of liberation, who awaited the Republic. Only now we await the socialist State, the real one, the Chinese one."[19] Couples who exchanged their "Communist I dos" marched to their outdoor potlucks to boisterous singing of "The Internationale," convinced that they were keeping an old tradition alive while they awaited the new "Chinese" state to come. In this and a myriad of other ways, Italian "Chinese" identified their fight for communism against the American occupier and the fascist functionaries as a continuation of their Partisan elders' battles against the Nazi occupier and the Fascist sympathizers. Reading and citing the Little Red Book served as a means to leave the world of Italian spiritual corruption and Cold War compromises behind while contemporaneously reverting to the traditions of a better, more heroic, Italy. China, thus, was far and near, and that's just what radical Italians were looking for.

Yugoslavia: *Kina je tako blizu a tako daleko* (China is so close and so far)

If in Italy the field was ripe for distribution of the Little Red Book because of the compromises and corruptions of the Italian Communist Party, the same could be imagined for Yugoslavia. In Yugoslavia, too, student demonstrations and university occupations erupted in Belgrade, Zagreb, and Sarajevo, with protesters claiming that Tito's socialism had lost its way and had forgotten its commitment to the proletariat. How else could you explain, students asked, the growing unemployment rates the country was facing in the late 1960s and 1970s while a capitalist culture of luxury accumulation was in full swing? How else could you explain the increased centralization of the state that disregarded the needs of its people? As was happening throughout Italy just on the other side of the Adriatic Sea, baby boomers were asking their communist leaders "what have you done *since* the war?" But unlike their Italian equivalents, they didn't use the symbol of the Little Red Book to do it.

Before investigating why not, it is useful to remember all the reasons why Mao could have proved a potent instrument for indictment. First, unlike the Italian case, in general terms Yugoslavia resembled much more the Chinese body politic. Like China, Yugoslavia was a multinational state par excellence. Like China, during World War II the country was the playground of imperialists and their gruesome "nationalizing" campaigns. And like China, it was also a country trying to realize the promises of socialism with a predominantly undereducated and

---

[19] Ibid., p. 210.

non-industrial proletariat. What is more, the People's Republic of China authored attacks against the League of Communists of Yugoslavia (SKJ) that were so biting that the jibes of *Divergenze* against the Italian Communist Party look fawning. In fact, Tito's brand of "non-aligned" socialism that manipulated American and Soviet interests to finance its own domestic economic and social reforms served as Mao's favorite punching bag when discussing the corruptions of "socialist revisionism." In countless speeches, pamphlets, and even the aforementioned *Divergenze*, Tito's Yugoslavia symbolized "false socialism," where Mao consistently described Tito's People's State as being an "accomplice" of American imperialism and a moral lesson of how quickly socialism can degenerate into capitalism if strong ideological foundations are not preserved.[20] In many ways, the Little Red Book was conceived as a means to ensure that China would not suffer the type of "socialist degeneration" that students in Belgrade and Zagreb decried. So, why did this same book not act as a guide and symbol of socialist renewal and liberation in Yugoslavia as it had in the Italian case?

Explaining why things didn't happen is a task that the careful historian should avoid when possible. But a few key factors can be identified. First of all, a major reason why Yugoslavs proved much less interested in Maoist handbooks on how to realize a revolutionary communist takeover is because they had already had one. While in World War II Italy Partisans fought tooth and nail to kick the Germans out and usher in a new republic, Yugoslavia's Partisans kicked out the Germans (and Italians), and then kept right on kicking until they didn't just have a republic, they had a People's Republic. As numerous studies have shown, this communist takeover was no bloodless affair. Historians estimate that around 100,000 Yugoslavs were killed to secure a single-party state.[21] And once this state was put in place, its toddler years were spent collectivizing, nationalizing, secularizing, and industrializing with a gusto that would have made Mao proud. Though after the 1948 Stalin–Tito split the country began to seek a socialist path on its own terms, including the self-management schemes and free-market incentives Mao so derided, none of this could have been possible without those first "revolutionary" years that by the 1960s were a long-forgotten memory. In fact, as Milan

---

[20] Some examples of these arguments can be found in Mao's speeches "Why it is Necessary to Discuss the White Paper" (August 28, 1949) and "Refutation of the So-Called Party of the Entire People" (July 1964).

[21] Though there are no trustworthy census reports for the immediate aftermath of World War II (because of population movements and the lacking infrastructures to confirm estimates), we can assume that at least 10.5 million people lived in Yugoslavia when Tito came to power.

Kusturica's 1995 film *Podzemlje: Bila jednom jedna zemlja (Underground: Once Upon a Time There was a Country)* so brilliantly evoked, state-sponsored cultural initiatives in Yugoslavia seemed to many a broken record of commemorating the Partisan-style heroics that had been required to found the "soft" socialist state of the 1960s.[22] Radios were inundated with tunes from the Partisan songbook.[23] One of the country's most successful soccer teams, Belgrade's Partizan, had fans donning Partisan regalia to support their team. Books, theaters, movie theaters, and later television programs featured one World War II era dramatic extravaganza after another retracing the Partisan sacrifices that would eventually lead to the founding of the Socialist Federal Republic of Yugoslavia.

One of the most visible examples of how the Yugoslav state promoted a cult of the Partisan to consolidate a socialist, federalist, and multinational postwar body politic can be seen in the Pioneer movement. Founded in 1941 and originally modeled along the Soviet Pioneer model, Yugoslav children were incorporated into the Communist Party by the same means that Lenin, Stalin, and later Mao applied. All schoolchildren were inducted into the Young Pioneers at age seven with an emphasis on converting future generations from "ideologically undecided" to "ideologically decided" members of the Communist Party. As was happening throughout the entire communist world, young Yugoslavs were made to learn the tenets of socialism and the role of the state in realizing revolution through the recitation of oaths and songs, all bedecked in triangular red scarves worn throughout communist Europe, Asia, Latin America, and Africa.[24] According to Ildiko Erdei, up until the Stalin–Tito split few

---

[22] Emir Kusturica, *Podzemlje: Bila jednom jedna zemlja (Underground: Once Upon a Time There was a Country)*, distributed by New Yorker Video, 1995.

[23] There has been an explosion of publications in ex-Yugoslavia and beyond about the fascinating interplay between top-down official state culture (epitomized by Partisan hagiography), state-sponsored consumer culture, and the rich counterculture that blossomed in most of Yugoslavia's republics. The most colorful example is Iris Andrić, Vladimir Arsenijević, and Đorđe Matić, eds., *Leksikon YU mitologije* [Lexicon of Yugoslav mythology] (Zagreb: Postscriptum and Belgrade: Rende, 2004). For more scholarly studies see Patrick Hyder Patterson, *Bought and Sold: Living and Losing the Good Life in Socialist Yugoslavia* (Ithaca: Cornell University Press, 2011); Jason Vuic, *The Yugo: The Rise and Fall of the Worst Car in History* (New York: Hill & Wang, 2010); Breda Luthar and Marusa Pusnik, *Remembering Utopia: The Culture of Everyday Life in Socialist Yugoslavia* (Washington, D.C.: New Academia Publishing, 2010); Hannes Grandits and Karin Taylor, *Yugoslavia's Sunny Side: A History of Tourism in Socialism (1950–1980)* (Budapest: Central European University Press, 2010).

[24] For a fascinating analysis of the Pioneer movement and its many transformations within the Yugoslav state throughout the postwar period see Ildiko Erdei, "The 'Happy Child' as an Icon of Socialist Transformation: Yugoslavia's Pioneer Organization," in John Lampe and Mark Mazower, eds., *Ideologies and National Identities: The Case of*

differences could be noted between the Yugoslav version of the Pioneer movement and the other sister organizations in Albania, Bulgaria, Romania, Hungary, Czechoslovakia, Poland, and the USSR, except for the ever-present *titovka*, the Partisan-uniform sidecap named after Tito himself. After the Stalin–Tito split, however, the Pioneers became one of the prime battlegrounds for differentiating Yugoslav socialism from Stalinism, where reforms of rituals, oaths, songs, and activities emphasized how Yugoslavia would avoid the pitfalls of the USSR and its satellite states by displacing extreme militarization and bureaucratization with the encouragement of creativity and individuality.[25] While young Pioneers in the USSR promised "to passionately love and cherish my Motherland, to live as the great Lenin bade us to, [and] as the Communist Party teaches us to," young Pioneers in Yugoslavia had a much longer list of vows to recite:

> *Today when I'm becoming a Pioneer*
> *I give my honorable Pioneer word*
> *That I will diligently learn and work*
> *Respect parents and teachers*
> *And be a faithful and honest friend*
> *Who keeps his word of honor;*
> *That I will follow the path of the best Pioneers,*
> *Appreciate the glorious deeds of Partisans*
> *And all progressive people of the world*
> *Who stand for liberty and peace;*
> *That I will love my Homeland*
> *Self-managing socialist Yugoslavia*
> *And its brotherly nations and nationalities,*
> *And that I will build a new life,*
> *Full of happiness and joy.*[26]

Liberty, peace, brotherly nations, and the glorious deeds of Partisans: Yugoslavs knew all about the necessary sacrifices for socialist revolution, national liberation, and the danger of imperialist powers wishing to encroach on their territory. In fact, they wore their partisan *titovka* hats to symbolize just such an awareness. And in case they ever forgot, the little red *Pionirske knjižice* (Pioneer booklets) they received upon initiation into the Pioneers could remind them. But the lesson of Yugoslav socialism intertwined the ever-present awareness of Partisan sacrifice with a sense of responsibility of what all that Partisan fighting had really been for. Partisan-adoring Yugoslavs had to move beyond the fighting: they needed to love "self-managing socialist Yugoslavia." They needed

---

Twentieth-Century Southeastern Europe (Budapest and New York: Central European University Press, 2003), pp. 154–72.
[25] Ibid., p. 170.   [26] Translation taken from ibid., p. 173.

Fig. 8. Slovenian Young Pioneer in loyalty oath ceremony, wearing
titovka and red scarf, holding out hand to receive his little red *Pionirska
knjižica* (Pioneer booklet). (Mitja Vidovič.)

to stand for "liberty and peace." And most importantly, they needed to
work at building a new, post-combative life "full of happiness and joy."
Mao's Little Red Book filled with barrels of guns and paper-tiger imperialists had some tough competition with the message of Yugoslavia's
universally distributed little red booklets.

   Mao's Little Red Book also probably failed to induce the same amount of
excitement in Yugoslavia because the anti-imperialist, Third World-
liberation arguments that so attracted Italian youth to Mao's cause were
initiatives that Tito's socialist state, too, was proposing. Throughout the
1950s, 1960s, and 1970s, Yugoslavia was one of the most visible actors
seeking aid to support Asia and Africa's bid to shed the chains of postcolonial indentured servitude. The consolidation of the Non-Aligned
Movement and Yugoslavia's criticism of America's involvement in Vietnam
and Israel are just some of the more famous instances of this commitment.[27]

---

[27] For the most-often cited English-language study of the non-aligned movement see Peter
   Willetts, *The Non-Aligned Movement: The Origins of a Third World Alliance* (London:
   Pinter, 1978). Studies of Yugoslavia's role in formulating and participating in a global

Though Mao interpreted the Non-Aligned movement as empty posturing, to everyday Yugoslavs it was very real, filling the pages of their newspapers and opening the arena of political action and imagination well beyond the Balkan peninsula to which they had formerly been relegated. Interestingly enough, it was this overlapping Chinese and Yugoslav commitment to the global anti-imperialist movement that probably sparked most interest in Mao's Little Red Book. For example, stories of activists demonstrating against British colonialism in the streets of Hong Kong splashed across the front pages of Yugoslavia's newspapers, where article after article (including pictures of heroic Maoists standing proud with Little Red Book held high) made explicit reference to the Little Red Book as a potent tool in the anti-imperialist cause.

The Yugoslav high-school student mentioned at the beginning of this chapter stated that he had sent away for a copy of the Little Red Book after seeing just such representations of Red Guards and anti-imperialist activists waving Little Red Books in newspapers and on the nightly news. Though for Yugoslavs the Little Red Book did not represent their own Bible or symbol for action against imperialism, it is clear that they recognized how it served its purpose with anti-imperialist comrades-in-arms.

Finally, we know that Maoist thought on revolutionary socialism was not the instigator of 1960s and 1970s movements to re-instill a more socialist orientation to Tito's Yugoslavia because the kind of "new socialism" Yugoslav protesters demanded was one that Mao himself would never accept. Belgrade, Zagreb, and Sarajevo students fought Yugoslav police and militia groups demanding a more *humanitarian*, not a more *revolutionary*, socialism. These rebellious youngsters were not acolytes of Lenin, Stalin, and Mao, as many of their equivalents in Italy were. Instead, most Yugoslav dissidents were the followers of "humanist" Marx, the Marx championed by some members of the Frankfurt School, Herbert Marcuse, the *New Left Review*, and Yugoslavia's own Praxis school.[28] Taken very abstractly, late 1960s and early 1970s student revolts in Yugoslavia resemble those of China's Red Guard: students decried the "bourgeois" corruption of their teachers

non-aligned movement have also witnessed an increase of interest in the last few years, as can be seen by the two-part workshop sponsored by Columbia University's Blinken European Institute on The Global Cold War in the Mediterranean Area. For particularly interesting examples see Rinna Kullaa, *Non-Alignment and its Origins in Cold War Europe: Yugoslavia, Finland and the Soviet Challenge* (London: I. B. Tauris, 2012); Ante Batović, *Non-Aligned Yugoslavia and the Relations with the Palestinian Liberation Organisation* (Florence: European University Institute, 2013).

[28] Nebojša Popov, ed., *Sloboda i nasilje: Razgovor o časopisu Praxis i Korčulanskoj letnjoj školi* [Freedom and outrage: discussion of the magazine *Praxis* and the Korčula summer school] (Belgrade: Res publica, 2003).

and elders and called for a more authentic socialism. To this call, Tito (just as Mao had done a few years before) surprised all and got on national television to concede: "The students are right."[29] But broad abstractions are dangerous beasts. Yugoslavs' Praxis-inspired young bloods were no Red Guards, and Tito's return to socialism translated into an increase in social protections, not a return to Marxist–Leninist orthodoxy or revolutionary politics.

Compared to the Italian case, Yugoslavs' limited enthusiasm for the Little Red Book point to two significant phenomena. First, the importance of the figure of the "Partisan" in both countries determined to a large degree a predilection toward changing the world through "the barrel of a gun." By the 1960s, many Italians, both young and old, had sanctified the Partisans' World War II struggles to such an extent that when faced with their own reformist, bureaucratic present they thirsted for action, and in some cases even blood. In Yugoslavia, Partisan violence didn't end when the Nazis left, and for years Yugoslavs licked their wounds hoping that all that violence and all those sacrifices would be worth it. By the 1960s and 1970s, Tito's Yugoslavia was working ever harder to prove that this was so. The last thing anyone wanted was another round of civil or political wars in the name of ideology. And dissatisfied Yugoslavs collaborated with Egyptian, Indian, German, British, and American "New Leftists" in demanding a more humane socialist turn. As the Chinese embassy that sent the Little Red Book to the curious Pakrac high-school student expected, Mao's message in Yugoslavia fell flat, while in Italy, where hagiographies of combat-ready Partisan communists dominated the popular imagination, interest in Mao, for a while at least, seemed unquenchable.

But where common cause amongst Italian and Yugoslav Little Red Book audiences could be found (and where Chinese embassies perhaps misjudged their audience) was on the question of anti-imperialism. Both Italians and Yugoslavs demonstrated respect for China's stance against imperialism, and American imperialism specifically. Both populations obtained their Little Red Books in part to show their support and to learn the secrets of China's anti-Western, anti-colonialist convictions. As can be seen by *Divergenze*, Chinese diplomats, propagandists, and strategists expected no less from their fellow "true" socialists in Italy. But in targeting primarily "in between" audiences instead of competing socialist readerships, a strategy described by Xu Lanjun, perhaps an opportunity was missed. In the hearts of many Yugoslavs, the Non-Aligned

---

[29] "Studenti su imali pravo," *Novi List* (June 9, 1968).

Movement was not an underhanded strategy of an imperial pawn: it was a *raison d'être*. Who knows what would have happened if China had approached Yugoslavia as a country not that far away, a country much closer than "Chinese" Italy, a country eager to hold up the Little Red Book as a common symbol against the menace of imperialism?

Nevertheless, by comparing the reception of the Little Red Book in two domestic contexts across Europe's southern reaches of the Iron Curtain one thing is clear: Cold War explanations do not clarify domestic receptions. In capitalist, US-sphere-of-influence Italy, Mao's Little Red Book was a best seller, regardless of the fact that much of its content was intended for an audience that in no way resembled the urban, industrially developed, and consumerist context of most Italians. This apparent paradox can be explained by the fact that the Little Red Book promised a way to retrace a continuity with the uncompromising past of World War II Partisan struggle and a new commitment against American imperialism. In socialist Yugoslavia, the Little Red Book garnered much less interest, and what interest there was had nothing to do with communism. Combat, sacrifice, and political power growing "out of the barrel of a gun" were state-sponsored, old (*titovka*) hat lessons for Pioneer-trained Yugoslavs, and failed to incite enthusiasm. What enthusiasm did exist was subsumed under the same anti-imperialist interests the Yugoslav state was already promoting. If there is a common history of why a student in Venice, Italy and a student in Pakrac, Yugoslavia sent away for Mao's mantras, it is not about World War II legacies, communism, and the Cold War. It is about anti-imperialism.

BIBLIOGRAPHY

Andrić, Iris, Vladimir Arsenijević, and Đorđe Matić, eds., *Leksikon YU mitologije* [Lexicon of Yugoslav mythology] (Zagreb: Postscriptum and Belgrade: Rende, 2004)

Batović, Ante, *Non-Aligned Yugoslavia and the Relations with the Palestinian Liberation Organisation* (Florence: European University Institute, 2013)

Colombara, Filippo, *Vesti la giubba di battaglia: Miti, riti e simboli della guerra partigiana* (Rome: DeriveApprodi, 2009)

Le Divergenze tra il compagno Togliatti e noi: Ancora sulle divergenze tra il compagno Togliatti e noi (Beijing: Casa Editrice in Lingue Estere, 1963)

Erdei, Ildiko, "The 'Happy Child' as an Icon of Socialist Transformation: Yugoslavia's Pioneer Organization," in John Lampe and Mark Mazower, eds., *Ideologies and National Identities: The Case of Twentieth-Century Southeastern Europe* (Budapest and New York: Central European University Press, 2003), pp. 154–72

Ferrante, Stefano, *La Cina non era vicina: Servire il popolo e il maoismo all'italiana* (Milan: Sperling & Kupfer, 2008)

Grandits, Hannes, and Karin Taylor, *Yugoslavia's Sunny Side: A History of Tourism in Socialism (1950–1980)* (Budapest: Central European University Press, 2010)

Judt, Tony, *Postwar: A History of Europe since 1945* (New York: Penguin, 2005)

Kullaa, Rinna, *Non-Alignment and its Origins in Cold War Europe: Yugoslavia, Finland and the Soviet Challenge* (London: I. B. Tauris, 2012)

Luthar, Breda, and Marusa Pusnik, *Remembering Utopia: The Culture of Everyday Life in Socialist Yugoslavia* (Washington, D.C.: New Academia Publishing, 2010)

Un Matrimonio Comunista (Milan: Edizioni "Servire il Popolo," 1972)

Niccolai, Roberto, "Intervista a Giuseppe Regis, Cofondatore delle Edizioni Oriente," in *Parlando di rivoluzioni* (Pistoia: Centro di Documentazione di Pistoia, 1998), pp. 70–76.

Patterson, Patrick Hyder, *Bought and Sold: Living and Losing the Good Life in Socialist Yugoslavia* (Ithaca: Cornell University Press, 2011)

Popov, Nebojša, ed., *Sloboda i nasilje: Razgovor o časopisu Praxis i Korčulanskoj letnjoj školi* [Freedom and outrage: discussion of the magazine *Praxis* and the Korčula summer school] (Belgrade: Res publica, 2003)

Vuic, Jason, *The Yugo: The Rise and Fall of the Worst Car in History* (New York: Hill & Wang, 2010)

Willetts, Peter, *The Non-Aligned Movement: The Origins of a Third World Alliance* (London: Pinter, 1978)

12 Badge books and brand books
The Mao Bible in East and West Germany

Quinn Slobodian

> Some people have read a few Marxist books and think themselves quite
> learned but what they have read has not penetrated, has not struck root
> in their minds, so that they do not know how to use it and their class
> feelings remain as of old. Others are very conceited and having learned
> some book-phrases, think themselves terrific and are very cocky; but
> whenever a storm blows up, they take a stand very different from that of
> the workers and the majority of the peasants. They waver while the latter
> stand firm, they equivocate while the latter are forthright.
>
> Study

West Germans bought over one hundred thousand copies of Mao's book
of quotations in 1967. Three editions were sold, each bearing a distinct
ideological imprint. Alongside the familiar, plastic-bound edition of the
Beijing Foreign Languages Press was a paperback published by the
left-liberal Fischer Press.[1] Translated and edited by West German
students of Sinology, the Fischer edition provided a scholarly perspective
on the Cultural Revolution that was broadly sympathetic, signaling its
orientation with a cover photograph of a young girl and an elderly woman
in a benign moment of intergenerational communication.[2] The third
edition of Mao's book of quotations, published by the anti-communist
Marienburg Press, had the title *The Mao Zedong Breviary: Catechism of
700 Million*. The editor, Kurt C. Steinhaus, both tapped into and
reinforced racialized anxiety in his introduction, warning of a "Far
Eastern-Asiatic system endowed with an inborn collectivism striving
uncompromisingly for world domination."[3] The publishers declared that

---

[1] The first German-language edition published by Foreign Languages Press was 13.8 cm x
9.4 cm, followed by the smaller "miniature" edition of 10.7 cm x 7.9 cm published in
1968. See Ingo Nentwig, "Die Mao-Bibel: Das Kleine Rote Buch der Zitate," in Helmut
Opletal, ed., *Die Kultur der Kulturrevolution: Personenkult und politisches Design in China von
Mao Zedong* (Ghent: Snoeck, 2011), p. 179.

[2] Mao Zedong and Tilemann Grimm, *Das rote Buch: Worte des Vorsitzenden Mao Tse-tung*
(Frankfurt am Main: Fischer, 1967).

[3] Fritz C. Steinhaus, "Zur Einführung," in Mao Zedong, *Das Mao Tse-tung Brevier*
(Würzburg: Marienburg-Verlag, 1967), p. 7.

their goal in releasing the book was to "show Mao in all his severity." "It is necessary," they said, "to give Germans and Europeans the creeps."[4]

West Germans read the Little Red Book for reasons ranging from fear to curiosity to the hope that Chinese communism might offer a way out for a left trapped between the consensus-minded functionaries of West German organized labor and the calcified bureaucratic socialism of East Germany (the GDR). Socialist student activists adopted the Beijing edition as an outward symbol of their distance from both the West German mainstream and the Soviet-led socialist bloc. It served as an accessory to the anti-authoritarian Maoism of an early phase of socialist student activism from 1966 to 1968 and an emblem of later turns to subcultural and sectarian Maoism from 1969 into the 1970s. In all cases, China was distant. The only real contact with Chinese came through trips of small numbers of activists to East Berlin to smuggle back films, copies of the *Peking Review*, and, most importantly, stacks of the Little Red Book to sell at political events.

In the GDR itself, there were no copies of Mao's book of quotations for sale in 1967. Yet China was nonetheless much closer, and the Little Red Book was a matter of state. Relations with China, worsening progressively since the Sino-Soviet Split of 1962–63, reached a low point for the GDR in 1967. For East German officials, the Little Red Book was a feared sight in the hands of Germans, but more so in the hands of the Chinese, including those who perpetrated a series of violent clashes with East Germans in both Berlin and Beijing in the course of the Cultural Revolution.

In both countries, Mao and the Little Red Book represented the intrusion of a political force from beyond Europe and North America. The book was seen in both countries as an instrument that could challenge, and was challenging, the powers that were. Observers in both countries, especially in Sinology circles where sympathy for Mao had been high in the 1950s, believed that the format of the Little Red Book distorted the Chinese leader's writings, but they also saw its aphoristic structure as the source of its success. The repackaging of decades worth of Mao's utterances and writings into pithy commandments transformed historically grounded analyses into scripture, theory into religion, and selections from the *Collected Works of Mao* into what was called, on both sides of the border, the "Mao Bible."

The following chapter focuses first on the Little Red Book as a material object and locates it within the print culture of the two Germanys.

---

[4] "Tiger aus Quark," *Der Spiegel* (July 3, 1967), p. 40.

Fig. 9. *Das Rote Buch*, a West German "brand book" edition of Mao's quotations, published by Fischer Verlag (1967).

It proposes the terms *badge books* and *brand books* to help conceptualize the different ways that the Little Red Book circulated and was received in liberal-capitalist and state-socialist countries. By badge books I mean books (and book-like objects) that expressed meaning through their outer form as much as through their content, and acted as identifiers of belonging in a particular political group. By brand books I mean books as commodities that were consumed within the space of the market and contained ideas debated within a depoliticized "marketplace of ideas," where political affiliation was not fixed. In the late 1960s, the Little Red Book sat at the blurred intersection of these two genres of books in the two Germanys. Exploring this distinction helps explain the popularity and the resonance of the Little Red Book in the West Germany of the late 1960s as a result of fortuitous timing that permitted it to resemble simultaneously an accessory of the classical workers' movement and a modish commodity of the educated elite. Meanwhile, the absence of an open commercial book market in East Germany and the official intolerance of the authorities for criticisms of the Soviet model of socialism meant that the Little Red Book could not be perceived neutrally, and remained a dangerous vector of potential sedition.

Badge books

Much has been made of the Little Red Book's format. Gerd Koenen refers to it as an "attractive gadget" that owed much of its charm to its novelty.[5] Yet the pocket-sized, primary-colored, plastic-clad format was not unprecedented. Indeed, in the two Germanys of the 1960s, it would have resonated with print practices pointing back to German socialist traditions, as well as to the most current trends in paperback publishing. Small-format books were common accessories of political membership in both East and West Germany, and provide the clearest example of badge books. Following a practice from early social democracy and 1920s communism, one proved membership in political parties or trade unions by carrying small, brightly colored booklets, often bound in a durable, and even plastic, cover. The membership books for the governing East German political party, the Socialist Unity Party (Sozialistische Einheitspartei Deutschlands, SED), as well as for the East German umbrella trade union (the FDGB), were close to the same size as the Little Red Book, and clad in leatherette. The East German statutes of the SED appeared in a new small edition with a durable red plastic cover in 1963, the year before Mao's Book of Quotations. Printed on parchment paper in a style reminiscent of the Bible, the statutes included numbers printed in red, dictating the guidelines for the obligations and proper conduct of a socialist.[6] As accoutrements of everyday life for party members, who made up only 10 per cent of the population but exercised disproportionate power in social life, both the membership books and statutes were outward markers of authority.

The West German Social Democratic Party (SPD) utilized a similar pocket-sized red membership book immediately after the war, but changed the color and the format when they abandoned the language of class struggle and the goal of nationalizing the means of production in a bid for electoral relevancy with the Godesberg Program of 1959. The switch from red to blue party books distanced them from their shared roots with communist parties and signaled a clear self-positioning within

---

[5] Gerd Koenen, *Das rote Jahrzehnt: Unsere kleine deutsche Kulturrevolution 1967–1977* (Cologne: Fischer, 2001), p. 147.

[6] Sozialistische Einheitspartei Deutschlands, *Der Statut der Sozialistische Einheitspartei Deutschlands* (Berlin: Dietz, 1963).

the Cold War camp of "the West."[7] Perhaps influenced by the success of the "gadget" of the Little Red Book in the late 1960s, the SPD switched to a pocket-sized format clad in plastic in the early 1970s, and back to a little red book a few years later.

The Soviet Union itself produced small, red-clad versions of both the statutes and the constitution in the 1930s, making the little red book an important part of the international print culture of the socialist movement. Perhaps out of an awareness of its symbolic effect in expressing and proving group membership, the red membership book was one of the elements appropriated cynically by the Nazi Party in the 1930s. The existence of these precedents provides a context for the Little Red Book in both Germanys. These traditions would have made the Little Red Book recognizable in both republics as a visible means of expressing political allegiance. Like the party books and statutes, it acted as a badge that stood outside the book market as such, intended to be shown as much as it was to be read.

Brand books

The Little Red Book resonated with changes in the West German commercial book market even as it echoed existing socialist traditions of badge books. Through the 1950s, the pocket-sized paperback had been identified with American-style dime novels (*Heftromane*) of true crime and Westerns. The format only became respectable in the early 1960s as publishers conscious of a rapidly growing university student population as a potential market began to produce inexpensive pocket paperbacks of philosophy, contemporary literature, and political commentary.[8] Publishers signaled their break with the pulpy content and chaotic covers of the 1950s through simplicity of design, including usually only one color, with a small, simple font. The most well-known example is the Edition Suhrkamp, which began publishing in 1963, and became what Adelheid von Saldern calls "*the* symbol for a quality social-critical product."[9] Even though the intention of the publishers, as she says, was to "express opposition to the commodity and point to the idea that it was the content not the form of the cover that mattered," the effect was quickly just the opposite. The austere covers became an

[7] See examples at www.hdg.de/.
[8] Mark W. Rectanus, "Literary Publishing in the Federal Republic of Germany: Redefining the Enterprise," *German Studies Review* 10.1 (Feb 1987), p. 98.
[9] Adelheid von Saldern, "Markt für Marx: Literaturbetrieb und Lesebewegungen in der Bundesrepublik in den Sechziger- und Siebzigerjahren," *Archiv für Sozialgeschichte* 44 (2004), p. 158.

aesthetic of their own, signaling one's status as a consumer of both books and ideas. Having the right books on your shelves, being seen reading them, and giving them as gifts, quickly became a symbol of "group belonging" in the countercultural and intellectual milieus of the 1960s and 1970s.[10] The books rewarded the repeat consumer, as they were designed to appear together on a shelf in the so-called Rainbow Series that showcased the polychromatic spectrum of their spines.

Highbrow publishers made an ascetic aesthetic out of the primary-colored, pocket-sized book in the 1960s, distinguished from what Deutsche Taschenbuch Verlag publisher called the "less than serious cultural pluralism of the American model" in favor of a book "with its own face and a demanding program."[11] As a serious book that was also an eye-catching commodity, the Little Red Book fit easily into this model and blended in well on a wall of Suhrkamp books. Parallel to the tradition of badge books, then, there was a rise in the 1960s of brand books, print objects that expressed cultural distinction through consumption, and offered a self-understanding mediated by the market. In a twist, serious paperbacks were commodities that disavowed their status as commodities, containing the theoretical arsenal of an emerging socialist New Left. Mao's face would appear in several iterations of these serious paperbacks, including his *On Guerilla Warfare* in 1966 on the widely read *rororo* series published by Rowohlt, a republication of Hungarian author György Pálóczi-Hórvath's *Emperor of the Blue Ants* by Ullstein in 1967, and an edition of quotations from Mao the same year titled *What Mao Actually Said* from the Molden press.[12] The Little Red Book itself acted as an important product in the emergence of an activist counter-public (*Gegenöffentlichkeit*). The proprietor of one of the first leftist bookstores, Roter Stern in Marburg, began by selling the Little Red Book at conferences, concerts, and on university campuses.[13]

Locating the Little Red Book between the status of badge books and brand books helps us to understand its effect and reception in the two Germanys. In West Germany, one could even say that the question of

---

[10] Ibid., pp. 167–68.
[11] Heinz Friedrich, quoted in Mark W. Rectanus, *Literary Series in the Federal Republic of Germany from 1960 to 1980* (Wiesbaden: Harrassowitz, 1984), p. 123.
[12] Mao Zedong, *Theorie des Guerillakrieges oder Strategie der Dritten Welt* (Reinbek bei Hamburg: Rowohlt, 1966); György Pálóczi-Hórvath, *Mao Tse-tung: Der Herr der blauen Ameisen*, 2nd edn. (Frankfurt am Main: Scheffler, 1967); Philippe Devillers, *Was Mao wirklich sagte* (Vienna: Fritz Molden, 1967).
[13] Lisa Borgmeister, "Politische Buchhandlungen im Kontext der 68er Bewegung in der BRD: Am Beispiel der Marburger Buchhandlung 'Roter Stern'," in Stephan Füssel, ed., *Die Politisierung des Buchmarkts: 1968 als Branchenereignis* (Wiesbaden: Harrassowitz, 2007), pp. 97, 108.

whether Mao's Book of Quotations was a badge book or a brand book became what was at stake. Was the attraction of the Little Red Book simple intellectual faddism? Was it one more shade of verbal radicalism with a Far Eastern flavor, like Bertolt Brecht's *The Good Person of Szechwan*, which appeared in the Suhrkamp Rainbow Series in 1964? Or was it a badge book, representing membership in a transnational political community that linked West Berlin to Beijing, with potentially destructive consequences? Could the interest in the Book of Quotations be folded into the dynamic of sensationalistic trend-chasing and detached intellectual consideration, or did it have to be taken seriously as a political force in the streets?

Critical voices on the left were quick to see the dynamic of Mao as a brand at work. Introducing a page of cartoons titled "Disarm Mao with Fashion" in the satirical magazine *Pardon* in August 1967, Chlodwig Poth observed that Brigitte Bardot and Sammy Davis Jr. had been seen wearing "Mao suits" and Jean-Luc Godard, "the quickest of the quick among the cineastes," had produced *La Chinoise*, where "the first wave of Mao Fashion could be seen." The Little Red Book was a prominent feature in the film. The students in the film, dressed in the characteristic caps and blue jackets of Chinese workers, built barricades out of the small books and worked in front of bookshelves filled with hundreds of copies of it. One of Poth's cartoons depicted a boutique selling "Mao suits" while a Chinese man ran furiously on a treadmill behind a curtain. The clerk promised "the very latest, my dear lady: an authentic Red Chinese sweats our suits through here with guaranteed pure worker sweat." The text brought the satirist's irony to a sharp point, reading:

German readers can choose from three editions of Mao's collected quotations, and the leftist students in Berlin are discussing the Cultural Revolution. But the events in the giant Chinese empire and Mao's thoughts and deeds still hold much possibility and variety for us. And we should make use of them all. Because, when you think about it, everything that is revolutionary is an absolute danger for our form of economy and society. So let's make it into fashion fast and turn Mao into an amusing gag.[14]

Poth identified what had been the standard means of dealing with the challenge of youth culture in West Germany since the late 1950s, when "hooligan riots" (*Halbstarkenkrawalle*) still troubled those in power: namely, to see it "as an amusing gag," that is, to sociologize rebellion as a phase of adolescence assimilable into the dynamic of a consumer culture.[15]

---

[14] Chlodwig Poth, "Entschärft Mao mit Mode," *Pardon* (August 1967), p. 38.
[15] See Uta G. Poiger, *Jazz, Rock and Rebels: Cold War Politics and American Culture in a Divided Germany* (Berkeley: University of California Press, 2000), pp. 110–20.

In a review of *La Chinoise* following its West German premiere in January 1968, Alf Brustellin wrote that the film "does not appraise Maoists, ideologies or student communes; rather, it manifests through images the possibility that the capitalist West has to be rid of them." It proved that "everything is fashion for the West. Even the most immediate horrors can be re-digested playfully by our (sub)culture industry [and] the mechanisms of aestheticization work so splendidly that Mao can be turned into a trendsetter." At the theater, he observed, "there is a glass vitrine – across from the refreshments – full of pretty red Mao Bibles (two deutsche marks each)."[16] Brustellin saw the adoption of Chinese communist accessories by young Western Europeans as a limit case of depoliticized consumption. In 1972, Helga Novak's *Moral Morals from Bible-Babble: Romantic Affairs while reading the Mao Bible* made a similar point. In a radio play produced for a major radio station, she played newspaper reports about Davis Jr. and Bardot's Mao suits alongside jazz music, suggesting that it was one lifestyle choice among others.[17] She also linked the Little Red Book to the "serious paperbacks" phenomenon with a fake announcement advertising "five series with twenty-five opinions, printed in provocative pop colors."[18] These critics saw Mao defanged and recoded as a passing fashion in the hyper-visual culture of the late 1960s. They implied that the Little Red Book, despite its ostensible status as an anti-consumerist commodity, could not escape its role as a marker of distinction within a commercial market.

The alternative analysis was to take the interest in the Little Red Book in deadly earnest. Werner Titzrath, who would become editor of the Springer-owned *Hamburger Abendblatt*, did so when he portrayed the Little Red Book as the node of a global revolutionary network in 1968. In an article titled "Vietnam – in Germany too?" Titzrath wrote that the Vietcong, "the machine pistol aimed, already practices insurgency: They want revolution. The others," referring to West German students, "Mao Bible under their arms, attempt at least, to experiment with it."[19] He said that the Vietcong and West Berlin activists "have Mao as ideological instructor. Both possess – one more so, the other less so – the recipe whereby militant minorities can terrorize indifferent majorities and, when possible, govern them."[20] In a clear attempt to label the Book of

---

[16] Alf Brustellin, "Kommune für einen Sommer," *Süddeutsche Zeitung* (January 22, 1968).

[17] Roman Luckscheiter, "Maos mediale Absorption: Helga Novaks Hörspiel Fibelfabel aus Bibelbabel (1972) im Kontext," www.iaslonline.de/index.php?vorgang_id=2695 (September 16, 2007).

[18] Quoted in ibid.

[19] Werner Titzrath, "Vietnam – auch in Deutschland?" *Die Welt* (February 7, 1968), p. 2.

[20] Ibid.

Quotations as a badge book, Titzrath cast Mao as the source of subversive knowledge and strategy, and the nodal point linking international struggles lined up against the West.

Student activists themselves played with the swing between political badge and consumerist brand. Appropriations of Mao by socialist student activists from 1967 to 1969 were characterized by an attitude that can be called serious irony. In a review of the Little Red Book in April 1967, Reimut Reiche, president of the primary socialist student organization, the Socialist German Students' Union (Sozialistischer Deutscher Studentenbund, SDS), noted that a shift in student opinion had taken place recently from the Soviet "traditionalist" geopolitical interpretation to the Chinese position.[21] He expressed fear in the irony involved in the identification with the Chinese position. "Six months ago," he wrote, "no-one would have dared to quote Mao at an SDS gathering, today it occurs constantly, but amidst the affected laughter of reader and listeners."[22]

What did it mean to declare oneself "Chinese" and quote Mao but to do so while laughing? The ambivalences of this position can be seen in a short film called *The Words of the Chairman* made by film student Harun Farocki in 1967 and screened repeatedly in West Berlin that year. Beginning with an image of the Little Red Book spinning while Chinese choral music played, the text quoted an adapted version of Lin Biao's introduction while a woman clothed in a Mao suit and cap tore a page from the book, folded it into the fledges of an arrow and affixed a pin to it. As the voiceover read "We must cleverly transform [Mao's words]. In our hands they must become weapons" the viewer sees the arrow flying into a bowl of soup, splashing a cartoonish version of the shah of Iran and his wife (primary targets of socialist student criticism) with liquid, leaving the shah appearing as if he has been shot. The short film ends with another shot of the spinning Little Red Book.[23] Tilman Baumgärtel has pointed out that *The Words of the Chairman* was the first piece by activist film students that made any

---

[21] On the substantive reception of Chinese communism in the West German socialist student movement see Laura K. Diehl, "Die Konjunktur der Mao-Images in der bundesdeutschen '68er'-Bewegung," in Sebastian Gehrig, Barbara Mittler, and Felix Wemheuer, eds., *Kulturrevolution als Vorbild? Maoismen im deutschsprachigen Raum* (Frankfurt am Main: Peter Lang, 2008); Sebastian Gehrig, "(Re-)Configuring Mao: Trajectories of a Culturo-Political Trend in West Germany," *Transcultural Studies* 2 (2011), pp. 190–210; Quinn Slobodian, *Foreign Front: Third World Politics in Sixties West Germany* (Durham: Duke University Press, 2012), pp. 53, 57, 171–81.

[22] Reimut Reiche, "Worte des Vorsitzenden Maos," *Neue Kritik* 41 (April 1967), p. 10.

[23] The film was made shortly after the climactic demonstration in West Berlin during the shah's visit on June 2, 1967. See Slobodian, *Foreign Front*, chapter 4.

reference to violence.[24] Farocki has downplayed literal readings of the film, claiming that "people understood then that over-obviousness is also a form of irony."[25]

Farocki explained the citation of Mao's book retroactively as a camp provocation with no earnest intent. Yet the lines between playful representations of violence and actual violence were indistinct. In February 1968, another student from the German Film and Television Academy (DFFB) in West Berlin, Horst Mahler, presented a film with step-by-step instructions for building a Molotov cocktail. This apparent provocation happened within two months of extensive attacks with just such weapons against the building of the mainstream tabloid Springer press by socialist students in West Berlin.[26] Mahler himself went on to become a member of the leftist terrorist group the Red Army Faction (RAF). In court after their first action, the arson of a department store, two other founding members of the RAF, Andreas Baader and Gudrun Ensslin, showed how provocation and actual violence could go together when they waved Little Red Books in the air during their trial.[27] The socialist activist Rainer Langhans went further, reading long passages from Mao's Book of Quotations aloud during his trial in 1967.[28]

In activist provocations from 1967 to 1969, the Little Red Book acted as the textual equivalent of a tomato, a projectile favored by socialist students. When the police in Freiburg protested that students had no permit to sell books in 1968, they sold tomatoes "two deutsche marks each with a Mao as a bonus," likely implying that the tomatoes could be thrown rather than eaten.[29] At times, the book itself was literally thrown. In May 1969, a student in Heidelberg hurled two Italian-language copies of the Little Red Book at a university instructor while screaming insults at him (and had the chutzpah to charge the janitor with theft for taking the books afterward).[30] At other times, the Little Red Book appeared amid an arsenal of colorful provocations. A faculty member recalls finding a Bible spray-painted red after the evacuation of the occupied German Studies building at the Free University (Freie Universität Berlin, FU) in

---

[24] Tilman Baumgärtel, *Vom Guerillakino zum Essayfilm: Harun Farocki* (Berlin: B Books, 2002), p. 63.

[25] www.farocki-film.de/.

[26] Siegward Lönnendonker, "Kleine Zeittafel für die Jahre 1945–1973," in Karol Kubicki and Siegward Lönnendonker, eds., *50 Jahre Freie Universität Berlin aus der Sicht von Zeitzeugen* (Berlin: Zentrale Universitätsdruckerei, 2002), p. 329.

[27] Diehl, "Mao-Images," p. 196.   [28] Gehrig, "(Re-)Configuring Mao," p. 202.

[29] "Zur Sonne," *Der Spiegel* (June 24, 1968), p. 50.

[30] Staatsanwaltschaft bei dem Landgericht Heidelberg an Christian Boblenz. 28 Aug 1969. International Institute for Social History Archive, Neue Linke, Studentenbewegung, Außerparlamentarische Opposition in Deutschland Collection, File 82.

May 1968, where a banner referencing Mao had hung reading "All Professors are Paper Tigers." The red Bible was likely a pun on the "Mao Bible," and an attempt to playfully transubstantiate the *Urtext* of German letters – Martin Luther's Bible – into an accessory of revolt.[31] In July 1968, SDS members interrupted a talk by Interior Minister Ernst Benda organized by Christian democratic youth. While a nine-year-old boy read Mao's quotations aloud, a female student rang a cowbell, activists threw colored eggs at Benda, and two young men in uniforms with Nazi emblems patrolled the stage.[32]

The bluntness of the Little Red Book seemed to be part of its charm. In 1969, German–French socialist activist Daniel Cohn-Bendit went to Italy to convince Godard to help him make a Western.[33] According to a newspaper report, it was going to be about "miners and cowboys who conspire against their boss and found a cowboy commune."[34] One of the three roles was to be played by a horse that would quote Mao.[35] As with the provocative demonstration, Mao's quotations were cast as a zero point of political education, able to be performed by both a child and an animal. The universal accessibility of the book was its virtue, but these depictions also satirized its simplicity. To be understood by a child was also a condemnation. The socialist student left shared this understanding of Mao's book with the mainstream. The cover for the German translation of Jan Myrdal's 1971 book, *Return to a Chinese Village*, featured a child gazing fixedly over the top of a Little Red Book that was quite large in his small hands.[36] The fact that the book approached normal size in the hands of a child suggested that it was in fact a child's book, written for someone at a basic level of literacy and comprehension.

From right to left, the discourse around Mao's Little Red Book revolved around its epigrammatic, scripture-like nature. If activists treated this fact with irony, others were more concerned. A case in point was the Fischer Press version of the Little Red Book, which would sell close to twenty thousand copies in its first three months of publication and would make top-ten bestseller lists in June and September 1967.[37]

---

[31] Ursula Hennig, quoted in Karol Kubicki and Siegward Lönnendonker, "Die Freie Universität im Feld der politischen Spannungen," in Kubicki and Lönnendonker, eds., *50 Jahre Freie Universität Berlin*, p. 130.

[32] *Frankfurter Rundschau* (July 2, 1968).

[33] "Ach, wie gut," *Der Spiegel* (May 24, 1976), p. 93.

[34] "Mao-Western," *Die Zeit* (March 28, 1969), p. 2.

[35] "Ach, wie gut," *Der Spiegel* (May 24, 1976), p. 94.

[36] Jan Myrdal, *China: die Revolution geht weiter: Bericht über den Fortschritt in Liu Ling* (Munich: Nymphenburger Verl.-Handlung, 1971).

[37] "Bücherspiegel," *Der Spiegel* (June 19, 1967), p. 127; "Bücherspiegel," *Der Spiegel* (September 18, 1967), p. 183.

The book was a new translation from the Chinese by Sinologist Tilemann Grimm assisted by Chinese journalism student Tien-Mu Cheng and a team of students at the Ruhr University in Bochum.[38] Grimm had translated a multiple-volume set of Mao's writings earlier in the decade, and was sympathetic to him as a philosopher and poet. What galled him about the Little Red Book was its excision of Mao's writings from their original context, giving them an "apodictic coloring" that made them seem more like military-style "commands" than the conclusion of a "chain of reasoning."[39] He compared the recitation of long quotes from the book by the Chinese to the "liturgical responsory" of Christian monks.

Grimm acknowledged that these simplifications were necessary for the use of the Little Red Book as a means of mass mobilization, especially to those who were working at a basic level of literacy, but warned that this would have consequences. As he put it, "We must realize that in the minds of millions upon millions, it is these writings edited to take on a much more penetrating tone that represent what Chairman Mao has said in what might be the first book of their lives. There is much that cannot be understood but can still be 'repeated as a prayer'."[40] Grimm feared that the transformation of Mao's writings into decontextualized axioms not only travestied their original meaning but gave them the danger of mass, weaponized misinterpretation.

The *Catechism* version of the Little Red Book, which would also sell 20,000 copies by June 1967, was much more direct in its criticism.[41] Marienburg Press, and its affiliated Holzner Press, which had produced military publications in the Nazi period, had specialized in Sinophobic assessments of geopolitics since the late 1950s. Authors such as Steinhaus and Wilhelm Starlinger, whose work was admired by Chancellor Konrad Adenauer, made frequent predictions of a coming race war led by the Chinese.[42] Steinhaus, a functionary at the Ministry of Economics, translated the book into German from English, and described it as part of the Chinese campaign for "global victory" that "will still stand at the end of the Cultural Revolution as a new and unsettling sign of a communist-Asian power arming itself in preparation for a catastrophe of historical proportions (*Geschichtskatastrophe*)."[43] The power of attraction that the Little Red Book might have for

---

[38] "Tiger aus Quark," *Der Spiegel* (July 3, 1967), p. 40.

[39] Mao and Grimm, *Das rote Buch*, pp. 13–14.   [40] Ibid., p. 14.

[41] "Zeitmosaik," *Die Zeit* (June 9, 1967).

[42] See Wilhelm Starlinger, *Hinter Rußland China* (Würzburg: Marienburg-Verlag, 1957); Walter Leifer, *China schaut südwärts* (Würzburg: Marienburg Verlag, 1961).

[43] Mao Zedong, *Das Mao Tse-tung Brevier*, p. 20.

non-white populations was of particular concern. Steinhaus was certain that the quotations would "have an enduring effect on the people in many developing countries, especially in Asia but also in black Africa, if only because of the unforgivingly aggressive tone that it takes against imperialists and colonialism." He felt that the book would cement China's reputation as the "champion of the 'oppressed nations'," setting the stage for a world under Chinese domination that he predicted would be established by the year 1985.[44]

Designating the Little Red Book as either a fad or a bible sought to place it outside of politics proper, as an artifact of either pre-rational taste-driven consumption or pre-rational religious thinking. While some leftist students celebrated the weapon-like qualities of the Little Red Book as a tool of mobilization, the mainstream press worried about the effects of its pared-down political theology in China and beyond. For conservative observers such as Steinhaus and Titzrath, the "Mao Bible" was a manual for world revolution being taken up by both external and internal enemies.

The Little Red Book in the East

The first assessments of the Little Red Book from East German officials sounded remarkably similar to those of West German Sinologists. Gerd Kahlenbach, a secretary at the East German embassy in Beijing who had been in China for over ten years, wrote of the Little Red Book in May 1967:

In reality, this is a collection of statements by Mao completely torn from their context, chosen and compiled by the leadership clique because they respond to their current political needs, originating from the most diverse works and the most diverse periods of the history of the CCP, and transferred in a dogmatic and completely undialectical way to the current moment and the current developments. They had to be severed almost completely from their concrete content for this to happen. In the process, they have become empty phrases, which can be used to prove everything and nothing, and can be used by the "opponents" for their own ends.[45]

---

[44] Fritz Carl Steinhaus, *Rot-Asien 1985. China bereitet die Geschichtskatastrophe vor* (Würzburg: Marienburg-Verlag, 1966).

[45] Kahlenbach. Embassy of the GDR in Beijing. "Zu einigen Aspekten des gegenwärtigen 'Studiums der Mao Tse-tungs' in der Volksrepublik China," 16 Mar 1967. Politisches Archiv des Auswärtigen Amts (hereafter PA-AA), C 495, 75; Kahlenbach was the attaché at the embassy from 1957 until 1961 when he became the third secretary. Werner Meissner and Anja Feege, eds., *Die DDR und China 1949 bis 1990: Politik, Wirtschaft, Kultur: eine Quellensammlung* (Berlin: Akademie, 1995), p. 459.

Reporting firsthand from the Chinese capital in early 1967, Kahlenbach wrote that "the deluded youth and other 'rebels' are sent out with the 'Little Red Book' in their hands to destroy the party organizations and replace and inhumanely mistreat functionaries, who have usually followed the 'directives' coming from above and done their work accordingly." The quotations themselves had become ubiquitous, functioning as literal badges in the Beijing streets. "Every publication from the leaflets of the Red Guards to the *People's Daily* begins with a quote from Mao," he wrote, "there are quotes affixed to every wall, in every house, on all vehicles and public transit, on every bicycle. Quotes from Mao on silkscreened paper are used as wallpaper in apartments; quotes in the form of a badge are worn on clothes." Like Grimm, Kahlenbach sought to save Mao from the simplifications of his work at his own hands, saying of the Little Red Book: "This cannot be called a true study of the work of Mao Zedong."[46]

The official East German line was that the creation and distribution of the Little Red Book and the promotion of Mao Zedong Thought over all other socialist ideology was part of the campaign of geopolitical expansion being undertaken by Mao and his "petit bourgeois group" driven by "adventurist great power-chauvinism."[47] Yet circumstances meant that the East Germans were not able to assess the situation from a distance as Grimm and other West Germans had done. Rather, they were brought into direct contact with the mobilized Red Guards of the Cultural Revolution both at home and abroad. East German diplomats had been victim to a series of attacks in China since the middle of 1966, including in February 1967 when youth stormed the automobile of the East German ambassador at the airport in Beijing chanting the slogan from the Little Red Book, "Fear no sacrifice!" and dousing the car and its inhabitants with black paint, the color of reaction.[48] In East Berlin itself, Chinese embassy employees, suspicious that authorities had helped cause a car accident in which four Chinese diplomats had died, hung the embassy building with signs in June 1967 quoting from the Little Red Book about the need to fight "so long as a single man remains" and the threat that "blood must be answered with blood!"[49] When the embassy

---

[46] Kahlenbach, "Aspekten."
[47] Martina Wobst, *Die Kulturbeziehungen zwischen der DDR und der VR China 1949–1990: kulturelle Diversität und politische Positionierung* (Münster: Lit, 2004), p. 77.
[48] Kahlenbach. "Material zur 'Kulturrevolution,'" Attachment 7, 1 Jun 1967. PA-AA, C 495, 75; "Farbe der Schande," *Der Spiegel* (February 13, 1967), p. 86.
[49] SED Berlin District Headquarters. Party Organ Department. Report on the Events at the Chinese Embassy in Berlin-Karlshorst on 28 Jun 1967. 29 Jun 1967. Bundesarchiv (hereafter BArch), NY 4182, 1222.

director, Liu Pu, visited the East German Ministry of Foreign Affairs in August 1967, he laid a copy of the Little Red Book on the table demonstratively at the beginning of the discussion, and later read out a section predicting the inevitable downfall of reactionaries.[50]

In East Germany, the brandishing of the Little Red Book by Chinese functionaries was a clear indicator of the radicalization of the conflict between Mao's China and the Soviet Union and its allies. The Sino-Soviet split had meant an abrupt U-turn in East German publishing at the beginning of the 1960s. After the publication of hundreds of thousands of copies of Mao's writings in the late 1950s, the Chairman's books had abruptly disappeared from East German libraries and bookstores after the first disagreements between the Chinese and the Soviets in 1960. With the intensification of the split after 1963, East German officials banned the importation of all printed material from China and directed that all Chinese entering the country be "thoroughly searched" for any newsletters or brochures.[51] The Chinese responded by producing their own translations of polemics in the embassy in East Berlin and handing them out to workers, functionaries, and foreign students around the country.

After the Little Red Book entered mass production, it became a primary product smuggled into East Germany by the Chinese and out by others, usually West German students, who made day trips from West Berlin to the embassy. According to Werner Sollors, a student at the Free University in the 1960s, a good portion of the operating budget of the primary socialist student organization, the SDS, and the rental of their headquarters came through the sale of Little Red Books acquired for free from East Berlin.[52] Dieter Kunzelmann recalls that they also received the books by direct post from Beijing and could sell them in large numbers at student events. He conceded wryly that the right-wing tabloids "were, in this regard, a little bit right when they claimed sensationalistically that we were financed from Beijing."[53] Little Red Books and other publications were acquired despite the best efforts of the East German security forces. In March 1967, a journalist saw East German border police find a copy

---

[50] Transcript of conversation between Kurt Schneidewind, leader of the Far East Department and the Deputy Ambassador of the PRC, Liu Pu, 14 Aug 1967. PA-AA, C 1058, 73.

[51] Wobst, *Kulturbeziehungen*, p. 50; Honecker, SED to Hager. 22 Aug 1963. BArch-Stiftung Archiv der Parteien und Massenorganisationen der DDR im Bundesarchiv (hereafter SAPMO), DY 30, IV A 2, 221.

[52] Personal conversation, Tufts University, Medford, Mass., March 31, 2010.

[53] Dieter Kunzelmann, *Leisten Sie keinen Widerstand! Bilder aus meinem Leben* (Berlin: Transit, 1998), p. 55.

of the *Peking Review* on an FU student during a search and hold it in the air saying, "Rat poison!"[54] In 1968, the Chinese embassy received copies of the Little Red Book in English, Spanish, French, and German translation.[55] Among the steady stream of two or three visitors a day were many foreigners studying and visiting West Berlin, which had become a node of the international confluence of counterculture and socialist student activism by the last years of the decade.[56]

Far from encouraging the interest of young people in the Far Eastern socialist critique of capitalist democracy, East German authorities joined the right-wing Steinhaus in seeing Chinese communism as having potentially globally destructive effects, especially for the white nations of Europe, which they felt would face the brunt of anger as the erstwhile (and partially ongoing) imperial powers. The East German authorities were especially concerned about the attraction of the Chinese model for their own youth. The Chinese embassy had begun concerted efforts to court young East Germans in September 1967.[57] Traffic to the embassy peaked the following month with as many as sixty-three young East Germans a day entering and leaving with Mao buttons and Little Red Books.[58] Students at high schools were reported to be reading the book and wearing homemade Chinese-style caps emblazoned with the words "Mao fan."[59] Questioned about their motivations, two students said that wearing a Mao button was "ultra-modern" (*hochmodern*) and they wanted to be the first at their high school to have one.[60] Even in the face of such suggestions of the superficial attraction of Maoism, the East German authorities could not dismiss the Chinese challenge to the authority of the Soviet Communist Party and its "brother party," the SED, as a passing fad. In January 1968, the government prohibited access to the embassy for East German citizens.[61] Armed guards turned would-be visitors away at the gates, leaving East Germans only secret

---

[54] "'Lassen Sie bitte Ihre Hose runter,' Ostberliner Grenzpolizisten auf der Suche nach Mao Tse-tungs Schriften," *Die Zeit* (March 24, 1967).

[55] HA XX/2. Semi-Annual Report. 29 Nov 1968. Die Behörde für die Unterlagen des Staatssicherheitsdienstes der ehemaligen Deutschen Demokratischen Republik (hereafter BStU) Ministerium für Staatssicherheit (hereafter MfS), HA XX, 10775, p. 48.

[56] HA XX/2. Periodic Report. 10 Sep 1970. MfS, HA XX, 11054, p. 173.

[57] "Einzelinformation über die Beeinflussung Jugendlicher durch die chinesische Botschaft in Berlin-Karlshorst." 25 Sep 1967. MfS, ZAIG, 1329, p. 23.

[58] "Die Beeinflussung von Jugendlichen durch Mitarbeiter der Botschafter der VR China in Berlin-Karlshorst." 23 Oct 1967. Ibid., p. 28.

[59] Gräfe, Secondary School Inspectorate, Department Head. Report of the Greater Berlin Secondary School Inspectorate. n.d. PA-AA, C 1058, 73.

[60] "Einzelinformation," 25 Sep 1967, p. 25.

[61] Schröder. Abt. XX/2. "Periodische Berichterstattung zur politische-operativen Situation." 22 Feb 1968. MfS, HA XX, 10775, p. 2.

meetings with Chinese embassy employees and the closely observed postal service for further literature from Beijing.

Conclusion

There was no ambiguity about the status of the Little Red Book in East Germany. It was immediately deemed a badge book and a marker of membership in a political community that had set out to displace the Soviet Union as the leader of the socialist world. Lacking the free market of the West, the distinction between badge and brand could not and did not exist in the GDR. Provocations could not be seen as part of the froth of pop culture or the forgivable rambunctiousness of youth. The government owned and controlled the publishing houses, and publications were monitored and dictated by review through internal mechanisms of ideological oversight.[62] All books published outside party presses, whether fiction or non-fiction, were deemed a potential threat.[63] Unable to fold the book into a dynamic of apolitical consumption, and thus neutralize it, the East Germans ended up taking Mao's book of quotations much more seriously than West Germans. If the free market was able to "disarm Mao with fashion" in the Federal Republic as Poth had implied, in the GDR the only option was the always elusive goal of total proscription.

Yet even as they criticized the Little Red Book, both East and West German authorities paid it the compliment of imitating it as a weapon of propaganda. The GDR published a Little Red Series (Kleine Rote Reihe) of pocket-sized booklets for the youth organization it funded in West Germany in the early 1970s. The publications featured much material about the history of German socialism, including an article called "Forward, Young Guards" intended perhaps to reassert the national roots of working-class radicalism against the internationalist temptation offered by Mao's China.[64] In West Germany, the Ministry of Defense contracted the leftist publisher Rowohlt to print 50,000 copies of a gulag memoir in the format of Mao's book of quotations bound in green plastic. The West German army shot the books over the border with rockets and floated them over with balloons, displaying a curious devotion to the power of the printed word in years when the

---

[62] See Dominic Boyer, "Censorship as a Vocation: The Institutions, Practices, and Cultural Logic of Media Control in the German Democratic Republic," *Comparative Studies in Society and History* 45.3 (2003), pp. 511–45; Gunter Holzweißig, *Zensur ohne Zensor: Die SED-Informationsdiktatur* (Bonn: Bouvier, 1997).

[63] Dime novels (along with films) from the West were condemned as catalysts of counterrevolution in 1950s East Germany. See Poiger, *Jazz, Rock and Rebels*, chapter 2.

[64] Georg Rohde, *Arbeiterjugendbeschlüsse 2* (Dortmund: Weltkreis, 1972).

majority of East Germans had already tuned into television and radio signals coming from the West.[65] The materiality of the Little Red Book remained worthy of emulation even in the late 1960s, when scholars see visual media dominating text as a source of information.[66] As a politicized commodity, the "Mao Bible" illustrated the continuing cultural power of the printed and bound book as a material object even as social commentators declared print culture dead.

BIBLIOGRAPHY

Baumgärtel, Tilman, *Vom Guerillakino zum Essayfilm: Harun Farocki* (Berlin: B Books, 2002)

Borgmeister, Lisa, "Politische Buchhandlungen im Kontext der 68er Bewegung in der BRD: Am Beispiel der Marburger Buchhandlung 'Roter Stern'," in Stephan Füssel, ed., *Die Politisierung des Buchmarkts: 1968 als Branchenereignis* (Wiesbaden: Harrassowitz, 2007), pp. 91–158

Boyer, Dominic, "Censorship as a Vocation: The Institutions, Practices, and Cultural Logic of Media Control in the German Democratic Republic," *Comparative Studies in Society and History* 45.3 (2003), pp. 511–45

Devillers, Philippe, *Was Mao wirklich sagte* (Vienna: Fritz Molden, 1967)

Diehl, Laura K., "Die Konjunktur der Mao-Images in der bundesdeutschen '68er'-Bewegung," in Sebastian Gehrig, Barbara Mittler, and Felix Wemheuer, eds., *Kulturrevolution als Vorbild? Maoismen im deutschsprachigen Raum* (Frankfurt am Main: Peter Lang, 2008), pp. 179–202

Fahlenbrach, Kathrin, *Protest-Inszenierungen: visuelle Kommunikation und kollektive Identitäten in Protestbewegungen* (Wiesbaden: Westdeutscher Verlag, 2002)

Gehrig, Sebastian, "(Re-)Configuring Mao: Trajectories of a Culturo-Political Trend in West Germany," *Transcultural Studies* 2 (2011), pp. 190–210

Holzweißig, Gunter, *Zensur ohne Zensor: Die SED-Informationsdiktatur* (Bonn: Bouvier, 1997)

Koenen, Gerd, *Das rote Jahrzehnt: Unsere kleine deutsche Kulturrevolution 1967–1977* (Cologne: Fischer, 2001)

Kubicki, Karol, and Siegward Lönnendonker, "Die Freie Universität im Feld der politischen Spannungen," in Kubicki and Lönnendonker, eds., *50 Jahre Freie Universität Berlin*, pp. 104–42

Kubicki, Karol, and Siegward Lönnendonker, eds., *50 Jahre Freie Universität Berlin aus der Sicht von Zeitzeugen* (Berlin: Zentrale Universitätsdruckerei, 2002)

Kunzelmann, Dieter, *Leisten Sie keinen Widerstand! Bilder aus meinem Leben* (Berlin: Transit, 1998)

Leifer, Walter, *China schaut südwärts* (Würzburg: Marienburg-Verlag, 1961)

---

[65] Von Saldern, "Markt für Marx," p. 156.
[66] On the rise of the visual in the 1960s see Kathrin Fahlenbrach, *Protest-Inszenierungen: visuelle Kommunikation und kollektive Identitäten in Protestbewegungen* (Wiesbaden: Westdeutscher Verlag, 2002), p. 11.

Lönnendonker, Siegward, "Kleine Zeittafel für die Jahre 1945–1973," in Kubicki and Lönnendonker, eds., *50 Jahre Freie Universität Berlin*, pp. 294–347

Mao Zedong, *Theorie des Guerillakrieges oder Strategie der Dritten Welt* (Reinbek bei Hamburg: Rowohlt, 1966)

Mao Zedong and Tilemann Grimm, *Das rote Buch: Worte des Vorsitzenden Mao Tse-tung* (Frankfurt am Main: Fischer, 1967)

Meissner, Werner, and Anja Feege, eds., *Die DDR und China 1949 bis 1990: Politik, Wirtschaft, Kultur: eine Quellensammlung* (Berlin: Akademie, 1995)

Myrdal, Jan, *China: die Revolution geht weiter: Bericht über den Fortschritt in Liu Ling* (Munich: Nymphenburger Verlag-Handlung, 1971)

Nentwig, Ingo, "Die Mao-Bibel: Das Kleine Rote Buch der Zitate," in Helmut Opletal, ed., *Die Kultur der Kulturrevolution: Personenkult und politisches Design in China von Mao Zedong* (Ghent: Snoeck, 2011), pp. 177–81

Pálóczi-Hórvath, György, *Mao Tse-tung: Der Herr der blauen Ameisen*, 2nd edn. (Frankfurt am Main: Scheffler, 1967)

Poiger, Uta G., *Jazz, Rock and Rebels: Cold War Politics and American Culture in a Divided Germany* (Berkeley: University of California Press, 2000)

Poth, Chlodwig, "Entschärft Mao mit Mode," *Pardon* (August 1967), p. 38

Rectanus, Mark W., "Literary Publishing in the Federal Republic of Germany: Redefining the Enterprise," *German Studies Review* 10.1 (Feb 1987), pp. 95–123

Literary Series in the Federal Republic of Germany from 1960 to 1980 (Wiesbaden: Harrassowitz, 1984)

Reiche, Reimut, "Worte des Vorsitzenden Maos," *Neue Kritik* 41 (April 1967), pp. 9–10

Rohde, Georg, *Arbeiterjugendbeschlüsse 2* (Dortmund: Weltkreis, 1972)

Slobodian, Quinn, *Foreign Front: Third World Politics in Sixties West Germany* (Durham: Duke University Press, 2012)

Sozialistische Einheitspartei Deutschlands, *Der Statut der Sozialistische Einheitspartei Deutschlands* (Berlin: Dietz, 1963)

Starlinger, Wilhelm, *Hinter Rußland China* (Würzburg: Marienburg-Verlag, 1957)

Steinhaus, Fritz Carl, *Rot-Asien 1985: China bereitet die Geschichtskatastrophe vor* (Würzburg: Marienburg-Verlag, 1966)

"Zur Einführung," in Mao Zedong, *Das Mao Tse-tung Brevier* (Würzburg: Marienburg-Verlag, 1967), pp. 5–20

von Saldern, Adelheid, "Markt für Marx: Literaturbetrieb und Lesebewegungen in der Bundesrepublik in den Sechziger- und Siebzigerjahren," *Archiv für Sozialgeschichte* 44 (2004), pp. 149–80

Wobst, Martina, *Die Kulturbeziehungen zwischen der DDR und der VR China 1949–1990: kulturelle Diversität und politische Positionierung* (Münster: Lit, 2004)

13   Principally contradiction
The flourishing of French Maoism

Julian Bourg

> If in any process there are a number of contradictions, one of them must be the principal contradiction playing the leading and decisive role, while the rest occupy a secondary and subordinate position. Therefore, in studying any complex process in which there are two or more contradictions, we must devote every effort to finding its principal contradiction. Once this principal contradiction is grasped, all problems can be readily solved.
>
> Methods of Thinking and Methods of Work

French Maoism flourished in the decade between 1966 and 1976, coinciding precisely with the Chinese Cultural Revolution. Having germinated slowly since the 1940s, French Maoism thrived in the wake of the Sino-Soviet split and as a result of converging international and domestic circumstances. It wilted in the wake of Mao's death, amidst the ongoing decline in far-left activism in the late 1970s, and has largely faded, except for a residual cross-pollination in intellectual life that continues even today.[1] The reception of Maoism in France, as elsewhere, was subject to the vicissitudes of "traveling theory" – the dislocation and creative appropriation that attended the translation of Maoist thought into different cultural contexts.[2] Ironically, Mao's rough-and-ready peasant communism proved especially influential because it took root among the intellectual elite, notably with students at the prestigious École Normale Supérieure and among luminaries such as Louis Althusser, Jean-Luc

---

[1] For readable introductions see Christophe Bourseiller, *Les Maoïstes: la folle histoire des gardes rouges français* (Paris: Plon, 1996) and Richard Wolin, *The Wind from the East: French Intellectuals, the Cultural Revolution, and the Legacy of the 1960s* (Princeton: Princeton University Press, 2010). I refer throughout this chapter to details found in Julian Bourg, "The Red Guards of Paris: French Student Maoism of the 1960s," *History of European Ideas* 31 (2005), pp. 472–90 and Julian Bourg, *From Revolution to Ethics: May 1968 and Contemporary French Thought* (Montreal: McGill-Queen's University Press, 2007).

[2] Edward Said, "Traveling Theory," in *The World, the Text, and the Critic* (Cambridge, Mass.: Harvard University Press, 1983), pp. 226–47; Edward Said, "Traveling Theory Revisited," in Nigel Gibson, ed., *Rethinking Fanon: The Continuing Dialogue* (Amherst, N.Y.: Humanity Books, 1999), pp. 197–214.

Godard, Julia Kristeva, Jean-Paul Sartre, and Philippe Sollers. Maoism arrived in France at a fortuitous time, its international promotion by China in the 1960s coinciding with openness in France toward alternative radicalisms. The efforts of the Foreign Languages Press in Beijing, yielding the Little Red Book and, perhaps more importantly, the multi-volume *Selected Works*, coincided with domestic circumstances in such a way as to allow the seeds of *la pensée Mao* to fall in particularly fertile soil.

Maoism was a dissident communism in France. By the mid 1960s, the Soviet-aligned French Communist Party had been discredited in the eyes of some of its followers and sympathizers. The party's ambivalent positions over the Algerian war, which concluded in 1962, had reflected a tone-deafness toward anti-colonialism, and its rigid commitment to class-based politics sidelined questions of empire and race. Older communists were furthermore disappointed with the decline of the fighting spirit of the French Resistance and the party's embrace of de-Stalinization. As elsewhere, younger French radicals in the 1960s found inspiration in decolonization and "Third-Worldism" writ large: China, Cuba, and Vietnam. Protests by young Maoists against the American war in Southeast Asia, leading to violent street clashes with right-wing students, precipitated the student and worker revolts of May–June 1968, which grew into the largest general strike in twentieth-century Europe. The stolid Communist Party initially condemned those events – before trying to capitalize on them, but it was too late. May 1968 opened a period characterized by political radicalism and the precipitous decline of the established Communist Party. Maoism proved to be among the most recognizable and influential of the tendencies to emerge during "the '68 years."

The generational split between older communists and younger radicals also gave rise to the primary distinction among French Maoists – namely, what A. Belden Fields once described as the difference between "hierarchical" and "anti-hierarchical" Maoism.[3] The "adult" dissidents of the Communist Party, packing their bags after the Sino-Soviet split, formed their own movement in June 1966, which in December 1967 became the Maoist-oriented French Marxist–Leninist Communist Party.[4] This party lasted until 1976 and was organized according to Leninist principles: strict discipline, order, and clandestineness. More intriguing to many scholars has been the anti-hierarchical brand of French Maoism that developed among students and young radicals after

---

[3] A. Belden Fields, *Trotskyism and Maoism: Theory and Practice in France and the United States* (New York: Praeger, 1988), pp. 87–88, 94ff.

[4] The Mouvement communiste français and then the Parti communiste marxiste–léniniste français.

1968. The roots of that phenomenon can be traced to students at the École Normale who, while studying Marx with their teacher Althusser, had formed their own Maoist "circle" in 1964.[5] After trying to take control of the Communist Party's student organization from within, they broke away and formed their own group in December 1966: the Union of Marxist–Leninist Communist Youth.[6] That month, their rupture with the French Communist Party was consummated when they published a special issue of their journal *Marxist–Leninist Notebooks* on the Great Proletarian Cultural Revolution (to which Althusser contributed an unsigned article).[7] Caught up with their own inner political and theoretical debates, remarkably, the Maoists at the École Normale largely skipped the events of May 1968 – a missed appointment that led to masochistic self-criticism and the group's dissolution that fall.

In October 1968, the core of the École Normale Maoists joined forces with the anti-authoritarian leaders of the May events to form the Proletarian Left, a movement that for the next six years became synonymous with Maoism in the public eye.[8] "Of all the Maoist organizations after May 1968," Christophe Bourseiller has observed, "the most important numerically as well as in cultural influence was without question the Proletarian Left."[9] The group worked in cities, working-class suburbs, immigrant communities, and rural areas. It had divisions dedicated to high schools, universities, the media, propaganda, the military, women, cinema, health, abortion, international leftism, prisons, and, of course, factories.[10] Although the Proletarian Left courted terrorism, it never went down the road as far as the era's German and Italian leftists did. It furthermore attracted prominent intellectuals to its cause: Sartre took over as nominal director of its paper when the real editor was arrested; on

---

[5] Camille Robcis, "'China in our Heads': Althusser, Maoism, and Structuralism," *Social Text 110* 30.1 (Spring 2012), pp. 51–69. For a judicious account by a former student who situates Althusser's intellectual projects within the context of the distinctive ambience of the École Normale, see Étienne Balibar, "Althusser and the Rue D'Ulm," *New Left Review* 58 (July–August 2009), pp. 91–107.

[6] The Union des jeunesses communistes marxistes–léninistes. The Communist Party's student organ – the Union des étudiants communistes – had been refounded in 1956.

[7] Anonymous [Louis Althusser], "Sur la révolution culturelle," special issue on *La Grande révolution culturelle prolétarienne (I)*, *Cahiers marxistes-léninistes* 14 (November–December 1966), trans. Jason E. Smith as "On the Cultural Revolution," *Décalages* 1.1 (2010), scholar.oxy.edu/decalages/vol1/iss1/9, accessed September 1, 2011. Two more issues of the *Cahiers marxistes–léninistes* on the Cultural Revolution appeared, in January–February 1967 and April–June 1968. See Frédéric Chateigner, "D'Althusser à Mao: les *Cahiers Marxistes–Léninistes*," special issue on *Prochinois et maoïsme en France (et dans les espaces francophones)*, *Dissidences* 8 (May 2010), pp. 66–80.

[8] The Gauche prolétarienne.   [9] Bourseiller, *Les Maoïstes*, p. 105.

[10] Dossier, France, Gauche prolétarienne, F Δ Rés. 576. Bibliothèque de documentation internationale contemporaine, Nanterre, France.

the margins of Maoist militancy, Michel Foucault helped animate the Prison Information Group, investigating the conditions of political and common-law prisoners. Leaving behind the structural rigidities of the party form, the anti-hierarchical Maoism of the Proletarian Left sought to channel the rebellious energies of 1968, to diversify the sites of struggle, and above all to make culture and everyday life into the material of emancipatory, transformational politics. Ultimately, the group's anti-hierarchical sensibility expressed itself in an incapacity to maintain organizational coherence, and it dissolved in 1974.

Militant French Maoism reached a crescendo in the years after 1968, but even before the May events Maoism percolated throughout French popular culture more generally. The French-language version of the Little Red Book appeared exactly at the moment when small, inexpensive paperbacks were capturing the European book market.[11] *Citations du président Mao Tsé-toung* was published twice, first by the Foreign Languages Press in December 1966 and then a year later by the French publishing house Éditions Seuil.[12] The Chinese Communist Party's own decision to publish a "great quantity" of Mao's writings had been announced in mid August 1966, and the Foreign Languages Press edition was first advertised in the weekly *Pékin Information* in mid November.[13] The Foreign Languages Press also published volumes I and IV of *Selected Works* in 1966, although unofficial French translations of Russian editions had earlier been available.[14] *Pékin Information* had primed French audiences for the Little Red Book earlier in the year through swooning depictions of the Cultural Revolution and the power of *la pensée Mao Tsé-toung* – the "soul of revolutionary peoples," a "red flag" to be lifted high, a "red sun" rising to "light up the entire

[11] Ben Mercer, "The Paperback Revolution: Mass-Circulation Books and the Cultural Origins of 1968 in Western Europe," *Journal of the History of Ideas* 72.4 (October 2011), pp. 613–36.

[12] Jean-Claude Guillebaud, interview by François Dosse, 7 July 2011. I am grateful to Dosse for sharing this interview with me. At that time, communist China was not a signatory to international copyright conventions. See Stephanie L. Sgambati, "China's Accession to the Berne Convention: Bandaging the Wounds of Intellectual Property Piracy in China," *Fordham Intellectual Property, Media and Entertainment Law Journal* 3.1 (1992), pp. 139–74.

[13] "Le Comité central du P.C.C. decide de publier en grande quantité les oeuvres du président Mao," *Pékin Information* 33 (August 15, 1966), pp. 13–15. *Pékin Information* 46 (November 14, 1966). Alongside *Les Cahiers de la Chine nouvelle*, *La Chine*, and *La Chine en construction*, *Pékin Information* was one of the main sources of official Chinese news in French. Beginning in February 1967, each issue of *Pékin Information* opened with several choice Mao citations. See *Pékin Information* 8 (February 20, 1967).

[14] *Pékin Information* 22 (May 30, 1966). I can longer support an earlier claim that the four-volume *Oeuvres choisies* were published 1962–68. The story is more complicated. See Bourg, "The Red Guards of Paris," p. 473.

world" with its "radiant influence," an "inexhaustible source of wisdom and courage" opening a "new era."[15] Readers were exhorted to "study and apply *la pensée Mao Tsé-toung* in a creative way"; the "entire country" was to be a "great school" for Mao's thought.[16] The almost-magic powers of Mao's thought were extolled in stories, such as that about Drill Team No. 3211, which relied on the Chairman's aphorisms to fight and extinguish a massive industrial fire.[17] With the Little Red Book, anything was possible! The Cultural Revolution's cult of youth and the rhetoric of renewal were placed front and center. For instance, French students could consider the claim that, as part of the Cultural Revolution, Chinese students had proposed an entirely new system of human science education.[18] French readers in particular would have been attuned to a four-part article series lauding the Paris Commune on its ninety-fifth anniversary.[19] As the Little Red Book arrived in France, *Pékin Information* reported its success in places such as Australia and Brazil.

In late December 1966, Robert Guillain claimed in *Le Monde* to have acquired one of the first French-language copies of the *Citations*.[20] Comparing it to a "missal" and "catechism," he called this "Gospel of

---

[15] "Levons haut le grand drapeau rouge de la pensée de Mao Tsé-toung: participons activement à la grande révolution culturelle socialiste," *Pékin Information* 19 (May 9, 1966), pp. 29–35; "Une nouvelle victoire de la pensée de Mao Tsé-toung," *Pékin Information* 24 (June 13, 1966), pp. 3–5; "Vive la grande révolution culturelle prolétarienne," *Pékin Information* 25 (June 20, 1966), pp. 7–13; "La Pensée de Mao Tsé-toung est l'âme des peoples révolutionnaires," *Pékin Information* 40–41 (October 6, 1966), p. 31; "Le Vaste rayonnement de la pensée de Mao Tsé-toung: les experts chinois à l'étranger," *Pékin Information* 48 (November 28, 1966), pp. 25–27; "Une nouvelle époque marquée par l'établissement vigoreux de la suprématie complete de la pensée de Mao Tsé-toung," *Pékin Information* 50 (December 12, 1966), pp. 13–17; Tong Siao-hai, "La Pensée de Mao Tsé-toung: inépuisable source de sagacité et de courage," *Pékin Information* 51 (December 19, 1966), pp. 21–25.

[16] Wang Kié, "Étudier et appliquer dans une façon creatrice la pensée de Mao Tsé-toung," *Pékin Information* 30 (July 25, 1966), p. 31; "Tout le pays doit être une grande école de la pensée de Mao Tsé-toung," *Pékin Information* 32 (August 8, 1966), pp. 6–8. The phrase "grande école" has particular meaning in France, where it refers to the small set of elite institutions in humanistic, scientific, and administrative fields. Cf. "Le Peuple chinois est determine à faire de chaque branche d'activité une grande école de la pensée de Mao Tsé-toung," *Pékin Informtion* 36 (September 5, 1966), pp. 22–27.

[17] "La Pensée de Mao Tsé-toung dirige notre bataille," *Pékin Information* 40–41 (October 6, 1966), pp. 32–37.

[18] "Des étudiants proposent un nouveau système d'éducation pour l'enseignement supérieur des lettres et des arts," *Pékin Information* 30 (July 25, 1966), pp. 22–24.

[19] Cheng Tche-se, "Les Grandes révélations de la Commune de Paris," *Pékin Information* 15 (April 11, 1966), pp. 13–16; *Pékin Information* 16 (April 18, 1966), pp. 17–20; *Pékin Information* 17 (April 25, 1966), pp. 27–29; *Pékin Information* 18 (May 2, 1966), pp. 28–31. In November, Italian Maoists compared the Cultural Revolution favorably with the Paris Commune: "La Grande révolution culturelle chinoise rang aux côtés de la Commune de Paris," *Pékin Information* 46 (November 14, 1966), pp. 26–27.

[20] Robert Guillain, "Le Petit livre rouge," *Le Monde* (December 24, 1966), pp. 1, 3.

communism according to Mao ... *the* book" of the moment, a "universal and obligatory *best seller*." Yet, the text was "neither easy nor short"; Mao's thought was abstract and challenging, opaque to those who did not speak in Marxist tongues. Guillain encouraged his readers to avoid mocking the image of millions of Chinese clinging to their breviaries, for a serious development was underway. The Little Red Book provided "coherent thought" that, directing concrete actions, might enable the Chinese people to "escape their immobilism," especially the disabling inheritance of the Confucian tradition. Guillain invoked the classic stereotype of China as the "sick man of the East" in contrast with the "explosive health" of the Red Guards. By January 1967, four thousand copies of the Little Red Book had been sold in Paris alone.[21] In February, French newspapers reported that the English-language *Quotations* were selling out in the United States and that massive efforts to memorize Mao's citations were underway in China.[22]

In June 1967, in full Orientalist splendor, the men's magazine *Lui* published an eight-page photo-shoot of Asian women scantily clad in Chinese jackets, or entirely naked – each image adorned with quotations by the Chairman himself. By then the fashionable boutique O'Kennedy was selling "Mao collar" jackets at a premium off the Champs-Elysées.[23] In many respects, the high point of pre-1968 cultural Maoism arrived with the August 1967 release of Jean-Luc Godard's film romp *La Chinoise*, which centered on a youthful Maoist sect in Paris composed of a philosophy student, a painter, a chemist, an actor, and a farmer fresh in the capital from the provinces.[24] The film included Claude Channes's upbeat soundtrack single, "Mao-Mao," known for its tag line, sung by a child's voice, "It's the Little Red Book that makes everything finally move." Although one critic at the Avignon film festival debut complained that the film "ruined" everyone's evening, Godard helped lay the groundwork for its success at the September 1967 Venice film festival through an interview with *Le Monde*.[25] Linking his efforts to Sergei

[21] Bourseiller, *Les Maoïstes*, p. 74.

[22] "Les Chinois apprennent par coeur les citations du petit livre rouge," *Le Monde* (February 15, 1967), p. 3; "Les 'Citations de Mao Tsé-toung' ont du succès aux États-Unis," *Le Monde* (February 26–27, 1967), p. 6.

[23] Bourseiller, *Les Maoïstes*, pp. 64–65.

[24] Jean-Luc Godard (dir.), *La Chinoise*, 96 min., Anouchka Films, 1967. James S. Williams has drawn attention to the serious anti-terrorist message of *La Chinoise*: James S. Williams, "'C'est le petit livre rouge / Qui fait que tout enfin bouge': The Case for Revolutionary Agency and Terrorism in Jean-Luc Godard's *La Chinoise*," *Journal of European Studies* 40.3 (September 2010), pp. 206–18.

[25] Nicole Zand, "Béjart et Godard au Festival d'Avignon," *Le Monde* (August 8, 1967), p. 9; "'La Chinoise': quelques individus-types avec pour seul point commun la jeunesse" (Jean-Luc Godard, interview by Yvonne Baby), *Le Monde* (August 24, 1967), p. 10.

Eisenstein, Maxim Gorky, Igor Stravinsky, Luigi Pirandello, and even Fidel Castro, and referring to himself as a "receiver–transmitter," Godard described how the film was a paean to contemporary youth – both the perpetual renewal of young people (who "do not yet wear masks") and the historical specificity and significance of the postwar generation ("a cultural fact without precedent"). The young people depicted in the film were "in movement … passing from one social structure to another," and in this process they had found a "friend": Mao Zedong. Or, as he otherwise put it, they were "Robinsons whose Friday is Marxism." What youth in France and the "Third World" shared was "the will to be different than their parents," and Godard had sought to mobilize such "primordial sincerity" against the "spoiled kingdom of Western cinema." Several weeks later, Jean de Baroncelli echoed Godard's estimation of the value of this film, calling it the "most important, passionate, and revolutionary film" at the Venice festival, meriting the Golden Lion award.[26] Also in September 1967, Radio Peking announced that 59 million copies of the *Quotations* had been published in the first twelve months of the Cultural Revolution.[27] By the end of the year, Nino Ferrer's pop hit "Mao et moa," tracing the link between red wine and the Red Guards – *Le quart de rouge, c'est la boisson du garde rouge* – could be heard on French radios.

After 1968, beyond the precincts of committed militancy, Maoism also permeated French culture more generally. In the late 1960s and early 1970s, a slew of "little red books" appeared on a variety of subjects. A satirical volume, *The General's Little Red Book*, an edited collection of some of Charles de Gaulle's choice absurd quotes, such as "A great country has no friends" and "I have too many eunuchs around me," was followed by other collections of citations on the "free woman," the sexual revolution, transvestites, revolutionary violence, the Cannes film festival and cinematic eroticism, schoolchildren and high-school students, and even acupuncture – each distilling the aphoristic essence of its theme.[28] The prominence of sexuality in these chapbooks was notably out of

[26] Jean de Baroncelli, "'La Chinoise' de Jean-Luc Godard: un film qui 'eclipse' tous les autres," *Le Monde* (September 6, 1967), p. 16. On the other hand, Samuel Lachize complained in the Communist Party paper, *L'Humanité*, that Godard overlooked the Soviet Union's support of the North Vietnamese: "'La Chinoise' vue par 'L'Humanité'," *Le Monde* (September 7, 1967), p. 11.

[27] "59 millions d'exemplaires des 'pensées de Mao'," *Le Monde* (September 2, 1967), p. 3.

[28] Robert Rocca, ed., *Le Petit livre rouge du general: pensées choisies (et parfois commentées)* (Paris: Éditions de la pensée moderne, 1968). For instance, André Laude and Max Chaleil, eds., *Le Petit livre rouge de la révolution sexuelle* (Paris: Debresse, 1969); Giovanni Sciuto, *Le Petit livre rouge des travestis pas comme les autres: le 4è sexe, une enquête*, preface by Louis Vidal (Soisy-sur-Seine: Éditions du Senart, 1974).

step with the original Little Red Book. Maoism's cultural influence in 1970s France was pervasive. The avant-garde revue *Tel Quel* made its Maoist turn in 1970;[29] Jean Yanne's farcical film *Les Chinois à Paris* (1974) fantasized a Chinese Red Army invasion of Paris;[30] in 1977, the Little Red Book was submitted to close academic reading, a clinical postmortem for Maoism the year after the Chairman's death.[31] In 1980, the former militants Claudie and Jacques Broyelle pronounced definitively in their farewell to Maoism, *Apocalypse Mao*, "China was *in . . .* [Now] it is *out . . .* we are no longer Maoists."[32]

Intellectual engagement marked the beginning and end of Maoism's flourishing in France. Given their social status and political impact, it matters that certain influential thinkers engaged with *la pensée Mao*, either directly or on its margins. Even today echoes of Maoism can be heard among the intellectual elite of France. In the 1960s, Maoism proved useful for criticizing Soviet-aligned French communism, accused of being stuck in revisionism, economism, or humanism. Not all themes and concepts of Maoist thought took hold to the same degree. The language of democratic centralism, self-criticism, the "creative masses," overcoming the difference between intellectuals and the people, the preeminence of ideological and cultural struggle – all of this was in the air. Mao's language of violence had a certain rhetorical appeal, too, although French Maoists never took the terrorist route. The concept of "investigation" was put into practice even before 1968, as École Normale Maoists went to factories and farms to learn what books could never teach. The strategy of the investigation returned in 1971–72 through the efforts of Foucault and the Prison Information Group. Another compelling example of an almost hand-in-glove fit between Maoism and French intellectual life concerns the coincidence between the Maoist critique of Confucian humanism and French anti-humanism. Although the forms of this trend in postwar French thought were varied, the structural Marxism of Althusser played a pivotal role in it, not least because his students were among the most potent theorists of post-revisionist Marxism and eventually of post-Marxism and neo-Marxism. Given the rigor, sophistication, and density of their analyses, the four-volume *Selected Works of Mao Tse-tung* proved influential in ways

---

[29] Patrick ffrench and Roland-François Lack, eds., *The Tel Quel Reader* (London: Routledge, 1998), p. 13. See Wolin, *The Wind from the East*, chapter 6, on *Tel Quel* and Julia Kristeva.

[30] Jean Yanne (dir.), *Les Chinois à Paris*, 115 min., Ciné Qua Non, 1974.

[31] François Marmor, *Le "Petit livre rouge," Mao Tsé-toung: analyse critique* (Paris: Hatier, 1977).

[32] Claudie and Jacques Broyelle, *Apocalypse Mao* (Paris: Grasset, 1980), p. 8.

that the Little Red Book could not be. One essay in particular, Mao's "On Contradiction" (August 1937), proved crucial for Althusser and others.[33] Although quotations from "On Contradiction" appeared in the Little Red Book, it was its argument as a whole that was extracted, decontextualized, refashioned, and put to work.

Althusser observed in 1972 that Maoism was a "contradictory critique." Over the previous four decades, he said, "the only *historically existing* (left) 'critique'" of Stalinism had been found in the Chinese revolution: "A silent critique. A critique *from afar*. A critique 'from behind the scenes.' ... A *contradictory* critique," but nevertheless one "from which one can learn [and that can] help us to see our own history more clearly."[34] Contradiction became the touchstone of Althusser's longstanding engagement with Maoism, beginning with his first published mention of Mao in 1953, in which he referred to the "recent text," "On Contradiction."[35] Throughout the 1950s and 1960s, as he continued to emphasize the theme of contradiction, Althusser the theorist was less interested in the Little Red Book than in Mao's longer philosophical essays.[36]

Mao's "On Contradiction" was written in 1937, as the civil war between Chinese communists and nationalists was suspended in favor of a united front against imperialist Japan. Alongside the distinction between antagonistic and non-antagonistic contradiction,[37] the main

[33] "On Contradiction" first appeared in French in *Cahiers du communisme* 29.7–8 (1952), pp. 673–816. After mid-1950s French translations from Russian, it was published by the Foreign Languages Press as a brochure in 1957 and in Mao's *Quatre essais philosophiques* and volume I of the *Oeuvres Choisies* in 1966.

[34] Louis Althusser, "Reply to John Lewis," in *Essays in Self-Criticism*, trans. Grahame Lock (London: New Left Books, 1976), pp. 92–93.

[35] Louis Althusser, "On Marxism," in *The Specter of Hegel: Early Writings*, ed. and intro. François Matheron, trans. G. M. Goshgarian (London: Verso, 1997), p. 249. Mao Tsetung, "On Contradiction," in *Selected Readings from the Works of Mao Tsetung* (Peking: Foreign Languages Press, 1971). The essay was singled out for praise during the Cultural Revolution. See Fan Fou-ken, "En s'appuyant sur 'De la pratique' et 'De la contradiction,' une horloge de fréquence de type chinois a été fabriqué," *Pékin Information* 25 (June 20, 1966), pp. 29–33.

[36] On contradiction in the thought of Althusser, see Louis Althusser Archives, Institut Mémoires de l'Édition Contemporaine, Saint-Germain-la-Blanche-Herbe, France, AL T2. A57–03.01 and AL T2. A57–04.01. I am indebted to Camille Robcis who kindly shared her research notes with me.

[37] Here were seeds of what would later appear in the 1957 essay "On the Correct Handling of Contradictions Among the People" (Mao, *Selected Readings*, pp. 432–79), namely, the difference between, on one hand, contradictions among the people and, on the other hand, contradictions between the people and their class enemies. This essay was republished with "On Contradiction," in Mao Tse-tung, *Quatre essais philosophiques* (Peking: Foreign Languages Press, 1966). See "En publiant un texte ancien de Mao Tsé-toung la presse chinoise demande la juste solution des contradictions au sein du peuple," *Le Monde* (June 21, 1967), p. 6. On Althusser's reading of this text see Robcis, "'China in our Heads'," p. 59.

innovation of "On Contradiction" concerned Mao's distinction between principal and secondary contradictions, and between primary and secondary aspects of a contradiction. He also advanced the related notion of uneven development in the essay. Complex phenomena are traversed by multiple contradictions, said Mao, but one contradiction could always be identified as "play[ing] the leading role" at a given time and place, and moreover one aspect of the contradiction could be identified as ascendant. So, for example, the classical Marxian interpretation holds that the principal contradiction of the capitalist era is between the bourgeoisie and the proletariat, while the contradiction between imperialism and colonized peoples is secondary; moreover, the proletariat forms the principal aspect of the contradiction, and must eventually prevail over the bourgeoisie. But while such propositions might be true generally, complex phenomena develop dynamically and unevenly, with considerable variation from place to place. Contradictions were never frozen in place; their aspects could shift position. An indigenous bourgeoisie might be connected to foreign colonialists, or they might make common anti-imperialist cause with fellow nationals. Given historical variety, development was thus "uneven." Still, notwithstanding multiple contradictions traversing complex phenomena, for Mao, one contradiction could always be identified as "play[ing] the leading role" at a given time and place. Therefore, the basic conflict between capitalists and workers that characterized some Western societies might be less acute than the contradiction between the colonial and the colonized in the "semi-feudal, semi-colonial" conditions of 1930s China. Even then, multiple outcomes were possible: foreign-imperial/Chinese-elite coalitions might be arrayed against the popular classes, or China could experience "national unity" in the face of imperialism. In essence, Mao was arguing against Marxist "dogmatists" to say that while the conflict between the communists and nationalists represented the principal contradiction in general, it was temporarily subordinated by the particular historical contingency of Japanese invasion.

There were practical–strategic lessons to draw from this re-injection of contingency, variability, and inversion into dialectical thinking. The theory of the mobile reversibility of contradictions and their aspects would enable one to decipher when to act and how, and therefore reading circumstances correctly was a prerequisite to meaningful action. In this light, Mao concluded his discussion of principal and secondary contradictions with an appeal for the relative autonomy of *theory*. This assessment would play a pivotal role for Althusser and his students. In "certain conditions," Mao said, revolutionary theory could play "the principal and decisive role" in a given contradictory matrix. Against a dogmatic "mechanical materialism" that crudely reduced cultural superstructure to an economic base, in contrast, "dialectical materialism" was attentive to circumstances and advantageous combinations of principal and secondary contradictions (and their primary and secondary aspects). Thus cultural revolution could take precedence over the economic. That is, theory was both a weapon of class struggle *and* the arena in which to wield it.[38]

Althusser's fullest engagement with Mao's essay "On Contradiction" appeared in two articles published at the height of the Sino-Soviet split: "Contradiction and Overdetermination" (December 1962) and "On the Materialist Dialectic" (August 1963), both reprinted in his landmark 1965 volume, *For Marx*.[39] The cornerstones of Althusser's structuralist Marxism were laid here, including his use of the psychoanalysis of Sigmund Freud and Jacques Lacan and his articulation of the notion of "theoretical practice." After first chiding Mao for keeping his discussion "abstract" and "descriptive," Althusser pursued the notion that a contradiction is "inseparable from the total structure of the social body in which it is found." Because contradiction is shaped by its historical conditions *as well as* affecting those conditions, he said, it can be considered to be "overdetermined in its principle."[40] Complexity was to be the byword.

Following the critique of Mao's descriptive abstraction and the attempt to embed contradictions in their sociohistorical conditions, in the 1963 essay "On the Materialist Dialectic," Althusser observed that even if contradiction was a "universal" phenomenon (and Mao gave it almost metaphysical standing) it only appeared in particular situations. "Contradiction," he wrote, "is always specific and specificity universally appertains to its essence." With this in mind Althusser turned to the "three very remarkable concepts" Mao had expressed in his 1937 essay: principal and secondary contradictions; primary and secondary aspects of the contradiction; and uneven development. These elements added up to great complexity: there was never just one contradiction, but many that proceeded unevenly. Nevertheless, viewed systematically, a "structured complex unity" came into focus. For the Marxist, this unity was governed by a single principal contradiction, namely, that between domination and subordination. Althusser's language here enabled him to sidestep the issue of how the contradictions between bourgeois and

---

[38] Mao, "On Contradiction," in *Selected Readings*, pp. 85, 110–17.

[39] Louis Althusser, "Contradiction and Overdetermination" and "On the Materialist Dialectic," in *For Marx*, trans. Ben Brewster (New York: Pantheon Books, 1967).

[40] Althusser, "Contradiction and Overdetermination," pp. 94n6, 101.

proletariat and between imperialism and the colonized were related, and which one was privileged. This question was important to his confrères in the French Communist Party, and Althusser was trying to fly slightly below the radar. Domination formed the "condition of existence" for secondary contradictions (just as, dialectically, they in turn formed the conditions of existence for domination).[41] Overdetermination now meant, for Althusser, not only the "reflection of the conditions of existence of the contradiction within itself," but also the "reflection of the structure articulated in dominance that constitutes the unity of the complex whole within each contradiction."[42]

Turning next to Mao's emphasis on "concrete reality ... in which the *identity of opposites* is supreme," Althusser introduced explicitly psychoanalytic language in order to distinguish principal and secondary contradictions and their primary and secondary aspects. The "exchange of roles between contradictions and their aspects" he called "*displacement.*" The primacy, say, of capitalism over imperialism or economics over ideology could be repositioned, the minor term changing places with the major. The "'identity' of opposites in real unity" Althusser called "*condensation*" and "fusion." To Mao's contention that "'at every stage in the development of a process, there is only one principal contradiction which plays the leading role'," he commented that "this principal contradiction produced by *displacement* only becomes 'decisive,' explosive, by *condensation* (by 'fusion')." That is, "'the dissolution of (the existing) unity'" in a "revolutionary *mutation*" and "*recrystallization*" becomes possible once contradictions condense to the point that they "fuse" and in a sense *light the fuse*, thus displacing domination. In sum, the false unity of domination, through the displacement and condensation of its contradictions, led dialectically to revolutionary change. Althusser concluded that uneven development "constitutes [the] most intimate essence" of contradiction; it is a kind of "primitive law ... internal to ... social formation[s]." Contradictions are many and complex because the whole is invariably structured by dominance – dominance is "*the precondition for the concrete variation of the contradictions* that constitute it." Dominance was a kind of Unmoved Mover of the whole, and at the same time, domination only existed through the

---

[41] Althusser noted that the "principal ... term" of the principal contradiction was "relation to nature," which was "organically part of the 'conditions of existence'": "On the Materialist Dialectic," p. 208.

[42] Ibid., pp. 183–206. The point is reminiscent of Gottfried Wilhelm Leibniz's argument that the universe is composed of monads and that each monad contains the entire universe within it.

complex contradictions that expressed it, thus dialectically opening the possibility of moving and overcoming that Unmoved.[43]

Althusser got into trouble with the Soviet-aligned French Communist Party for his sympathetic engagement with Maoism. In November 1963, he submitted a written response to accusations of deviationism made by the philosopher Lucien Sève. Unpublished at the time, the text displayed a slippery candor. In making imperialism and not capitalism into the primary contradiction, he acknowledged, the "Chinese leadership" had misused a useful theory. Their "false reasoning" had resulted in a political error and "fraud" (*imposture*). For his part, however, Sève had naïvely taken the Chinese line at face value, "falling into the trap of the Chinese leadership." Nevertheless, Maoist ideas, specifically the difference between principal and secondary contradictions, had "a very substantial theoretical value." The Chinese had merely erred in the "content" and "political, practical application" of an otherwise valuable theory by substituting imperialism for capitalism as the leading term in the principal contradiction.[44] In 1974, Jacques Rancière observed that during this episode "Althusser set in motion an inversion mechanism that [was] a regular feature of his rhetoric: there [was supposedly] no relationship at all between his theoretical position and the political argumentation of the Chinese."[45] Such a position became habitual to Althusser because he often found and put himself in the interstices of conflicting worlds: critical of the Communist Party while refusing to resign his membership, lambasting dominant ideology from the shelter of the École Normale. In spite of its materialist aspirations and dialectical framing, however, such theory tended to be uprooted and context-free. Some of his students made this connection and attacked theoretical practice as idealism.

A final and highly significant text in which Althusser engaged with Maoism via the theory of contradiction appeared in November–December 1966. Unsigned, the article, "On the Cultural Revolution," was published in the fourteenth issue of the *Marxist–Leninist Notebooks*, the bulletin of his Maoist students at the École Normale. As I mentioned earlier, this issue, subtitled "The Great Proletarian Cultural Revolution," was the first one published by the newly formed Union of Marxist–Leninist Communist Youth after their rupture with the French Communist Party's student

---

[43] Ibid., pp. 210–13.

[44] Louis Althusser, "Réponse à une critique," *Écrits philosophiques et politiques*, vol. II, ed. and intro. François Matheron (Paris: Éditions Stock/IMEC, 1995), pp. 380–85; Bourg, "The Red Guards of Paris," p. 480n27.

[45] Jacques Rancière, *Althusser's Lesson*, trans. Emiliano Battista (London: Continuum, 2011), p. 36.

group. For Althusser, the *"unprecedented"* and *"exceptional* historical fact" of the Cultural Revolution required a "political" analysis and a reflection on "Marxist theoretical principles." The basic "conjuncture" of China in 1966 concerned not international circumstances, such as Sino-Soviet relations, but rather dynamics "internal" to Chinese society itself. Here, Althusser, like most other French Maoists, tended to take Chinese self-understanding (and propaganda) at face value.[46] Chinese communism, he said, faced the alternative of the "two roads": forward-moving revolution or dead-end capitalist "regression." The Cultural Revolution was a response to the danger that a socialist country could appear superficially revolutionary while substantively recreating the capitalist world it was supposed to overcome; in other words, the worry was that China might maintain the "outward [economic and political] *forms*" of socialism while its revolutionary essence became "progressively neutralized." This analysis reached back to the 1937 essay on contradiction and the uneven reversal of contradictions and their aspects. In 1966, a *"mass ideological revolution"* was required in order to create "a corresponding [socialist] *ideological superstructure"* to supplement political and economic developments.[47] In principle, such an ideological revolution would be "made by the masses themselves" and target ideas, "ways of thinking [and] acting," and customs and mores. Furthermore, the Cultural Revolution seemed to involve a structural innovation: it was driven by mass organizations that were the "result of initiatives from the base" and in which youth were the "vanguard." Though different from unions and the Party, such organizations nevertheless operated "under the direction of the Party," which, together with "Mao Tse-tung *Thought,*" provided orientation and a check against harmful spontaneism.[48] The clear tension between mass movements from below and party direction from above might have raised doubts about Chinese versions of the Cultural Revolution. However, instead of stimulating deeper reflection on contradiction, in this case Althusser let these loose ends fray. And yet, as we will see, it was precisely the friction between party and mass that would feed the long-term Maoist commitments of Althusser's student Alain Badiou.

Althusser then turned to the *"theoretical* problems" posed by his political analysis of the Cultural Revolution. Again, the Chinese situation

---

[46] Without downplaying the interest of Maoist ideas or projecting a historical clarity that usually emerges in hindsight, it nevertheless remains striking how *marxisant* intellectuals often combined critical thinking and gullibility in complex ways. In other words, the ambiguities of the fellow traveler still require analysis and explanation.

[47] See, for instance, "Une grande révolution idéologique qui détruit l'ancien et établit le nouveau," *Pékin Information* 35 (August 29, 1966), pp. 16–17.

[48] Anonymous [Louis Althusser], "On the Cultural Revolution," pp. 1–10.

highlighted the possibility of capitalist "regression" under socialism: "an *original* form of capitalism" could emerge "beneath socialist 'appearances'." Class divisions could still exist in a socialist society, and thus class struggle could "continue quite virulently" at the "political ... and above all the ideological level." For Althusser, the "essential" innovation of the Cultural Revolution was that "the *ideological* can become the strategic point at which everything gets decided ... The future depends on the ideological." Here is where his earlier assessment of Maoist ideas about contradiction resurfaced. Marxists beholden to mechanistic economism, for whom the materialist base structure determined everything "*in the last instance,*" did not understand the differences between principal and secondary contradictions and their primary and secondary aspects. In short, Althusser was repeating Mao's diatribe against 1930s Chinese communist "dogmatists," only his target in 1966 was a French Communist Party caught between economism and humanism. Mao and the Cultural Revolution were offering the lesson that "*class struggle can unfold in its purest form* (par excellence) *in the ideological sphere.*" Marx and Lenin had already arrived at the insight, but "for the first time in the history of the workers' movement" present-day China found itself "*capable*" of putting the theory of ideological struggle into practice. Before concluding on the feeble observation that the mass organizations of the Cultural Revolution were separate from the party (contradicting without reflection his earlier support for placing such organizations under party supervision), Althusser made some rather provocative suggestions on "the domain of the ideological." If the economic base structure and political superstructure could each be compared to a "floor" of a building, ideology ought to be considered as "cement" that "seeps ... into all the rooms." It "*distinguishes* and *cements*" and "regulates [individuals'] relation" to practices, objects, and relations themselves. Ideology did not just involve ideas and beliefs; rather, it incorporated and expressed "*objective social relations,*" mores, and practices. The floor metaphor and the polyvalence of ideology would return in Althusser's famous 1970 article on "ideological state apparatuses."[49] In spite of his general enthusiastic endorsement of the Cultural Revolution, in this anonymously published 1966 text, he nonetheless qualified his support: events in China were "surprising and disconcerting"; "*errors,* inevitable in every movement, will happen"; "in no case" should there be

---

[49] I agree with Robcis on this point: Robcis, "'China in our Heads'," p. 62. Louis Althusser, "Ideology and Ideological State Apparatuses: Notes Toward an Investigation," in *Lenin and Philosophy and Other Essays,* intro. Fredric Jameson, trans. Ben Brewster (New York: Monthly Review Press, 1971).

"recourse to violence"; there was no question of "exporting" the Cultural Revolution even if communists around the world might "borrow" and "benefit from" its *lessons.*" The position, however, that final judgments needed to be withheld since the Cultural Revolution was still underway, of course, can be read either as a thoughtful openness toward the ambiguities of the moment or as a failure to think through the contradictions at hand.[50]

While it is tempting to apply Mao's theory of contradiction to the French reception of Maoism itself – the primary contradiction between China and France and secondary contradictions among various phases and factions within France – in conclusion, it might be more fruitful to emphasize the longevity of French Maoism. Mao's essay on contradiction continued to fuel theoretical reflection after 1968. Philippe Sollers, editor of *Tel Quel,* published an article in 1971, in which he riffed on the "categorio-gram" of the Chinese character for contradiction, translated literally by him as "javelin and shield." Leaning explicitly on Althusser, he suggested that dialectical thought itself was not simply a Western import but that it lay deep in the history of Chinese philosophy itself.[51] Althusser's former student Alain Badiou more explicitly parted company with his teacher in his 1975 book *Theory of Contradiction.*[52] Reflecting on Mao's slogan "It is right to rebel against the reactionaries," Badiou argued that the phrase was neither simply an "observation [of] objective contradictions" nor a "directive [of] subjective mobilization." The notion that it was "right" to rebel meant that it was "correct" to rebel – in other words, that there were "reasons" to rebel. Reason, Badiou suggested, "is contradiction ... every reason contradicts." Embracing Mao's proposition that, at a given time, "theory could temporarily play the main role," Badiou nevertheless dismissed Althusser's version

---

[50] Anonymous [Louis Althusser], "On the Cultural Revolution," pp. 2, 8, 10–19.

[51] Philippe Sollers, "Sur la contradiction," *Tel Quel* 45 (1971), rpr. in Philippe Sollers, *Sur le matérialisme: de l'atomisme à la dialectique révolutionnaire* (Paris: Seuil, 1974), pp. 121–57.

[52] Alain Badiou, *Théorie de la contradiction* (Paris: François Maspero, 1975). Alain Badiou, "An Essential Philosophical Thesis: 'It Is Right to Rebel against the Reactionaries'" (a translation by Alberto Toscano of chapter 1 of *Théorie de la contradiction*), *Positions: East Asia Cultures Critique* 13.3 (2005), pp. 669–77. This issue of *Positions*, edited by Tani E. Barlow, is dedicated to Badiou's Maoist writings and to the group with which he was associated in the 1970s and early 1980s: the Union of Marxist–Leninist Communists of France (Union des communistes de France marxistes–léninistes). See also Wolin's excursus on Badiou in *The Wind from the East*, and Florent Schoumacher, "La Grenouille, les puits et Alain Badiou: les aventures de la dialectique maoïste au sein de l'UCFML," Special issue on *Prochinois et maoïsme en France (et dans les espaces francophones), Dissidences* 8 (May 2010), pp. 131–55.

of theory on the grounds that it paid insufficient attention to how reason (that is, knowledge) involved both theory *and* practice.

Badiou is a crucial figure for assessing the afterlives of French Maoism and its continuing fertilization of critical thought in the West.[53] Forty years later he maintains a positive assessment of Maoism. He could claim in 2005 that Maoism "was the only innovative and consequential current of post-May 1968" and in 2008 that "I am probably now one of [Maoism's] few noteworthy representatives."[54] We are "contemporaries" of 1968, he says, in the sense that our present-day view of politics emerged at that moment.[55] Specifically, Badiou takes from Maoism the attack on the form of the political party. We saw earlier the ambiguities of Althusser's description of the Cultural Revolution as operating, so to speak, "from above" and "from below." Badiou, too, has noted this tension, observing that the Cultural Revolution itself reflected the "historical development of a contradiction" between mass action and the desire not to destroy the Communist Party.[56] Although the "political innovations" of China remained limited by the local historical conditions in which they emerged, their effect circulated more broadly, marking "the end of the party-state" and "the strict logic of class representation"; in other words, "*a new politics of the negation of the negation.*"[57] For Badiou, the issue has seemingly been resolved. Politics itself concerns events, indeterminacies, and possibilities that are irreducible to the earlier, by-definition exclusive, hierarchical, and conservative structure of political parties. "Mao's *Little Red Book*," he writes, "has been our guide, not, as fools say, in the sense of a dogmatic catechism, but on the contrary, so that we can clarify and invent new behaviors in all sorts of disparate situations that were unfamiliar to us."[58] Baidou is aware of the irony, or better, contradictions of his own position. "'Mao' is a name that is intrinsically contradictory in the field of revolutionary politics," he admits, while sometimes gesturing toward the rehabilitation of the Leninist party model he elsewhere so clearly abjures.[59] Contradiction à la Mao thus remains at the heart of Badiou's reflections. Mao's dictum

---

[53] See Bruno Bosteels, "Post-Maoism: Badiou and Politics," *Positions: East Asia Cultures Critique* 13.3 (2005), pp. 575–634. See also "Roads to Renegacy" (Badiou, interview by Eric Hazan), *New Left Review* 53 (September–October 2008), pp. 125–33. François Laruelle has attacked Badiou's Maoism, which he vaguely associates with "the reeducation of philosophy by mathematics," in *Anti-Badiou: sur l'introduction du maoïsme dans la philosophie* (Paris: Éditions Kimé, 2011), p. 7.

[54] Alain Badiou, *The Century*, trans. Alberto Toscano (Cambridge: Polity Press, 2007), p. 61. Alain Badiou, *The Communist Hypothesis*, trans. David Macey and Steve Corcoran (London: Verso, 2010), p. 262, cf. p. 101.

[55] Badiou, *The Communist Hypothesis*, p. 62.   [56] Ibid., pp. 113–14.

[57] Ibid., pp. 115–16, 263.   [58] Ibid., p. 103.   [59] Ibid., pp. 153, 270.

that "one divides into two" serves him as a discriminative principle
distinguishing those who maintain a commitment to leftist emancipatory
conflict from those who, pursuing the opposite formula – "two fuse into
one" – cling to comfortable conservative order.[60] Badiou's continuing
investment in Mao's two essays on contradiction from 1937 and 1957 led
him to write in 2005 that "the complete and utter disappearance of
these texts from all bookstores, without exception, is a sign of the
times, when we would instead be happy to see them included in some
university syllabus or other."[61] Badiou's desire was fulfilled in 2007 when
Verso republished Mao's writings on contradiction and practice.[62]
Responding in a public letter to Slovoj Žižek's introduction to this
volume, Badiou opined, "The first question must therefore be: what
problems do we and Mao still have in common?"[63]

The modest claim I would like to make is that, as the case of "On
Contradiction" makes clear, beyond the popular-culture influence of the
Little Red Book, Mao's writings have been taken seriously in France
and submitted to rigorous, if sometimes challenging, theoretical analysis.
In addition to the decontextualization and creative elaboration found in
other places, the French appropriation of Maoism has been characterized
by close reading, abstraction, and systemization. The story of the Maoist
concept of contradiction, from the 1930s until today, a history that
has emphasized the priority of theory, ideology, and culture and that
has underscored the openness and variation of dialectical thinking, provides us with a prime example of the flourishing of French Maoism.
A final suggestion to make – speculative and thus immodest – is that
the French theoretical reception of Maoism in the 1960s and 1970s
has played a decisive role in wide-ranging intellectual developments over
the past forty years: from contemporary neo-Marxism to complexity
theory and the cultural turn.

BIBLIOGRAPHY

ARCHIVAL SOURCES

Gauche prolétarienne, F Δ Rés. 576. Bibliothèque de documentation
    internationale contemporaine, Nanterre, France
Louis Althusser Archives, Institut Mémoires de l'Édition Contemporaine, Saint-
    Germain-la-Blanche-Herbe, France

---

[60] Badiou, *The Century*, p. 60.   [61] Ibid., p. 212n40.
[62] Mao Tse-tung, *On Practice and On Contradiction: Žižek Presents Mao*, intro. Slavoj Žižek
    (London: Verso, 2007). A French edition followed in 2008.
[63] Badiou, *The Communist Hypothesis*, p. 269.

GENERAL SOURCES

Althusser, Louis, "Contradiction and Overdetermination" and "On the Materialist Dialectic," in *For Marx*, trans. Ben Brewster (New York: Pantheon Books, 1967), pp. 87–128 and 161–218

"Ideology and Ideological State Apparatuses: Notes Toward an Investigation," in *Lenin and Philosophy and Other Essays*, intro. Fredric Jameson, trans. Ben Brewster (New York: Monthly Review Press, 1971), pp. 127–86

"On Marxism," in *The Specter of Hegel: Early Writings*, ed. and intro. François Matheron, trans. G. M. Goshgarian (London: Verso, 1997), pp. 241–57

"Reply to John Lewis," in *Essays in Self-Criticism*, trans. Grahame Lock (London: New Left Books, 1976), pp. 33–99

"Réponse à une critique," in *Écrits philosophiques et politiques*, vol. II, ed. and intro. François Matheron (Paris: Éditions Stock/IMEC, 1995), pp. 380–85

Anon. [Louis Althusser], "Sur la révolution culturelle," special issue on *La Grande révolution culturelle prolétarienne (I)*, Cahiers marxistes-léninistes 14 (November–December 1966), pp. 5–16; trans. Jason E. Smith as "On the Cultural Revolution," *Décalages* 1.1 (2010), pp. 1–18, scholar.oxy.edu/decalages/vol1/iss1/9

Badiou, Alain, *The Century*, trans. Alberto Toscano (Cambridge: Polity Press, 2007)

The Communist Hypothesis, trans. David Macey and Steve Corcoran (London: Verso, 2010)

"An Essential Philosophical Thesis: 'It is Right to Rebel against the Reactionaries'," trans. Alberto Toscano, *Positions: East Asia Cultures Critique*, 13.3 (2005), pp. 669–77

"Roads to Renegacy" (interview with Eric Hazan), *New Left Review* 53 (September–October 2008), pp. 125–33

Théorie de la contradiction (Paris: François Maspero, 1975)

Balibar, Étienne, "Althusser and the Rue D'Ulm," *New Left Review* 58 (July–August 2009), pp. 91–107

Belden Fields, A., *Trotskyism and Maoism: Theory and Practice in France and the United States* (New York: Praeger, 1988)

Bosteels, Bruno, "Post-Maoism: Badiou and Politics," *Positions: East Asia Cultures Critique* 13.3 (2005), pp. 575–634

Bourg, Julian, "The Red Guards of Paris: French Student Maoism of the 1960s," *History of European Ideas* 31 (2005), pp. 472–90

From Revolution to Ethics: May 1968 and Contemporary French Thought (Montreal: McGill-Queen's University Press, 2007)

Bourseiller, Christophe, *Les Maoïstes: la folle histoire des gardes rouges français* (Paris: Plon, 1996)

Broyelle, Claudie and Jacques, *Apocalypse Mao* (Paris: Grasset, 1980)

Chateigner, Frédéric, "D'Althusser à Mao: les *Cahiers Marxistes–Léninistes*," Special issue on *Prochinois et maoïsme en France (et dans les espaces francophones)*, *Dissidences* 8 (May 2010), pp. 66–80

ffrench, Patrick, and Roland-François Lack, eds., *The Tel Quel Reader* (London: Routledge, 1998)

Laruelle, François, *Anti-Badiou: sur l'introduction du maoïsme dans la philosophie* (Paris: Éditions Kimé, 2011)

Laude, André, and Max Chaleil, eds., *Le Petit livre rouge de la révolution sexuelle* (Paris: Debresse, 1969)

Mao Zedong, "On Contradiction," *Cahiers du communisme* 29.7–8 (1952), pp. 673–816

    On Practice and On Contradiction: Žižek Presents Mao, intro. Slavoj Žižek (London: Verso, 2007)

    Quatre essais philosophiques (Peking: Foreign Languages Press, 1966)

    Selected Readings from the Works of Mao Tsetung (Peking: Foreign Languages Press, 1971)

Marmor, François, *Le "Petit livre rouge," Mao Tsé-toung: analyse critique* (Paris: Hatier, 1977)

Mercer, Ben, "The Paperback Revolution: Mass-Circulation Books and the Cultural Origins of 1968 in Western Europe," *Journal of the History of Ideas* 72.4 (October 2011), pp. 613–36

Rancière, Jacques, *Althusser's Lesson*, trans. Emiliano Battista (London: Continuum, 2011)

Robcis, Camille, "'China in our Heads': Althusser, Maoism, and Structuralism," *Social Text 110* 30.1 (Spring 2012), pp. 51–69

Rocca, Robert, ed., *Le Petit livre rouge du général: pensées choisies (et parfois commentées)* (Paris: Éditions de la pensée moderne, 1968)

Said, Edward, "Traveling Theory," in *The World, the Text, and the Critic* (Cambridge, Mass.: Harvard University Press, 1983), pp. 226–47

    "Traveling Theory Revisited," in Nigel Gibson, ed., *Rethinking Fanon: The Continuing Dialogue* (Amherst: Humanity Books, 1999), pp. 197–214

Schoumacher, Florent, "La Grenouille, les puits et Alain Badiou: les aventures de la dialectique maoïste au sein de l'UCFML," Special issue on *Prochinois et maoïsme en France (et dans les espaces francophones), Dissidences* 8 (May 2010), pp. 131–55

Sciuto, Giovanni, *Le Petit livre rouge des travestis pas comme les autres: le 4è sexe, une enquête*, preface by Louis Vidal (Soisy-sur-Seine: Éditions du Senart, 1974)

Sgambati, Stephanie L., "China's Accession to the Berne Convention: Bandaging the Wounds of Intellectual Property Piracy in China," *Fordham Intellectual Property, Media and Entertainment Law Journal* 3.1 (1992), pp. 139–74

Sollers, Philippe, "Sur la contradiction," *Tel Quel* 45 (1971); repr. in Philippe Sollers, *Sur le matérialisme: de l'atomisme à la dialectique révolutionnaire* (Paris: Seuil, 1974), pp. 121–57

Williams, James S., "'C'est le petit livre rouge / Qui fait que tout enfin bouge': The Case for Revolutionary Agency and Terrorism in Jean-Luc Godard's *La Chinoise*," *Journal of European Studies* 40.3 (September 2010), pp. 206–18

Wolin, Richard, *The Wind from the East: French Intellectuals, the Cultural Revolution, and the Legacy of the 1960s* (Princeton: Princeton University Press, 2010)

14 By the book

Quotations from Chairman Mao and the making
of Afro-Asian radicalism, 1966–1975

Bill V. Mullen

> We must give active support to the national independence and
> liberation movement in countries in Asia, Africa and Latin America as
> well as to the peace movement and to just struggles in all the countries
> of the world.
>
> War and Peace

A defining moment in the history of US radicalism's Maoist turn remains
Black Panther Party (BPP) founder Bobby Seale's recollection of the role
of *Quotations from Chairman Mao* in building the Panthers' organization
and ideology. As Seale recalls it, in early 1967 he and Huey Newton
came up with the idea of purchasing sixty copies of the Little Red Book
from China Book Store in San Francisco in order to sell them for $1
apiece on the University of California Berkeley campus. The money was
to be used to purchase weapons to arm BPP members against police
brutality on the streets of Oakland. Ideologically, Seale writes, the book
also became the Panthers' urtext for internationalizing black struggle in
the USA:

> Me and Huey and the brothers in the core organization used the Red Books and
> spread them throughout the organization, because Huey made it a point that the
> revolutionary principles so concisely cited in the Red Book should be applied
> whenever they could ... Huey would say, "Well, this principle here is not
> applicable to our situation at this time." Where the book said "Chinese people
> of the Communist Party," Huey would say "Change that to the Black Panther
> Party. Change the Chinese people to black people." When he saw a particular
> principle told in the Chinese terms, he would change it to apply to us.[1]

The facility of Seale's account belies a deeper truth. Newton was well
read in Mao's writing before 1966, and like many African American
radicals had been paying close attention to China, especially after Mao
released his August 8, 1963 "Statement Supporting the Afro-American
in their Just Struggle Against Racial Discrimination by US Imperialism."

[1] Bobby Seale, *Seize the Time: The Story of the Black Panther Party and Huey P. Newton* (New
York: Vintage Books, 1970), p. 82.

Yet most of the new BPP members were young, inexperienced, and not yet politically fluent (few of them also spoke or wrote Chinese). Mao's *Quotations* provided a recruitment tool and shorthand distillation of twentieth-century Chinese and revolutionary history even *formatted* so as to appear ready-made to the innumerable challenges facing new cadre: building a party, party discipline, fomenting national liberation struggle, advancing the class struggle, fighting sexism. As such, the Little Red Book was literally *sui generis*: a provisional textbook for building a revolutionary organization that challenged both the form and formalism of earlier historical models. *Quotations* was especially appealing for young African American and Asian American radicals seeking an alternative to what they perceived as a largely Eurocentric body of revolutionary theory. Other writers included in Panther study circles were Frantz Fanon, Malcolm X, and Che Guevara. Yet precisely because Maoism insisted on the tactical application of ideas emerging directly from struggle, *Quotations* seemed to offer a blueprint for translating events such as the Great Proletarian Cultural Revolution onto African American battles being waged miles away. Revolutions could be made, it seemed, by the book.

This chapter will examine the historical conditions and political objectives that contributed to the popularization of Maoism and the Little Red Book in the 1960s and 1970s US left. It will argue that Maoism entered the ideological current of the US left most forcefully as a tool for building a Third World anti-imperialist internationalism created by African American and Asian American activists who saw in the Little Red Book a syncretic device for conceptualizing and advancing their own national self-determination struggles. It will also argue that the Little Red Book's emphasis on revolutionary culture had a lasting impact on Afro-Asian artists and activists especially in the university, who used its edicts in part to help build successful campaigns for ethnic studies and the inclusion of non-white students. At the same time, the chapter will argue that *Quotations from Chairman Mao* contributed through its mash-up form and content to an epistemic horizontalism that took multiple forms: proliferating political sectarianism; irresolution about the relationship of ethnic national movements to proletarian internationalism; and a template for what became multiculturalism in both liberal public and academic spheres. These tendencies, especially immanent in US assimilation of Maoism, also served to displace class struggle and key Marxist political conceptions (such as the importance of building a mass working-class organization). Finally, the gap in objective conditions between revolutionary China and the world's most advanced imperialist superpower made the practical application of Maoist thought a constant, and in the end insurmountable, challenge. As a result, the intellectual and political usages of the Little Red Book in the USA also came to symbolize the difficulty of building a sustained socialist alternative to capitalism.

Maoism and Maoist thought emerged at the forefront of 1960s Afro-Asian political struggles through two dialectically related events. On June 1, 1962, a gathering of approximately fifty ex-Communist Party (CPUSA) members met in the Hotel Diplomat in New York to found the Progressive Labor Movement (PL). The members conceived PL as an anti-revisionist organization siding with China and Maoism in its recent split with the Soviet Union.[2] In 1964, PL sponsored a trip to Cuba and recruited several radical black students from the East Bay to attend.[3] By 1965, PL had become the Progressive Labor Party with a membership of more than 600. As Robin D. G. Kelley and Betsy Esch demonstrate, the PLP began dedicated to the idea that black workers were the "key revolutionary force" in building revolution, and had some initial success in recruiting in black communities such as Harlem. Yet by 1968 PLP was attacking all forms of revolutionary nationalism as "reactionary" including the Vietnamese liberation struggle, the Black Panther Party, and even affirmative action.[4] The latter positions especially alienated many younger radicals in a widening movement – especially radicals of color – who began to build their own organizations using Maoist ideas. The second event was the solidarity established between China and African Americans between the time of W. E. B. Du Bois's well-publicized visits to China in 1959 and 1961, Mao's statement of support of "Afro-American" liberation released to the USA in 1963, and China's backing of anti-colonial movements in Africa, especially Nkrumah's Ghana, a touchstone for many black leftists such as Amiri Baraka, Malcolm X, and Du Bois himself. In combination, these events seemed to affirm Mao's exhortation that the "spirit of internationalism" could be defined by "a foreigner selflessly adopt(ing) the cause of the Chinese people's liberation as his own."[5] Mao's declaration from *Quotations* that China "must give active support to the national independence and liberation movements in Asia, Africa and Latin America as

---

[2] A. Belden Fields, *Trotskyism and Maoism: Theory and Practice in France and the United States* (New York: Autonomedia, 1988), p. 185.

[3] Robin D. G. Kelley and Betsy Esch, "Black Like Mao: Red China and Black Revolution," in Fred Ho and Bill V. Mullen, eds., *Afro-Asia: Revolutionary Political and Cultural Connections Between African Americans and Asian Americans* (Durham: Duke University Press, 2008), p. 109.

[4] Ibid., p. 102.

[5] Mao Tse-Tung, *Quotations from Chairman Mao* (Peking: Foreign Languages Press, 1966), p. 177.

well as to the peace movement and to just struggle in all the countries of the world" also helped Asian American and African American radicals relate their own positions as racial minorities in the USA to anti-colonial struggles outside the country.[6] Maoism thus became a primary tool to combat what they perceived as both domestic and international colonialism. It joined their First World experiences of racism to Third World national liberation struggles while simultaneously becoming a tool for building interracial, inter-ethnic solidarities.

Quotations from Chairman Mao quickly became the most available, accessible, and *fastest* way for young radicals to imagine themselves undertaking these tasks. At the same time, because the book was never intended for young *American* radicals, it lent itself to exceptionally fluid application and adaptation, becoming simultaneously a blueprint and a blank check for African American and Asian American activists. Its low cost and portability also made the book a mobilizing model for a wide range of political tactics and ideas unified by its broad emphasis on the widely interpreted slogan "Serving the People." "Our point of departure is to serve the people whole-heartedly and never for a moment divorce ourselves from the masses, to proceed in all cases from the interests of the people and not from one's self-interest or from the interests of a small group, and to identify our responsibility to the people with our responsibility to the leading organs of the Party."[7]

Thus after 1966 a mushrooming of study circles, affiliate groups, and new parties began to use the Little Red Book as the basis for political activity. The leadership and notoriety of the new Oakland Black Panther Party as well as the sizable presence of Asian American activists there made the Bay Area a focal point for much of this work. For example, in 1967, a group of young Asian Americans in San Francisco's Chinatown formed Leway, a contraction of the words "Legitimate Ways." According to historian Fred Ho, Leway wanted to unite and politicize street youth and gangs and to fill a vacuum for social services and community youth programs particularly in the Chinatown area of San Francisco. Leway organizers used a pool hall on Jackson Street in Chinatown to "hold sessions reading Mao Zedong's Red Book" and screen films on Third World liberation struggles.[8] Organizer Alex Hing recalls that he came to Leway after working with Black Panthers on the Peace and Freedom Party campaign which petitioned in California to run Eldridge Cleaver

---

[6] Ibid., p. 66.   [7] Ibid., p. 171.

[8] Fred Ho, "Introduction," in Fred Ho with Carolyn Antonio, Diane Fujino and Steve Yip, eds., *Legacy to Liberation: Politics and Culture of Revolutionary Asian Pacific America* (San Francisco: AK Press and Big Red Media, 2000), p. 5.

for president.[9] Hing recalls that a "core group" within Leway, encouraged by Panthers Bobby Seal and David Hilliard, began building a "revolutionary organization" similar to the Panthers. Hing and other Leway members began attending study sessions on Marxism and Leninism at Cleaver's house. "It started with the Red Book, which we had already been reading," recalls Hing, "and then we went from the Red Book to longer tracts of Mao like 'On the State,' 'On Contradiction' and 'On Practice' and we were basically studying the same thing the Panthers were studying."[10] Out of the study group, Leway and Panther members hit upon the idea of forming the "Red Guard Party," a paramilitary-style organization named in tribute to its Chinese counterpart. In 1969, the Red Guard released "Red Guard Program and Rules" modeled closely on the Panthers' ten-point program and patterned on sections of the Little Red Book. "Program and Rules" called for decent housing, education, exemption from state military service, an end to police brutality, full employment, and for US government recognition of the People's Republic of China. The document referred to "Our leader Mao Tse-Tung" and cited this material from Chapter III of the *Quotations*, "Socialism and Communism": "The Socialist system will eventually replace the Capitalist system; this is an objective law independent of Man's will."[11] The document also laid out a twelve-point "Rules of the Red Guard" and reprinted verbatim "Points of Attention" and "3 Main Rules of Discipline" from section XXVI on "Discipline" from *Quotations*.[12] The latter were drafted originally as instruction to the People's Liberation Army in 1947 and first published in *Selected Military Writings*.

In 1971, the Red Guard merged with the New York City-based I Wor Kuen (IWK). I Wor Kuen is Cantonese for "Society of the Harmonious Righteous Fist," a moniker taken from the Boxer Rebellion in China at the turn of the century. IWK was formed as a revolutionary collective mainly of radical students and working-class youth in November, 1969. Like the Red Guard Party, it organized "Serve the People" programs based on the Black Panther Party Survival Programs.[13] In March 1970, IWK began a door-to-door tuberculosis testing campaign in New York's Chinatown at a time when Chinatown had no hospital facilities or Chinese-speaking staff.[14] It also organized childcare school programs.

---

[9] Alex Hing, former minister of information for the Red Guard Party and founding member of I Wor Kuen, interviewed by Fred Ho and Steve Yip in Ho et al., eds., *Legacy to Liberation*, p. 283.

[10] Ibid., p. 285.   [11] Mao, *Quotations*, p. 24.

[12] Ho, "Introduction," p. 404; Mao, *Quotations*, pp. 256–57.

[13] Ho, "Introduction," p. 6.   [14] Ibid.

When IWK and the Red Guard Party began discussions about a merger in 1970, a "two-line struggle emerged between day-to-day grassroots organizing for revolution versus a terrorist or ultra-militarist position that advocated armed urban guerilla actions to 'incite' the people to revolution."[15] Debates about paramilitarism led to discussions of male chauvinist practices – recalling the Little Red Book's Chapter XXXI on "Women," and resulted in the development of collective childcare to allow female cadres to participate in political work.[16] In July, 1971, when they merged, the groups retained the name I Wor Kuen and released a twelve-point program inspired by the Black Panther Party and Young Lords Party, a New York-based Puerto Rican organization that had also in part been inspired by Maoist ideas. The twelve-point program broadly paraphrased major principles from *Quotations*, calling for self-determination for all colonized and oppressed peoples, an end to male chauvinism, an end to US imperialism (including the "Amerikan military" and an end to "immigration and emigration harassment"), and finally an open call for a socialist society.[17]

Before its demise, the Red Guard Party carried out public marches to commemorate China's May Fourth movement, supported the Third World Student Strike at San Francisco State University and UC Berkeley, collaborated with San Francisco Newsreel (later Third World Newsreel) on weekly film screenings, attempted a Breakfast for Children Program under the Panthers' direction, and worked in coalition with organizer Alice Barkley to fight the gentrification of Chinatown.[18] Testimonials from contemporary activists demonstrate the symbiotic nature of those activities in radicalizing Bay Area activists and the role of the Little Red Book in that process. For example, Steve Yip recalls entering Berkeley in the fall of 1969 specifically to hook up with the new Asian American Political Alliance formed through the Third World Student Strike. One result was new Ethnic Studies programs at San Francisco State and Berkeley. As a freshman in the fall of 1969, Yip recalls being introduced to Mao's *Quotations* in the newly founded Asian Studies course. "As radical intellectuals," he writes, "many of us were particularly struck by Mao's comment that 'If you want knowledge, you must take part in the practice of changing society. If you want to know the taste of a pear, you must change the pear by eating it yourself ... If you want to know the theory and methods of revolution, you must take

---

[15] Ibid.   [16] Ibid., p. 7.
[17] I Wor Kuen, "12 Point Program and Platform" in Ho et al., eds., *Legacy to Liberation*, p. 407.
[18] Hing, interview, in Ho et al., eds., *Legacy to Liberation*, p. 288.

part in revolution.'"[19] Inspired specifically by the Cultural Revolution's call to Chinese students to "serve the people," Yip and other activists left Berkeley in December 1969, and opened the Asian Community Center (ACC) in one of the basements of the International Hotel on Kearny Street in Chinatown. The I-Hotel, as it was known, famous as a low-cost haven for Chinese immigrants and Chinatown residents, would become something like an unofficial headquarters for the Asian American Bay Area left, and the site of a long campaign against the eviction of tenants and destruction of the hotel. Yip and comrades contributed by opening Everybody's Bookstore to disseminate news and information about China and other Third World liberation struggles. "All literature from China were priced cheaply as part of socialist China's policy to assist revolutionary forces internationally," recalls Yip, "whether it was Mao's little Red Book and collected works, pamphlets by Marx, Engels, Lenin, Stalin, or periodicals from China."[20] The ACC also published a political platform in its newsletter modeled closely on the Black Panther Party ten-point program, the Red Guard Program, and the Little Red Book's taxonomic structure of political themes: "What we See"; "What we Want"; "What we Believe."[21] (Indeed, the publication of programmatic lists of principles and demands by many US left organizations should best be understood as a generic convention modeled on both the Black Panther Party ten-point program and on the Little Red Book itself.) The list included demands for adequate housing, medical care, employment, and education, and called for Asian unity built by cadre-style discipline reminiscent again of the Red Book: "Our people must be educated to move collectively for direct action."[22]

The ACC and Everybody's Bookstore laid the groundwork for the formation one year later of Wei Min Shu (WMS), a Maoist, anti-imperialist group formed in partial response to the 1968 "Statement by Mao Tse-Tung, Chairman of the Central Committee of the Communist Party of China, in Support of the Afro-American Struggle Against Violent Repression," published in the wake of urban rebellions in the USA triggered by the assassination of Martin Luther King, Jr. Yip became active in WMS, as did Dolly Veale. Veale, whose family had left China in 1955, transferred to Berkeley in early 1970 and became active in the campus anti-war movement when the USA invaded Cambodia in April that year. Veale was arrested and banned from campus for taking part in student protests after the May 1970 shootings of students at Kent

---

[19] Steve Yip, "Serve the People – Yesterday and Today: The Legacy of Wei Min She," in Ho et al., eds., *Legacy to Liberation*, p. 17; Mao, *Quotations*, p. 209.
[20] Yip, "Serve the People," p. 18.   [21] Ibid., p. 29.   [22] Ibid.

State and Jackson State. She also rode buses to Vancouver, Canada to meet women from North and South Vietnam to discuss the war. "Though we didn't fully comprehend all that was involved at the time," she recalls, "many of us were greatly attracted to the revolutionary and internationalist stance emanating from then-Maoist China."[23] The turning-point in her political education came when she heard a member of the Red Guards quoting from Mao's Little Red Book at a mass meeting at the I-Hotel. Veale recalls her mother's warnings never to "listen to reds," but "the whole youth upsurge of that time forced me to be open minded. So I read it and found that it actually made sense!"[24] Inspired especially by Mao's "Serve the People" edict, Veale, like Yip, dropped out of college and joined Wei Min Shu, helping to launch an alternative health clinic in Chinatown. According to Yip, WMS had "been working to make a class analysis of the community, investigating the class structures among Chinese people" including the role played by Chinese immigrant workers in US labor. In 1974, WMS published a book titled *Chinese Working People in America*. In the same year, WMS members joined workers in Lee Mah, an electronics sweatshop whose workers had been locked out by the company. WMS helped to mobilize white, black, and Latino strikers to join the Lee Mah picket line, and encouraged Lee Mah workers to step outside of Chinatown to take part in police shootings of African Americans in San Francisco.

WMS's legacy helps to illuminate political tendencies that proliferated in Maoist-inspired political work of the post-1966 period. The free health clinic Veale helped to start – like the Black Panther and Red Guard breakfast programs – was short lived, undone by restricted funding and limitations on quality of care. As Veale recalls, student volunteers who had effectively "gone to the countryside" had limited effect and capacities operating in an advanced capitalist society. "While dressing the wounds," she recalls volunteers wondering, "how do we get rid of the great wound maker – the profit system?"[25] Veale attempted to solve this problem by becoming a member of the Revolutionary Communist Party, to this day the US revolutionary left party most identified with anti-revisionist Maoism. The party remains small and marginal, in part because it struggled – like its precursor the Revolutionary Union – to engage wide bodies of the working class beyond its student membership, something that similarly limited WMS's impact and duration – it ended in 1974. At the ideological level, WMS also struggled to resolve the relationship between nationalism and proletarian internationalism.

---

[23] Dolly Veale, "Mao More Than Ever!" in Ho et al., eds., *Legacy to Liberation*, p. 184.
[24] Ibid., p. 185.   [25] Ibid., p. 191.

Yip recounts the difficulty of translating the highly localized experience of mainly Chinese immigrants and Chinese American students in San Francisco into a workable theory of working-class internationalism. WMS's fairly selective appropriation and application of ideas from Mao's *Quotations* is telling here. Sections from *Quotations* on party-building, class and class struggle, and socialism and communism appear from activist accounts to be less essential to political work than sections on militarism and combating imperialism, lightning rods for recruitment during US wars in Vietnam and Cambodia. As was the case with the Panthers and Red Guard Party, who tended to focus on strategies of direct action rather than party building, *Quotations* became for WMS members a book whose selective use anticipated limits to its application, particularly up against the massive weight of American capitalism and capitalist class structures.

Maoism's important role in Asian and Asian American ethnic self-determination struggles is also evident in its adoption by Hawaii Pacific Islander and Japanese American activists during the period 1966–75. Ray Tasaki, for example, a third-generation Sansei Japanese American interned at Heart Mountain, Wyoming, during World War II, was living in the Bay Area in 1971 when Japanese American cadres within the Red Guard Party began organizing a study group in the Japanese community in Japan Town San Francisco. According to Tasaki, the group read Mao's writings such as "On Practice" and paid special attention to discussion and debate about Mao's "serve the people" edict. From the discussion group came a "core" known as the Japan Town Collective (JTC). The Collective sought strategies to redress "the root causes of people's oppression, alienation and internalized racism and psychological self-effacement particular to Japanese Americans from being interned during World War II."[26] The JTC worked in the Asian Women's Health Team and, following the example of the Panther's "survival programs," offered legal services, health care, and a prison program. The JTC also held anti-war marches, film screenings about Third World struggles, and forums about the role of Japanese American Nisei farmers in struggles of the United Farm Workers.[27] After two years in the JTC, Tasaki left to join I Wor Kuen, which later became the League of Revolutionary Struggle, a merger of African American, Chicano, Puerto Rican, and Asian American national liberation struggle organizations.

[26] Ray Tasaki, "New Dawn Rising: History and Summation of the Japan Town Collective," in Ho et al., eds., *Legacy to Liberation*, p. 54.
[27] Ibid.

In April, 1971, the organization Third Arm was set up in downtown Honolulu's Chinatown. Third Arm, a mainly student organization whose name was taken from William Hinton's popular and sympathetic study of Chinese village life, *Fanshen*, began an anti-eviction campaign to protect Chinatown residents, screened films from China such as *Red Detachment of Women*, sponsored a free health clinic, and released a "12-point program" in July, 1971 modeled on both the Panther program and the epigrammatic polemical model of the Little Red Book, especially Chapter IV, "The Correct Handling of Contradictions Among the People":

> What is a universal contradiction that all or most of the interest groups face having to exist or work or hang out in Chinatown? What problem or contradiction will rally the most support in the community? If such a contradiction is found and usually through investigation a contradiction of this nature will emerge, organizing of the various elements within the community must begin to happen. But it doesn't happen without any effort, energy or struggle being expended.[28]

The primary means of resolving contradiction for Third Arm was self-determination: "In order for people to have self-respect they must have direct control over their daily lives ... Only in this way – community control – can our needs be met."[29] Third Arm, which described its politics as Marxist–Leninist–Maoist, consisted in part of former members of Kaimuki House, or the "Pacific Rim Collective," begun in 1970, a study group whose readings ranged from Fanon to Che Guevara and whose study focused in part on the relationship of Hawaii's colonial history, anti-colonial struggles, and the Vietnam War. As Peggy Myo-Young Choy summarizes the transition from Kaimuki House to Third Arm, "For the activists, the ideas of Marx, Lenin and Mao point to the need to 'serve the people, serve the workers, and to meet the people's needs'."[30]

China's role in supporting anti-colonial struggles in Asia and Africa, its standing as the leading non-white revolutionary country in the world, and Mao's oft-repeated declarations of support for black liberation

---

[28] Peggy Myo-Young Choy, "Return the Islands Back to the People: A Legacy of Struggle and Resistance in the Ka Pae' aina," in Ho et al., eds., *Legacy to Liberation*, p. 127.

[29] Ibid., p. 126.

[30] Ibid., p. 113. Struggles around anti-colonial national sovereignty also motivated the formation of Maoist-oriented Asian American organizations such as the KDP (Katipupnan ng mga Demokratikong Pilipino, or Union of Democratic Filipinos) formed in 1973. The KDP was a largely West Coast-based group that traced its roots to the Katipunan in the Philippines founded in 1892 by the working-class leader Andres Bonifacio. The KDP was also the US liason to the CPP (Communist Party of the Philippines) whose New People's Army used Maoist tactics in its guerrilla warfare against the Marcos regime. For more see Helen C. Toribio, "Dare to Struggle: The KDP and Filipino American Politics," in Ho et al., eds., *Legacy to Liberation*, pp. 31–46.

struggle in the USA were also essential to inspiring Asian American activists to unite with African and black liberation struggles in tandem with Asian American struggles. As we have seen, African American revolutionary leaders such as Bobby Seale and Huey Newton took inspiration from China's lead to build solidarity with Asian American political struggles. The Little Red Book was key to advancing this conception of conjoined Afro-Asian national self-determination struggle, and to providing what might be called a racialized analysis of traditional Marxist ideas. Chapter II on "Classes and Class Struggle" included an excerpt from Mao's August 8 1963 "Statement Supporting the Afro-American in their Just Struggle Against Discrimination by US Imperialism" written in the wake of the March on Washington Movement. The statement declared that, "in the final analysis, national struggle is a matter of class struggle," and centered black and non-white struggle in its analysis of capitalism and imperialism, effectively calling for a non-white united front to defeat both:

The speedy development of the struggle of the Afro-Americans is a manifestation of sharpening class struggle and sharpening national struggle within the United States . . .

I call on the workers, peasants, revolutionary intellectuals, enlightened elements of the bourgeoisie and other enlightened persons of all colors in the world, whether white, black, yellow, or brown, to unite to oppose the radical discrimination practiced by US imperialism and support the black people in their struggle against racial discrimination.[31]

Combined with their personal experiences of anti-Asian racism, exposure to the Black Civil Rights Movement and Black Panther Party – "in particular their emphasis on the Little Red Book and the teachings of Chairman Mao and his serve the people line" – activists such as Moritsugu "Mo" Nishida found themselves turning from Mao to Amilcar Cabral, founder of the Party of Revolution of Guinea-Bissau and the Cape Verde Islands in order to combine anti-colonial struggle and interracial activism.[32] Similarly, Maoism enabled African American radicals to develop a more expansive, inclusive definition and application of "black" liberation struggle. Inspired in part by the Little Red Book's call for an internationalism that "opposes both narrow nationalism and narrow patriotism,"[33] black revolutionaries sought to define what leaders of the Revolutionary Action Movement described as a "World Black

[31] Mao, *Quotations*, pp. 10, 92–93.
[32] Moritsugu "Mo" Nishida, "Personal Liberation/People's Revolution," in Ho et al., eds., *Legacy to Liberation*, p. 214.
[33] Mao, *Quotations*, p. 177.

Revolution" or "Black Internationalism" as opposed to simply "black nationalism." The distinction between these sometimes turned in internal debates over both the meaning of Maoism and the place of texts such as the Little Red Book in building political movements.

The most important US location for advancing these debates was Detroit. The city might be considered the triangulated point of an axis –Beijing–San Francisco/Oakland–Detroit – around which turned much of the proliferation and advance of Maoist thought and ideas in the 1960s and early 1970s USA. In general, much of the Maoist-influenced activism among Detroit radical leadership served as both a dialectical counterpoint to and even critique of activism which it perceived as narrow, superficial, and inadequately historicized. In some ways, this critique centered on the exaggerated role of the Little Red Book itself in building what we have seen were sometimes itinerant and contradictory radical movements centered on the West Coast. For example, Grace Lee Boggs, along with her husband James Boggs, the pioneer of many currents of Detroit radicalism, criticized the Black Panther Party for a shortsighted and ahistorical approach to Maoist thought:

> Like everyone else, the founders of the Black Panther Party were not prepared for the flood of aspiring revolutionaries. Even if they had wanted to, they had not had the time to create a revolutionary philosophy and ideology and a structure and programs to develop the thousands who were knocking at their door. So they borrowed virtually intact Mao's Little Red Book, without distinguishing between what is appropriate to China or a postrevolutionary situation, and what is appropriate to the United States, or a potentially revolutionary situation.[34]

Boggs's assessment, written years after the 1960s, refers both to the Panthers' own testimonials about selective use of Mao's writing, largely confined for some members to strategies for armed struggles, and to their allies such as the Red Guard Party whose tactics at times replicated what Boggs calls the "militarism and adventurism" in the Chinese Communist Party during the period of the Cultural Revolution.[35] The Boggses thus challenged what they perceived as a short-sighted application of Mao Zedong by replacing questions of tactics and strategies with questions of revolutionary philosophy and ideology: "We are not faced with the task of applying the ideas of Marx or Mao to the United States," they wrote,

---

[34] Grace Lee Boggs, *Living for Change: An Autobiography* (Minneapolis: University of Minnesota Press, 1998), p. 145.
[35] Robin D. G. Kelley and Betsy Esch note that Eldridge Cleaver represented a wing of the Black Panther Party more interested in guerrilla warfare than long-term planning for revolution, and that many Panthers limited their reading of Mao (and others such as Che) to their writings on "revolutionary violence and people's war." See Kelley and Esch, "Black Like Mao," p. 126.

"but with that of developing a new concept of human identity as the basis for the revolution in America, a concept which must extend the dialectical development of humanity itself."[36] Maoism's emphasis on ethical conduct, self-criticism, and the concept of *fanshen* or "self-overturning" became the basis of what the Boggses called "dialectical humanism," a political practice "built on unselfishness, on serving the people, the country and oppressed peoples all over the world."[37] The cornerstone of dialectical humanism was their argument that black liberation struggle in the USA was central to developing what they called, after Mao, a "New Man" and "New Woman": "the Negro revolt is ... not just a narrow struggle over goods and for the development of the productive forces ... The burning question is how to create the kind of human responsibility in the distribution of material abundance that will allow everyone to enjoy and create the values of humanity."[38]

The Boggses' expansive analysis of the meaning of black liberation effectively altered the canon, political assimilation, and application of Maoism and Maoist thought by the US left. It both decentered and contextualized its fetishization best symbolized by the sometimes contradictory and inconsistent use of its "primer," the Little Red Book. They forced new and young activists in particular coming into the movement to consider their political work and struggles in a broader philosophical (and international) framework similar to the way Fanon had challenged black nationalists to think about the epistemology of anti-colonial struggles. Towards this end, the Boggses established revolutionary study groups in Detroit in which large sections of Mao's *Selected Writings* were paired with work by Lenin, James, and Cabral in order to work out conceptions of "dialectical humanism." Following a Maoist ethos, this theoretical work was perceived as the basis for revolutionary practice. Most important in this regard was James Boggs, a leader of the Boggses' study circle as well as a Detroit auto worker. Boggs served as liason, mentor, and intermediary to both a generation of young black radicals inspired by the general upturn of black nationalism and anti-colonialism, and to workers in Detroit auto plants where shopfloor struggles became a testing-ground for Maoist ideas.

For example, according to founding member Max Stanford, James Boggs served as "ideological chairman" for the Revolutionary Action Movement (RAM), a loosely affiliated nation-wide organization headquartered in Philadelphia but with chapters in northern California,

---

[36] James Boggs, *Racism and the Class Struggle: Further Pages from a Worker's Noteboook* (New York: Monthly Review Press, 1970), p. 126.
[37] Ibid., p. 80.   [38] Ibid., p. 18.

Cleveland, Detroit, and other cities. RAM's early years included work with the Student Nonviolent Coordinating Committee and leadership from, among others, students at Central State University in Ohio. In 1963, the party formed a provisional government and elected Robert Williams premier-in-exile from Cuba.[39] RAM's "Code of Cadres," as Robin Kelley and Betsy Esch note, was modeled closely on the "Three Main Rules of Discipline" section of *Quotations* and even borrowed verbatim the edict to "not take a single needle or piece of thread from the masses."[40] Yet in large part because of James Boggs's advisement, RAM's relationship to Maoism well exceeded the maxims of the Little Red Book. In 1965, RAM published the essay "The Relationship of Revolutionary Afro-American Movement to the Bandung Revolution." The essay referenced the 1955 meeting of decolonizing African and Asian countries in Indonesia as the birth of a new era dubbed "Bandung humanism," a clear recasting and retitling of the Boggses' conception of dialectical humanism. It defined Bandung humanism as a "revolutionary revision of Western or traditional Marxism to relate revolutionary ideology adequately to the unprecedented political, socio-economic, technological, psycho-cultural developments occurring in the post World War II era."[41] The essay was a companion to a second published in 1965, "The World Black Revolution," which featured a cover photograph of Mao and Robert Williams, citing China's 1949 revolution as the starting-point of the Bandung era. The essay synthesized citation of Malcolm X, Robert Williams, James Boggs, and Mao's "Statement in Support of Afro-America" into a call for an international revolutionary action movement which would "in order to be

---

[39] Williams was a North Carolina NAACP organizer who in 1960 fled the US to Cuba after he was falsely accused by the FBI of kidnapping. He became an ardent supporter of Castro's revolution until a falling out forced him to move to China in 1966. From China he published and distributed his newspaper *The Crusader* which was widely read by RAM members. RAM frequently published or republished articles by Williams in its own newspaper, *Black America*. Upon his return to the USA in 1969, Williams remained an important touchstone and totem for Afro-Asian activists. Yuri Kochiyama, close friend and associate to Malcolm X and a pioneer of Asian American and Afro-Asian liberation struggles in the USA, recalls that Williams gave her her first copy of the Little Red Book. For more on Williams see Timothy Tyson's *Radio Free Dixie: Robert F. Williams and the Roots of Black Power* (Chapel Hill: University of North Carolina Press, 1999). For more on Kochiyama see Diane Fujino's *Heartbeat of Struggle: The Revolutionary Practice of Yuri Kochiyama* (Minneapolis: University of Minnesota Press, 2005). For more on Afro-Asian collaboration generally see Diane Fujino, *Samurai Among Panthers: Richard Aoki on Race, Resistance and a Paradoxical Life* (Minneapolis: University of Minnesota Press, 2012).

[40] Kelley and Esch, "Black Like Mao," p. 113.

[41] Revolutionary Action Movement, "The Relationship of Revolutionary Afro-American Movement to the Bandung Revolution," *Black America* (Summer–Fall 1965), pp. 11–12.

successful ... have to organize a People's liberation army on a world scale."[42] RAM's manifesto might be considered the theoretical apex of efforts by black radicals to weld Maoist notions of dialectical transformation to Third World internationalism. It offered budding black and Asian activists a theory and practice that seemed the apotheosis of Maoism's promise to develop an anti-colonial Third World united front.

Finally, Detroit-variety Maoism found a home on the shopfloor of the city's massive auto industry where, uniquely on the American left in this period, the Little Red Book's maxims on "Class and Class Struggle" became the centerpoint of both theory and practice. Key organizations here were the League of Revolutionary Black Workers and DRUM (Dodge Revolutionary Union Movement). Both groups were spearheaded by black workers from Detroit with Maoist roots and training. These included Luke Tripp, Charles "Mao" Johnson, Charles Simmons, and General Baker. All four had participated in a 1964 trip to Cuba sponsored by the then still Maoist Progressive Labor Movement. Under their leadership, the League and DRUM carried forward the early 1960s Maoist/PL emphasis on the black worker as the vanguard of revolution while using Little Red Book slogans such as "Dare to Fight! Dare to Win!" to organize black workers on the shop floor. Because the factory rather than the university was the primary site of their political work, the League and DRUM were critical of what they called "bourgeois" or "porkchop" nationalism, and used Cultural Revolution-style slogans to proclaim their difference from other (mainly West Coast) Maoist and black nationalist organizing efforts: "One Class-Conscious Worker is Worth 100 Students."[43] By 1972, both the League and DRUM had morphed again in two directions that sustained its Maoist legacy: one group split to form the Black Workers' Congress (BWC), while other members joined the Maoist Communist League.[44] The Black Workers' Congress in particular instantiated ideas from Chapter V, "War and Peace," from the Little Red Book cited earlier: "We must give active support to the national independence and liberation movements in countries in Asia, Africa and Latin America as well as to the peace movement and to just struggle in all the countries of the world."[45] In its self-published manifesto, the BWC called for the right of self-determination for Africans, Chicanos, Puerto Ricans, Asians, and

---

[42] Revolutionary Action Movement, "The World Black Revolution" (1965), Box 2, Robert Franklin Williams Papers, Bentley Historical Library, p. 32.

[43] *South End* 21.104 (April 14, 1969).

[44] Max Elbaum, "Maoism in the United States," first published in Encyclopedia of the American Left, 2nd edn., 1998. See www.marxists.org.

[45] Mao, *Quotations*, p. 66.

Indians living in the USA and for a "Black United Front and third World Alliances."[46] In a final echo of *Quotations*, the BWC manifesto invoked a "unity of opposite which includes various classes" in calling for a Third World labor strike to help end the Vietnam War, restore a Palestinian homeland, and prompt US divestment from South Africa.[47]

Arguably, the Little Red Book's greatest long-term impact was felt not in the politics but the left culture of the USA. Section XXXI, "Culture and Art," became one of the sections most referenced by African American and Asian American artists and writers seeking to develop a theory of the role of the arts in social change. Particularly influential were passages from Mao's May 1942 "Talks on the Yenan Forum on Literature and Art," his call for artists to conjoin their work to mass struggle, and this passage from *Quotations* from the 1940 essay "On New Democracy":

Revolutionary culture is a powerful revolutionary weapon for the broad masses of the people. It prepares the ground ideologically before the revolution comes and is an important, indeed essential, fighting front in the general revolutionary front during the revolution.[48]

In 1967, RAM leader-in-exile Robert Williams spoke in Beijing to commemorate the twenty-fifth anniversary of Mao's Yan'an talk. Echoing Mao's Yan'an address urging that "all our literature and art are for the masses of the people," as well as the idea of revolutionary culture as part of a revolutionary "front," Williams urged African American artists to develop a "new revolutionary approach to propaganda" and encouraged black writers in the USA to work with the newly formed international Afro-Asian writers' association. The intent of Afro-Asian art, he wrote, was to "serve to stimulate revolutionary zeal" and become "a mechanism to detonate the explosion of rebellion."[49] In the USA, black and Asian writers and artists began applying Mao's theory of culture in a manner described in the Little Red Book as "Letting a hundred flowers blossom and a hundred schools of thought contend."[50] In Detroit, separate black arts conferences were held in 1966 and 1967 dedicated to the relationship of revolutionary art to revolutionary politics. James and Grace Boggs, who helped shape the agenda for the 1966 conference, described the urgency of the role of culture in creating revolutionary optimism:

---

[46] Dodge Revolutionary Union Movement, "Third World People: Unite" (1971), Box 1, Detroit Revolutionary Movements Collection, Walter P. Reuther Library of Labor and Urban Affairs.

[47] Ibid.   [48] Mao, *Quotations*, pp. 299–300.

[49] Robert F. Williams, "Speech, 25th Anniversary of Mao's 'Talks at the Yenan Forum on Literature and Art'" (1967), Box 3, Robert Franklin Williams Papers, Bentley Historical Library.

[50] Mao, *Quotations*, p. 302.

"A people building a national movement needs the conviction that history is on their side and ultimate victory is certain because as a people they have an inherent dignity which no amount of brutalization and degradation can destroy."[51] In California, Maulana (Ron) Karenga created the 1968 manifesto "Black Cultural Nationalism" which, as Robin D. G. Kelley and Betsy Esch have shown, derived many of its principles from Mao's "Talks at Yenan" including the idea that culture must be both artistic and social and of use to the broad masses of people.[52] In Newark, New Jersey, poet Amiri Baraka developed poetry and theater that tried to combine elements of Marxist–Leninist–Maoist thought with Black Arts Movement technique in order to challenge what it considered narrow forms of cultural nationalism. The Little Red Book even generated direct imitators. In 1970, Earl Ofari, a former member of SNCC and then graduate student in sociology at Cal State Los Angeles, published *The Black Book*. The thirty-two-page broadside is comprised of sayings by Frantz Fanon, Malcolm X, and W. E. B. Du Bois, organized, like *Quotations*, around key political questions: Black Culture and Art; Black Unity; Africa; Imperialism; Socialism; The Third World. Even in its production the book echoed the Yan'an creed from *Quotations* that literature and arts are "created for the workers, peasants and soldiers and are for their use."[53] The book was published by the Radical Education Project, a Students for Democratic Society project based in Detroit; its title page indicated that it was "printed by movement labor."[54]

The Black Arts Movement influenced an entire generation of Black and Asian artists and writers, from the poet Sonia Sanchez, who visited China in the early 1970s, to the contemporary musician Fred Ho. Indeed in combination with "Culture and Art," the ultimate section of the Little Red Book, the section titled "Study," may represent at least symbolically how the Little Red Book helped to forward a truly *cultural* revolution in the USA. We have already noted the role the book played both inside and outside of university settings in generating political momentum for ethnic studies, Black Studies and Asian Pacific American Studies curricula on university campuses. Indeed Black Studies, Asian American Studies, and Ethnic Studies alive and well on university campuses today have expanded the canon of academic study to include non-Western histories and cultures in a manner similar to the way the Little Red Book

---

[51] Inner City Organizing Committee Papers, James and Grace Boggs Collection, Box 5, Folder 7 (1966), Walter P. Reuther Library of Labor and Urban Affairs, p. 1.
[52] Kelley and Esch, "Black Like Mao," p. 138.
[53] Mao, *Quotations*, p. 300.
[54] Earl Ofari, ed., *The Black Book* (Detroit: Radical Education Project, 1970), p. 1.

expanded the *genre* of political writing in the 1960s. An important primary source example of this development is the "Asian Studies Manifesto" created by the Asian Students' Committee of City College, New York, in 1973. Authored by Boreysa Tep, Richard K. Wong, and Jean Yonemura, the Manifesto noted that the successful fight for the development of a department of Asian Studies at City College had emerged to serve the needs of Asian students after a successful struggle for open admissions. The Manifesto criticized previous university curricula offerings on Asia as Eurocentric and demanded, in ten-point program style, that Asian Studies function as a vehicle to "service" Asian students: to provide world perspective on Asia, to involve students in policy-making decisions, to present the history of Asians in America, to present an Asian perspective on Asian history, to provide employment for Asians, and to promote understanding of the common struggles of Third World peoples. The Manifesto also called for the hiring of more Asian faculty members, and for the admission of more non-white students.[55] In perhaps the most direct echo of the Red Book's admonition that real political knowledge can only come "through practical work and close contact with the masses of workers and peasants," the Manifesto insisted that "Asian Studies can play a role in bringing students back to the community by exposing them to the community's problems and needs, by learning from the community people themselves, by helping students to find ways to solve the community's problems."[56]

The Asian Studies Manifesto, with its easy substitution of academic "service learning" for "serving the people," in many ways symbolizes both the horizons and limits of Mao's *Quotations* as a tool for building revolutionary movements across the time and space of the late 1960s/ early 1970s US left. The Manifesto demonstrated the rapidity, ingenuity, and dedication with which movement activists sought to translate their political education into practice, and how ripe for change the objective conditions on the ground really were, especially for non-white radicals. Yet owing to concurrent events well beyond the scope of the American university – China's alignment with reactionary Third World governments, political conflicts within China during the Cultural Revolution, and the ill timing of Mao hosting Nixon in 1972 when the USA was still waging war in Vietnam – Maoism soon lost significant traction as a basis for sustained political organizing. For African American and Asian American radicals, China and Maoism's loosening hold was also related

---

[55] Boreysa Tep, Richard K. Wong, and Jean Yonemura, "Asian Studies Manifesto" (1973) in Ho et al., eds., *Legacy to Liberation*, pp. 408–11.
[56] Mao, *Quotations*, p. 312; Tep et al., "Manifesto," p. 410.

to the splintering of at times parallel, at times intertwining movements into multiple sectarian streams as well as a refocusing onto numerous ethnically based movements (including academic ethnic studies) which have persisted to this day. At the same time, the US economic crisis of the 1970s, the emergence of neoliberal economic politics and policies globally, and the permanent repressive apparatus of the US state – which included the infiltration and assassination of movement leaders such as the Black Panther Party's Fred Hampton – all helped to diminish the growth and impact of Afro-Asian solidarity struggles.[57] The Little Red Book should be understood in context as a metonymy for these processes. The book's polyvalent usages and applications, disparate and at times self-contradictory messages, and incomplete relevance to social conditions in the USA made it as much a symbol for an oversized and itinerant dream – a successful Chinese-style revolution in America – as a prism onto that dream's irreconcilability with US capitalist imperialism. At the same time, the book's iconographic form and content made it something like a textual flag for a new world in the making – a People's Republic stretching from Tiananmen Square to the San Francisco Bay – whose specter still haunts the dreams of US empire today. That specter, recognizable in the Maoist-influenced battle cries against neoliberalism reaching from rural India to Occupy Oakland, make it unlikely that the Little Red Book and its legacy will fade from the revolutionary imagination any time soon.[58]

---

[57] In August 2012 American journalist Seth Rosenfeld published a book alleging that Richard Aoki, a Japanese American member of the Oakland chapter of the Black Panther Party, had been an FBI informant. Aoki is described as the "radical Japanese cat" in Bobby Seale's *Seize the Time* who gave the Panthers their first guns in late 1966, which were to be used to defend against police brutality in Oakland. Diane Fujino's *Samurai Among Panthers* details how Aoki encouraged the Panthers to take up Maoist ideas and helped to build the organization. While the evidence against Aoki is inconclusive, FBI infiltration of the Black Panthers and other left groups such as the Socialist Workers' Party is well documented. See especially Jim Wanderwall and Ward Churchill, *The COINTELPRO Papers: Documents from the FBI's Secret Wars Against Dissent in the United States* (Boston: South End Press, 2001) and *Agents of Repression: The FBI's Secret Wars Against the Black Panther Party and the American Indian Movement* (Boston: South End Press, 2001). For more on Aoki see Fujino, *Samurai Among Panthers* and Seth Rosenfeld, *Subversives: The FBI's War on Radicals and Reagan's Rise to Power* (New York: Farrar, Straus & Giroux, 2012) and these redacted FBI files also made available by Rosenfeld: www.documentcloud.org/documents/423064-fbi-files-richard-aoki.html

[58] For a popular account of the resurgence of Maoism (and Naxalism) in contemporary India see Arundhati Roy's *Walking With the Comrades* (New York: Penguin, 2011). In February 2012, the international journal *Maoist Road* affiliated with the Maoist Communist Party of Italy expressed its solidarity with Occupy Oakland's call for a nation-wide general strike on May 1, 2012. The strike did not materialize. See maoistroad.blogspot.com/2012/02/maoist-road-supports-call-occupy.html.

264   Bill V. Mullen

BIBLIOGRAPHY

Belden Fields, A., *Trotskyism and Maoism: Theory and Practice in France and the United States* (New York: Autonomedia, 1988)

Boggs, Grace Lee, *Living for Change: An Autobiography* (Minneapolis: University of Minnesota Press, 1998)

Boggs, James, *Racism and the Class Struggle: Further Pages from a Worker's Noteboook* (New York: Monthly Review Press, 1970)

Choy, Peggy Myo-Young, "Return the Islands Back to the People: A Legacy of Struggle and Resistance in the Ka Pae' aina," in Ho et al., eds., *Legacy to Liberation*, pp. 99–134

Dodge Revolutionary Union Movement, "Third World People: Unite" (1971), Box 1, Detroit Revolutionary Movements Collection, Walter P. Reuther Library of Labor and Urban Affairs

Fujino, Diane, *Heartbeat of Struggle: The Revolutionary Practice of Yuri Kochiyama* (Minneapolis: University of Minnesota Press, 2005)
    Samurai Among Panthers: Richard Aoki on Race, Resistance and a Paradoxical Life (Minneapolis: University of Minnesota Press, 2012)

Ho, Fred, "Introduction," in Ho et al., eds., *Legacy to Liberation*, pp. i–vi

Ho, Fred, with Carolyn Antonio, Diane Fujino, and Steve Yip, eds., *Legacy to Liberation: Politics and Culture of Revolutionary Asian Pacific America* (San Francisco: AK Press and Big Red Media, 2000)

Inner City Organizing Committee Papers, James and Grace Boggs Collection, Box 5, Folder 7 (1966), Walter P. Reuther Library of Labor and Urban Affairs

I Wor Kuen, "12 Point Program and Platform" in Ho et el., eds., *Legacy to Liberation*, pp. 405–07

Kelley, Robin D. G., and Betsy Esch, "Black Like Mao: Red China and Black Revolution," in Fred Ho and Bill V. Mullen, eds., *Afro-Asia: Revolutionary Political and Cultural Connections Between African Americans and Asian Americans* (Durham: Duke University Press, 2008), pp. 97–154

Mao Tse-Tung, *Quotations from Chairman Mao* (Peking: Foreign Languages Press, 1966)

Nishida, Moritsugu "Mo," "Personal Liberation/People's Revolution," in Ho et al., eds., *Legacy to Liberation*, pp. 211–16

Ofari, Earl, ed., *The Black Book* (Detroit: Radical Education Project, 1970)

Revolutionary Action Movement, "The Relationship of the Revolutionary Afro-American Movement to the Bandung Revolution," *Black America* (Summer–Fall 1965), pp. 11–12
    "The World Black Revolution" (1965), Box 2, Robert Franklin Williams Papers, Bentley Historical Library

Rosenfeld, Seth, *Subversives: The FBI's War on Radicals and Reagan's Rise to Power* (New York: Farrar, Strauss & Giroux, 2012)

Roy, Arundhati, *Walking with the Comrades* (New York: Penguin, 2011)

Seale, Bobby, *Seize the Time: The Story of the Black Panther Party and Huey P. Newton* (New York: Vintage Books, 1970)

Tasaki, Ray, "New Dawn Rising: History and Summation of the Japan Town Collective," in Ho et al., eds., *Legacy to Liberation*, pp. 53–58

Tep, Boreysa, Richard K. Wong, and Jean Yonemura, "Asian Studies
     Manifesto" (1973), in Ho et al., eds., *Legacy to Liberation*, pp. 408–11
Toribio, Helen C., "Dare to Struggle: The KDP and Filipino American Politics,"
     in Ho et al., eds., *Legacy to Liberation*, pp. 31–46
Tyson, Timothy, *Radio Free Dixie: Robert F. Williams and the Roots of Black Power*
     (Chapel Hill: University of North Carolina Press, 1999)
Veale, Dolly, "Mao More Than Ever!" in Ho et al., eds., *Legacy to Liberation*,
     pp. 183–96
Wanderwall, Jim, and Ward Churchill, *Agents of Repression: The FBI's Secret Wars
     Against the Black Panther Party and the American Indian Movement* (Boston:
     South End Press, 2001)
     *The COINTELPRO Papers: Documents from the FBI's Secret Wars Against
     Dissent in the United States* (Boston: South End Press, 2001)
Williams, Robert F., "Speech, 25th Anniversary of Mao's 'Talks at the Yenan
     Forum on Literature and Art'" (1967), Box 3, Robert Franklin Williams
     Papers, Bentley Historical Library
Yip, Steve, "Serve the People – Yesterday and Today: The Legacy of Wei Min
     She," in Ho et al., eds., *Legacy to Liberation*, pp. 15–30

15 Conclusion
In the beginning is the word: popular democracy and
Mao's Little Red Book

Ban Wang

All erroneous ideas, all poisonous weeds, all ghosts and monsters, must
be subjected to criticism; in no circumstance should they be allowed to
spread unchecked. However, the criticism should be fully reasoned,
analytical and convincing, and not rough, bureaucratic, metaphysical
or dogmatic.

Classes and Class Struggle

Religion as politics

Mao's Little Red Book represented a scriptural authority and emanated a
sacred aura during China's Cultural Revolution. An intense religious
atmosphere surrounded the activities and rituals of Mao's words.
Everyday life was immersed in study sessions, discussions, lectures,
public performances of Mao's poems and quotations, ritualistic confes-
sions of one's errant thoughts, and nightly diary-writing aimed at
self-criticism. The study sessions may be seen as a form of text-based
indoctrination that resembles religious hermeneutics and catechism,
which were not meant to disseminate knowledge and truths but to
foster faith, loyalty, and conviction. And the rituals were widely diffused
in popular life: the posting of Mao's quotations on shop fronts, the
singing and performing of quotation songs in the streets, the wearing of
Mao badges, group sessions for discussing what lessons or wisdom one
could learn from Mao's texts. These activities can be described as a broad
aesthetic experience aimed at converting individuals into true believers.

Mao's Little Red Book was enveloped in a compelling aura of religi-
osity, and stood at the center of a massive movement. In her recent study
Barbara Mittler draws our attention to a propaganda poster entitled
"Let's Set Off a New Upsurge in the Study of Mao's Works." The poster
shows a group of people in a sea of pinkish flowers, with three major
figures of worker, peasant, and soldier in front. Each member of this
study group holds a copy of Mao's Little Red Book in hand, all looking
up with a smile to a bright future. All the books are open, suggesting that

faithful readers have been intensely reading and studying. Rather than taking up the center of the poster, Mao's works are spread out in copy after copy and in one hand after another. What is striking is not the elevated image of Mao's book but its wide dissemination and populist following among the masses.[1] The religious ambiance created by the repetitive book images and avid reading seemed to inspire confidence and faith in the future of the country.

Associating Mao's book with the religiously venerated canons of classics, Charles Fitzgerald noted that Mao Zedong Thought has "become to his own people in his own age what the sayings of Confucius were to the Chinese people for the past two thousand years: a source of inspiration and guidance in matters social, political, and moral."[2] The format of quotation, *yulu*, not only echoes the terse and fragmented maxims of Buddhist sayings and Daoist epigrams, but most significantly the *lunyu*, the *Analects of Confucius*. In this lineage Mao became a modern sage-king by virtue of a reactivation of China's long-entrenched text-based heritage.[3] The widespread and constantly enacted rituals of reading, studying, and discussion of Mao's quotations and writings, the telling of success stories in applying Mao's teachings to all occasions and looking for answers to all problems, the passionate intensity with which readers adhere and defend Mao's words – all this warrants religious terms in the characterization of Mao's Little Red Book.

Rather than textual fetishism, Mao's texts were a spiritual guide to scientific and social practice in changing the world. Premised on the belief that the political spirit drives productivity and material advances, the practitioners viewed Mao's words as effective means for investigating the truth and promoting scientific discovery. A 1968 Red Guard publication contended that the sciences must be informed with and guided by Mao Zedong Thought, and expert knowledge is not valid unless it is so guided. The new scientists, uttering Mao's familiar quotation "be resolute, fear no sacrifice, and surmount every difficulty to win victory," could scale the height of scientific achievement. In another testimony, a soldier learning to be a veterinarian runs into difficulty in castrating pigs for peasants. Confronting his anxiety about possible failure and losing face, he studied Mao's story of the Foolish Old Man who Removed the Mountains, which cured his selfishness, and gave him courage and resolve. Invocations of Mao's quotation served to purge his selfishness and to clear the way for his technical success. Another narrative

[1] Barbara Mittler, *A Continuous Revolution: Making Sense of Cultural Revolution Culture* (Cambridge and London: Harvard University East Asian Center, 2012), p. 189.
[2] Quoted in ibid., p. 193.   [3] Ibid.

recounted how, in a village plagued by drought, studying and pronoun-
cing Mao's words made the people more resourceful and enabled them
to discover water. Still another shows how peasants, inspired by Mao's
words, discovered a way to create rockets that would disperse the clouds
to prevent hailstorms in an effort to protect the crops.[4]

The quasi-religious practice of the canonical texts is firmly in China's
revolutionary tradition. Treating Yan'an's burgeoning culture as a
discourse community, David Apter and Tony Saich note that the text-
centered activities in Yan'an's mass learning environment contained
"certain proto-religious characteristics intertwined in a secular theory
of politics that identified logos with power."[5] Nowhere is this aspect
more prominent than in the rectification campaign that succeeded
in elevating Mao's texts to the status of orthodoxy. The same proto-
religious activity resurged with passionate intensity during the Cultural
Revolution. The study session and other ritual uses of Mao's Little
Red Book have been seen as forms of thought control and political domination. In the Cultural Revolution, Mao encouraged the rebellious and
critical spirit, yet rebellious believers submitted to and remained enthralled
to the new icon. This seems paradoxical. But the paradox is possible
partly due to a negative view of religion, one that sees religious beliefs
and activity as nothing but illusory and deceptive, as false consciousness
imposed on believers by the ruler. Commentators have discussed the
charismatic features of the Mao cult and the Cultural Revolution.[6]

In this chapter I will challenge the purely negative view of religion by
rethinking Mao's Little Red Book and the Mao cult from the perspective
of charismatic politics and political theology. In Andreas Kalyvas' analysis of Max Weber writings on prophetic religion, charismatic politics
addresses "religious movements striving to control their communities
by challenging the existing dominant beliefs, symbolic significations,
and institutions."[7] This religious cultural revolution was to create a
new collective will in order to transform the existing structure of
political power while affecting the moral orientation of human behavior.
Charismatic religious leaders and charismatically inspired groups
engage in a "plural and contested terrain" where different spiritual
and ideological groups compete for the control of symbolic power and

[4] Ibid., pp. 212–14.
[5] David Apter and Tony Saich, *Revolutionary Discourse in Mao's Republic* (Cambridge, Mass.: Harvard University Press, 1994), p. 3.
[6] Daniel Leese, *Mao Cult: Rhetoric and Ritual in China's Cultural Revolution* (New York: Cambridge University Press, 2011).
[7] Andreas Kalyvas, *Democracy and the Politics of the Extraordinary: Max Weber, Carl Schmitt and Hannah Arendt* (New York: Cambridge University Press, 2008), p. 47.

of the legitimate meanings. The charismatic leader of a religious movement, "by virtue of a personal call and of some charismatic qualities," will "proclaim a new set of values and a new substantive vision of the world, seeking to respond to the growing fears and distress of the masses and to capitalize on their shaky but gradually increasing disillusionment vis-à-vis the established authority."[8]

From this perspective, the religious trappings of the Cultural Revolution may have been as much rebellious and subversive as obscurantist and authoritarian. On the one hand, when devotees studied and recited Mao's magic words, they might have been caught up in a discursive net. On the other hand, actual discursive practice also put authoritative words on uncertain ground. Personal, opinionated, unorthodox interpretations frequently erupted and collided, opening up explorative spaces conducive to controversy and argument and leading to different trajectories as people acted on Mao's words. Such text-centered practice is a subjective, aesthetic experience that reshapes feelings, impacts the mind, and forges collective bonds among the insurgent groups in their struggle, and yet may be beyond the control of any single authority. It is thus hasty to reduce this critical potential to a simplistic view of Mao's discourse as no more than a religious orthodoxy aimed at controlling the minds and hearts of the faithful. On the contrary, the discursive practices associated with Mao quotations could be volatile and dynamic – empowering and energizing social action and fueling the critique of the powers that be.

Linking political discourse with religious ritual also renders revolutionary discursive practice open to an analysis in terms of political theology. Political theology inquires into the source of ultimate authority and conceives the sovereign ruler as a godly, omnipotent figure. This approach holds that religious concepts and practices, often thought to be relics of the benighted, unenlightened era, persist in supposedly secular society and liberal politics. The German philosopher Carl Schmitt contended that all the concepts of the modern theory of the state are secularized theological concepts.[9] As Christian Sorace puts it, "secular political institutions and concepts are theological in disguise."[10] In contrast, liberal politics insists on the separation of Church and state and claims that the modern political system has superseded its theological past, and that religion is only a private ethical choice. Taking issue with this liberal suppression of religious or cultural residues in politics,

---

[8] Ibid., pp. 52, 57.
[9] Carl Schmitt, *Political Theology* (Cambridge, Mass.: MIT Press, 1985), p. xv.
[10] Christian Sorace, "Saint Mao," *Telos* 151 (Summer 2010), p. 175.

political theology asserts that theological modes of politics and social organization are indeed very much alive in modern politics.

The Mao cult according to Alain Badiou

In the decade of the Cultural Revolution (1966–76), Mao's Little Red Book exerted a tremendous impact on international politics and resonated with the aspirations of the decolonizing, anti-establishment movements around the world. While acknowledging a new obscurantism in the Mao cult, Alain Badiou, keeping faith with the Cultural Revolution, challenges the quasi-religious interpretation of its activities as merely illiberal and conservative. Skeptical of liberal democracy whereby politics is reduced to formal, bureaucratic procedure, Badiou sees the personality cult as a sign of a vibrant political movement conducted as a symbolic struggle in revolutionary social change. The personality cult may be dynamic and empowering to the cultists, thanks to the stirrings of popular democracy in a quasi-religious movement.

The recital of Mao's words and directives may suggest a form of absolutist authority, but interpretation of the text evinced an active process of remaking and transforming their meaning. The Red Guards, organizations, and groups would deploy Mao's words in debates and demonstrations. In constantly arguing over the "true" meaning of the text, the center of the "sacred" text was decentered and fragmented into heterogeneous readings. Textual authority was embroiled in a war of words and split apart through contradictory interpretations. While it is true that the sacred words functioned as an imperative rhetoric, their exegesis (Badiou's term) was "in a state of constant flux."[11] Instead of condemning the ritual of reading and rereading as scholastic and doctrinal, Badiou urges us to reconsider the similar flux in religious practice in the West.

The Mao cult was the pinnacle of a much wider educational movement centered on the cult of revolutionary heroes in the manner of religious hagiography. Nowhere is hero worship more remarkable than in the Three Constantly Read Articles (*Lao sanpian*). A supplement to Mao's Little Red Book, the *Lao sanpian* puts emphasis not on the leader but on heroes imbued with revolutionary spirit and altruistic ethics. Linking hero worship to personality cult, Badiou points to its romantic, creative, and populist impulses. Modern liberal culture in the West does not dispense with hero worship, and has transferred godlike creativity

---

[11] Alain Badiou, "The Cultural Revolution: The Last Revolution?" *Positions: East Asia Cultures Critique* 13. 3 (Winter 2005), p. 504.

to the individual artist endowed with extraordinary imagination and genius. The romantic sacralization of the artist in modern times is a cultural practice carried over from Christianity, as words of high aesthetic value are uttered and memorized with reverence by school-children. But this religious respect for the humanist tradition is considered liberal education rather than indoctrination. If liberal critics value the creative genius of the artist and treat him or her as expressive of the cultural ethos, Badiou continues, why should they look askance at a politically engaged artist – a political creator? The romanticized image of Mao, by virtue of his power to rally young students and disenfranchised workers into a revolt against the corrupt bureaucratic and party apparatus, is the image of a popular hero, one who is out to create a new world by destroying the defunct one. If it is not inept to sacralize the artist, then it is much more risky and dangerous, and indeed more subversive, to glorify a hero of a political movement. This is because the political innovator seeks to change the world by rallying popular support: in Mao's case, inspiring and galvanizing young people and workers into rebuilding society and reinventing culture. Badiou writes, "It is less inept or more meaningful to sacralize political innovators, because political creation is rarer, more risky, and more immediately addressed to all."[12]

How does the political artist/innovator address the multitudes, like a priest or a prophet? The priest among his flock – does this image mean that the leader is the pinnacle of authority? One premise for the Cultural Revolution was that the party apparatus and the state system had lost the spirit of revolution and were out of touch with the ordinary working people. Having atrophied into a top-heavy, elitist bureaucratic apparatus, the party was pursuing policies that aggravated the divide between the elite and the grassroots, the cities and the countryside, and industry and agriculture. Though capable of leading and representing the people in the past, now the party was seen as engaged in the bureaucratic entrenchment of elite powers, rapidly becoming estranged from the Chinese people. Badiou writes that there was little that could guarantee that the party represent the people or be the "source of rationality."[13]

In this vacuum of political representation, which amounted to a crisis of legitimacy, there arose the need for a Rousseauian expression of popular will, for "a representation of the representation."[14] With no other institutional guarantees available, something singular and unique, something powerful and charismatic, should take the place of

---

[12] Ibid., p. 505.   [13] Ibid.   [14] Ibid.

the routine, institutional representation. Badiou paints a scenario of religious–aesthetic representation of the popular will:

Finally, one person, a single body, comes to stand for the superior guarantee, in the classical aesthetic form of genius. It is also curious . . . to see that, trained as we are in the theory of genius in the realm of art, we should take such strong offense at it when it emerges in the order of politics. For the communist parties, between the twenties and sixties, personal genius is only the incarnation, the fixed point, of the double representative capacity of the party. It is easier to believe in the rectitude and the intellectual force of a distant and solitary man than in the truth and purity of an apparatus whose local petty chiefs are well known.[15]

The personality cult, in other words, functions like a religious/political focal image in rallying popular support in radical social movements. The Cultural Revolution targeted the political superstructure of the party-state. Mao's prophetic visions warned that the party-state was leading China down the road of capitalism. "Capitalism" here did not refer to the familiar categories of private property and free market, but to the bureaucratic routinization of the post-revolutionary party apparatus. The charge was directed at the fact that the "officials in the upper echelon of the bureaucracy, by virtue of their power and privilege in the state apparatus, were acquiring material privileges and prestige and exploiting society as a whole."[16] The party-state apparatus had a vested interest in preserving the status quo and became conservative in its intransigency to any social change.

The popular appeal of the Cultural Revolution met Mao's attempt to go outside the party and to reconnect with the people in a push for social change. Thus "Mao incarnates not so much the party's representative capacity" as a personal, charismatic focus for rallying political energy from outside the party against the capitalist and bureaucratic tendencies within it. Going against his own party, Mao proclaimed that it was just to rebel and encouraged the revolutionary masses to bombard its headquarters. The image of Mao, a political innovator rather than the chief of the party apparatus, figures prominently with a religious aura in the mass study sessions and rituals. It is a "revenge of singularity on representation."[17]

Our God is none other than the people: examples from literature

"The Foolish Old Man who Removed the Mountains" is the title of an essay in the Three Constantly Read Articles. In his speech at the Seventh

---

[15] Ibid.
[16] Maurice Meisner, *Mao's China and After*, 3rd edn. (New York: Free Press, 1999), p. 370.
[17] Badiou, "The Cultural Revolution," p. 506.

National Congress of the Chinese Communist Party in 1945 in Yan'an, Mao invoked the Daoist fable of the indefatigable old man. In it, an old man urged and led his sons in an enterprise to dig away two mountains in front of their house. This impossible but resolute undertaking touched the gods, who sent fairies to carry the mountains away. At the moment of speech, the United Front between the Guomindang and the Communists was breaking apart, and the fight continued against the Japanese. Mao says:

Today, two big mountains lie like a dead weight on the Chinese people. One is imperialism, and [the] other is feudalism. The Communist Party has long made up its mind to dig them up. We must persevere and work unceasingly, and we, too, will touch God's heart. Our God is none other than the masses of the Chinese people. If they stand up and dig together with us, why can't these two mountains be cleared away?[18]

Rather than imposing God's decrees from the top down on the people, the fable suggests that the leader and people work together. With concerted effort the people's power may match that of the gods and prevail over adversity. These concerns resonate with the themes of the mass line and the notion of the people as master of their own fate. Linking political theology to the mass line policy in the relation between leader and led in Mao, Christian Sorace sees "a widening of the religious divide between himself and the people."[19] On the other hand, Sorace also argues that the story works to suture the gap between heaven and earth, the leader and the led. As Mao says, "We too, will touch God's heart. Our God is none other than the masses of the Chinese people." Hinting at the link between popular democracy and religious imagery, the story not only puts the leader back among the led but also strives to render the masses into their own leaders.

That the people with right ideas, political consciousness, and dynamic energy are sublime masters of their destiny was exemplified by Mao's poem "Farewell to the God of Plague." During the Great Leap Forward, a campaign was underway to wipe out the plague of Schistosomiasis in Yu Jiang County, Jiangxi Province. Written to honor the victory of a public health campaign in wiping out the disease, the poem begins with a bleak scene of desolation. For all the idyllic "green mountains and emerald streams," the plague has ravaged the land and left villages ghost-inhabited and overgrown with brambles. As the peasants battle and finally prevail over the disease, the poem takes a fanciful flight toward a

---

[18] Mao Tze-tung, *Selected Works of Mao Tze-tung*, vol. III (Peking: Foreign Language Press, 1965), pp. 321–22.

[19] Sorace, "Saint Mao," p. 176.

mythical, heavenly realm, where the legendary Cowherd asks about the situation on the earth. Although the Cowherd and Weaving Maid are mythical figures residing in the heavens, they are from peasant stock and have humble roots. Their earthly concern is greeted with the good news of people's sovereign power in defeating the disease:

> Borne by the breezes of spring,
> A host of soft green willow twigs dance in the air.
> In this land of ours,
> We are all worthy of Yao and Shun in deed and in name.
> Rain of red petals will change into waves if we so desire,
> And green mountains will turn into bridges at our command.[20]

The spring and renewed landscape are back in the magic land of China, *shenzhou*. The handiwork not of gods but of the people, the landscape is restored to its green health and bathed in a divine aura. But the honor is due to each and everyone involved in the health campaign: "The people are worthy of Yao and Shun in deed and in name." Yao and Shun are legendary kings in Chinese antiquity, reputed for their deep commitment to caring for the well-being of ordinary people as the fundamental principle of governance. But in socialist China ordinary working people are taking the place of the ancient rulers. The people are both leaders and led, mythical and plebian, the agent of their own emancipation. Like the mythical figure of the Foolish Old Man who Removed the Mountains, the people are capable of transforming the sky and changing the earth:

> With our silver hoes
> We till the five majestic peaks that pierce the clouds;
> With our arms of iron
> We shape the three mighty rivers that flow across the land.[21]

These lines celebrate the sovereign power of the people, who are capable of leading themselves, organizing their labor, taking on challenges, and changing the world. The poem taps into the inexhaustible reservoir of energy, intelligence, and power of the masses in shaping their own destiny. But all these accomplishments are still graced by the aura of kingly Yao and Shun, inspired by the Foolish Old Man, and Mao's elevated charisma. These transcendent figures are elite saviors of the people, leading them in a campaign of self-emancipation.

---

[20] The translation of Mao poems is by Ma Wenyee. See Ma Wenyee, *Snow Glistens on the Great Wall: A New Translation of the Complete Collection of Mao Tse-tung's Poetry* (Santa Barbara: Santa Barbara Press, 1986), pp. 110–11.

[21] Ibid., p. 111.

Cao Zhenglu's recent novel *Course on Democracy* (*Minzu ke*) (2011) stresses similar themes. Set in a campaign to implement the policy of assisting the left-wing organizations in the Cultural Revolution, the novel depicts how an army officer curbs the Red Guards' rebellious impulses and unruly behavior. Staying away from scenes of violence against political victims and of the ransacking of cultural heritage, Cao presents an unconventional narrative of the Cultural Revolution by exposing the power elites in their corruption, usurpation, and personal vendettas. Most relevant to the theme of this chapter is the protagonist Xiao Ming, a Red Guard who engages in study sessions, soul searching, and thinking about China's future.

Like all other practitioners of the Mao cult, Xiao Ming cites the quotations, shouts slogans, attacks the administration, and writes a diary. Yet in addition to reading Mao's texts, she also reads Marxist volumes, such as Engels' *Gotha Program*. Aspiring to emulate the Paris Commune, an exemplar for spontaneous mass social movements, she thinks deeply about issues of popular democracy and has constant discussions with her associates and friends, raising and trying to deal with the questions of capitalism and socialism and the plight of ordinary people.

As a focus of the novel's title, "the course on democracy" (*minzhu ke*) invokes the Cultural Revolutionary theme of mass democracy (*da minzhu*). It recalls the mass campaign that exhorted people to exercise their democratic rights to speak out and rebel, to critique and to protest, and to publicize their views with big-character posters. The class on democracy also reveals a thoughtful, educational process based on reading, studying, and discussing. A telling episode toward the end of the novel sums up this lesson. Reflecting on her experience in the Cultural Revolution as *minzhu*, Xiao Ming realizes that *minzhu* literally means that people are masters of their own fate and should participate in the business of shaping their own affairs. Rather than being passively guided by the Little Red Book, political participation is one of discursive practice: active study, discussion, and argument in seeking the truth. This happens in the process of poring over and thinking about ways in which Mao's quotations are open to contrary interpretations. In a dialogue with a friend with rigid belief in Mao's words, Xiao Ming says that she has had a revelation: any one of Mao's statements about the revolution can be contradicted by another. To her shocked friend, she proceeds to conduct such a thought experiment in the clash of quotables by juxtaposing one Mao quotation in contradiction with another. For instance, Mao teaches that the masses are true heroes and we (party leaders) are often inexperienced and laughable. Yet Mao also says that the truth is held in the hands of few. Who is the creator of history? Mao says it is the people. Yet Mao also says that millions of people remain unclear about the purpose of the revolution.

What is significant about this experiment is not how self-contradictory Mao quotations are, or how subversive this word game is. Rather, the very process of seeking the truth by discussing and thinking, by unraveling Mao's words as specific, contextual responses to diverse circumstances and to complex situations constitutes a vibrant enlightenment. Xiao Ming writes in her diary:

Years later, whenever I recall this episode, my heart is filled with mixed feelings. In those sincere and faithful years, how many such debates did we carry on? What is the significance of this activity? The meaningfulness of our purposes, the tortuousness of thought process, the narrowness of our path, the burden of our feelings, plus all kinds of helplessness. Are all these unnecessary? No, this is precisely a class on democracy. On the blackboard is written: "We educate ourselves."[22]

It is this passionate seeking for truths, this deep commitment to public affairs, the constant discussion to identify problems and issues of the nation and the world, and the self-styled, self-assigned leadership role for my own society and community that mark the true meaning of democracy. In sharp contrast with the liberal, representative system, in which you cast a ballot for a representative who speaks on your behalf, Xiao Ming defines democracy as people's self-education and self-organization. "What is democracy?" she asks. It is self-confidence in discoursing on all important issues of the nation and the world and being able to get angry about them. It is a daily atmosphere of participation, involvement, and effective talk. It is a sense of responsibility as the master of the house. In this discursive process, there are no boundaries for a thinking person. Anything can be put on the table for discussion. Truths fear no discussion. Truths should stake out a position and meet objections.

This notion of democracy is one legacy of the Cultural Revolution's release of discursive energy and venting of political passion. It is the democratic side of the scriptural, charismatic authority in the practice of Mao's Little Red Book.

BIBLIOGRAPHY

Apter, David, and Tony Saich, *Revolutionary Discourse in Mao's Republic* (Cambridge, Mass.: Harvard University Press, 1994)
Badiou, Alain, "The Cultural Revolution: The Last Revolution?" *Positions: East Asia Cultures Critique* 13.3 (Winter 2005), pp. 481–514

[22] Cao Zhenglu, *Minzhu ke*. See Zuo'an wenhua wang (Leftbank website), www.eduww. com/article/201108/30477html.

Kalyvas, Andreas, *Democracy and the Politics of the Extraordinary: Max Weber, Carl Schmitt and Hannah Arendt* (New York: Cambridge University Press, 2008)

Leese, Daniel, *Mao Cult: Rhetoric and Ritual in China's Cultural Revolution* (New York: Cambridge University Press, 2011)

Mao Tze-tung, *Selected Works of Mao Tze-tung*, vol. III (Peking: Foreign Language Press, 1965)

Ma Wenyee, *Snow Glistens on the Great Wall: A New Translation of the Complete Collection of Mao Tse-tung's Poetry* (Santa Barbara: Santa Barbara Press, 1986)

Meisner, Maurice, *Mao's China and After*, 3rd edn. (New York: Free Press, 1999)

Mittler, Barbara, *A Continuous Revolution: Making Sense of Cultural Revolution Culture* (Cambridge, Mass., and London: Harvard University East Asian Center, 2012)

Schmitt, Carl, *Political Theology* (Cambridge, Mass.: MIT Press, 1985)

Sorace, Christian, "Saint Mao," *Telos* 151 (Summer 2010), pp. 173–191

Index